GENRES OF RECOLLECTION

ARCHIVAL POETICS AND MODERN GREECE

PENELOPE PAPAILIAS

GENRES OF RECOLLECTION
© Penelope Papailias, 2005.

All rights reserved. No part of this book may be used or reproduced in any manner whatsoever without written permission except in the case of brief quotations embodied in critical articles or reviews.

First published in 2005 by
PALGRAVE MACMILLAN™
175 Fifth Avenue, New York, N.Y. 10010 and
Houndmills, Basingstoke, Hampshire, England RG21 6XS
Companies and representatives throughout the world.

PALGRAVE MACMILLAN is the global academic imprint of the Palgrave Macmillan division of St. Martin's Press, LLC and of Palgrave Macmillan Ltd. Macmillan® is a registered trademark in the United States, United Kingdom and other countries. Palgrave is a registered trademark in the European Union and other countries.

ISBN 1–4039–6105–0 hardback
ISBN 1–4039–6106–9 paperback

Library of Congress Cataloging-in-Publication Data is available from the Library of Congress.

A catalogue record for this book is available from the British Library.

Design by Newgen Imaging Systems (P) Ltd., Chennai, India.

First edition: February 2005

10 9 8 7 6 5 4 3 2 1

Printed in the United States of America.

Library
University of Texas
at San Antonio

103778
B000127

Genres of Recollection

ANTHROPOLOGY, HISTORY, AND THE CRITICAL IMAGINATION publishes works dealing with theoretical and methodological developments in history, anthropology, and historical anthropology. Books in the series analyze the ways in which accounts of the past are produced, circulated, and consumed in an increasingly global marketplace of commodities, identities, and cultural practices. The series is committed to making sense of the form and content of historical imagination across the world, to new ways of writing history, and to how both these concerns may animate critical currents in ethnographic method and social theory. The publisher and editors of this series seek, among other things, to foster work that might broaden dialogue between anthropologists, historians, and those from other fields who engage with both.

SERIES EDITORS
Ann Stoler, New School for Social Research
John L. Comaroff, University of Chicago and American Bar Foundation

ADDITIONAL TITLES IN THE SERIES
Beyond Memory: The Crimean Tatars' Deportation and Return, by Greta Lynn Uehling

WITHDRAWN
UTSA Libraries

In memory of my parents,
John and Mary Jane Papailias

Contents

Acknowledgments

I think I can pinpoint when I began writing this book (though, of course, it was hardly yet *this* book). I was still in college, on a trip with my father to his natal village. We were visiting with my great aunt Yiorgia, who had ushered me into her living room to show me some old photographs of the family. I spoke to her enthusiastically with my little Greek, asking her questions and making observations. She responded just as enthusiastically. Only later did I realize she was almost deaf. These are the kinds of fortuitous circumstances in which one takes the first step.

Around the same time, in the Modern Greek Studies program at Harvard, I was encouraged to view my growing interest in things Greek as an opening to think about the politics of culture more generally. I am particularly indebted to Meg Alexiou, Vangelis Calotychos, and Charles Stewart for posing the initial challenges.

My teachers at Michigan, Brink Messick, Ann Stoler, Bruce Mannheim, Sally Humphreys, Val Daniel, and Artemis Leontis, in turn, inspired me to undertake a project at the intersection of anthropology, history, and literary criticism. For those who know their work, the imprint each has left on this text will be clear. I am especially grateful to Sally Humphreys for her close readings of early drafts of this manuscript and mentoring throughout the writing process.

My cohort in the graduate anthropology program at the University of Michigan was legendary because of its size, but I like to think for other reasons as well. Without the endless conversations but also the personal support in dire times, it is hard to know how this project would have been started, let alone completed. In so many ways, Rachel Heiman, Laura Kunreuther, Mani Limbert, Charles Lord, Janet McIntosh, Ellen Moodie, Esra Özyürek, and Karen Strassler created the conditions of possibility for this book.

A number of institutions and granting agencies provided generous support for my research and writing, including the Fulbright Program, the Wenner-Gren Foundation for Anthropological Research, the Phi Beta Kappa Society (Mary Isabella Sibley Fellowship), and the Horace Rackham School of Graduate Studies at the University of Michigan.

During the course of my research, I was fortunate to meet numerous people who graciously agreed to speak with me about their historical practice. I am most thankful to all of them. I am also grateful to the staff at several Greek archives and libraries for their assistance and willingness to discuss their work with me: especially, the late

Maria Asvesti, Ioanna Petropoulou, Stavros Anestidis, Yiannis Koutis, and Olga Mavromati. A special word of thanks must be extended to Yiorgos Mandas for entrusting a stranger with precious stories. Stamatis Spirou and Mihalis Fotiadis both offered a patient and listening ear as I first began to work out some of the arguments in this book. Last, but hardly least, Athena Triandafyllidis extended me her warmth and nurture at various critical junctures during the long period over which the research and writing of this book has stretched.

Since I have yet to come "home" from the field, I have also greatly profited from the many opportunities to share this work in formal and informal settings with historian and anthropologist colleagues in Greece, including Athena Athanasiou, Rika Benveniste, Effi Gazi, Antonis Liakos, Eleni Papagaroufali, Akis Papataxiarchis, Yiannis Papatheodorou, and Riki Van Boeschoten. While this dialogue proved invaluable to me as I reformulated some of my arguments, needless to say, I take full responsibility for choices of emphasis and, of course, any "historical errors."

Assistance came from various other directions as well. Aslı Iğsız, Esra Özyürek, and Ilay Ors elucidated the contours of Turkish memory politics. Kathleen Canning provided an engaged reading from the perspective of a European historian. Vangelis Calotychos, Panagiotis Roilos, and Lukas Tsitsipis gave me the benefit of their Greek linguistic and literary expertise, and Zeese Papanikolas his insight into the experience of Greek migrants in the United States.

Athena Athanasiou, Laura Kunreuther, Eleni Papagaroufali, Karen Strassler, and two anonymous readers read through the whole or parts of this manuscript at various stages of its final preparation. I so appreciate the time and care they put into detailed critical responses that helped me see this work with other eyes.

Finally, my greatest debt is to Triandafyllos, who saw me through every moment of this project. The flower buds in the tiny vase on my desk, the mini cappuccinos, and the midnight dinners in Athens and Stemnitsa always managed to bring me back to life during the struggle of writing. The conclusion of the book was hastened by Alexandros's arrival. Even though I cannot say he gave me the rest to finish, getting to return to play with him was incentive to let go.

This book is dedicated to my parents for what they taught me and what I learned in thinking about their lives and, above all, for their boundless affection and unqualified support. My pleasure at seeing this book go out into the world cannot but be partial in having lost them as readers.

Note on Transliteration
and Translation

Before Greek fonts were mounted on computer operating systems, Greek speakers began exchanging e-mail messages with each other using the characters of the Latin alphabet and the symbols of the computer keyboard in idiosyncratic and creative ways. Later, when Greek fonts became widely available, some people still kept writing this way. As might be expected, this new script enraged the Greek philological establishment: Greek was being Americanized, phonetic spellings were going to ruin Greek students' spelling, and, worst of all, the apogee of "Western" writing was being reduced to "primitive" hieroglyphics (some people, you see, were transcribing letters visually, for instance, using an "8" to represent "θ," *theta*). The heterogeneity of these practices, however, personally comforts me. For one, this new cyberGreek (or Greeklish, as it is called) confirmed something that people had been feeling for a long time: namely, that the way a word *looks* matters. Second, the advent of Greeklish exposed the inevitable multiplicity of transcription systems and their relation not to some "natural" way that acoustic signals should be visualized or the Greek alphabet Latinized, but to diverse language ideologies and always changing technologies of inscription.

Despite my theoretical understanding of what was at stake in all of this, I have to admit that I still had hoped to find an unobjectionable system, only to give up in the end and accept that I, like everyone else, would have to navigate my own course: between the Scylla of orthographic transliteration (the choice of the philological establishment, since it respects the authority of written language and acknowledges a continuity with ancient Greek through historical spellings) and the Charybdis of phonetic transliteration (the usual choice of anthropologists and linguists, since it challenges the philological establishment's excessive reverence for the ancient past at the expense of the modern Greek present and, through an emphasis on local inflection, supports ethnographic realism and the romance of the oral). In other words, ideology all around. Sympathizing with the latter position (up to a point), I decided to begin with a phonetic approach. Since most of the material I transliterate comes from handwritten or printed texts, however, it seemed misleading to go too far in this direction (by oralizing the diphthong "ou" to *u*, for instance). I also decided against including accent marks, on which purists of either camp might insist, as I believe they would only confuse English speakers. Finally, in some cases, I have preferred unorthodox semiphonetic, semihistorical spellings (as in "typografiko," instead of the phonetic "tipografiko" or the historical "typographiko"). The relatively greater familiarity of the word spelled this way not only makes Greek more accessible (rather than deliberately more "exotic") but also, in calques such as this, acknowledges Western modernity's ideal of antiquity—not, as some would have it, modernity's "debt" to Greek origins.

Unless otherwise indicated, English translations of passages cited from Greek and other non-English sources are my own.

Prologue

When I finished college, I set off on a journey to find my "roots" in a Greek mountain village. Buoyed along by the valorization of ethnicity in U.S. society, I left for
Greece with assumptions I now understand as problematic about what I would find
and how I would find it and what I would do with it when I found it. Growing up
in New York City, I had been tempted to see the village, by contrast, as a small place,
a community that might be grasped and known. The fact that the people I met on
walks along overgrown mountain paths would tell me, after first asking "to whom I
belonged," that they had known my long-deceased grandfather and eaten at his
restaurant in Athens seemed to me tangible evidence of the village's intimacy and the
resilience of its inhabitants' memory. The patent difficulty of daily life in the village
in the past, the scars of war and political turmoil, the pathos of the stone skeletons
of houses abandoned to migration all seemed more real and closer to life-and-death
than anything I had known growing up and, thus, worth exploring and writing
about. The longer I stayed and tried to untangle local stories, however, the more
opaque the "village" became, the more labyrinthine and far-flung the social networks
through which it was imagined, and the more complex and multifaceted the discourses through which its past had been conceived and documented.

One of my profound realizations of that year was that the village was already written—and extensively at that. Letters; newspapers; folklore collections; poems; political satire; local histories; registers of birth, marriage, death, and baptism; deeds of
sale; and community records unfurled scriptural routes in any direction one might
wish to pursue. How had I thought that I would be the one to write this story? Even
more remarkably, how had I thought that I would write about the village on the basis
of speaking with people? Beyond my own personal naïveté, this innocence can be
traced back to a whole way of seeing the world and Others from humanity's hypo-
thetical "center" and "future": a perspective deeply engrained, as many have argued,
in the "Western" knowledge project itself. At that point in my life, though, I was
largely oblivious to the legacy of disciplines such as literary criticism and history, the
backbone of my liberal arts education, in the power games of nation and empire.
Later, during my graduate studies in anthropology, these issues would be at the fore-
front of discussion, and I would have the opportunity to rethink my earlier attempts
to write about the village. In the process, though, I was drawn away from the puzzle
of the village ("mine" or any other) to the puzzle of the inquiry itself: all the conversations and journeys set in motion, the subjects and questions taken for granted, and
the cassette tapes, journal notes, and photographs generated in the wake of such

earnest quests. The fact that I *knew*, without having been taught, how to gather stories of immigration from old relatives in the United States or of village ways from my grandmother in Greece while I entirely missed asking other questions, for instance, about the street battles in which my father fought in December 1944 in Athens, led me to wonder how people learn the habits of history and come to frame their experience and that of those close to them in particular and often quite limiting ways.

Instead of disowning my nostalgia and destroying the traces of these earlier inquiries, I decided—or, it would be more correct to say, I was compelled—to turn the mirror around to examine the practices of others who, following some kind of innate historical common sense, had engaged in their own acts of documentation. Most simply put, this book is about *that* common sense: about the way certain historical topics, sources, and witnesses, and not others, come to present themselves to the eager seeker and how specific routines of research and forms of historical writing become established and widespread.

This project seemed urgent to me for several reasons. For one, given that political legitimacy and cultural identity are so often staked on claims to the past, these practices clearly represent a key site to examine the production of social subjectivities, negotiations of local and global power, and redefinitions of citizenship and community. Second, common sense regarding *how* to collect evidence, transcribe testimony, and compose historical narratives clearly shapes *what* can be recorded; in usually escaping observation, however, these conventions effectively normalize silences in the historical record and, for this reason, especially deserve critical attention. Finally, mapping the densities of historical production in relation to particular historical themes, archival arrangements, and "genres of recollection," including historical fiction, local historiography, memoirs, letters, and fieldnotes, brings into relief the cultural politics of witnessing as well as the obverse: the *unwitnessability* of the many traumatic experiences that have marked twentieth-century modern Greek history. In this study, I view the tension between modes of historical documentation and archiving aimed at possessing, accumulating, and domiciling the past and forces of dispossession, fragmentation, and dislocation as a cultural, historical, political, and poetic problematic of central importance.

Much, nonetheless, was against my doing this project. In conversations about my research, people often seemed disappointed that I had chosen to focus on forms of historical practice that could hardly be considered "exotic." Couldn't I have traced alternative histories in the embroidered lines of women's trousseaus? Hadn't I discovered a particularly Greek way of doing history, a distinctly Hellenic sense of time, or an unusual Greek Orthodox memory rite? If not, why didn't I at least seek out the disenfranchised who had had long been excluded from dominant historical narratives and taken on the role of scribe myself? Despite these pressures, when I looked around, I kept finding myself surrounded by great numbers of people engaged in, what seemed in my eyes, quite familiar practices of historical documentation. If there is something Greek about this project, then, it has more to do with the place of Greece in global histories (and historiographies) of colonialism, nationalism, industrialization, and war than with the isolation of a uniquely "Greek" (i.e., non-"Western") ontology of history. Situating this inquiry within a tensed global field, in turn, I suggest, raises questions about the politics and poetics of historical production and archival formation that are not always evident at history's imputed heart (i.e., the academic historiography and state archives of powerful nations).

Doing research for this book entailed turning the historian's archive into an anthropological "field" and interrogating history's and anthropology's foundational empiricisms. The various historical producers with whom I spoke often assumed that I was interested in writing history rather than in the writing *of* history, and it was sometimes difficult to make documentation itself materialize as an object of inquiry. Over time, I came to realize that *talking* with people about their writing represented a comforting anthropologizing of my subject: a series of cassette tapes to hold on to. Ultimately, I found that I had to claim reading more decisively as an anthropological method and look in literary and linguistic ways at, for the most part, nonliterary texts. During the course of my research (September 1997 to December 1999), I was first based in the provincial city of Volos and thereafter in Athens; however, my "archival field" really was constituted by local and national networks of historians and archivists, diverse authorities on the past (academics, elites, witnesses, descendants, critics, politicians) and public and private sites of textual documentation, preservation, and circulation (archives, libraries, bookstores, exhibitions, home archives). The *time* of my research was punctuated by moments of local and national discussion and debate over historical representations (public lectures, conferences, commemorative events, book readings, newspaper exchanges). Reading various genres of historical writing, going over translations and transcriptions, analyzing characters, plots, and allusions, and discussing the interpretation of particular texts with new acquaintances and old friends proved to be yet another dimension of this research; my reading notes are definitely also "fieldnotes."

While writing this book involved displacing reflection on historical practice from me to others, it did occasion a return of sorts to objects and stories that had been passed on to me: unsorted black-and-white photographs neatly gathered in a worn envelope at the back of a family drawer, a copper jug my grandfather used to measure wine for sale at his vineyard, some Greek books on a shelf in my father's closet. Among the latter were local histories that my father had promised to sell to compatriots in New York on behalf of a childhood friend who had channeled his Marxist politics into writing utopian histories of village artisans and their labor collectives. These objects crystallized my nostalgia for a past that was not my own, for a world that, because I did not always know Greek, I could not for a long time decipher. With little pieces of paper still taped to them, prices scrawled beside awkward dollar signs by someone clearly more comfortable with drachma than dollars, these books embodied the inscrutability of this world and its concerns. Here I return to these materials, but in a new way, refracted through the inquiries of strangers and their multifarious desires for and claims on the past. The point was never, of course, these particular artifacts or some past to which they purportedly refer, but the conditions in which ephemeral collections and painstaking re-collections take shape, the sheer proliferation of some stories and the forgetting and forbidding of others, and the inclusions and exclusions from collective histories that emerge out of all this restless recording.

Chapter 1

Introduction:
Taking Testimony, Making Archives

This book explores the politics of historical representation in Greek society through an ethnography of documentation, archiving, and historical writing. Against the backdrop of the late 1990s, the first decade of the post–Cold War era, I take up central traumatic moments of twentieth-century Greek history—refugee crisis, labor migration, urbanization, and civil war—in order to trace the various historical and political contexts, archival constructs, and textual and technological formats in which accounts *about them* have been documented. My aim is twofold: to bring into relief the cultural mediation of historical knowledge and consider the way that "re-collecting" the past contributes to the production and reproduction of cultural difference, socioeconomic distinction, and political community.

This inquiry is sited in history's disciplinary, epistemological, and geopolitical gray zone: it engages tense points of contact and friction between academic and amateur historians, personal and state archives, and Greek and European historiographies. In these marginal spaces of historical production, history as we know it is constantly being undermined: the authority of public stories by the whispers of family secrets, the archive as monument to national accumulation by the centrifugal forces of transnational labor and colonial expropriation, the rhetoric of fact by the truth of fiction, and the transparency of referential statement by the impact of performative utterances. Rethinking historical praxis in a broad way will lead me to propose an archival poetics to account for documentation's double status as material practice that keeps memory "in place" and ethical response to the discourse of others.

Re-collecting the Past

Many people in Greece appear to have taken history into their own hands. How else to explain the proliferation in the past fifteen years of autobiographies, local histories, and illustrated coffee-table books composed around their authors' connection to a particular place or series of events? Technologies of historical research from tape recorders to computer word processors are widely available while methods of historical inquiry, ranging from research in local archives to the conducting of interviews, seem to be a matter of common sense. For most academic observers, this historical "graphomania," to use Svetlana Boym's term for the Russian literary disease of "writing too much, plagiarizing too much, behaving too much like a writer" (1994: 169), is a problem, if not an embarrassment. A reviewer of a local history of a former ethnic Greek neighborhood of Istanbul, for instance, complains that "these kinds of works" do not follow the "rules" of any genre, leaving scholars "paralyzed" when forced to evaluate them. The author's proposed solution: separate the wheat from the chaff so real historians can get back to work.[1]

Such a response to the phenomenon of popular historical writing, however, does not seem entirely satisfying. Policing the boundaries of "good" and "proper" writing in the name of criticism is always an effective way to defend the exclusiveness of disciplinary knowledge. It runs the risk, however, of substituting academic elitism for cultural analysis. Instead, taking up Nietzsche's (1874) famous condemnation of the "consuming fever of history" in his day might lead us to ask what all this historical work is *doing*. All around Greece, in living rooms and courtyards, in local libraries and municipal archives, the rituals of historical inquiry are being performed daily. In the process, arguments are being woven connecting, but also separating, social collectivities and political positions of the past and present. Rather than an obstacle that needs to be overcome or a hindrance in the path of serious scholarship, the historical practice of those who admit they are "not historians" might be a central concern for students of historical production, cultural memory, and textual culture. Precisely those qualities that discredit the products of these independent labors in the eyes of professional historians—their blatant partiality, sentimental tone, verbosity, and outdated or inconsistent methodologies—testify to the availability of history as a discourse on the self as well as to the tremendous investment that people have made in documenting and witnessing a past that they—or others—consider their "own."

The subjects on whom this book centers all approach history as avowed amateurs who, nonetheless, have dedicated themselves with passionate intensity to creative acts of historical documentation. Their social backgrounds, ideas about history, modes of archiving and writing, not to mention the milieus in which their efforts were conceived and brought to fruition, could not be more different. The cases I will treat include the living room archives and source book histories of amateur local historians in a provincial Greek city, the transcription of oral testimony from thousands of Greek refugees from Anatolia (Turkey) at an independent research center that had been established by a cosmopolitan Greek aristocrat, the reception of a controversial novel about the Greek Civil War written by a nationally acclaimed author of documentary fiction, and the writing and editing of a Peloponnesian potato farmer's memoirs of transatlantic migration and wartime loss. What these diverse historical producers shared was a sense that they must, both for their own existential well-being and that of some collectivity (family, local community, ethnic group, social class, nation, humanity), document and preserve accounts of a past that was being forgotten, elided, or actively repressed in public discourse, official history, and/or academic scholarship.

Personal archives served as the principal field sites for my ethnography.[2] A first definition of the personal archive might be a textual, material, and theoretical construct that marks the borders between secrets and revelation as well as between private lives, state authority, and national imaginaries. The personal archive can be constructed to stand beside or even compete with state archives, but it can also be a hiding space in which subversive memories are stored and preserved for possible future disclosure. It can refer to the home and its contents, which through calculation or circumstance take on the status of historical evidence. The word *personal* highlights the control and management of archives by individuals, families, or groups and the manner in which they knit their identities and histories into them.

While the fact that an archive is personally held can endow it with a stamp of authenticity and an anti-institutional aura, this independence, idiosyncrasy, and association with the "feminine" sphere of the home can undermine the authority of histories written from its materials and reconfirm established hierarchies of scholarship. It would be naïve to think of personal archives as existing outside the orbit of official taxonomies: often enough they simply reproduce the categories of dominant historical narratives and domesticate them, as it were. Sometimes, however, by dint of an explicit agenda or simply as an outgrowth of diasporic and cosmopolitan practices of communication and community formation, personal archives transcend national borders that state archives are so often constructed to define and defend. In short, as a gesture to the feminist dictum "the personal is political," the word *personal* is intended to de-center expected boundaries between the personal and the official, the private and the public, and home and the world, while also bringing particular emphasis to the gendering of history.

I am aware, though, that my use of the word *archive* in this context, aside from maddening professional historians and archivists, might seem a provocative contradiction when coupled with *personal*. Given the archive's explicit connotations of the public, the institutional, and even the state itself, some might have expected (and preferred) that I use the word *collection*, which first brings to mind the individual and the concept of private property.[3] As processes of gathering and organizing material signs and objects into circumscribed spaces and holding on to them, collecting and archiving can be seen as closely related, even overlapping, practices that mediate between display and concealment as well as between private and public spaces. The archive and the collection nonetheless differ in several important respects that bear centrally on the subject of this book.

For one, archives seek not to erase, but to preserve, signs of the original contexts from which their materials come: they are about reference. The most fundamental principle of archivistics is provenance, and the famous French stricture "respect des fonds" directs the archivist to attend to the scrupulous reproduction of the original order in which records were inscribed, interpreted, and transmitted. The collector, on the other hand, as Hannah Arendt has pointed out in her commentary on Walter Benjamin's famous essay "Unpacking My Library," is a consummately modern subject: ostensibly a paragon of conventionality and throwback to an older age, the collector does not, in fact, revere tradition and its authority, but instead is set on shattering the inheritance of the past. In Arendt's reading, Benjamin's collector enthusiastically "destroys the context in which his object once was only part of a greater, living entity" (1955: 45). By bringing various objects and artifacts into the collection's new order, or, in Benjamin's terms, its "magical circle," the collector aims to "renew the old world" (60–1). As opposed to collectors, most of the personal archivists in this book do not see themselves as recreating the world and putting the fragments of the past into a new order, but precisely as "salvaging," "redeeming," and even "resurrecting" the "old world" and, by extension, revealing history as self-evident, self-present document.

Second, while the collection often constitutes a highly deliberate arrangement, orchestrated by the demanding vision of a finicky collector, the archive is the product of a significantly more chaotic process of accretion, shaped by the automatic and sometimes careless procedures of state functionaries as well as by the haphazard (or intentional) destruction of materials that otherwise might have ended up there. Admittedly, the fact that I am looking at personal, not public, archives, many of which were constructed from newly produced documents (e.g., transcribed oral testimony), blurs the sharpness of this distinction. Nonetheless, the term *archive* underscores the conviction of many of my interlocutors that more is better and that the future, not the present, should be the final arbiter of what stays. My preference for the word *archive* over *collection* also reflects the fact that this book focuses on written texts rather than objects (though the status of the document as artifact and possession will be of paramount importance, especially in the chapter on local history). Furthermore, although collectors can also be "peddlers" and the objects in their collection potential commodities to be sold (Chow 2001), personal archivists see themselves as serving the public good and scrupulously avoid looking at their labors in commercial terms. Finally, using the term *archive* in this capacious way allows me to draw attention to the relationship—sometimes implicit and unconsciously mimetic, other times ironic and directly confrontational—which diverse documentary assemblages establish with real (or imagined) public archives and the place these acts of historical documentation and archiving occupy in national and global debates over historical knowledge and practice.

Recollection, at least in an unhyphenated form, might strike some readers as a strange term on which to anchor this project, invoking as it does a Platonic vocabulary that casts memory as a technique of recall from a preexisting stock of knowledge. The view of history and memory that informs my analysis in this book could not be more different. What I am actually interested in is *re-collection*, a spelling of the word I use to highlight the resourceful and dynamic phase of collecting, documenting, and archiving involved in historical production, but also to underscore the frequency with which the historicity of historical practice *is* ignored or concealed, and cultural and textual mediation made to appear secondary and exterior to a purportedly "original" utterance or "firsthand" experience.

In her important work on trauma and narrative, Cathy Caruth (1996) has argued that traumatic moments in people's lives constitute "unclaimed experience," which while relentlessly possessing them, so often cannot be possessed *by* them. Although in this book I will focus, by contrast, on the *claiming* of history and the circumstances that enable historical "experience" to be materialized and textualized as archivable content, the tension of this book lies precisely at those points in which practices of historical re-collection aimed at generating knowledge of a past reality are stalled or deflected by silence or run up against uses of language that fail to represent, or exceed mere reference to, a given event.

Anthropology and Archive

The contemporary politicization of the past witnessed by the feverish construction (and destruction) of monuments, the calling forth of countless survivors to testify to historical injustices, and the performance of collective mourning rites has contributed, unsurprisingly, to the burgeoning of academic research on the politics of memory.[4] This cultural criticism, though, has not always escaped an *uncritical* romance of memory (cf. Stoler and Strassler 2000).[5] Thus, while "memory" is often depicted as a wellspring of popular cultural resistance and an alternative archive of a past reality occulted by the powerful, "history" has tended to be treated as a monolith, a catchall for the official, the hegemonic, the written, the deeply inauthentic. As a result, the projects that I will be examining in this book, ones that flirt too close to the borders of conventional historical scholarship in their emphasis on writing the past, are precisely the kind to fall through the cracks of academic interest. Ironically, tacking a wide circle around the sign of history in the name of a more "democratic" memory concept can have the effect of snubbing common and accessible forms of historical production and disregarding the diversity and internal contestation of discourses labeled historical.

Even though my inquiry has been informed by a vibrant interdisciplinary discussion on cultural memory,[6] I thus have to admit that I am not quite ready to give up on history. Many of the cues for my research have been drawn from a growing body of research in postcolonial studies and historical anthropology that examines the social production of the past and political struggles over the control and definition of historical knowledge.[7] This work is highly critical of history as discipline and ideology, but wary of the failure to engage it.

While Hayden White (1973, 1978, 1987) famously located the historical *product*—the historiography (and specifically the masterwork of famous historians)—at the center of critical historical reflection, recent studies in historical anthropology have shifted attention to the conditions of historical produc*tion*.[8] White's assault on historical reference and his assertion that the "truth" of historical texts is largely determined by political forces external to them opened the way for inquiry into the power/knowledge nexus of nation and empire in which historiography occupies a central place. Yet, as Michel-Rolph Trouillot has pointed out, in much critical history, "narratives are occasionally evoked as illustrations, or, at best, deciphered as texts, but the process of their production rarely constitutes the object of study" (1995: 22). Rejecting the extremes of both positivism and constructivism, Trouillot has underlined the importance of attending to the historicity of historical narration itself. In a study on Haitian history and historiography, he has examined the charged political terrain in which historical narratives become authoritative and dominant in national and global contexts as well as the way that glaring silences have been incorporated into the historical record as a result of the unequal access different groups have to the means of historical production.[9] Deliberately de-centering historiography from his analysis, Trouillot asks how silences enter the process of historical production at other sites, such as those of source creation, archive making, and metanarration.

While theorists of history still might treat historiography as the central locus for their meditations on historical practice, for those working in the interstices of history and anthropology, it is the archive that has proved to be an important conceptual figure and research destination. Pointing to a new interdisciplinary interest in archives as subjects, not just sources, for research, Ann Stoler (2002b) suggests that we think of an "archival turn" following close on the heels of the "historical turn" in the social sciences, as archives have started to be approached "not as sites of knowledge retrieval but knowledge production." Thinking of the archive as a "process whereby texts are written" rather than as a mere "accumulation" of documents, to use the words of literary critic Roberto Echevarría (1998: 24), has provided openings for the "ethnography" or "biography" of the archive (Stoler 1992; Dirks 1993). The shift from thinking of archives as depositories of records to *archiving* as a mode of record making draws attention, in other words, to the social and political relationships, rhetorical forms, and layered temporalities generated by and generating diverse archival constructs.[10]

The currency of the term *archive* can be traced back to Michel Foucault's critical work on the history of the human sciences. For Foucault, the archive represents not what has been said by a particular society, but what *can* be said: the archive defines the mode of occurrence of discourses as well as the principle of their differentiation. Posing a radical break with the traditional hermeneutic goals of historical research, he argues: "if there are things said—and those only—one should seek the immediate reason for them in the things that were said not in them, nor in the men that said them, but in the system of discursivity, in the enunciative possibilities and impossibilities that it lays down" (1972: 128). Following Barthes (1977), Foucault (1977) fundamentally displaced the "author" and the "work," the classic categories of intellectual history, from the center of the study of texts and, of course, of history itself. Instead, Foucault's archaeology, as an alternative history of thought, places emphasis on what makes it possible *or impossible* for texts (in the sense of discursive formations) to take shape.

Despite Foucault's admonition that his notion of archive not be confused with the "library of all libraries" or the "sum of all the texts that a culture has kept upon its person as documents attesting to its own past, or as evidence of a continuing identity" (1972: 128–9), social scientists armed with his insights have returned to these literal archives and seen them in productive new ways. Beyond searching there for the "voices" of the lower classes or the colonized—or, more interestingly, identifying the rhetorical tactics and narrative templates, from pardon tales and radical philosophy to rumor and gossip, which they have employed in their confrontations with the state and the law (e.g., Ginzburg 1980; Davis 1987; Stoler 1992; White 2000)—historians, anthropologists, and scholars in other disciplines have begun to examine archival categories and conventions as imprints of governance, traces of imperial imaginaries, and products of discourses and technologies of documentation (statistics, demography, ethnology, law, etc.) marshaled by the state to describe, manage, and rule various "problematic" populations (e.g., Hacking 1990; Comaroff and Comaroff 1992; Richards 1993; Guha 1994; Echevarría 1998; Stoler 2000b, c, forthcoming; Dirks 2001, 2002; Asad 2002).

Before getting too far ahead of the story, though, I need to backtrack and consider how anthropology got into the archive in the first place. The presence of the anthropologist in the archive would seem to break disciplinary etiquette: anthropologists, after all, have traditionally kept their distance from archives, viewing them as sites of historical research homologous to, but nonetheless distinct from, the ethnographic "field." Although there were always isolated voices of dissent, anthropology and history were long seen as compatible inquiries into discrete spheres of alterity (the past, elsewhere). As Lévi-Strauss noted with assurance several decades ago, the anthropologist "conceives [history] as a study complementary to his own: one of them unfurls the range of human societies in time, the other in space" (1966: 256). Disciplinary divisions of labor could be explained in relation to a series of oppositions (writing/orality, history/memory, time/space, conscious/unconscious, the "West"/"the Rest") that, in turn, gave substance to that between archive and field. While the labor of writing has been stressed in both disciplines, the less-explored contrast of historical reading (of a "dead" text) versus anthropological listening (to a "live" voice) might be added to these other pairs. For both historians and anthropologists, however, the journey to a *place* of contact with the "real," whether archive or field, and the exhausting and sometimes dangerous sojourn there have constituted a rite of passage integral to the formation of professional identities with their racial, gender, and ethnic inflections.[11]

Notwithstanding the supposed complementarity of the two disciplines, as late as 1990 James Clifford could puzzle (in something of an overstatement) that "as yet no systematic analysis exists concerning the differences and similarities of [historical and anthropological] research *practice*, juxtaposing 'the archive' with 'the field'—seen both as textual, interpretive activities, as disciplinary conventions, and as strategic spatializations of overdetermined empirical data" (54–5). In the discipline's classic statement on fieldwork, however, Bronislaw Malinowski had explicitly likened the anthropologist to a historian, but one bearing the extra burden of producing documents prior to analyzing them: "In Ethnography, the writer is his own chronicler and *the* historian at the same time, while his sources are no doubt easily accessible, but also supremely elusive and complex; they are not embodied in fixed, material documents, but in the behavior and in the memory of living men" (1922: 3). Just as the historian cannot make a "mystery of his sources" or speak of the past "as if he knew it by divination," anthropologists, argued Malinowski, would also need to document their sources in writing. An incidental effect of this "chronicling" was that the anthropologist became de facto the originary archivist for peoples lacking written historical records. Thus, Malinowski would note with no little pride that the native texts that he had taken down in the local Kiriwinian language formed a *corpus inscriptionum Kiriwiniensium*, a textual archive of local culture analogous to those used by classical philologists in their study of ancient societies (23–4).

With the critique of anthropology's colonial legacy (Asad 1973; Fabian 1983; Said 1989), the imputed differences between anthropology and history would come to be overshadowed by their shared empiricism and common service in colonial knowledge production (Cohn 1980). In turn, the repudiation of the archive's and field's "metonymical power to stand in for the imaginary totalities of anthropology and history" (Axel 2002: 13) set the stage for the remolding of the structural dualities on which the two disciplines have been premised. The deconstruction of those foundational oppositions (and especially the central one of writing/orality), though, might be said to have been foreshadowed by the mimeticism of Malinowski's *corpus*. If the historian's archive preserves "preexistent" documentary collections, what are we to make of the anthropological penchant for *creating* documents (Asad 1986: 144; cf. Cohn 1987: 6, 9)?[12] How does this *poesis* reveal the inevitable "incompleteness" of the archive as well as the linguistic and social construction of the sources "embodied in fixed, material documents"? In the simultaneous reverence and banishment of writing symbolized by Malinowski's *corpus*, emerges the paradox whereby anthropology, the discipline defined by its association with "orality" and the "behavior and memory of living men" might become a suitable epistemological space to rethink the archive as a "process whereby texts are written."

At first, this does seem an unlikely claim: in an overview of the relation of anthropology to written culture, Brinkley Messick (1993b) has argued that the omission of writing as source and subject of anthropological research represents an organizing principle of the discipline.[13] While Messick credits the Geertzian interpretive turn of the 1970s for creating conditions in which an "ethnography of writing" (hypothetically) could develop, he points out that Geertz himself only spoke of the text as *metaphor* for culture and studiously avoided engaging the complex textual heritages and indigenous intellectual traditions of the societies about which he wrote.[14] Geertz's influential writings, thus, could be said to have extended anthropological common sense regarding the exclusion of writing from cultural analysis: namely, anthropologists would continue to study "the text of culture," while the analysis of actual written texts would be left to specialist colleagues in other fields, such as historians and literary critics. As evidenced by the flurry of publications in the 1980s and 1990s that addressed anthropological writing practices and the status of ethnographies as texts (Marcus and Cushman 1982; Clifford and Marcus 1986), anthropologists have proved quite capable of examining the stylistic subtleties of their rhetorical practices. What they consistently have failed to do, as Messick notes, is accord anything near the amount of interest in their subjects' textual productions as they have in their own.

It would be wrong, however, to assume that written culture has just slipped through the cracks of disciplinary concern. Rather than a subject of neutral indifference, writing has something of a bad name in the discipline. The association of writing with Western power and the elite classes of indigenous societies has made it easy for liberal-minded anthropologists to justify focusing on those disenfranchised by writing as well as (strangely) viewing the study of written cultural practice as analogous to "ignoring the voices of the weak" and capitulating to the textual guiles of the powerful. Although highly sensitive to the nuances of verbal communication and their import for social analysis, linguistic anthropologists, for their part, have also typically defined the subject of their research as *speech* not writing (or even speech *against* writing), reflecting the legacy of how language has been conceptualized in structural linguistics.[15] As Derrida has famously pointed out, Saussure viewed writing as inherently *exterior* to "natural" speech: as a secondary semiotic system that had so fundamentally distorted our understanding of language that it could be likened to "a garment of perversion and debauchery, a dress of corruption and disguise, a festival mask that must be exorcised, that is to say warded off, by the good word" (1976: 35). In his critique of Saussure's metaphysics of the sign, Derrida would end up demanding a redefinition not only of orality, but also of writing itself. As he notes, the "violence of writing does not *befall* an innocent language. There is an originary violence of writing because language is first . . . writing" (37). For Derrida, then, "writing" does denote the graphic mark of the signifier, but "dissemination": the "breaking force" (*force de rupture*) that sets the sign adrift in chains of citation (1988: 9). From this perspective, "writing" can be said to be characteristic of all language and even "experience" to the extent that it cannot be disassociated from the "field of the mark" (1988: 9–10).[16]

Be this as it may, given the suspicion of writing (in the conventional sense) that permeates the discipline, it is little wonder that a backlash to the linguistic turn was voiced from many quarters in the 1990s. For instance, those promoting phenomenological approaches to anthropology have challenged, in Valentine Daniel's words, "our collective logocentric inclinations, our privileging of language over labor, words over acts" (1996: 199) and argued for the importance of bringing the senses, emotion, and embodied practice—in other words, nonverbal spheres of human perception, expression, and communication—into the center of anthropological inquiry (cf. Seremetakis 1994; Jackson 1996). Other critiques of anthropology's verbal bias have been voiced by analysts of visual culture who point to the field's stunning lack of attention to the complexities of visual representation (Taylor 1994). Still others have not stopped to argue the point, but in their urgent inquiries into globalization and the new politics of labor, citizenship, and identity seem to imply that the time for "stories" is over. At this point, one might be tempted to jettison the project of textual anthropology entirely as obsolete, even reactionary. On the other hand, the importance of written discourse in anchoring relations of power and domination has hardly been eclipsed, and anthropological investigations of writing practice, far from having reached their saturation point, could be said to have barely begun.

In this book, then, I hope to push the critical discussion on the archive in some new directions while, at the same time, demonstrating how a textual anthropology might enable and be enabled by a theory of archive. Much recent work on archives by historians, anthropologists, and archivists has been focused on *archives of power:* archives of former colonial regimes, archives holding wealthy collections, archives for which extensive information about day-to-day management has been preserved, and archives in which new technologies and innovative archival policies have been pioneered.[17] By contrast, in this book I am asking what might be learned by looking at archiving in a society from which "primary" sources—archaeologist's classical "treasures" and prehistoric shards, philologists' folk songs and funeral laments, and ethnographer's observations of peasant life—have long been mined and removed for "Western" knowledge projects. Already in the "margins of Europe," I push history even further to its limits by focusing on personal rather than public archives, on often outdated technologies and epistemologies of historical research, and on historical practices conducted by people who are not professional historians or archivists.[18] In their banality and creativeness, their conformity and confrontation with hegemonic global and national historical narratives and practices, these independent acts of documentation, I will suggest, constitute unexpectedly generative sites to study the cultural politics of archives and archiving.

Second, rather than looking at archives to study a particular system of rule, I bring these ideas back to the historian's archive in order to open up an ethnography of historical production. Locating this project outside the province of disciplinary history (and canonical historiography) and focusing on moments when "proper" historical form, practice, and method are deemed by the historical establishment to have been transgressed or distorted, in turn, enables me to consider how hierarchies of scholarship shape and are shaped by social distinctions as well as how conventions of authoritative historical discourses themselves delimit the content of the historical. Writing of the identification of amateur history with women's writing practices in nineteenth-century Europe, Bonnie Smith, for instance, has argued that "it was in dialogue with the more popular amateur vision—that is, with femininity, everyday life, and their attendant superficiality—that historical science took shape as a matter of national importance, as genderless universal truth, and simultaneously as a discipline mostly for men" (1998: 9–10). Class, I would add, represents another important axis of social identification around which supposedly objective professional standards are established: the pseudointellectualism of the educated middle classes often forms the required counterpoint to give substance to academic elitism. While modes of historical re-collection inspired by modernist conceptions of witnessing and authenticity entail the mobilization of the lower classes as informants and speakers of oral testimony, it always seems to be middle-class *writers*, especially "graphomaniac" local historians wedded to positivist models of historical scholarship, who arouse the ire and mockery of the scholarly establishment and have to be "put in their place."

Finally, despite their obvious centrality to archives and archiving, processes of entextualization have yet to be explored in any depth in recent theorizing of the archive (Axel 2002: 36). In this book, though, I am keenly interested in the discursive constitution of the archive and the linguistic and technological aspects of historical documentation more generally. As has been implied by my comments thus far, the textual anthropology I have in mind to carry out this project is not a matter of providing a "sociological context" for particular texts by flushing out cultural and historical allusions, sketching biographies and social backgrounds of writers, examining the composition of audiences, and then once again ceding more "technical" linguistic and stylistic matters to text-savvy colleagues. Rather, I intend to actively claim reading as anthropological practice and address language as cultural performative through engagement with the linguistic "details" and "insides" of texts. Before I consider the contours of the Greek archival landscape and the particulars of my case studies, I thus want to elaborate on the archival poetics underpinning this ethnography, placing emphasis first on the document as material artifact and textual property, and then on documentation as citational act.

Keeping Memory in Place

In introducing a materiality often sorely lacking in treatments of history as narrative, a theory of archive draws attention to the political economy of historical production. While masterworks of historiography tend to be radically dematerialized, reproduced, circulated, and analyzed without particular regard for their status as objects, in the archives, texts are first and foremost artifacts. An acknowledgement of this materiality forces reflection on central issues at the core of history's epistemology and even metaphysics. If death turns meaning (a loved one, an important leader) into mere materiality (corpse, ashes, dust), it is history that offers the promise of transforming materiality back into meaning (cf. Stewart 1993: 140). Thus, for de Certeau, writing history "exorcises death by inserting it into discourse" (1988: 100). To arrest and reverse this regenerative process and treat the archive as an end rather than a "means to," by contrast, entails dwelling on the document as fetish and the archive itself as *dwelling*. Insisting on the materiality of the archive illuminates the status of history as patrimony as well as the way that unequal control, possession, and transmission of documentary assemblages contributes to legitimating political authority and anchoring social identities.

In historians' anecdotal accounts of their research, archives often appear as emblems of abstract deterritoriality and timelessness, magical portals to utopia or the afterlife itself. French historian Arlette Farge has likened historical research to an immersion, a plunge in the sea (1989: 10). The archive, for British historian Carolyn Steedman, is not a place, but "a boundless, limitless space" of unfettered memory where the historian can lose herself in speculation in a "striking reversal of the general impulse of modernity, to turn space into place, and to find a home in the world, by literary and other means" (2001: 83). Historians often describe the actual (rather than virtual) archive as a cold, empty place cut off from the daylight and bustle of the unfolding present, a sepulchral catacomb that isolates the historian from (contemporary) humankind. As Steedman suggests, Michelet was "the first to show us this capacity among historians to be alone, not only in the act of writing, but in the archive itself. The Archive allowed the imagining of a particular and modern form of loneliness . . ." (2001: 72).

In the archive, furthermore, the materiality of the document can reassert itself at any moment: the flip side of the archive as symbol of possession and accumulation is its status as a pile of fragile and destructible papers, an irresistible target for acts of incineration and obliteration (cf. Geary 1994; Derrida 1996). The gradual physical decay of archives' contents makes them "monumental repositories of death's debris and documents lacking currency" (Echevarría 1998: 177). Thus, for many historians, the journey to the archive is above all a journey to death, a descent into Hades, which affords them an opportunity to meet with the dead whom history has the capacity (and, for some, the responsibility) to "resurrect." As a result, archival research is characterized by a strange blend of present lifelessness and past liveliness, posing "a startling contradiction" between solitude and submersion in a wallowing "mob" of formerly living beings (Farge 1989: 21).

In some historians' accounts, this archival death drive is inverted into a sexual one as the emptiness of the archive renders it an exotic *terra incognita*, like the "blank spaces" on the colonial map, ripe for historical "penetration" and exploration. Writing of "sex in the archives," Smith has noted the sexual language used by nineteenth-century male historians to speak of their insatiable desires for physical contact with documents, preferably being "touched" by them for the first time: Ranke, for instance, once described working with an "absolutely virgin" collection of documents and having a fling with the "object of my love, a beautiful Italian" (1998: 119). Interestingly, as she points out, historians were writing in these exuberant tones about their archival obsessions and love affairs with document-fetishes at the same time that the historical discipline was in the process of acquiring the trappings of professionalism. Over time, even though this voracious desire to get in touch with the past would come to be attributed to the amateur, historical authority has still remained largely hinged on the presence of the historian in the archive and the mystique of the "primary" source, as Anthony Grafton (1997) has demonstrated in his study of the footnote, that ultimate homage to the archive.

Although these kinds of archival fantasies and nightmares are integral to disciplinary mythologies, there is good reason to counter the persistent abstraction of the archive as imaginative space as well as the archive's primary identification with the professional historian. Indeed, when one ceases looking at the archive from the vantage point of the solitary historian-hero, one cannot but be struck by the archive's *busyness:* a great diversity of social actors, including civil servants, archivists, informants, donors, and researchers are involved in creating, maintaining, and using them. The archive as social world emerges at the nexus of intense textual traffic. Most of the dramas and intrigues played out there have nothing to do with the historian's brief sojourn.

From the materiality of the archive also follows the important point that archives are always *placed*. In taking up place with their bulk, they simultaneously *make* place, even if in the virtuality of cyberspace.[19] A topographical structure appears to be essential to the archive's ability to accumulate and memorialize (as Derrida says, a "domiciliation" necessary for archives to "take place").

Since taking place *takes time*, the archive's structure could properly be said to be *chrono*topic. Even though the mystique of the archive as origin conceals, or attempts to render irrelevant, the conditions of its repetition and reproduction—always with the hope, as Derrida has written of memory in psychoanalysis, to "return to the live origin of what the archive loses while keeping it in a multiplicity of places" (1996: 92)—this unfolding beyond the singularity of the original event constitutes the time of the archive. As an ongoing process of reading and writing, archiving draws attention to the fluidity and interpenetration of temporalities and the dialogic and transferential relationship between past and present involved in historical production (cf. LaCapra 1985a; Rebel 1991). Driven by desires about which they are not always (or often) reflexive, archivists and researchers constantly review and reread archives as they seek "unknown" dimensions of the past, unavoidably projecting present concerns onto historical analogues. The new materials "miraculously" discovered preserved among the archive's holdings through obsessive "grubbing," to use LaCapra's term (1985b), and the shifts in which parts of an archive seem most relevant and noteworthy at different points in time underscore the historicity of historical practices and epistemologies.

Although archives represent the very essence of beginning and origin, this unceasing shuffling and reshuffling of documents make their orientation toward the future seem equally important. The construction of archives is always bound up with what their present makers and managers believe *should* be left to coming generations and the kinds of histories they imagine to be enabled (or disabled) by the architecture and contents of the archive as quintessential work-in-progress. The sense of panic generated by the sheer volume of documents in the archive and the urgency of locating those that have yet to be "salvaged" (from the jaws of destruction and before the death of the last surviving witness) creates a moral hierarchy in which *acting* to collect and preserve is usually privileged over *thinking* about the archival process, thus insuring that the "preliminary" work of documenting never gets done "in time" for analysis to become a priority.

The archive, of course, is as much about bringing together documents, people, and times and keeping them "in place" as it is about dividing, excluding, and keeping out. A notion of home as site of concealment, hoarding, possession, and (un)limited access, thus, appears to be central to the concept of the archive.[20] Archives mark borders between exterior and interior, public and private, visible and invisible. To quote Derrida: "No archive without outside." An archive's monumental exterior is what generates a sense of mystique and secrecy surrounding the contents held within. That is why opening formerly closed archives, such as those of totalitarian or dictatorial regimes, is usually anticlimactic: what is found are not the scandalous secrets of the regime but the banality of its everyday mechanisms of surveillance.[21]

Limiting access to archives, even ones that are ostensibly public, has a long history, linked to social hierarchies pertaining to different cultural and historical contexts. In nineteenth-century Europe, for example, women, children, and men lacking credentials were often barred from entering archives and libraries, while during the same period men's studies at home began to be defined as off-limits for other members of the family (Smith 1998: 127). The digital age, though, appears to be preparing the way for a new democratic ideal of global archival access. In Internet "archives without walls" not only is a broader public able to use archival holdings, but the holdings themselves can be greatly expanded through links to other archival collections; as a result, archival ownership also is being fundamentally transformed since documentary collections can remain in the custody of their original producers or owners and still be broadly accessible (Cook 2000). Despite these radical possibilities, as has become increasingly clear, much is also being invested in preventing the free circulation of discourse online. It might be more appropriate, then, to speak not of access, but of "fictions of access" (Stoler 2002b), and consider how the transparency of knowledge (as myth) has operated as a technology of liberal governmentality aimed at constituting citizens as rational, self-governing, and self-improving political subjects (Joyce 1999).

While critical discussion of historiography has centered primarily on the scripting of national fantasies of origin and continuity, archiving draws attention to the relationship of history to the state and, by extension, to law, bureaucracy, and citizenship. In saying this, I do not mean to imply that the state is the practical or real instantiation of the nation's imaginary. The state's magic is just as spellbinding as the nation's. The difference lies in the fact that the state is typically depicted as the

"transcendent unifying agent of the nation" (Coronil 1997: 4): in other words, as
that entity that can turn the dream of the nation into a reality. As records of the
state's interaction with its citizens as well as sign of the state's capacity to preserve,
organize, and monumentalize the nation's past, archives can be seen as one of the
many potential arenas in which the state depicts itself as able to bridge the hyphen
between nation and state. To understand the degree to which archives have come to
symbolize the state and project its political legitimacy, one need only consider the
French national archives, the prototype of the modern archive, whose establishment
was one of the founding acts of the revolutionary government. On a symbolic plane,
the granting of public access to the French national archives, over which, in fact,
there would be much discussion on a practical level (as regards the setting up of a
reading room, the job description of the archivists, the publication of catalogues of
holdings, etc.) signaled a radical break with patriarchy and heredity and the adoption of a new ethic of governance in which an unfettered conduit between state and
citizenry was touted (cf. Milligan forthcoming).

More often than not, however, archives have been used less to display the state's
accountability to its citizens than its capacity for brute power and domination over
them and the state's enemies. In absconding archival material from other European
countries and bringing it to Paris to fill a new Palais des Archives, Napoleon turned
archival acquisition into a sine qua non of expanding states. With his defeat and the
return of most of the documents to their original owners, archives became a national
priority across Europe, thus enabling scholars to demonstrate their patriotism
through efforts to secure or publish collections of documents (Smith 1998: 116–7).
At the height of European colonialism, archival formation represented a practical
and symbolic instantiation of imperial rule. Thomas Richards, for instance, has
described the archives of Victorian England as a "utopian space of comprehensive
knowledge" that constituted "a virtual focal point for the heterogeneous local knowledge of metropolis and empire" (1993: 11). Although the (theoretically) open
archives of liberal democracies always had their "forbidden" parts (Combe 1994), in
the twentieth century it was the communist archive that emerged as the paragon of
the "closed" archive, perfectly fusing the modalities of secrecy and transparency
at the heart of the archive concept. While the obsessive bureaucratic machine of the
Party served as the cornerstone of its radically egalitarian ideology, its apparatus
of surveillance and totalitarian grip on power rendered its archives the epitome of
distrust, obscurantism, and arbitrary power.

Although for Derrida, the archive occupies a "privileged *topology*" (1996: 3) close
to power, it might be more useful to think of archives as simply located in some kind
of relation to power. The monumentality of archives—or their conspicuous *lack* of
monumentality, dispersion, disorganization, decay, and even burial in that most
mythical and crypt-ic of archival locations, "in the basement in boxes"—symbolize
the relative coherence or incoherence of the collectivities that have created them,
whether families, nation-states, political parties, or transnational communities. Since
archives often do not succeed in establishing a permanent home for themselves, but
are frequently housed "temporarily" (in a rented space, an extra room in a building
with another function, etc.), it might be more useful to think less in terms of place

than of pla*cing*, and to attend to the incessant movements (relocations, dislocations, even exile) of archival collections and their textual properties. Thus, between the early travels—and travails—of the American Constitution and Declaration of Independence and their "permanent" housing in a specially constructed "Shrine of Freedom" in the U.S. National Archives, one can trace the consolidation of the American state as well as its increasing need and ability to monumentalize its history.[22] If one looks beyond the prototype of the modern archive as a completed monument centered in the capital of a powerful nation with a colonial past, it becomes clear that maintaining an archive over time, controlling access to its holdings, and encasing it in a sufficiently imposing and grand exterior is not such an easy matter. At the same time, surviving political domination can be hinged on keeping things in many places and out of sight.

Geopolitical relations and asymmetries of power, as I will suggest in this book, can be studied in unexpected ways in the absence and destruction of archives, in dreams of archival totality never achieved, and in documents displaced, lost, exiled, or distributed in transnational circuits as well as in personal archives established to offset these deficits, expose historical injustices and oversights, or set the terms of historical knowledge on another footing. Just as an archive of power asserts its autonomy and self-sufficiency by centralizing its holdings and importing materials from other locations to subsume to its categories, the inability to hold on to important documents and halt their materialization as paper, pulp, garbage, or ashes can be a telling sign of political subordination or persecution.

Inscribing Origins, Authorizing Genres

Given its centrality in defining historical knowledge and professional identity, the archive, surprisingly, has not proved an important subject of theoretical analysis by historians. As the unnamed figure of authority, the archive has been left to the anecdotal margins of disciplinary discourse: to corridor talk and autobiographical reflections on the experience of research. For most historians and philosophers of history, the collecting of documents and the consultation of archives represent the all-important *first* step. Writing of the "historiographical operation," de Certeau, for instance, has asserted that "in history everything begins with the gesture of setting aside, of putting together, of transforming certain classified objects into 'documents.' This new cultural distribution is the first task" (1988: 72). While Ricoeur maintains that his three "phases" (documentation, explication, representation) refer to different methodological levels, not chronological stages, of historical practice, an evolutionary schema positing historiography as endpoint remains implicit (2000: 170). A similar teleology is also apparent in historians' informal essays. Meditating on her research in eighteenth-century judicial archives, Farge reminds her reader that "history is never the repetition of the archive" (1989: 93) and concludes with a final chapter entitled "Writing," in which she considers how the fragmented discourses of dead voices might be transposed into the historian's final written account.

Commenting on the "feverish" (figuratively and literally speaking) impatience of researchers to find what they are seeking within the "dust" of the archive, Steedman describes British social historians' haste to leave the provincial town where the Public Record Office is located and *finally* get home to write (2001: 29).

Breaking with guild narratives of the progression from documentation (the archive, the archival encounter) to history, I propose to de-center a genre (academic historiography) and a textual practice (writing) from the discussion of historical practice and rhetorics. This move has at least three implications. First, while viewing historiography as the representation of a given historical "reality" confirms a text-context understanding of the relationship of language to historical experience, a focus on archiving obviates such spurious categories. Thinking in terms of the archive means shifting attention away from narrative (and its "closure," "coherence," and "meaning") to open-ended acts of citation that cut across textual utterances, archival formations, and the fact-fiction divide: in other words, to the "he-said-she-said" of historical discourse and the links of listening and trust of which historical knowledge is inevitably composed.[23] Framed in terms of transmission rather than verification, citation alerts us to the ethics of history.

Second, the shift from historical product to historical production entails a shift away from the "author" and the "work" to the power-laden intertexual borders between reporting and reported discourse within and between conventionally defined textual units. As a result, even when addressing "traditional" texts of literary, historical, or anthropological analysis (e.g., fiction, historiography, oral narrative), media studies theory that reconceptualizes the work as an effect within a network can be instructive.[24]

Finally, in de-emphasizing the finished, authoritative text of historiography, the turn to archive brings into relief a multiplicity of textual practices *besides* writing (or, if we follow Derrida, *as* "writing," as dissemination) and a plethora of genres of historical writing involved in documenting the past. Highlighting this textual spectrum makes clear the extent to which the differential credibility of various genres normalizes the uneven distribution and legitimation of social knowledges. Furthermore, this textual panoply exposes the degree to which the monolingual and referential frame of normative historiography excludes "foreign" (a-syntactical, untranslated/ untranslatable, nondenotative, noncausal) discourse as a "mere" matter of form.

Intertextuality and the Archival Gap

A discursive theory of archive cannot be anything other than a theory of intertextuality. Taken as a whole, the archive is characterized by a complex and almost haphazard juxtaposition of documents. As Echevarría has suggested, one of the fundamental functions of the archive as "grab-bag of texts" is to "generate an inchoate, heteroglossic mass: a mass of documents and other texts that have not been totally, and sometimes not even partially absorbed, that retain their raw, undisturbed original existence as evidence of the non-assimilation of the Other" (1998: 176). As opposed to the collection, the hallmark of the archive, as I have noted above, is its retention of the link between a particular document and the original context of its production and use. A turn to archive, thus, brings into relief a multiplicity of technologies and textual practices (and nontextual, even antitextual practices) involved in creating, replicating, or eradicating the "primary" source, such as copying, touching, transcribing, translating, listening, reading, collecting, classifying, annotating, citing, donating, xeroxing, handwriting, typewriting, computer-processing, photographing, taperecording, videotaping, hiding, hoarding, exposing, censoring, and forging as well as, of course, tearing, shredding, burning, and deleting. Needless to say, historians themselves engage in many of these archival functions as they compose personal, (ex)portable archives of transcribed sources from which to write their histories.

History might not (or should not) be the "repetition of the archive," but repetition remains the most fundamental fact of the archive. Remarking on the endless hours she has spent in the archive "recopying, without changing a word," Farge reflects on the seeming "imbecility" of "this banal and strange exercise," this "industrious and obsessive occupation," but concludes that something ultimately is gained through the physical, sometimes grueling passage of the archive through the historian's body (1989: 24–6). De Certeau similarly explains that history begins with the process of "producing" a series of documents "by dint of copying, transcribing, or photographing these objects, simultaneously changing their locus and their status" (1988: 72). Even though, for Ricoeur, the archive represents the "first writing," he acknowledges, "in the archives, the historian is by profession a reader" (2000: 209). A focus on the archive thus gives pride of place to practices central in narratives of historical research and archival "survival," ranging from the valued intellectual capacity to read and judge what is important (and what is missing) in a surfeit of materials to the humbling manual and mechanical labor of copying and transcription.

Despite the fact that the archive attempts to put a lock on provenance, the archive-in-practice is testament to the constant drift of written signs into new textual compositions. Contrary to the principle of provenance (namely that utterances can best (or only) be understood in relation to their original contexts), Derrida has pointed out that signs prove eminently readable and communicative even if we do not know what their (supposed) author meant to say at the moment of their inscription: they can always be "grafted" into new chains of signs and not only not lose their ability to function but also gain new possibilities for expression. This essential "iterability" precludes the ability of any context to totally enclose the sign's identity (1988: 9). As a result, as Bakhtin has suggested in a similar vein, when we speak we are never really using "our own" words. Discourse does not just point to a referential object; it always also recognizes the word of the other and carries over its ideological accents. Against a cultural (and legally codified) conception of private textual property, Bakhtin reminds us that the "word in language is half someone else's" (1981: 293).

These "decontextualizations" and "recontextualizations" of discourse, in turn, represent a promising site for the anthropological study of the interface of textual and social power. In a discussion of studies on performance in linguistic anthropology, Richard Bauman and Charles Briggs argue that scholars have spent enough time demonstrating that verbal art must be contextualized within particular social worlds and performance routines (instead of treated as a static philological text-artifact); they suggest that a more urgent project is to examine the linguistic processes and social circumstances enabling the *de*contextualization of discourse (whether for the purposes of social science research or in the course of local negotiations of power): "Taking the practice of decontextualization as the focus of investigation, we ask what makes it possible, how it is accomplished in formal and functional terms, for what ends, by whom, under what circumstances, and so on" (1992: 72). From this perspective, the "banal and strange exercise" of gingerly holding, reproducing, and transmitting a series of "original" graphic marks in the course of historical research appears to be a culturally elaborate, sensual ritual with political import.

Historical writing in the historicist tradition has endorsed (even required) the large-scale decontextualization and recontextualization of various kinds of supporting evidence. In historiography, these textual appropriations tend to be emphasized, not concealed, since evidence is usually cited in a maximally intact state as metonym for a given historical "experience," period, or identity position. As in journalistic and judicial discourse, loosening the quotation marks and paraphrasing a given stretch of text usually diminishes its persuasiveness. As V. N. Vološinov notes: "Judicial language intrinsically assumes a clear-cut discrepancy between the verbal subjectivism of the parties to a case and the objectivity of the court" (1929: 123). It is this piercing of historical discourse with innumerable other cultural performatives that makes it particularly open to examination as *social* text. As Messick has written of judicial testimony, texts constructed from quoted discourse are particularly valuable for social analysis because they comment on discourse itself: "theirs is a discourse about discourse, about other texts both written and oral" (1995: 168). Extending this observation, one might add that quoting evidence also establishes an inter*medial*, not only intertextual, relationship between framing discourse and cited text, which implicitly comments on, compares, and hierarchizes media technologies (e.g., when a handwritten document is referred to and reproduced in print).

Rather than a routine and unremarkable matter, citation might be viewed as a politically and morally loaded response to another's voice and accorded a place at the center of a textual ethnography of historical production. In his well-known discussion of reported speech, Vološinov describes three kinds of relations that a reporting context can establish with the speech it reports. The first is a balanced relation in which reporting and reported speech maintain clear borders. The second entails a colonization of the reported speech by the author's discourse ("Language devises means for infiltrating reported speech with authorial retort and commentary in deft and subtle ways"). In the third kind, the reported speech is more powerful than the reporting context and undermines its authority (1929: 120). This last case is marked by the permeation of the framing text with alien ideologies and agendas from the perspective of the author's (putative) intentions. Bakhtin has described the resistance of reported speech to appropriation and assimilation as entailing the assertion of quotation marks against the will of the speaker: "Language is not a neutral medium that passes freely and easily into the private property of the speaker's intentions; it is populated—overpopulated—with the intentions of others" (1981: 294).

A special case of citation practice, which often coincides with the relationship of oral (reported) speech to written (reporting) discourse, involves the translation of foreign language (including dialects, varieties, and antiquated forms of the "same" language) into a "standard" or "modern" national tongue. Rather than the starting point for historical writing and (national) archival formation, monolingualism can be viewed as one of its most important products. The requirement that foreign languages be translated so that a text speaks a *single* language necessarily renders unreadable forms of historical discourse that speak multiple languages and, worst of all, do not clearly hierarchize them.

Translation, of course, is never just a transparent exchange of currency in a free market circulation of language but, as many scholars of colonialism have stressed, a relationship between unequal languages. Given that some languages are "more likely to submit to forcible transformation in the translation process" (Asad 1986: 157–8; cf. Rafael 1993), the "complementarity" of languages belies the fact that their "discursive and cultural *modes of signification* are in conflict with each other, striving to exclude each other" (Bhabha 1994: 227). The token citation of a few exotic words in a foreign language can authenticate the translating discourse while reducing the translated language to a list of key words "roughly translated," as in glossaries found in area studies monographs (Chakrabarty 2000: 17) or the *vocabulaire* of colonial explorers who oriented themselves toward "*using words*, rather than *speaking*" (Fabian 1986: 19). Even though translation can often involve "linguistic alienation," (Friedrich 1989) as speakers are forced to conform to a dominant language, it is important not to fetishize the "mother tongue," which itself can be the product of nationalist campaigns of standardization and the eradication of multilingual practices. In demanding that equivalences be found for different languages, registers, and alphabets, translation as institutional practice can be said to support the ideal of an unmixed, pure, "native" language and the innate separation of (national) languages.[25] Nostalgia for what is "lost in translation" also can elide the performative aspect of translation as a "staging of cultural difference" (Bhabha 1994: 227) as well as the way that the *translating* language is transformed through encounter with the "foreignness" of other languages, as Benjamin (1968) has famously argued.

Given the fetish of the primary source, mediation as social, linguistic, and technological process and power relation tends to be downplayed, even erased, in the name of isolating and illuminating the original word. As Derrida has suggested, the belief in the primacy of live memory is dependent on defining the "technical prosthesis" as a "secondary and accessory exteriority" (1996: 92). Freud himself dreamed of recovering memory in its original temporality in the way that an archaeologist unearths stones that seem to speak the truth of the past without the need for an archivist-mediator. Yet, as Derrida points out, Freud's own model of the psyche and memory was shaped by concepts of inscription, temporality, archivization, circulation, reproduction, and impression related to a particular kind of mediated communication: namely, handwritten correspondence. Media theorist Friedrich Kittler, on the other hand, has argued that as "talking cure," Freudian psychoanalysis was inspired by new technologies of voice recording, which in documenting *sound* (noise, babble) shattered the philological category of discourse, the text (i.e., meaning). Despite the phonological principles at work in psychoanalysis and its focus on the "nonsense" (parapraxes, puns, slips of speech), Kittler partly corroborates Derrida by concluding that the written psychoanalytic case study represents a "final attempt to establish writing under media conditions" (1999: 90). For our purposes, two points must be stressed about technologies of documentation. For one, despite the fact that these technologies crucially shape archivable content, the persistent denial of mediation in various practices of historical re-collection can be essential to truth claims based on access to the authenticity of a primary source, whether an "original" written document or a "live" voice. Second, the mixing of media (as in Freud's case) might be seen not just in terms of technological determinism—in other words, as an incomplete cultural and historical shift (e.g., from philological transcription to phonography, from the (good) hand-writing of the European high bourgeoisie to the typewritten texts of global mass culture)—but as an index of socioeconomic hierarchies and competing cultural, aesthetic, political, and moral positions.

In this book, I will consider techniques and technologies of documentary inscription and archival repetition from several vantage points, including that of the "textual archive" of primary sources, the written transcription of oral testimony by educated mediators, and the transliteration and translation of foreign languages or dialects into a "standard" literary language. The textualized archive turns up in numerous guises in this book: the "source books" of local historians eager to amass the documents needed for a historical analysis of the local past (to be written in the future, by someone else, someone trained); the archival activism of professional historians, who (temporarily) don "the uniform of the archivist" to secure the necessary "proof" to write forgotten or forbidden histories; and so-called documentary fiction. The published archive of primary sources is a legacy of nineteenth-century historicist scholarship when books and journals often boasted titles such as "Archive of . . ." or "Cabinet of . . ."[26] In comparison to historiography, these works appear to be banal and "primitive" genres of historical re-collection, which simply reproduce the textual collocation of existing archives or create new ones from evidence that is "out there." However, the selection, framing, and "remediation" (Bolter and Grusin 1999) of these sources into other media formats (through typing, printing, computer processing, digitization) effects a change in locus and status that, as de Certeau has pointed out, is always productive, not derivative. At the same time, on a more existential level, the abiding belief in the document as access point to the presence and intention of the author is integral to the way in which the archival origin comes to be desired, claimed, embodied, and brought home during the course of historical research.

A necessary correlate to the textual profusion of the archive is the mystique of its gaps; the overwhelming textual clutter and its semblance of fullness is offset by the recognition of just how much is not there, of what has been lost, destroyed, confiscated, made off-limits, or never written down in the first place. This lack of closure "underscores the fact that gaps are constitutive of the Archive as much as volume" (Echevarría 1998: 182). As Trouillot has argued, the silences in the historical record should not be considered mere or incidental absences; instead, silences and mentions constitute "dialectical counterparts." In his view, the archive is not a passive accumulation but a dynamic arena that prepares particular facts for "historical intelligibility" (1995: 48–52). Over the course of the twentieth century, there have been significant changes in the idea of why archives exist; a juridical-administrative model of archives serving the internal needs of the state has given way to a sociocultural one, reflecting the sway of historians in the training of archivists as well as archives' wider public use. While insuring government accountability, the protection of personal rights, and the continuity of the administrative apparatus are still acknowledged as key functions of archives, increasingly citizens expect documentary collections to provide them with a touchstone for their identity, a sense of place, and a repository for cultural memory (Cook 2000). As a result, many archivists have reimagined themselves as *creators* of archives, selectively sifting through a massive corpus of documents but also identifying and filling in the archive's perceived "gaps" by generating or seeking other kinds of documents to compensate for the overrepresentation of certain powerful record collectors (Wallot and Fortier 1998). This attempt to compensate for silences by filling in "gaps," whether through the production of new documents (via ethnography, oral history, or even historical fiction) or the designation of new categories of papers and artifacts as "historical documents" (i.e., the records of a factory, personal letters, diaries, audiovisual materials) in accordance with changing criteria of historical knowledge, however, often represents less of a critique of the "archive system" than a capitulation to the positivist dream of archival totalization. Furthermore, documenting the "experience" of groups excluded from the historical record through this additive process of archival expansion can end up, ironically, reifying their identities rather than addressing the way that subjects are discursively constituted as "different" to begin with (Scott 1992).

While all the personal archives I consider in this book were constructed in order to expand the documentary base, some also make explicit bids to *reform* archival categories through the generation of new kinds of documents. Given the prominence of testimony as a mode of historical production in the latter half of the twentieth century, the transcription and citation of oral sources has occupied a central place in these projects of archival reform. The use of oral sources, of course, is of particular interest because of their radically variable status in different historical epistemologies and political ideologies. For the historicist, orally transmitted information is dubious: it always must be "double-checked" and matched against written sources.[27] With the emergence of testimony as a profoundly compelling mode of cultural representation, however, the oral discourse of the testifier has taken on a new validity in relation to written sources. In modernist and Marxist historical approaches, oral sources can *heighten* a text's authority by introducing the viewpoint of the "lower classes" and the "common person" who has usually been "written out" of history.

Yet, the burden of the witness, according to Felman and Laub, lies in the fact that testimony is "solitary" and "noninterchangeable"; it cannot be "relayed, repeated, or reported without thereby losing its function as a testimony" (1992: 3). How, then, can oral testimony be *written* and still remain "authentic"? Given the ethical and emotional aspect of testimony, the position of the scribe as "honest" mediator takes on especial importance. Since the verbatim transcript of oral speech rarely sounds as true and as moving as literary representations of the oral, literary traditions of testimony, in fact, can create expectations about "real" testimony that affect how it is both heard and documented. As a result, it becomes pressing to identify implicit textual templates (but also actual recording technologies) that shape the reified text unit ultimately expropriated from interactional contexts. Furthermore, to the extent that the voice of the witness can be used strategically to empower the mediator, the terms of authorship on which these dialogues and communicative exchanges are undertaken must be considered as well as the instances when quoted testimony escapes the semantic control of the masterful mediator-writer. Finally, rephrasing Gayatri Spivak's famous question, we must also ask, "can the subaltern *write*"?

Genre and the Performative

Along with citation, genre is the other concept on which I have relied in this book to move beyond a mechanistic text/context model of the relation of language to society toward a more nuanced understanding of the co-construction of linguistic forms and social relations as well as to de-emphasize authorial intent. Like reported speech, genre is a pivotal site in which language, culture, and ideology intersect. In his *Introduction to Poetics*, Tzvetan Todorov explains that the study of genre requires both formal and ideological analysis, "for genre is as closely related to linguistic forms as it is to the history of ideas" (1981: xxxi).

In sketchy but insightful comments in the late essay "The Problem of Speech Genres," (1986) Bakhtin suggested how this stodgy category of literary criticism, traditionally focused on parsing typological distinctions between particular literary genres (epic, drama, etc.), could be transformed into a useful tool for social analysis. He did so, for one, by radically expanding the notion of genre to encompass the diversity and heterogeneity of human verbal expression, both written and oral, prosaic and poetic. Thus, speech genres, for Bakhtin, include forms of conventionalized discourse of varying degrees of elaboration, ranging from business documents to short rejoinders of daily dialogue, proverbs to multivolume novels, and personal letters to legal contracts, military commands, and scientific arguments. Second, he emphasized the connection of speech genres to specific spheres of communication and pointed to the ongoing "restructuring" and "renewal" of speech genres in situations of political and ideological struggle. Finally, as opposed to a view of genre as a distinct and closed verbal form, Bakhtin drew attention to the relationship *between* them, pointing out that secondary (or complex) speech genres (such as novels, ethnographies, etc.) typically "absorb and digest" primary ones (letters, oral reports, etc.). In this way, genres create frames between themselves and other genres (i.e., history is what is "not fiction"), but also act *as* frames for other discourses that they incorporate. Thus, genres can be said to put the world together in specific ways by arranging other discourses into a selective, often hierarchical, discursive order.

Drawing on Bakhtin, Charles Briggs and Richard Bauman (1992) have considered the implications of generic intertextuality for anthropology. Once genre ceases to be viewed as a series of linguistic features immanent to a text and understood as a relationship between a text and a tradition of discourse, it can be used to describe how textual coherence *and incoherence* are effected. On the one hand, a notion of genre gives structure and depth to textual production and orients the reception and interpretation of texts by creating links between them and their antecedents. In projecting a sense of "tradition," this intertextuality can be instrumental in the consolidation of certain kinds of authority (not everyone, for instance, is equally capable of casting discourse successfully within the constraints of a particular genre). The stability of genre, thus, can be fundamental to the integrity, autonomy, and identity of a given community or intellectual tradition: consider, for instance, the importance of historiography in establishing both the reality of the nation's "life" and of the historical discipline itself. On the other hand, as Briggs and Bauman point out, since texts never perfectly fit any generic model, an "intertextual gap," by definition, will always present itself. In some discourses, this gap is concealed in order to present an ideological façade of textual—and social—continuity (this impulse, I will argue, is strong in local historiography). Other discourses, by contrast, highlight a break with the past in order to emphasize authorial creativity and textual innovation (e.g., modernist writing) or ideological reform (e.g., Marxist historiography). Just as genre endows a sense of order and boundedness to texts, it also exposes the composition of texts from a variety of other genres, which, as in the case of citation, pull a given work in multiple, unpredictable directions. The authoritativeness of a particular genre can often be gauged in terms of its ability to effectively "contain" and "control" the other genres it incorporates.

Genre, thus, might be defined less by what it *is* than what it *does*, and brought into dialogue with theories of the performative. This move creates the possibility of displacing reference as the sole or ultimate function of historical discourse. As J.L. Austin (1962) has pointed out, even denotative statements can constitute speech acts to the extent that they inform; as we know from ideology-laden texts such as dictionaries, descriptive language can also be highly *prescriptive* (Bourdieu 1991: 60–1). The performative dimension of historical discourse is particularly pronounced in witnessing. In their important study on testimony, Felman and Laub (1992) have argued that testimony should not be treated simply as a report of the facts but understood as a speech act that addresses a listening other. In their view, testimony records the force of events not fully understood: "As a performative speech act, testimony in effect addresses what in history is *action* that exceeds substantialized significance, and what in happenings is *impact* that dynamically explodes any conceptual reifications and any constative delimitations" (5). In her work on trauma, Caruth (1996) similarly explains that theories of testimony do not deny reference, but refigure it as the repetitive and inescapable reenactment of traumatic events.

This conceptualization of reference in theories of trauma and testimony resonates with philosopher C.S. Peirce's semeiotics and, particularly, his notion of the Interpretant.[28] Peirce's tripartite model of the sign avoids locking the signifier and signified into a mirrored relationship (as Saussure suggested by likening the sign to two sides of a sheet of paper, joining the idea on the front and the acoustic image on the back). Thus, while the sign vehicle (what Peirce calls the Representamen) stands for something (an object), it always "addresses somebody, that is, creates in the mind of that person an equivalent sign, or perhaps a more developed sign" (§2.228). The "effect of the sign" and its "signification," the third component of the sign, what Peirce terms the Interpretant, *registers* the impact of an event, but not in mimetic terms. As we will see in many cases in this book, it is precisely discourse that cannot be reduced to reference in the conventional sense of a description of "what happened"—and yet is strikingly *true* to events—that various genres of historical discourse either blindly excise or struggle to express and record.

Viewed as a boundary marker and point of intersection for various discursive forms and cultural performatives rather than as a set of rules for the production of self-sufficient units of discourse, a concept of genre enables an appreciation of textual economies. In this book I present a wide spectrum of genres of historical writing, including local historiography, autobiography, historical fiction, and even records of historical research and archival formation (the "archivists' manuscripts").[29] I do not view this range of genres as representing a series of "choices" for potential historical authors, but rather as a hierarchy of discursive forms whose textual conventions (chronotope, linguistic register, handling of reported speech) strongly delimit the kinds of stories they can narrate.

Although I do not examine academic historiography directly in this book, at various junctures I draw attention to the dynamic by which scholarly discourse establishes its authority through discrediting and distancing itself from the vast and diverse realm of historical writing produced by nonprofessionals. Describing such processes in relation to literature and literary criticism, Boym has argued that the emergence of the Russian literary masterpiece was dependent on "graphomania," which she defines as a "practice of writing perceived as unhealthy in its own time, whether excessively banal, ideologically incorrect or culturally improper." She notes that concern about graphomania developed along with rising literacy in the nineteenth century, while in the postcommunist world it appears to be on the wane, along with the cultural status of literature itself. During its heyday, though, graphomania illuminated "the tenuous relationship between the art of writing in the singular, and the art of writing in the plural; between literature, which in some cultures constitutes the core of national identity, and everyday writing, which could jeopardize it" (169). Similarly, the phenomenon of historical logorrhea in Greek society can be seen as a sign of the importance accorded to the historical in Greek national culture.

While the place occupied by literature within textual economies might always merit special attention, in marking the crucial fault line between "fact" and "fiction," literature takes on added significance in a discussion of historical rhetorics. As counterpoint to the world of "real" discourse, literature has often served in times of political repression as a refuge or storehouse for aspects of historical experience and social critique that could not be expressed in discourses claiming to speak the truth. Literature, as Felman and Laub have pointed out, can represent a "precocious mode of witnessing" that inscribes "what we do not yet know of our lived historical relation to events of our times" (1992: 6). At the same time, with the advent of testimony, the boundaries between public and private knowledges and poetry and prose have been irrevocably shifted: in Mallarmé's phrase, "Verse is all there is" [*le vers et tout*] (cited in Felman and Laub 1992: 20). In monopolizing the "author function" in particular historical and cultural contexts, literature, according to Foucault (1977), also has been, disproportionately, a site of the systematic practice of transgression. With its "imaginative license" to mimic other speech genres, the novel has the potential to expose the rhetorical construction of authoritative discourses. This power might lie precisely in the fact that the novel *lacks* a genre of its own and, as Roberto Echevarría suggests, "has persisted for centuries without a poetics, always in defiance of the very notion of genre" (1998: 6). In often being as persuasive as factual discourse (if not more!), the novel can be extremely threatening to the historical discipline. To the extent that this is the case, it becomes problematic, if not impossible, to speak of historical discourse without taking into consideration the novel, especially the so-called historical novel.

Against a view of literature as "mirroring" life, Felman and Laub have underscored the dynamic reinscription and reworking of historical experience enacted by the text. Since context always must *read* and cannot just simply be known, they propose that the contextualization of text be complemented by a *textualization of context*. Similarly, in his discussion of history and the novel, Dominick LaCapra notes how context is always discovered *through* texts, a fact that is consistently obscured by the demand for context to play the role of a "determinative force with full explanatory power" (1985a: 128). From his perspective, literature should not be treated as secondary to historical scholarship (i.e., redundant of the facts it confirms) or merely suggestive of a given period, but as a use of language that inscribes contexts in ways that bear on some of the most important and subtle processes of life even if its insights cannot be "double-checked." Locating the novel *within* a broader textual economy rather than marking off a sphere of "historical fiction" as a subfield of literary production, thus, can break the deadlock of asking the nonquestion of how history inspires or is served by literature. Literature, instead, might be understood as an important kind of historical discourse in its own right as well as an irreplaceable guide to the cultural poetics of documentation.

"Greece" in the Archives

In the meantime let us hope that the state will show a livelier interest in our work, commensurable with that which we have so often demonstrated. While everywhere in the world states themselves found museums and erect luxurious buildings worthy of housing the historic heirlooms [keimilia] of the Nation and the written monuments of its history, here instead, after having ourselves created the museum of Greece from nothing, we have been threatened with expulsion and submitted to the dangers of the most arduous and expensive relocation so that, after a long course, we will end up with the most unsuitable of buildings in Athens to house our collections and even this will be under new and greater threats of provisionality . . .

—Konstandinos Rados, *Minutes of the Historical and Ethnological Society of Greece, 1916*

Focusing on Greece as a site of archival production interrupts certain expectations about where it might be most interesting and important to think about the politics of knowledge. Derrida (1996) has made much of the ancient Greek etymology of the archive but, as in so much else, the modern Greek *archeio* differs profoundly from its ancient counterpart. The residence of the ancient magistrates and storehouse of documents over which they possessed jurisdiction and exclusive interpretive control symbolized the perfect coincidence of political and textual authority. But those archons and their grand dwellings went missing long ago and contemporary Greece does seem, at first, a most unpromising place to study archiving and documentation.

Indeed, if the monumental architecture of the state archives of other European countries imposingly proclaims their colonial pasts and contemporary authority, the fact that Greece's General State Archives were not settled into a permanent building until 2003, nearly a century after their establishment and following decades of nomadic existence, uncatalogued and scattered in basements of public buildings and rented spaces around Athens, speaks eloquently to Greece's position in the global hierarchies.[30] This situation underscores the degree to which "Greece" has succeeded in projecting the image of a fully realized nation-state to the outside world, not to mention to its own citizens.

Predictably, the first efforts to gather documents relating to the country's modern history were undertaken not by the state, but by private individuals and groups, goaded into action by the state's failure to act as responsible guardian to national memory. In 1901, Yiannis Vlahoyiannis, a philologist, author, and dogged historical collector, would write of his Sisyphean attempts to stem the daily destruction of historical documents and their transformation into—or mistaken identification as— paper or garbage. Given the lack of public interest in preserving the records of contemporary Greek history, he explains how he took it upon himself to "salvage" documents from grocery stores where they were being used to wrap sold items and to scour "Athenian alleys and stockyards and basements and cheap dives to collect the priceless national treasure, which ignorance and negligence had condemned to total obliteration" (iv). Over the course of a lifetime of historical collecting, Vlahoyiannis even had occasion to save documents from the annihilating hand of the state itself: in 1893, when the national Audit Department decided to sell off old state documents in a massive public auction, he would buy many valuable documents pre-dating the rule of King Otto. After some years, though, he ended up donating these materials, along with his own vast personal archives, "back" to the General State Archives, where he served as first director and whose very establishment in 1914 is typically attributed to his tireless lobbying (Topping 1952: 249).[31]

For some Greeks, the state's failure to archive properly is just one more item in a long list of national disgraces whose enumeration forms a leitmotif as much of daily conversation as of social science rhetoric. As far back as 1882, the Historical and Ethnological Society of Greece had been founded by private citizens to collect historical artifacts, documents, and ethnological material relating to medieval and modern Greek history and philology. The group's goal was to create a historical archive and museum similar to the Hôtel de Cluny in Paris or the Kensington Museum in London. Although a private initiative, the society was established with the aim of ultimately turning its collections over to the nation as its "sacred trust" (iera parakatathiki): this phrase suggests the religious-patriotic zeal with which society members undertook their labors, as do descriptions of documents and artifacts as "relics" (leipsana) of national "life" (vios).[32] By 1916, even though they "were not any more in the first days of this" and their cases and cabinets were overflowing, the state, however, not only had failed to underwrite the society's efforts, but had barely protected them from eviction—or, as Konstandinos Rados, society president at the time, more dramatically described it, their "catapulting" (exesfendonizometha)—into even more inappropriate quarters.[33] Almost a century later, in a newspaper article about the General State Archives, a conservative party parliament member opined in terms remarkably similar to Rados's: "Greece, indifferent in a provocative manner toward the unique and irreplaceable sources of our national history, is the last state in Europe to allocate a building for its National Archives."[34] Although many Greek observers would agree with this condemnation of the state, others have faulted the "collective mentality" of the "average Greek" and the "culture of the Neohellene" and his or her lack of "historical sensitivity" to any period of history except antiquity or select, highly mythologized events of the contemporary past, such as the 1821 War of Independence and the resistance movement of World War II (cf. S. Matthaiou 1988; Droulia 1991). An added embarrassment for some stems from the fact that in such a "historical place" as Greece, the development of the infrastructure for modern historiography could be so stunted.[35]

While some Greeks have taken up archiving with, if not starry-eyed idealism, at least a firm resolve to strive for a European standard, others have viewed archives skeptically from the start, seeing in them a manifestation of sovereignty, while also suspecting, along with Benjamin, that "there is no document of civilization which is not at the same time a document of barbarism" (256). It is no great secret that much of the material needed to write a history of modern Greece is housed in foreign archives, such as those of the British Foreign Office, the American State Department, and the former Venetian and Ottoman empires, testament to various regimes of direct and indirect domination and rule in the region. Rather than a mirror of liberal rationality and good governance, the bloated Greek state bureaucracy from which the national archives, or at least a significant portion of them, are constructed generates a good deal of paperwork, but hardly boasts the most up-to-date archiving technologies or instills much faith in its citizens concerning the transparency of their relations with the state (Herzfeld 1992: 41). On the other hand, new systems of trans-European administration have not been greeted with any greater enthusiasm; thus, leftists often join the Orthodox in vocally protesting the European Union's "electronic filing" (*elektroniko fakeloma*), as they refer to the Schengen Treaty's personal information data bank.[36]

Perhaps the only truly "successful" archiving project in modern Greek history was that undertaken by the security police. Thus, for many Greeks, the words file (*fakelos*) and archives (*archeia*) bring to mind political surveillance long before historical scholarship. So bad were the memories (and so ineffectual the protests of historians) that in August 1989, to mark the formation of the first post–Civil War coalition government (the so-called *synkyvernisi*), police files kept on individual citizens, some dating as far back as the interwar years and others continuing through the Civil War (1946–49) and the military dictatorship (1967–74), were burned in the blast furnace of a steel plant with the apparent aim of purging decades of social stigma and political scapegoating. Blatantly breaking its own laws and procedures regarding the destruction of documents, the state, in an instant, turned millions of files into paper, pulp, *ashes*.[37]

All the repetitive discourse of lack and belatedness surrounding Greek archives probably should not be taken at face value, nor should the fact that modern Greek history has ended up being told by historians across the political spectrum as a story of sluggish industrialization, delayed class formation, and intractable patronage relations.[38] As scholars associated with the Subaltern Studies Collective have stressed, such accounts of national "incompleteness" speak to Western historiography's success in establishing European history as the objective standard for global history. As Ranajit Guha has noted, once Indian history was calibrated to "Europe" through the ruse of the universal narrative of capital, it would "henceforth be used as a comprehensive measure of difference" between the peoples of India and Britain (1997a: 3).

For some, including modern Greek history (and historiography) in a discussion of the colonial and postcolonial situation might seem like a strange and rude affront. As the putative origin of "Europe," "Greece" (or at least *ancient* Greece) has not only been incorporated into narratives of "Western civilization," but also given a place of honor (Herzfeld 1986, 1987a; Skopetea 1988a; Gourgouris 1996). After gaining "independence" in 1830 and passing from Ottoman rule to a Bavarian monarchy imposed by the European Great Powers, Greece, as Gourgouris has pointed out, was fated to become a nation "ideologically constructed by colonialist Europe without having been, strictly speaking, colonized" (1996: 6). While there remains a certain pathos in the continual reference made in Greek discourse, institutional as much as casual, to the ancient past as "ours," it is not surprising that Philhellenism, with its gushing praises for the Greeks, was taken literally and has proven difficult to recognize as a kind of Orientalism[39] (or Balkanism[40]). Given the prominence of ancient Greece in Western historical narratives, not to mention the more ambiguously received, but still unquestionably "impressive" legacy of the Byzantine past, it is little wonder that the history of the modern Greek state in its doomed-from-the-start catch-up game with Europe would seem unworthy of scholarly attention not only by foreigners, but even by Greeks themselves.

While the historiography of modern Greece remains largely a product for internal consumption and has rarely been seen as an authoritative platform from which to say something about European history more generally (Skopetea 1992), by contrast, a sizable body of foreign-language scholarship has developed on the "anthropology of Greece," as an important subfield of Europeanist anthropology.[41] Located on the capitalist side of the "Iron Curtain" and the "underdeveloped" southeastern edge of Europe, Greece emerged as an obvious site for anthropological research in the wake of postwar decolonization and the onset of the Cold War (de Pina-Cabral 1989: 400).[42] Enabled by the Redfieldian paradigm for the study of "complex societies," anthropologists working in Greece would study the so-called Little Tradition of oral village culture while leaving the "Great Tradition" of written culture and history to philologists and historians. In recent years, even though history and memory appear to have replaced "honor and shame" as "gatekeeping"[43] concepts in anthropological research on Greece, the methodological bias against writing persists.[44]

Following trends in anthropological research in general, a number of recent anthropological studies have addressed historical consciousness, local history, historical preservation, and popular memory in modern Greek society. One strand of this recent work has centered on describing a specifically Greek "historicity" and ontology of history, distinct from the "Western" linear, historical sensibility enshrined in conventional historiography.[45] In a related, but more politicized move, Greek historical consciousness has been mapped in order to theorize an alternative Greek modernity and morality resistant to the hegemony of the Western technorationalist capitalist order.[46] Yet another trajectory of contemporary anthropological work has focused on the "uses of history," primarily as related to the preservation of historical monuments. In this case, ethnography has been marshaled to document struggles between local communities and representatives of national or global institutions and agencies over the meanings ascribed to historic landscapes as well as over the rights to management and custodianship of particular monuments, buildings, and neighborhoods. In this work, the "local" people tend to be cast as victims of (European) History and its prerogative to define the most valuable and important dimensions of the past.[47] A last category of recent research could be termed "ethnohistorical" and has involved the use of ethnographic and oral historical methods by anthropologists (and some historians) to locate and record the historical memory of social groups elided or deliberately erased from official accounts of the past.[48]

Although this final field of research has incorporated an explicit theorization of collective memory and historical subjectivity, oral discourse, for the most part, has continued to be treated by anthropologists and anthropological historians as a natural repository for the countermemories of socially and politically marginalized groups. As in colonial and postcolonial studies, in which, as Ann Stoler and Karen Strassler have argued, the romance of the oral flourishes, subaltern memory often appears to be an unproblematic "access-point to untold stories of the colonized" since it is always "official memory that is on the line" (2000: 7–8). Ironically, as Andrew Shryock has suggested, ethnohistorical approaches, while privileging oral discourses about the past in order to critique hegemonic forms of written historiography, frequently end up overwriting alternative memory practices in the interest of producing a radical, but nonetheless linear, written historiography: a move, he deems, a form of "historiographical imperialism" (1997: 25–30). As a straw man in much recent work on social memory in Greece and elsewhere, *written* historical discourse produced by local agents is assumed to serve hegemony in such predictable ways that its production does not deserve scrutiny.[49] As a result, the internal diversification and contestation of written historical practices tends to be overlooked as well as the fact that these discourses are hardly in the hands of the state or the elite alone. Another incidental effect of an emphasis on "oral memory" is the circumvention of the history of language politics in Greek society, in which defending and documenting an oral vernacular (vs. the archaizing register of written *katharevousa*—i.e., "purified"— Greek) was for a century an established gesture of liberal and leftist folklore and literature. In implicitly supporting an "authentic" language (of the people), this privileging of the oral ultimately represents a failure to address the complex and power-laden relationship *among* the various languages, registers, and scripts through which modern Greek "experience" has been articulated.[50]

Given the place of modern Greek history and archives in a global context, isolating a sphere of Greek historical *a*synchronicity (call it historicity, memory, local identity) as the Other of "Western history," cannot be the route to "provincializing Europe," in Dipesh Chakrabarty's well-known phrase. To the extent that historical discourse played an important role in legitimating the colonial project, for formerly colonized people to "write their own history" cannot constitute in and of itself an emancipatory gesture: for, as he argues, "insofar as the academic discourse of history—that is, 'history' as a discourse produced at the institutional site of the university—is concerned, 'Europe' remains the sovereign, theoretical subject of all histories, including the ones we call 'Indian,' 'Chinese,' 'Kenyan,' and so on" (1992: 1). On the other hand, trying to "get out" of history and its discourse on capitalist progress, modern rationality, and liberal governance is equally doomed to failure: in seeking the "antihistorical," "antimodern" subject of a "different," "original" native culture, a quintessentially "anthropological" move, the ventriloquist-analyst simply inserts "untheoretical," "oral" voices into a narrative of "transition" that leads inexorably to modernity (18–19).

Instead, history (and historiography), according to Chakrabarty, must be faced as a field of global struggle. This move, for one, entails acknowledging that the constitution of Europe as sovereign subject of history and exemplar of modernity does not represent the natural outcome of national and domestic histories, but of a global history that centrally *includes* the colonizing enterprise. Second, the contribution of national elites of non-"Western" countries to making Europe *modern* has to be reckoned: there must be, as he notes, an "understanding that this equating of a certain version of Europe with 'modernity' is not the work of Europeans alone; third-world nationalisms, as modernizing ideologies *par excellence*, have been equal partners in the process" (21). Attention, thus, needs to be given to historical narratives produced by local elites extolling the emergence of the modern state form, capitalist development, and liberal citizenship at the expense of silencing the violence and racism attendant on their "successful" implementation.

Seen from this perspective, then, the kinds of independent projects of documentation and historical writing I examine in this book do not represent an irrelevant or supplemental site of historical production, but a charged, multivalent node of engagement with discourses of capitalist modernity and the nation-state as well as with the legacies of the colonialism itself. Despite (or probably because of) the vexed relationship of Greeks to their archives, the deficit of public confidence in the way that the past is being recorded, and historians' laments of national amnesia, Greek society could be said to be marked by a preoccupation with the *text* of history and its potential sources. Daily newspapers regularly carry special supplements on topics of Greek and world history and reprint excerpts from newly declassified U.S. State Department or British Foreign Office archives relating to controversial periods of the contemporary Greek past; intense discussion flares up periodically concerning the whereabouts of the personal papers of important Greek political figures; and, of course, the culture of the personal archive is extremely lively.[51] The political valence of personal archives, however, can vary widely, posing different, often divergent, arguments about the ideal relationship of citizens to the state and civil society as well as of "Greece" to "Europe." As instruments of historical research, they can also differ significantly in the degree of their commitment to the principle of democratic access to information.

For many local historians and historical collectors, the driving reason for composing personal archives remains the need to compensate for the "inadequacies" and "gaps" of Greek public libraries and archives. Following in the footsteps of Vlahoyiannis, many have made it their lifelong project to "salvage" documents and objects endangered by neglect or simply not (yet) recognized by others as of historical value, often with the long-term plan of donating their collections to the public. Yet others have literally built their lives and "names" around their collections by transforming their homes into miniature museums and archives, which they plan to entrust to their heirs to manage after their death. Some of the most important and certainly most well-managed Greek archives and libraries grew out of private collections and are not administered by the Greek state.[52] Notably, the contrast of these respected private institutions, whose importance to scholarship on modern Greek history has been amply demonstrated, to state-run archives and libraries, with their highly problematic functioning, has led, in one observer's opinion, to such a confusion of the "private" with the "public" that in common parlance the distinction between "archive" and "collection" has been lost (S. Matthaiou 1988: 139).

The prevalence of private libraries and archives in Greece and the extent to which the state appears to have relinquished its duties in this domain has not usually been viewed as a matter of public–private symbiosis, let alone of some kind of postnational privatization of historical knowledge, but rather as a sign of the tenacity of academic privilege and intellectual clientelism that a properly functioning state and intellectual culture should have expunged long ago. Historian friends often complained to me of the difficulty of working with private archives, even if they were ostensibly open to the public, and told me that they needed "connections" (*meson*) to gain access to them. Furthermore, they frequently suspected that people "on the inside" were holding onto choice materials in order to have the first opportunity to publish from them. Literary archives seem especially prone to this kind of hoarding and secrecy since they often end up in the hands of the critics who were originally given the opportunity to work with a particular author's unpublished manuscripts. The significance of privileged access to these archives is even greater in places, among which Greece could be included, where literary authors are treated as national-cultural heroes and, given the continued dominance of philological approaches to literature, publishing texts for the first time and commenting on them is seen as a principal function of literary criticism. As Caryl Emerson has written of the Bakhtin archive: "In Russia, as elsewhere (but perhaps more intensely in Russia where distrust toward official documents is matched by an enthusiasm for sacralized biography and relics), scholars with access to personal papers have tended to sit on them and trickle out their contents piecemeal to select petitioners" (1997: 55).[53] Through their policies of limited access, privately held archives and collections, thus, can be instrumental to creating and reproducing networks of scholarly patronage and lineage. As a result, the making of archives by individuals and private groups with a reformist agenda has often been aimed at challenging not only the categories and *modus operandi* of public archives but also the elitist and exclusionary practices of non-public ones.

Given the history of political repression in Greece, archiving has also been associated with political resistance, and the organizing of archives—the collective "dirty work" of historical scholarship—been considered an important practice of leftist activism. Historical circumstances led many leftists to *become* historians and, above all, archivists, taking upon themselves the task of creating archives "from scratch" in order to provide the sources—the *proof*—necessary to write histories critical of statist narratives. Until quite recently, the Greek General State Archives gathered documents almost exclusively according to juridical-administrative, not sociocultural, categories.[54] Needless to say, this limited definition of the historical, combined with a long history of political conservatism, explains why socially marginal, diasporic, and politically transgressive practices and actors (workers, unionists, refugees, communists, migrants, etc.) had been excluded from the map of potential historical knowledge, if not made explicit targets of official erasure. Interestingly, though, acts of documentary obliteration have also served as important *catalysts* for archival action. The 1989 destruction of the security files, for instance, could be said to have galvanized the archiving efforts of leftist historians in the 1990s: in that shocking instant of conflagration, it became apparent that the state, and not the historical establishment, had the final word on what papers it holds on to and, as a result, that the memory of the Left was most in jeopardy. The reconstitution and opening of the archive of the United Democratic Left (EDA) party, the legal leftist party that operated during the post–Civil War/predictatorship period (1951–67) when the communist party was banned, represents an example of this quickening of archival reflexes. In 1989, the decision to (re)construct this "persecuted" and "wounded" archive for the purposes of historical research led to the dynamic reclaiming of "waste paper" as historical document: EDA's records, which had been confiscated during the dictatorship, had to be literally extracted from the garbage bags in which they had been stuffed at the offices of the security forces.[55] As has become apparent in recent years, however, the obverse of this politicization of archiving has been that contemporary theoretical challenges to historical positivism are easily dismissed as "postmodern" and thus either apolitical or revisionist.

In addition to expanding and diversifying the possible subjects of history, independent projects of archival constitution have also aimed at introducing new historical epistemologies and models of archival construction, management, and use (new technologies and categories of documentation, standards of efficiency, democratization of access, conceptions of "memory work," etc.). Specializing in the history of social and political movements in contemporary Greece, the Archives of Modern Social History (ASKI), for instance, have been built around a core collection, including parts of the Greek Communist Party (KKE) archives and the archives of the Greek Communist Party of the Interior (KKE-*esoterikou*) as well as materials relating to other leftist and progressive political parties (including EDA); the women's, youth and antidictatorship movements; and the underground radio and press. In addition to a patent bid to redefine the potential subjects of modern Greek history, the collective of historians running ASKI, which was established in 1992, have also attempted to initiate a new kind of archival culture based on scrupulous documentation and an ethics of transparency. In the 1999 premier issue of ASKI's journal, *ArcheioTaxio* (i.e., "scaffolding," but literally the "order of the archive"), which by Greek standards represents a unique instrument for publicizing the archive's holdings, the historian Filippos Iliou triumphantly proclaimed the *openness* of these archives. The accessibility of the ASKI archives not only to "all researchers," but also to "any interested party," precludes the informal vetting of "qualified" scholars as in other private archives and also, most importantly, dispels the mystique surrounding the hermetically sealed communist archive.

Housed, symbolically enough, at the headquarters of the left-wing coalition party Synaspismos, ASKI poses itself as a clear critique of the Greek Communist Party, whose archives, located in the (recently flooded) basements of Perissos headquarters, remain programmatically shut to outside researchers, reflecting a philosophy of "closed" archives and an archival culture of restrictions, censorship, and "top secret" (*aporrito*) files.[56] The aura that continues to surround stories of the defeat and decades-long persecution of leftists in postwar Greece, however, has given an entirely different valence to Greek leftist history and archives than that in former communist countries. Through their peregrinations, losses, and dispersal, the archives of the Greek Communist Party, in contrast to their Soviet or Eastern European counterparts, testify to a history of imprisonment and exile, not totalitarian rule and surveillance. The communist party archives, which had already been much fragmented during the Metaxas dictatorship (1936–41), wartime occupation, and Civil War, would themselves go into "exile" in Eastern Europe, following the humbling path of refugee Greek communists after their defeat in the Civil War.[57] In this context, the return of the communist party archives to Greece could represent a much-awaited symbolic repatriation—and legitimation—of a history of political repression and harassment.

That a communist party archive could become a touchstone for the reform of archival practice and a paragon of archival efficiency and transparency, usurping a role associated with—and some might argue constitutive of—liberal governmentality, beyond telling us something about the distinct history of communism in Greece, underscores the fact that the politics of archiving and documentation in a "peripheral" state such as Greece are anything but straightforward or predictable. Accordingly, the independent projects of historical re-collection I consider in this book reflect various political visions and historical epistemologies, ranging from complicity with official patriotic discourses, historicist definitions of historical knowledge, and "European" ideals of capitalist development, political rationality, and nation-state consolidation to explicit attempts to critique and undermine them.

On Composing Historical Ethnography

In his study of memory in late-nineteenth and early-twentieth-century France, Matt Matsuda explains that he deliberately chose the "recognizable stuff of 'general' history" and made it "strange" by reading it back through the lens of memory (1996: 4). In other words, working from standard historical literatures on nationalism, imperialism, class struggle, and education, he traced the development of a modern conception of memory in the pedagogical use of mnemonics, the issuing of passports and identification cards by the French state, neurologists' theories of the brain as a center of memory, and even the buying and selling of "futures" on the stock exchange. I find this kind of use of the case study well suited to my objective in this book, which is to elucidate forms and structures of historical re-collection that cross-cut "recognizable" historical themes and periods.

Each of the four case studies presented in this book centers on a different historical event or process of late-nineteenth and twentieth-century Greek history in order to examine how it has been documented, archived, and narrated. My case studies all push up against academic history—its narratives, archives, institutions, methods, and jargons—as I seek moments in which scholarly discourse is defined against the unorthodox, outmoded, and unruly historical practices of nonprofessionals. Although the chapters of this book are intended to speak to each other on many levels, they can also be read on their own. What links them are a series of keywords: genre, personal archive, memory work, archival activism, document, testimony, event, voice, witness, scribe, archival gap, archival fiction, textualized archive, nostalgia, redemption, mourning, (dis)possession, transcription, translation, citation, technologies of documentation.

Upon first consideration, the most striking aspect of this book is its juxtaposition of case studies involving seemingly unrelated topics and junctures of modern Greek history that have been the subject of public discussion or scholarly reinterpretation in the 1990s. The first decade after the end of the Cold War was a period of ideological disengagement that saw the violent resurgence of nationalisms across the Balkans, but also the intensification of processes such as mass migration, deindustrialization, European Union integration, and the spread of global media culture that threw the fate of the nation-state—and the coherence of historical narratives about it—into question. Greece experienced these recent developments in ways that were importantly different from its neighbors and have affected its position among them. After the defeat of communist forces in the Greek Civil War in 1949, the "Iron Curtain" was pulled shut along Greece's northern border, effectively severing it from other Balkan states for forty years. The ideology of a diachronic Hellenism, legitimized by academic institutions at home and abroad, only served to confirm the self-sufficiency and seemingly solitary historical course of the Greek nation. With the redrawing and loosening of symbolic and political boundaries in southeastern Europe, however, the "Balkans" themselves have reemerged forcefully in regional and global consciousness (Todorova 1997; Bjelic and Savić 2002). In the 1990s, as the rest of the region was afflicted by armed conflict and severe economic crisis, Greece developed into the most stable and powerful Balkan state, a major investor in regional economies, and a magnet for new immigrants, primarily from former communist countries such as Albania.

Unsurprisingly, the decade following the fall of the Berlin Wall proved a dynamic moment in the reshaping of Greek historical narratives and archives as unhealed collective traumas of the recent past reasserted themselves in cultural memory. Each chapter of this book considers a different history that was actively contested and rewritten in the 1990s. For one, with the defusing of Cold War ideological polarities, the history of the Greek Civil War (1946–49) at long last started to be addressed in academic history as well as described in a flood of personal accounts (chapter 4). Similarly, the transformation of Greece into a country that "imports" rather than "exports" migrant workers has made the history of Greek labor migration a lively subject of public discourse and, for the first time, a topic on the agenda of academic historians (chapter 5). In the context of renewed nationalist fervor, a tremendous memory industry continued to proliferate around the celebration of the "lost homelands" of ethnic Greek populations of Anatolia (contemporary Turkey); however, the refugee crisis of 1922 and the multiethnic past of the former Ottoman Empire have also been looked to by *critics* of nationalism to counter the rising tide of xenophobia and the politics of ethnic superiority in the Balkans (chapter 3). Lastly, as the populist and nativist political rhetoric that marked the socialist 1980s has given way to a technocratic discourse on political and economic "convergence" with other states of the European Union, the history of earlier phases of Greece's industrialization and modernization have come to seem highly relevant for the nation's future by capitalism's enthusiasts and opponents alike (chapter 2).

Even though they treat different "chapters" of modern Greek history, the case studies of this book, when put together, are hardly intended to compose a "survey." Keeping in mind the needs of readers who come to this text with no particular knowledge of twentieth-century Greek history as well as those who are steeped in it, I have attempted to engage the respective literatures on these topics in a way that is informative and critical without being overly specialized. I do not make any pretence of having exhausted what, in many cases, are voluminous bibliographies. Indeed, I suspect that it is precisely mastery of these apparently autonomous subjects of research, with their dense webs of reference and internal debates, which closes off asking the kinds of questions I want to pose here: What accounts for the differential densities of interest formed around particular historical topics at specific moments in time? How has the intensity with which certain subjects have been documented in academic and popular historical discourses led to the systematic forgetting of others? When and with what consequences have historical events and processes been viewed as linked—or not? Why have certain topics seemed suitable for inscription in particular genres of historical writing (and not others), and how has this affected the degree to which knowledge about them has been disseminated and deemed credible and significant? Bringing causally and chronologically unrelated subjects within the frame of a single inquiry allows me to sketch the broader contours of contemporary Greek historical production and cultural memory and to consider how different moments and aspects of past experience have been re-collected and represented *in relation* to each other.

Although I might have chosen to discuss any number of historical themes, my reasons for choosing these and not others had to do not only with their salience as loci of historical reflection and contention in the 1990s but also with their relation to two principal historical modalities: the "event" and the "process." In a study of contemporary Indian society, Veena Das (1995) has proposed the term "critical event" to describe events that bring into being new modes of action and redefine traditional social categories. For Das, a critical event encompasses both world historical processes and the "inner life" of historical actors. Thus, the fact that a factory owned by a multinational corporation came to be located in Bhopal, India might have been the result of a conjunction of global forces; local people, however, did not become *conscious* of their place in the global order until the industrial accident radically transformed their lives, forcing them to navigate international legal systems and government bureaucracies in order to address the effect of the toxic leak on their bodies. Critical events fundamentally upset existing models of social relations and available categories of conceptual explanation, but the overwhelming need to narrativize them ultimately impels actors to "*invent* scripts" (200). As a result, we must attend not only to how historical experience transforms culture but also to how it transforms the meanings, purposes, and forms of historical practice and discourse themselves. In their study of testimony, Felman and Laub (1992) have described the "historical particularity" of traumatic events as lying, paradoxically, in their "unwitnessability." The traumatic event, they argue, *eliminates* its witness: "The event (the Plague—, the Holocaust) occurs, in other words, as what is not provided for by the conceptual framework we call 'History,' as what, in general, has no place in, and therefore cannot be assimilated by or integrated into, any existing cultural frame of reference" (104). The traumatic experience of World War II, would usher in a new kind of historical discourse, the testimony, and a new conception of history radically at odds with historicism's celebration of history as victory. As Felman notes in a later study, the new "reality of history is that of those traumatized by history"; history is now located in a "chain of traumatic interruptions rather than in sequences of rational causalities" (2002: 29–33). In the post-Holocaust era, victims were turned into witnesses and speaking subjects of history who were granted for the very first time "historical authority, that is to say *semantic authority* over themselves and others" (2002: 127).

In two of this book's case studies, I address periods of sharp social conflict, displacement, and violence that constituted central traumatic events of twentieth-century modern Greek history and that also changed the way that modern Greek history itself has been conceived and written. Both the 1922 "Asia Minor Catastrophe," as it is called in Greek, which resulted in an unprecedented "exchange" of almost two million people between Greece and Turkey, and the Greek Civil War (1946–49), which ended with the defeat of communist forces and now is regarded as one of the first conflicts of the Cold War, led to severe national economic crisis, personal dislocation, communal breakdown, and intense domestic social and political antagonism (between "locals" and "refugees" and the "Right" and "Left," respectively). Over the course of time, however, these events have been incorporated into public historical narratives and deployed in political culture in fundamentally different ways. The "Asia Minor Catastrophe" would be scripted as a quintessential tale of national defeat for which non-Greeks (Western Allies, Turks, etc.) could be blamed and would come to serve as a rallying point for nationalist nostalgia for "lost homelands" of Anatolia. The Civil War, on the other hand, has remained a profound cleft in national memory, alternately repressed through glorification of the "*national resistance*" (as a narrative of "noble struggle") and treated as a touchstone for ideological dogmatism.

While on the level of historical content, the "Asia Minor Catastrophe" and the Civil War have little in common, on a discursive and narrational plane, they are intimately bound together: both have formed key subjects for the elaboration of Greek literary and historical testimony. Treating these events in a single study sheds light on the significant role that projects of historical re-collection have played in shaping conceptions of historical subjectivity, agency, citizenship, patriotism (and, its obverse, treason) as well as in refiguring the relationship between personal and collective trauma, public mourning, and national redemption. A number of historical categories, concepts, and techniques—the identification of the "common person" and victim as witness to national history; the position of the scribe as one of empathetic projection or strategic disassociation from the experience of the witness-ing Other; the fluid relation between history and literature, and fiction and archive, attendant on constructing archives of oral testimony; and the application of new technologies of documentation to capture the voice of witnesses and the image of their suffering—have been developed, transferred, and critiqued *across* projects of re-collection involved in representing these two events.

In the other two case studies of this book, I turn to a consideration of open-ended historical processes and practices of historical re-collection centered not on highlighting stunning moments of rupture, loss, and conflict, but in marking routes of continuity among political orders, social groups, and forms of capitalist production. I do not want to overdraw the distinction between event and process because processes such as urbanization, industrialization, and migration have, of course, occasioned critical events of a wrenching kind, in which the global economy became part of people's experience and consciousness in profound ways. Insisting on a notion of process, however, allows me to center attention on the relationship of historiography to capitalism and consider the paper trails and institutions of docu-mentation that capitalist development inevitably generates. Historicist "histories of" (the nation, urbanization, industrialization), which posit a unified subject develop-ing toward a singular future (cf. Chakrabarty 2000: 23), might be passé in critical historical thought, but they persist and predominate in popular historical writing.[58] In this book, I will consider historical narratives of capitalism from two ostensibly opposed directions that in practice often come into contact (and conflict) over the interpretation of the same corpus of evidence: liberal historiography, on the one hand, as paean to modernity, capitalist accumulation, and nation-state expansion and consolidation, and its critique in Marxist and other critical historiographies, on the other hand, with their focus on labor exploitation, colonialism, and transnational communities and subject positions.

Although the two processes I discuss in this book—urbanization and transatlantic migration—occurred at roughly the same time (the turn of the twentieth century) and are clearly interrelated within a history of global capitalism, they notably have *not* been associated on a metahistorical level. In a first case study centered on the his-torical process, I examine the current interest of amateur local historians in writing the history of industrialization and urbanization. While the contemporary historiog-raphy of the modern Greek city represents a sharp break with a previous paradigm of nativist, anti-Western history and folklore, focused on "tradition" and the "indigenous," rural past, this new discourse on Westernization has precedents in a long bibliography of historical writing aimed at situating "Greece" within a "univer-sal" narrative of capitalist development. In the second case study in this framework, I consider, by contrast, a text without bibliography, references, or clear generic model: the memoirs of a Greek man who was a migrant worker in the United States in the beginning of the twentieth century. Despite the fact that when situated within world history, Greece's "industrial revolution" is insignificant compared to its export of labor power to other industrializing states, the history of Greek migration has only recently begun to be documented by academic historians and, to a lesser degree, by nonprofessional historical producers. On one level, it is clear why migration, in entailing the loss of human capital and producing (or perhaps simply drawing attention to) "mixed" cultures and languages, would be silenced from national historical narratives. Juxtaposing these two case studies, however, will allow me to ask how rhetorical forms and institutional structures have contributed to naturalizing this unequal narration. While urbanization can be told as the quintessential story of place, which with every passing generation enriches the stable chronotope of the nation-state, migration, as a story of movement and border crossing, cannot lay claim to such "roots" and thus appears unnarratable as collective history and more suited for description as an episode in an individual's picaresque life story. Comparing the different kinds of family archives from which histories of these subjects have been (or potentially could be) written—the archives of established, "founding" families versus those of the transnational working class (both their papers and their *bodies*)—also makes apparent how the differential ability of social groups to create and preserve documents related to their activities plays a central role in creating (and legitimating) uneven densities of historical narration.

On a second plane, then, each case study in this book revolves around a different permutation of the relationship among genres of historical writing, personal archives, and technologies of documentation. I begin with local historiography because it is the most dominant and commonplace genre of historical writing and archival practice in Greek public historical culture. Of the genres I will be considering in this book, it is also the most scorned and least examined by the historical establishment. Thus, in chapter 2, against the backdrop of deindustrialization in a provincial Greek city, I explore the emergence of a nostalgic historical discourse on the city's industrial past and lost urbanity produced by amateur local historians and to a large extent supported, if not catalyzed, by the municipality with its renovations of historic buildings and aggressive intervention into local historical production itself. Since most amateur writers viewed their task to be that of compensating for an archival lack rather than interrogating the exclusions of the historical record, their personal archives, I argue, functioned as supplements to existing public archives as well as as the means by which they internalized and "domesticated" established community and national historical narratives. The degree to which local history reproduces self-representations of the local elite class while repressing the presence of newcomers and experiences of local political and social conflict, I contend, has as much to do with positivist conventions of historical documentation and the genre of local historiography (the territorializing of history, the personification of the city as subject, reverence for citation) as with the explicit intentions and political agendas of writers and their sponsors. While denigrated by academic historians as outdated, the historicist reverence for the "primary" source that is evident in local historians' construction of their source-book histories and textualized archives reflects a romance of archive that is hardly a thing of the past in historical studies more generally and, furthermore, represents a prevalent and effective mechanism by which a select corpus of evidence is brought into historical semeiosis as *the* record of the past.

The projects of historical re-collection I consider in this book's two middle chapters both involve self-conscious bids on the part of historical producers to reform historical knowledge and practice through the solicitation, transcription, and archiving of oral testimony. In chapter 3, for example, I examine the case of the

Center for Asia Minor Studies, established in Athens in 1930 by a cosmopolitan Greek aristocrat to collect testimonies from ethnic Greek refugees about their "lost homelands" in Anatolia (Turkey) as well as about the refugee crisis itself. Its founder established this personal archive not so much to supplement Greek academic historical scholarship as to expose the silences of the historical record (i.e., the forgetting of Asia Minor Hellenism after the collapse of Greek irredentism) and demonstrate the inability of historicist methodologies to address the trauma of this unprecedented dislocation. In documenting the experience of a marginalized population and experimenting with new genres of literary testimony and technologies of documentation (voice recording, photography) associated with journalistic reportage and the bureaucratic management of refugee populations, this project, I argue, initiated an unprecedented opening to the victim as historical authority. In this chapter I do not actually focus on refugee testimony, but on genres of re-collection in the most literal sense: letters, fieldnotes, and informant biographies, which detail the circumstances of the archive's formation. In addition to attesting to the authenticity of the archive's contents, I suggest that the inscription of these texts and their emplacement in an archive in Athens contributed to shaping distinct social subjectivities (such as that of the middle-class "memory worker" and the "refugee informant" of "Eastern" Greek ethnicity). Despite the novel intentions underlying this project, over time the refugee crisis and the narration of Greek "lost homelands," as well as the mode of their re-collection (through the oral testimony of refugee-survivors), would become commonplaces of Greek popular historical production.

The subject of chapter 4, a 1994 novel about the Greek Civil War, written by an author renowned for his documentary fictions, similarly points to oversights in public historical narratives and official—as well as radical—archives, while provoking reflection on the new legitimacy of historiography based on oral testimony. This chapter examines the crucial place of literature in a discussion of historical discourse because of its ability to illuminate the rhetorics of historical writing (citation, voicing, transcription, tropes, dialogism) as well as serve as a repository for transgressive narratives. While national historiography did not begin to address the history of the World War II Resistance and the Civil War until the 1980s and 1990s, leftist fiction had begun to archive these memories almost immediately following the end of the war. In an apparent rejection of this tradition, this novel, which was heavily censured by the Left, represents the violence of communist partisans through a (seemingly) realist use of testimonial fiction. The controversy it stirred, I contend, had as much to do with the form of the novel as with its subject matter. As a fictional archive of oral testimony, the novel challenges an ideological essentialism that views the testimony of the individual speaker as a sign of a specific social or ideological position (e.g., the voice of the refugee, the voice of the Left). If literary testimony, but also historical testimony based (consciously or unconsciously) on literary models, attempts to circumvent the repetitions, meanderings, and dull spots of actual testimony through editing or excerption, making history read like fiction, the novel in question reverses this process by drawing into relief the linguistic and social mediation involved in transcription and archiving, the fragmentation and contingency of events testimony is supposed to clarify, and the performative dimension of testifying that does not necessarily "say" anything. By calling as witnesses the wounded Right, rather than the defeated Left, the novel also obliquely critiques liberal projects of "recuperating voice." Furthermore, by turning itself into a "court" in which the various speakers make depositions, the novel questions whether the Civil War has been constructively mourned in the public sphere, despite (or because of) the official "reconciliation" of Left and Right. In demonstrating that persuasive testimony can be constructed through rhetorical means, the novel ultimately blurs the borders of fact and fiction, suggesting that fiction can carry facts that history denies (or downplays) and that the factuality of historical discourse can be achieved through literary means.

In chapter 5, I reflect back on my discussion of local historiography by considering how a family archive might act not as an instrument for the reproduction of dominant historical narratives, but as a potential storehouse for counterhistories. I consider how forms of writing associated with migration and agricultural labor, the transhistorical and transgenerational practices of remembrance employed by the family as an institution of cultural memory, and even the body as archive enable the recording of the kind of story of migrant labor and communal violence typically occulted in local historiography. The text on which I focus is the autobiography of a Peloponnesian peasant, edited in 1996 after having been kept in a drawer for fifty years; it describes its author's experiences as a migrant laborer in the United States in the first two decades of the twentieth century and the deaths of his three sons in Greece during the Civil War. The circulation of these laser-printed and cheaply bound memoirs among a small circle of friends, relatives, and compatriots speaks to the continuing marginality of this unpatriotic story to hegemonic historical narratives centered on national and capitalist "progress" as well as to public networks of historical production and archival accumulation. Despite the obstacles of his limited education, the author had attempted to document his life experience in writing as no memory worker could have conceived to call on him in the 1950s. The difficulty he faces in writing in official Greek and the subsequent editorial interventions made to "correct" the text expose the relationship between writing and social position. That the author's faulty syntax, poor spelling, and incessant code switching render his text "unreadable," however, also underlines the stylistic and semantic limitations of normative historical prose with its demands for monolingualism, causality, and clear boundaries and hierarchies between reporting and reported speech. If the genre of local historiography is stabilized by reference to a particular place, it is much less obvious in what kind of genre to plot histories of lone strangers abroad and of new communities based on human friendship, not kinship or locality. Thus, even though autobiography would seem to be the genre *par excellence* for the bourgeois *Bildungsroman*, ironically, it proves the genre of historical writing most available to this writer. With its collocation of other genres, speech performances, and media contexts, this memoir does not succeed in regimenting its heteroglossia; instead, it records a complex phenomenology of interaction, testifying to its author's struggle to find a language to cast his experience of suffering and dispossession.

A last axis around which this book pivots is one of scale and positionality. Writing this book, I found that I could not fall back on the narrative structures of history, anthropology, or literary criticism—in other words, the linear metahistory of a particular event, the holistic description of a specific community of historical producers, or the linguistic and literary analysis of historical writing—but had to imagine another genre (a combination of these but, I hope, also something more) to capture the dynamism with which temporalities, social worlds, and textual forms interact in the archive. Although each case study attempts to create this genre by joining the analysis of historical discourse to that of archival practice, the book as a whole could be said to "progress" from a wide-angle exposition of the social and political contexts of historical production to the detailed examination of the poetics of particular texts, so sharply focused as to hone in on the significance of specific spelling "errors." While the first two chapters are broadly synchronic and diachronic in scope, the following two engage in the close analysis of particular texts and textual practices. Finally, juxtaposing these different case studies enabled me to identify and describe several of the subject positions constituted in the process of historical re-collection: copyist, archivist, scribe, scribe as witness to witnessing, witness, witness as scribe, academic, critic, publisher, sponsor, donor, dreamer of the archive, author, editor, translator, and, of course, reader.

Despite its breadth this book does not claim to exhaust the themes of twentieth-century Greek history or the sites of its documentation. Such an undertaking not only lies beyond the scope of a single monograph, but also would fundamentally misconceive the aims of this inquiry. Inertias associated with routinized divisions of disciplinary labor, established boundaries among related forms of social knowledge, and academic conventions, from historical periodization to bibliographies, inhibit asking the kinds of questions about historical production central to this project. Aesthetic and prosaic forms of language; provincial and cosmopolitan views of history; diverse archival formations and institutions of memory; divergent epistemologies of history, methodologies of historical research, and agendas for the reform of historical knowledge and practice; and local, national, and diasporic communities converge and contend with each other in the articulation of modern Greek historical experience. Bringing some of them together here is not so much a means to depict a fuller social reality or expand the terrain of History as to demonstrate how the politics of historical representation are fused to the poetics of archive in ways that matter profoundly for what ends up counting as "historical" and for who becomes an author, actor, or witness in histories of "Greece."

Chapter 2

Collectors of Sources: Local Historiography and the Possession of the Past

On a winter evening in 1998 in the provincial city of Volos, amateur local historians, representatives of the local historical associations, the city's mayor, and some prominent members of the Athenian academic historical community came together at an event entitled "Local History/National History." This gathering, which had been organized by the municipal history center to celebrate the compilation of a comprehensive bibliography of the city's local history, was one of numerous conferences, lectures, and exhibitions on historical topics that have taken place in recent years in the Spierer building, a renovated tobacco warehouse originally owned by a German company. With its exposed ceiling beams, rough wood plank floors, and sleek modern lighting, this building testifies to the city's former commercial past, current economic crisis, and European Union facelift. At the time of my research, along with gallery and auditorium spaces, "Spierer," as it was usually called, housed the municipal development organization and the municipal history center and archive. Before the event began, people milled around looking at the glass cases that displayed over two hundred books and offprints about the history of the city and the surrounding region: a material testament to the increase in interest in local history in the 1990s.

After a short while, the invited speakers took their places behind a row of microphones set up on a table at a short distance from the audience. In his talk "Sums without Addition: From National to Local History, not Vice Versa," a well-known economic historian and history professor at the University of Athens, Vassilis Kremmydas, decried the characteristic "pathologies" of locally produced scholarship, noting that such writing rarely "obeyed" disciplinary methods and could never piece-by-piece add up to an adequate vision of national history. He then made a call for local authors to fall into step with the "new history" (*nea istoria*), an approach to social and economic history that developed in Greece in the 1970s and

1980s.[1] In a similar vein, during the discussion period another prominent older historian associated with the "new history," Vassilis Panagiotopoulos, remarked:

> We have to understand that well-intentioned local scholars (*topikoi logioi*) . . . produce studies that are a little random, a little marginal . . . they somewhat burden the system. They don't bother me, though. The academic community has ways, has mechanisms to put this production in its place . . . to see it as a sign of the interest of local communities in their history and to leave it there. The social cost is insignificant. . . . Today we have the ability to judge this production, so it doesn't cause any problems . . .

Like most academic observers, these historians addressed the expanding and increasingly democratized field of historical production by highlighting the differences between high and low scholarship. In an oracular fashion, they proclaimed what they believed local history should be rather than examining what it *is*. Treating amateur historians as "second-class citizens" and "mere fact-grubbers . . . condemned to tunnel vision" (Samuel 1994: 4) and their labors as the "random accumulation of a miscellany of useful and useless data by magpies" (Humphreys 1997: 1) is, however, an effective way of demarcating hierarchies of scholarship. The local historians, many of whom had dressed up for the occasion, thinking they were to be rewarded in some collective manner, left in a huff.

While struggles over the authority to represent the past are involved in all the cases I will be examining in this book, local historiography undoubtedly constitutes the practice of historical re-collection that most raises the hackles of the historical establishment and to which it has most felt the need to respond. Academic historians can treat genres of historical writing such as testimony or autobiography as "primary sources" or look to historical novels to "give life" to a particular historical period, but local historiography cannot be so easily accommodated: it galls in poaching on historical methods and discursive forms (use of archives, footnotes, chronology) that comprise part of the standard repertoire of disciplinary history. The documentary fetish of local historians also brushes up too close to a lingering guild romance with making archives to be dismissed out of hand. Indeed, in generating such strong sentiments of repugnance, amateur local history appears to tap into the discomfort that some Greek historians feel when confronted with contemporary theoretical challenges to historical positivism. Indeed, any listener with Bakhtinian sensibilities would have detected in the stridency of Kremmydas's defense of the "new history" an absent audience to whom his words were equally addressed: that is, Greek historians associated with "postmodern" currents in historiography, whom he also has been known to challenge publicly.[2] Far from being irrelevant to academic history, then, debates over the status and value of amateur historiography provide an oblique view of contemporary conflicts within the discipline over the nature and purpose of historical knowledge.

On the other hand, the significance of amateur local history clearly is not exhausted by its relationship to academic history: it would be hasty to assume that the legitimacy of local history and the degree to which it reflects and shapes local political culture and lines of social distinction is primarily determined by the quality of its dialogue with scholarly history and not by some other criteria. Indeed, one thing that was striking about this gathering was the extent to which the encounter between the "local" and the "national" had been framed—one might even say staged—by the municipality itself. Brief opening comments by the director of the municipal history center, the active participation of the mayor in the discussion period, and the setting of this event in the municipality's renovated warehouse space combined to put symbolic quotation marks around the entire affair. Seen from this vantage point, local historiography appears not so much as an inferior version of its academic counterpart, but as a complex field of social contention in which various interested parties make claims not only to the city's past but also to control over the manufacture and deployment of historical discourse itself.

Furthermore, local historiography's reverence for the "primary" source draws attention to the materiality of historical practice not, as academics would like, as a sign of a previous, exhausted historical paradigm, but as a central obsession of archiving as a means of keeping memory "in place" in the construction and imagining of social and political collectivities. The archives that local historians in Volos were building in their homes and texts as well as their emotional and physical engagement with historical evidence and artifacts, such as yellowed newspapers and worn photographs, constituted affective—and effective—mechanisms through which they were forging meaningful and embodied connections to particular pasts. Seen ethnographically, then, local historiographical production and archival construction can be understood as performances of local belonging in which the borders of class, community, and citizenship were being actively enacted and negotiated.[3]

The empirical focal point of this particular inquiry was the provincial city of Volos, located along the eastern Aegean coast between Athens and Thessaloniki—or, to be more precise, the rhetorical production of that city in historical writing and local archives. A natural port at the apex of a horseshoe-shaped bay, Volos (population 120,000) experienced a brief but intense period of industrialization at the end of the nineteenth and beginning of the twentieth centuries. In the past twenty years, however, the city's manufacturing base has collapsed, generating for many residents a palpable sense of loss and distance from a once-prosperous past. At the same time, this impression of historical closure meant that Volos found itself in possession of precisely the kind of history in demand across many amateur and academic historical circles in 1990s Greece: namely, that of the neohellenic city, capitalist development, liberal reform, and bourgeois culture. Forming a notable break with the nativist, and often explicitly Left-oriented, history and folklore of the early postdictatorship period, this new paradigm of historical representation has centered on and, for the most part, celebrated the city's entrepreneurial past: the modernizing elite, their "European" outlook, and local commerce and industry.

While the other case studies in this book focus on the narrative constitution of historical rupture and displacement in first-person testimonies related to refugee crisis, war, and labor migration, here, by contrast, I am interested in exploring the rhetorics of continuity and emplacement in document-based historiographies of capitalist progress and liberal governance. Given the hegemony of local historiography as a "genre of recollection," with its demand that history be "grounded" in the biography of place, it is little wonder that the movements of the "unsettled" across the borders of city or state (because of migration, refugee flight, exile) would appear foreign to and untellable within the frame of a collective history. With its emphasis on the past as patrimony and symbolic capital, then, this chapter forms a counterpoint to the book's final case study in which I revisit from the perspective of a narrative of dispossession, displacement, and archival dispersal some of the same issues I take up here: namely, the relation between textual and social authority, the connection between history and home (and between "native" and "stranger"), the interface of family archives with public historical narratives, and the function of citation as a mechanism of social reproduction.

Academics and Amateurs

In the days following the "Local History/National History" event, I spoke with many of the local writers on the phone or at their houses over a cup of coffee. Most told me that they felt they had been subject to an unwarranted attack on their work. No matter what the professors say, one writer told me, local history is an aid (*voithima*) for later researchers, including academics. Others reminded me that they never had claimed to be historians in the first place. Indeed, the single most common remark local historians made to me was just that: "I am not a historian" (*Den eimai istorikos*).

On one level, this phrase simply states the obvious. In Greece, if one has not studied history on the university level, one is not a historian (and, by the same token, if one has a bachelor's degree in history, one *is*). To a large extent, academic and amateur historical practitioners do occupy different social worlds and intellectual milieus; they tend to know about each other's existence when there is a direct overlap in research interests and probably cross paths most often in the virtual space of the Sunday newspapers.[4] Yet, despite the apparent clarity with which historians and "nonhistorians" distinguish themselves from each other, the subjects and sources of amateur and academic historiography and the political orientation and social backgrounds of its authors, in fact, involve points of contact that defy a radical separation of their practices and the implied top–down model of how historical questions and methods change.

The tension between professional and amateur historians, of course, is hardly specific to Greece and is certainly not new to the politics of historical scholarship more generally, but developed in tandem with the disciplin(ing) of historical practice and the emergence of historicist methodologies.[5] The valorization of the "primary" source introduced a fundamental cleavage between "evidence" and "analysis," which, in turn, enabled a division to be made between the preliminary work of collecting sources (which "anyone" could do) and their interpretation (which had to be done by specialists). In a study of historical collecting in nineteenth-century Germany, Susan Crane explains that the relationship between amateurs (who amassed documents and artifacts) and experts (who studied and interpreted them) theoretically was based on a clear division of labor; in practice, however, this interaction was often strained. Scholars "feared that amateurs could do damage to the sources or that damage could be caused by 'irresponsible' interpretations and bad editing" while miffed amateurs frequently found themselves in the defensive posture of insisting that they were offering scholars a "valuable service" (2000: 16–17). Perhaps even more troubling to scholarly historians than amateurs' possible misuse or mishandling of sources, though, might have been the extent to which the amateurs' very existence demanded a recognition of the intense emotions and passions excited—even in the professional—by engagement with material signs of the past as well as an acknowledgment of the frequent "correspondences between the performance of ownership and the production of historical knowledge" (63).

For their part, local history writers with whom I spoke did not appear embarrassed to be writing history, despite their lack of credentials. Although an apology of sorts, I found that the statement "I am not a historian" rarely was made in an apologetic tone. After all, since the nineteenth century, if not earlier, important figures, including scholars, community leaders, and political figures, have encouraged local intellectuals to write the history of their native land or *topos*. Although amateur historians typically identified themselves simply as writers (*syngrafeis*), local writers (*topikoi syngrafeis*), or local researchers (*topikoi erevnites*), I found that trained historians and academics usually referred to them as historical researchers or *istoriodifes*, a word I only once heard a local writer use to describe his own practice. As I soon gathered from the tone in which academic historians used this word, the term *istoriodifis*, like the related *archaiodifis* (antiquarian) or *topikoi logioi* (local intellectuals), has somewhat derogatory connotations, recalling harmless and earnest, though sometimes also silly and misguided, habits of nineteenth-century historical research. The word *istoriodifia*, itself a nineteenth-century neologism based on the ancient Greek verb *difao* (to dive after, to hunt for), refers to the seeking and gathering of historical sources (documents, inscriptions, archives) and their recording for the sake of historical analysis in the future: in short, to the creation of an archive.

Most local historians with whom I spoke presented their practice to me less in terms of what it was than what it *wasn't:* namely "proper" history, interpretation, analysis. A former local journalist and one of the city's most prolific and respected history writers, Nitsa Koliou, insisted:

> No, I am not a historian. History is a discipline, which you have to study at university. To write history you have to be a historian. I write it, but I don't think that historians will criticize me for inaccuracies. To the contrary, I hear positive comments from them.

During my conversations with local writers, I found it difficult to get them to discuss their process of research and writing in any detail. Koliou was emphatic: "I didn't set any kind of program in my work, any kind of method. The subjects just came as they came, on their own. They came on their own." My questions about methods were usually "answered" by writers' demonstrations of technological gadgets related to text, image, and sound documentation and reproduction (scanners, mini-tape recorders, computers), or by queries about whether I could find devices such as handheld photocopiers for them in the United States. On more than one occasion, a local writer insisted we conduct our interview with his tape recorder running beside mine, rerecording the interview and taking the measure of our respective technological outfitting.

If forced to give a positive description of their labors, amateur local historians primarily depicted themselves as collectors or even "rescuers" of evidence that they had "unearthed" from their close personal surroundings. Given the prestige accorded to the ancient Greek past, it is little wonder that archaeological metaphors abounded in writers' descriptions of historical research.[6] Koliou, for instance, told me that during the politically conservative post–Civil War period, the stories of the wartime Resistance had "been hidden, been buried for some time" (*kryftikan, thaftikan gia kambosa chronia*) and that she had had to "bring them up to the surface" (*na ta anasyromai stin epifaneia*). The verbs she used to describe this historical labor— *skalizo* (turn up, as with a hoe) and *strangizo* (wring out, as a dishcloth)—suggest the degree to which she saw her work as a form of painstaking exertion. In the introduction to one of her recent books, she remarks: "Humble and insignificant ants of local History, let's try to come out of our little nests and start to collect the materials (*ilika*) for a new construction (*oikodomima*) that must be as perfect as possible" (1997: 8). This comparison of amateur local historians to "ants" underlines the industriousness and precision, as opposed to selectivity or creativity, which she saw as defining amateur historical research. The metaphor also suggests a view of history as collective project—the work of many hands—and of evidence as material artifact: a "building block" that exists prior to the questions that historians pose of the past.

This set toward history as a series of self-evident and self-present (if temporarily hidden or lost) documents led many local writers to accept a hierarchy of knowledge production in which they were clearly carrying out a lower-order function. However, since the final responsibility for determining "what happened" and "why" was consigned to someone else—someone young and trained, in some unnamed future—this arrangement actually freed writers from having to problematize their own practice; they could work furiously to hunt down and preserve the sources without having to fear that they had overstepped any boundaries. Dimitris Konstandaras, a school principal who had written a local history about refugees from Asia Minor settled in Volos, told me that he had called his book a "chronicle" (*chroniko*) because:

> in my book, really, I don't do, let's say, history, I almost just cite (*paratheto*) the sources for later when a young person can come to a conclusion about what happened. I myself avoid coming to a conclusion. I avoid adjectives. I cite the sources exactly as they are (*aftousies*). Others can then search more.

The use of *paratheto* here is telling: this word, which means to cite but also to juxtapose or place side-by-side, underscores the degree to which he saw his sources as concrete artifacts whose integrity should not be compromised if they were to be useful for a later work of historical interpretation. Like judicial testimony, historical discourse in this view should establish clear borders between reported speech and the reporting context: the value of evidence would be greatly diminished if the quotation marks were loosened and the discourse paraphrased. While contemporary Greek local history rarely constitutes a literal publication of the sources, its foundation in the reproduction of a personal archive of documents harkens back to the "textualized archives" of high historicism: namely, the print "museums" or "cabinets" of sources, which collectors and antiquarians published in eighteenth- and nineteenth-century Europe (Stewart 1993: 143; Crane 2000: 116). In Greece, one could point to Yiannis Vlahoyiannis's frequent use of the word "archive" to title his print editions of transcribed documents or testimonies (e.g., *Athenian Archive* [1901], *Archives of Modern Greek History* [1907]).

To the extent that they considered their practice to be a straightforward documentation or *katagrafi* (literally, a "writing down") of sources and facts, writers typically felt too much emphasis on writing, whether in the form of literariness or analysis, could compromise the authenticity of the materials they had collected. The author of a history of the municipal cemetery, Vassilia Yiasirani, for instance, told me that she did not wait to finish her research before starting to write; as soon as she gathered information about a particular area of the cemetery, she entered it directly into a file on her computer. Although several authors told me that they also liked to write poetry and short stories, most agreed that poetic or creative touches should be left for the introduction or for other explicitly nonhistorical works. Rafael Frezis, the author of a history of the Jewish community, told me, "I am not a writer (*logotechnis*, i.e., creative writer), let alone an historian." He noted that writing for him really was more of an obstacle than an end in itself, especially since having learned the formal register of Greek (*katharevousa*) in school, he had found it difficult to write in the demotic vernacular.

Since writers viewed their work first and foremost as a matter of collecting primary sources, they often were quite secretive about their research. Editing, revision, and collaboration, I found, played little part in the production of amateur local historiography: although put together, all this research might have been composing a richer picture of the local past, each "ant" was definitely carrying its own little load. When I asked Yiasirani if she had in mind a model for her text or had received help at any stage in the writing, she responded emphatically, almost as if she had been insulted, "No, no one, just myself, no one." She told me that she had discussed the subject of her book with some other local writers, but she did not show them the manuscript. "They saw it all at once when it was printed (*typothike*)," she explained. Writers typically spoke of their books as being "printed," rather than "published," suggesting that they saw their publishers as little more than printing presses. Many writers, including Yiasirani, rejected copyediting as unnecessary: "I am a philologist myself," she reminded me. Eleni Kartsagouli, the author of a history of Asia Minor (Turkey) from the perspective of local refugees, told me that she did not make many spelling errors and for her next book had decided not to pay for a copyeditor and instead take the manuscript directly to a typesetter.

Even though I initially thought that local histories had a limited circulation and readership, this assumption turned out to be incorrect. I found books of local history on the shelves of many acquaintances in the city, including those who did not consider themselves history buffs or even readers, for that matter. They told me that they did not necessarily read these books in their entirety: they might just flip through them, especially if they contained reproductions of rare period photographs. Others told me they simply liked to own them, as if their existence in and of itself represented a tangible sign of the region's historicity. Amateur history writers themselves turned out to be among the more avid readers of local history and many corresponded with local historians in other parts of Greece. (As I conveniently realized during the course of research, amateur writers are not difficult to locate since vanity presses usually print the phone number and addresses of authors on the inside of books' front cover). In 1990s Volos, the typical press run for local histories was 1,000, with the writer receiving a certain percentage of books to give away or sell.[7] Yiasirani's book on the cemetery was published on a local vanity press with funds from the municipality of Nea Ionia; of the 300 books that she was given after the first printing, she sold 200 and gave away 50. Giving away books actually seems to be a critical part of the circulation process, as I can attest from my own bookshelves. Leaving the home of local history writers, I inevitably would be loaded down with their books and other publications, usually enough to fill up a shopping bag. In Volos, as in most provincial Greek cities, there was one bookstore that stocked all the local history titles while other less-specialized bookstores or stationery stores usually carried a few books of local history, often featured in window displays. It is more difficult to find local histories in Athens, but some do make their way there; the capital's major bookstores often have a separate section for "local history" that includes select titles from all around the country. Whether they like it or not, these books also find their way on to the shelves of Greek academic historians—and sometimes into their footnotes as well.

While the "Local History/National History" event at the former tobacco warehouse made clear that the local/national distinction actually was a euphemism for amateur/scholarly (with "scholarly" glossed as "academic"), the division of historical labor on which it apparently rests (evidence vs. analysis, transcription vs. writing) has not, in fact, been so clear-cut over time.[8] In modern Greek historical studies, the exclusive identification of the "scholarly" with the "academic" occurred relatively recently (cf. Asdrachas 1993). This situation reflects, for one, the gradual process by which the historical discipline was professionalized in Greece. Even the so-called father of Greek nineteenth-century romantic historiography, Konstandinos Paparrigopoulos, was an autodidact who never completed conventional university studies. His appointment to a chair at the University of Athens came only after great delay, following lengthy negotiations with politicians of the day (Skopetea 1988b: 291; Gazi 2000: 69). Political circumstances in Greece, in particular the decades-long repression of leftist scholars, also impeded the convergence of "scholarly" and "academic" production: for many years, historians working outside the Greek academy, and often outside Greece itself, were considered more intellectually innovative scholars than those who taught in the conservative Greek university. One of the most important Greek intellectual historians, Konstandinos Dimaras, for instance, never held a university position in Greece nor did the early Marxist historian Yiannis Kordatos.

Yet another factor contributing to this ambivalence has to do with the marginal place occupied by *modern* Greek history in both Greek and international historical studies. Even as late as 1922, the Philosophical Faculty of the University of Athens hesitated to set up a separate chair of modern Greek history. Instead, a position in medieval and modern Greek history was proposed, reflecting the fact that modern Greek history was viewed as an extension of Byzantine (Liakos 1994: 191). The first independent chair of modern Greek history was established in 1936, but even this position subsumed Greek history within European ("Chair of History of Modern Europe and Particularly of Greece"). Scholars of modern Greek history also have been in a position of serious disadvantage in regard to archives when compared to colleagues working on more "prestigious" periods of Greek history, especially classical Greece, who have long had access to a well-established corpus of primary sources, a voluminous secondary literature, and a global network of scholars, research institutions, and funding opportunities. In a speech given in 1978, just four years after the end of the military dictatorship, the prominent Marxist historian Nikos Svoronos pointed out that while the sources for other periods of Greek history were widely available:

> we have just begun to catalog the sources of modern Greek history, the majority of which still remain unpublished, if not unidentified (*agnostos*). . . . And here is the difficulty: the historian of modern Hellenism has to be both a historian and a *istoriodifis*. The distinction that many people make in Greece between the supercilious (*megalofantasto*) historian and the humble *istoriodifis* seems, and is, dangerous and unrealistic. (1982: 32)

As this comment suggests, modern Greek historians often have had to compensate for the impoverished documentary base of modern Greek history by helping create archives before even beginning their research. This archival activism, unsurprisingly, has been particularly salient in connection with the historiography of politically sensitive topics and marginalized groups that were persecuted by, or simply remained invisible to, the state.

With the fall of the dictatorship in 1974 and the official recognition of the wartime Resistance by the socialist government in 1982, the status of modern Greek historiography transformed radically. Not only was an end brought to the postwar stigmatization of leftist scholars but, to a large extent, as in the United States and Europe following the social movements of the 1960s and 1970s, the situation was reversed, and leftist and liberal scholars assumed positions of power within the university as well as in national research centers and archives. Energized by the new freedoms following the regime change (*metapolitivesi*) as well as by access to institutional authority, modern Greek historiography rapidly expanded its thematic range and also began to be written in much greater quantities; in the last quarter of the twentieth century, production of historical monographs grew ninefold, with the greatest increase occurring between 1982 and 1990. In addition, the urgency about "setting the record straight" after decades of political repression inspired many people originally trained in other fields to *become* historians (Liakos 2001; cf. Asdrachas 1993).

These transformations in the broader social and political contexts in which academic history has been produced in Greece have also impacted amateur historical production, which similarly witnessed an exponential growth in the 1980s. After the fall of the *junta*, new political freedoms allowed long-suppressed stories to be brought forth into the public realm. The fact that the vernacular replaced the archaizing register of *katharevousa* as the official language of the Greek state also greatly democratized access to written discourse more generally. Tellingly, one of the first local histories published in Volos following the dictatorship was a two-volume history of the wartime Resistance in the city and the surrounding region. Published in 1985 by Nitsa Koliou, this book was also the first local history of Volos ever written by a woman. In the 1990s, municipal and other public sponsoring further encouraged the proliferation of local historical writing, as did technological advances such as the use of computers and desktop publishing.[9]

Major shifts in the topics of amateur historical writing also have been closely linked to those in academic historiography, even when methodologies and political agendas were at odds.[10] For instance, after the end of the dictatorship in 1974, the sharp drop-off in academic scholarship on the "patriotic" topic of the Greek War of Independence of 1821 had its counterpart in the waning of interest in this subject among writers of local history.[11] Academic historians often acknowledge that contemporary scholarly research on the wartime Resistance and the Civil War was to a large extent driven "from below" by the remarkable profusion of memoirs and regional histories of the conflict published throughout Greece in the 1980s and 1990s by nonprofessional historians (Margaritis 2000). Similarly, the lively interest in urban and industrial history evident in Volos as well as many other Greek cities cannot be separated from developments in academic history; specifically, in the 1980s the history of neohellenic city, centered on the problematic of "transition" from the Ottoman period to European modernity, emerged as a key *topos* of historical research, particularly for economic historians.[12] While for academics this topic was a touchstone for a critique of capitalism and colonialism, amateurs have more often expressed awe for a Europeanized Greek industrialist bourgeoisie in the pages of their histories.

The themes of amateur and academic historical writing, of course, do not always overlap, and these divergences often signal fundamental differences in opinion about the place of the political in historical scholarship. Despite the fact that the study of the Civil War became something of a boom industry among Greek academic historians in the 1990s, local history writers in Volos tended to steer a wide course around this sensitive subject. Sometimes, on the other hand, the archival material local historians collected was not only in step with academic interests, but in "advance" of them if judged by international developments in the historical discipline. Thus, since cultural history has been relatively little developed in the Greek academy, some of the documents and artifacts amateur historians have gathered relating to subjects such as bourgeois family life did not (yet) seem relevant to scholarly historical projects.

That academic and amateur historiographies are interrelated should be obvious: it is only the relative success of disciplinary tactics of self-definition, testified to by the resounding reverberation of the refrain "I am not a historian," which has made it necessary to argue this point in the first place. In bringing these practices of historical documentation and writing into a single discussion, I am not trying to construct a "complete" picture of different kinds of Greek historical discourses. Rather, my intention is to gesture to a key arena in which the authority to write the past is being contested as well as to expose the mystique of the archive, which the ritual banishment of the *istoriodifis* simply occults. Indeed, despite the fact that the postdictatorship period has seen the rapid development and institutionalization of modern Greek historiography as well as the legitimation of research on social history and on the political history of the Left, an aura continues to surround the "primary" (here in the sense of foundational rather than preliminary) work of archival constitution for modern Greek historical studies.

Nonetheless, the fact that local historians, in contrast to the other historical producers I will introduce in this book, were the least consumed with justifying their acts of documentation and also the glibbest of writers *is* startling. The acknowledgment "I am not a historian" was enough to justify and authorize the "straightforward" collection and publication of the "evidence." For this reason, then, although academics and amateurs alike were sure that they knew the genre of local historiography, I believe that it might be worth taking a closer look.

A Long Bibliography, or Capitalizing on History

Despite the sense of excitement with which local history was being taken up in Volos in the 1990s, the bookcases displayed during the municipal history center event revealed that the history of the city and the region has been written several times before, the earliest texts dating back to the eighteenth century. Indeed, the fact that local historiography is such an established and familiar genre on a national level might explain why Greeks have preferred to write their personal and family pasts into the fabric of local history, rather than foregrounding them in autobiography[13] or genealogy.[14] Given concrete form in rows of books in the library and entries in the bibliography, the tradition of local historical writing, in turn, has served as a potent centripetal force in contemporary local historical production, defining key events and figures as well as endowing local historiography with an air of autonomy in relation to both national history and academic scholarship. Older texts of local history form the common body of knowledge writers share, and the recent spate of republications of long out-of-print local histories has only made these books even more present in writers' consciousnesses.

Local historiography can be considered a quintessential form of national(ist) historiography, an ongoing response to the same kinds of educated middle-classes voices Ranajit Guha has described as calling on Bengalis in the second half of the nineteenth century to "write their own history" (1997a: 153).[15] However, given the complicity of historical discourse in legitimating colonialist rule and capitalist modernity, this mobilization, as Guha and others have argued, represented less a revolution in self-representation (Indians writing their own past) than a commitment to (and mass participation in) fitting "local" histories into global narratives of capital *in their guise as templates of universal historical knowledge.* From this perspective, each moment of local historical production in Volos could be said to entail a process of writing "Greece" into "Western" narratives of progress, development, and the international bourgeois class.

At the same time, local historiography, though framed as a continuous tradition, clearly makes up a diverse and fragmented field. Its literary form and sentimental register, but also the very sites and periods that constitute the "local past," have been in a constant state of flux, as have the groups who qualify as "real" Voliotes. Different, even contradictory, historical epistemologies and metanarratives of Greek national history (romantic, modernist, Marxist) have shaped what counts as knowledge about the past. One is led, then, to ask how local historiography has come to be seen as such a stable generic frame in which to cast discourse and what might be the political effect of this cumulative, recursive textual practice.

A first and most obvious way in which this heterogeneous body of writings has been held together under the sign of local history is through reference to the "life" of a common place. The personification of the city as a figure who is "born," "grows," and at some point goes into "decline," in turn, creates the impression that history must have a place to "take place."[16] Local historiography, thus, could be said to presuppose, but also produce, the chronotope of a localized (and nationalized) past. In describing the chronotope, Bakhtin has written: "Time, as it were, thickens, takes on flesh, becomes artistically visible; likewise space becomes charged and responsive to the movements of time, plot and history" (1981: 84). While Bakhtin wrote of literary chronotopes (the "road" of the picaresque novel, the "parlor" and "salon" of Balzac and Stendhal, the "threshold" of Dostoevsky), the chronotope also could be said to give "flesh" to historiography. Drawing on Benjamin's insight that secular modernity is characterized by "homogenous, empty time," much scholarly attention has been given to tracing the emergence of "national time" through the production and circulation of textual and media forms such as newspapers, novels, and, of course, historiography itself (Anderson 1983; Bhabha 1990).

In making time disproportionately problematic (through the "event" and "chronology"), historiography could be said, by contrast, to render the space (of the nation, of the city) *unproblematic:* an appended map suffices to "show" it. Elaborating on Nicos Poulantzas' observation that modernity entails the historicizing of territory and the territorializing of history, Fernando Coronil has pointed out that the relationship between time and space is rarely viewed in symmetrical terms: space is usually considered static and tangible and time dynamic and fluid. As a consequence, territories tend to be considered the "fixed, natural ground" on which histories are played out while histories are treated as fixed to unchanging, naturalized territories. This reification of geography, in turn, leads the "histories of interrelated peoples [to] become territorialized into bounded spaces" and makes shared histories seem divisible (1996: 77). In the case of local historiography, the obviousness of the *topos* of communal belonging creates the impression that the bourgeoisie live out their lives firmly rooted to a particular place, in a "village of natives," while newcomers and people living outside the city's perimeter appear (when they do) as temporary "interlopers." As a literary convention, the unity of place, thus, excludes certain historical actors before the research even begins.

A second way in which local historiography has come to seem like a unified genre is through minimizing, what Briggs and Bauman (1992) have called, "intertextual gaps" between the genre template and particular textual utterances.[17] In the brief review of Voliote local historiography that follows, I, therefore, have given emphasis not only to the chronotopes characteristic of different paradigms of historical representation, but also to the textual practices (citation, republication, prefacing, editing) that have played an important role in generating a sense of generic continuity and textual "tradition." Thus, I work on two planes at once: I sketch the outlines of major shifts in local historical discourses as seen against the backdrop of developments in modern Greek historiography more generally, while considering the selective way in which older texts were being read in the 1990s as sources on—but also as signs of—the city's "bourgeois revolution."

The End of History

The roads of the new city are clean and well kept, adorned with avenues of trees. And the houses are clean and have gardens. O, how fragrant the city is! Although it is commercial, it does not smell of tar, of coal, of smoke like Piraeus. It smells of roses and the fragrances of all kinds of flowers . . .

—E. Spyridakis, *Patridografia* (1934)

In the late 1990s, the history of Volos was being told as a narrative of rise and fall, of birth and death: in other words, as the story of a local industrial revolution that took off and then petered out. The widespread feeling that the city's history was over, however, has proved a catalyst for the current flourishing of historical writing about "old Volos": that "rose-scented" industrial center of the late nineteenth and early twentieth centuries. In the past fifteen years, as in many provincial cities and urban neighborhoods across Greece, local historiographical production in Volos has been devoted to subjects such as the development of manufacturing, industry, and transportation;[18] bourgeois cultural forms and social life;[19] neoclassical architecture and monuments;[20] religious and ethnic "minorities;"[21] and liberal social reform and left-wing protest.[22] As prosaic as the city's biography of industrial development might sound, its frequent reiteration in sources ranging from the municipality website and tourist pamphlets to local historical writing and grant applications made to European Union funding agencies is noteworthy given the fact that "Greece" for so long was defined by outside observers and Greek intellectuals as resistant (for good or for bad) to capitalist modernity and Western mores.

According to its thumbnail "biography," then, the "Greek" city of Volos was "born" in the 1830s. Although Volos, like the rest of the province of Thessaly, remained under Ottoman rule until 1881, the foundation of a nearby independent Greek state in 1830 spurred Greek investment in the city. Like European colonizers in the Middle East, the local Greek merchants chose to build a "New City," a commercial district oriented around a geometric grid of streets and set off at a symbolic distance from the Muslim town with its serpentine alleys (see fig. 2.1).[23] As commercial activity increased, people began to move to Volos from the mountain villages of Pelion, as well as in smaller numbers from Macedonia, Epirus, and other parts of Thessaly. Foreign consulates of Greece, England, France, Austria, Germany, Russia, and Italy were also established in the city at this time.

Until the 1912 annexation of Macedonia, Volos was the nation's northernmost port and its second most important industrial center, a hub for the manufacture of food products, textiles, and agricultural machinery as well as for the processing and export of tobacco. The modernization of the transportation infrastructure (railroad lines to the interior of Thessaly were completed in 1886 and a new port was built in the same period) would prove instrumental to the city's further economic development. The population, which was 1,500 in 1860, reached 5,000 in 1881 when Thessaly was

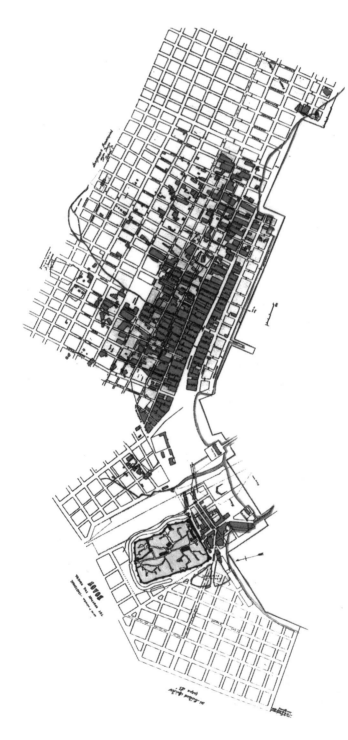

Figure 2.1 "Order" for a Turkish Town: "Old" and "New" Volos. Drawing by Vilma Hastaoglou.

annexed to the Greek state. Over the course of the following years, the city would quickly acquire the conventional trappings of an urban center: newspapers and journals; cultural organizations, including literary and theatrical clubs, music, dance, and art schools; photographers; a public library; private schools; and professional associations. In addition, with funding from private benefactors, important public buildings were constructed, including the town hall (1897), the commercial school (1900), a hospital (1903), and an archaeological museum (1908). Vilma Hastaoglou (1995), a professor of urban planning, has described the Volos of this time as a true "community of citizens" (*koinonia ton politon*), underscoring the dynamism of the local community and the large number of public works projects funded by wealthy citizens.

During the interwar period, the city's industrialization continued apace while class and ethnic conflicts also came to a head. After the settlement of 13,000 Greek Orthodox refugees from Turkey following the 1922 "Asia Minor Catastrophe" (see chapter 3), the city's population had reached 48,000.[24] The influx of refugees, who formed a pool of cheap but often skilled labor, further fueled the local economy. The increased prosperity of the city, however, did not bring better working conditions for the city's lower classes: wages fell between 20 to 50 percent after the refugee's arrival (Dimoglou 1999: 168). In February 1936, testament to the antagonisms between refugee and native populations, a makeshift market consisting of one hundred refugee-owned shacks was set ablaze by local Voliotes, killing a boy and destroying many refugees' fortunes (Mavrogordatos 1983: 195; Konstandaras 1994). In July 1936, major strikes took place in the city following on the heels of similar protests in Thessaloniki and Kavala in May. By the time World War II began, local industry was already in abatement, only to go into deeper decline after the Nazi Occupation and the Civil War.[25] While the local manufacturing economy did not contract decisively until the beginning of the 1980s in the wake of global deindustrialization, the devastating earthquake that struck the city in 1955 represents for many older residents the symbolic and emotional end point of the "old Volos."[26]

When I arrived in the city in 1997, unemployment was running at 17.4 percent and talk of the city's chronic economic problems was on everyone's lips.[27] The "old Volos" alluded to in casual conversations and being actively brought to the surface in local historiography and architectural renovation projects referred not only to the world of liberal reformers, cultural sophisticates, and dynamic entrepreneurs once engaged in building a "new city" but also to a sense of optimism about the future. With the destruction of many of the city's neoclassical buildings and the construction of modern cement apartment blocks in their place, Volos at the end of the 1990s looked much like any other provincial Greek city. Its urbanity had gone underground, preserved in the memories, photo albums, and private papers of the city's older residents as well as in the pages of old historiographies of the city and region, many of which have been reprinted in recent years.

Modern Argonauts

In an important essay on conceptions of national time in Greek historiography, Antonis Liakos (1994) notes that prior to the 1821 War of Independence, Greek intellectuals had envisioned the modern Greek nation as a "phoenix," which would resurrect the glories of ancient Greece from out of the "ashes" of the Ottoman present. In introducing a tremendous gap of time between antiquity and modernity, the resurrection metaphor, however, soon proved inadequate to the task of plotting national time. Gradually, and in dialectic with Western scholars' changing valuations of different periods of Greek history, especially the initially much-maligned Byzantium (but also Macedonian, Roman, Venetian, Frankish, and Ottoman periods), the "middle" time was filled in to form a metanarrative of Greek historical "continuity." In his multivolume *History of the Greek Nation*, published between 1860 and 1874, Konstandinos Paparrigopoulos definitively established the tripartite model of diachronic Hellenism (ancient–medieval–modern),[28] which remains enshrined in Greek history curricula and popular historical consciousness to this day. As Stathis Gourgouris has argued, Paparrigopoulos's insistence on describing the Byzantine period as medieval ("medieval Hellenism, so-called Byzantium") could be seen as an "unconditional surrender to the European model of national history": in other words, to a view of modernity as developing out of a "dark age" (1996: 259). Within this framework, Ottoman rule (1453–1821) could be depicted as a period of decline and degeneration that justified the great discrepancy between the civilizational heights of ancient Greece and the humble realities of the modern Greek nation.[29] Despite fundamental differences between the "revival" and "continuity" models of national historical time, Liakos notes that they converge in positing antiquity as an almost metaphysical force propelling "Greece" into the future.

Written in a formal archaizing register of Greek and replete with references to ancient texts, late-nineteenth-century local historiography of Volos and the surrounding region clearly espouses this temporally and spatially expansive vision of Hellenism. Since the province of Thessaly was not annexed until more than fifty years after the founding of the new Greek state, this discourse unabashedly presents the case for Hellenic "manifest destiny" to extend political and economic control into the region. In these historiographies, "old Volos" denotes the Ottoman past, a legacy that must be overcome if the city is to develop in step with modern Western society. Reconnecting to *ancient* Volos, it is suggested, will provide both the prototype and authority to do so. In striking contrast to contemporary local history, the future, not the recent past, represents the utopia toward which these texts are oriented.

Since Volos occupies the site of ancient Iolkos, the settlement from which Jason and the Argonauts supposedly set sail, the pursuit of the Golden Fleece serves in many early local histories as a protocapitalist mythology for the city. In his 1880 *Thessaly*, which was republished in 1995, Nikolaos Georgiadis, a doctor, explains that Volos is "fated because of its location to compete with its ancestress in wealth and size" (150). He considers Jason and the Argonauts' travels in the Black Sea and Asia Minor the mythic precursor to nineteenth-century Greek emigration and mercantile activity in the East, noting that "just as their ancestors, the Argonauts, who were the first of the Greeks to journey to Asia, sailed from the coast of Magnesia in pursuit of the Golden Fleece, so their descendants who are very fond of emigrating are settled everywhere around the globe" (98). In a similar vein, the cover of the 1901 *Guide to the Prefecture of Volos*, which was republished in 1997 by the Volos Commercial Association (*Emborikos Syllogos Volou*), depicts Hermes, the ancient god of commerce, resting his elbow nonchalantly on barrels and crates marked "Volos." In the guide, statistical and practical information about the city are prefaced by an overview of local history, mythology, and topography. Modern capitalist expansion is depicted as the fulfillment of antiquity's promising beginnings: the "dwarf Argo," the guide's introduction explains, has become a fleet of "steamer-colossi," while Minoan ancestors are hailed as the "forerunners of the colonial fever of the Greek race" (6).

The later prosperity of the city, then, would seem to bear out the views of nineteenth-century authors, who argued that Hellenism's true destiny could only be achieved by transforming a stagnant city, ruled over by "lazy" Turks, into a hive of activity directed by "industrious" Greeks. In 1836, a travel writer commented enthusiastically that even leisure time among the city's Greeks was more productive than that of the Turks: "In the few good Buildings are found Coffee-Houses with Rooms for billiards, where Greeks imitating Europeans gather together to discuss various commercial affairs." On the other hand, the Turk is described as sitting out in his kiosk on the slopes of the nearby Mt. Pelion "sweetly drinking his coffee, and drawing on his pipe (*tsibouki*)" (Leonardos 1836: 115). In these texts, the old market area around the Ottoman fort represents the precapitalist indolence and "Eastern" past from which the city's elite would like to distance itself. In a travelogue published in 1860 and republished in 1985, Nikolaos Magnis complains about the weekly bazaar held in the "Old City"; in the winter, he notes with disgust, the mud reaches a visitor's knee: "Yes to the knee. A place worthy for pigs not rational beings" (54). Repeating the complaints of earlier writers, he notes that Volos "should" be big and commercial, but the Ottoman authorities seem to prefer to "devastate it rather than to civilize it."

Ironically, at the turn of the twentieth century, the old Ottoman fort, which occupied the site of earlier Byzantine and ancient Greek settlements, represented the primary place where history (in other words, ancient Greek history) could be uncovered. Conveniently enough, archaeological excavation and urban planning would converge in its destruction once the city came into Greek hands. During his tenure as mayor, Georgiadis himself would take on the task of "cleaning up" the Ottoman neighborhood and ridding the city of material signs of its Turkish past. As he notes with satisfaction in a report originally presented in 1903, "the labyrinthine neighborhood of the *Palia* ('Old [Town]') was literally gutted (*exekoiliasthei*)" and, as a consequence, the opening up of roads and squares in the area allowed residents to enjoy the beneficial effects of "the flowing in of light and air" (1997: 21).

As originary histories, these early local historiographies are, at root, narratives of ethnic purity and cultural essentialism, quivering with anxiety about racial mixing. In the essay "History of the Founding of Volos," which was originally published in 1933 but remains within this paradigm of historical continuity, Dimitris Tsopotos depicts Volos as the resurrection of the ancient Iolkos and the Voliotes as descendants of the ancient Minoans: "the rapid progress and development [of the city], testifies that the ancient genius for forward development and *tireless entrepreneurialism* really is indigenous to this wondrous corner of the Pagasitic gulf" (1991: 10; *emphasis his*). Anticipating questions about the relative "Greekness" of the local population posed, for instance, by the settlement of Slavs and Ottomans in the region during that long stretch of time "between" antiquity and modernity, Tsopotos hastens to note that "true" Voliotes hail from the adjacent Mt. Pelion; at times of invasion or crisis, they simply retreat to their mountain villages. After quoting an Italian source that mentioned the presence of Jewish families in the old Ottoman fort, Tsopotos similarly reminds his reader that during the late Ottoman period Voliotes were not yet residents of the city; their businesses were in Volos but their homes (and the "women and children") were back in their mountain villages. Georgiadis is similarly emphatic that the Ottoman occupation had not compromised the reproduction of a native stock nor left an alien trace in Greek blood; the Greek and Turkish populations, he notes, were unmixable like "water and oil" (97).

These older texts of local historiography have all been republished in recent years by the municipality and local cultural groups. Their contemporary value clearly lies less in their analyses of Ottoman history or archaeological speculations than in the insight they provide into the "New City" of the late nineteenth and early twentieth centuries, whose fledgling beginnings form the fitting conclusions to these optimistic histories. Thus, the final chapters of Tsopotos's history, which detail the establishment of the city's urban infrastructure (streets, railroad, irrigation, industry), read like an index to the subjects amateur writers and the municipality were eagerly researching and documenting at the time of my research. With their erudite references to foreign language scholarship, old local histories also testify to the educational level of the city's former elite class. Their republication (usually in a facsimile format that highlights old-fashioned typographical features) suggests the importance of these texts as material artifacts in their own right. It is not without consequence, however, that their reprinting puts blatantly ethnocentric discourses back into circulation as so many unquestioned treasures of the local past.

Nostalgia for the "Old City"

In *The Country and the City*, a study of British literary representations of the idealized rural past, Raymond Williams argues that nostalgia for a lost golden age has been a constant throughout modern history. While the quest for a time *before* nostalgia might be futile, Williams notes that "what seemed a single escalator, a perpetual recession into history, turns out, on reflection, to a be a more complicated movement: Old England, settlement, the rural virtues—all these, in fact, mean different things at different times, and quite different values are being brought to question" (1973: 12). For Williams, the changing location and meaning of each epoch's "golden age" is correlated with contemporaneous social and economic transformations. Although he focused on the romance of the countryside, Williams predicted that the city would become a new frontier of nostalgia as ideals once associated with country life (community, reciprocity, aesthetics) were attributed to urban neighborhoods of the past. In the case of Volos, the first stirrings of nostalgia for the "old city" were recorded in the interwar period, as industrialization and refugee settlement led to the development of sharp new class and ethnic tensions in the city.

In his slim 1934 *Chronicle of Volos*, journalist Athos Trigonis dares to present the city's history in the form of a literary sketch, written in a self-conscious demotic Greek and illustrated with impressionistic woodcuts. Republished in 1987 by a local cultural association, this history focuses on the city's recent past, not the march of history from "antiquity to the present." Time, in his account, does not form a continuum, but is plotted as a contrast between a "before" and "after," a "then" and "now," symbolized most clearly in the juxtaposition of the Turkish bazaar (*pazari*) and the Greek market (*agora*). With curiosity, not contempt, Trigonis remembers the Ottomans sucking on their water pipes in local cafés and the scene in the muddy square of the old bazaar with "the Peliorites in their breeches, with their animals roped and loaded with walnuts and figs and silk and cocoons, the Almiriotes in *foustanellas* withloads of tobacco and the worn-out *karagounides*, with their animals, wheat and corn" (64). In contrast to the industrial development that was taking place in Volos at the time he was writing, this market scene with costumed Greek peasants from different parts of Thessaly appears to represent a reassuringly comprehensible and *visible* form of commodity exchange and regional difference.

Throughout his text, Trigonis juxtaposes precapitalist and capitalist economic forms by depicting a historical palimpsest: a remembered landscape of Ottoman monuments located just behind the contemporary "Western," industrial one:

> It does not seem difficult to me, if we close our eyes, to imagine what and how Volos used to be, around 1850 or 60: if you go behind the gas works a little further west and search, you will see, even today, a half a ruined arch of a stone bridge. (63)

A little further on, he notes:

> Behind this acropolis ran the west side of the exterior wall, which also had a small gate, the Kara Kapu, as they called it (in between Loulis's flour mill and Tsalapatas's factory). (64–5)

The "escalator" of nostalgia has moved on and in the 1990s "old Volos" referred to the city in the interwar period; the then-new factories Trigonis parenthetically mentions ("in between Loulis's flour mill and Tsalapatas's factory") represent key symbols of that past: the latter factory has even been slated as the site of a future museum of industrial heritage.

The "old city" of memory is never really a place, but a community. While charmed by the Ottoman period, Trigonis is not nostalgic for the Ottomans themselves; rather, he is fascinated by the Voliote "pioneers" who lived alongside them and established the fledgling institutions of bourgeois cultural life. Much of his book is taken up with documenting major events of the *modern* life of the city: the first concert, the first masked ball, the first dance, and even the first beach cabins for swimmers. Similarly, in a series of articles written in 1928 (and republished in book form in 1998), Nikolaos Gatsos, a lawyer, senator, and judge, writes with a mixture of awe and fascination about the city's founding families, the building of the first house and street, the establishment of various cultural institutions, the staging of the first cultural events, and the development of the city's commercial infrastructure. Writing in the formal register of Greek, Gatsos, who himself was a descendent of a local founding family, depicts the Volos of the mid- to late nineteenth century with the sentimental exoticism of someone describing a lost village community. Invoking a folkloric idiom, he notes that "our fathers" managed their business without banks because then "everything was simple, mores (*ithi*), customs (*ethima*), commercial exchanges" (89). Speaking of the nationalist aims of the city's philological association, he explains, "Then there were no class differences, nor was the creation of a commercial, agricultural or bourgeois or worker's consciousness an issue" (34). As this comment makes clear, nostalgia is almost always bound up with a defensive discourse on citizenship, one that distinguishes people of a certain class and social background. This nostalgia for a group of "real" Voliotes must be set in the context of the interwar period in which these texts were written and understood as a response to, among other things, the growing radicalization of the local working class and tensions brought on by the settlement in the city of a linguistically and ethnically heterogeneous population of impoverished Asia Minor refugees.

In the 1990s, I found that Volos residents were also using nostalgic discourses to lament the changed constitution of the local population as a result of postwar and contemporary immigration. Voliotes with whom I spoke often took pains to distinguish themselves from the "peasants" (*vlahi*) of the Thessalian plain.[30] As one elderly writer of local history told me: "In my neighborhood, we are all still living in *monokatoikies* [single-residence homes]. We think we are in our kingdom. But the *Kambos* [the Plain] has come here—Karditsa, Farsala, Larisa [other Thessalian urban centers]. It mixed up the local element. A lot of people have come here who do not love Volos." Echoing a sentiment that I heard on numerous other occasions, another older local writer told me that the local bourgeoisie had mostly left and gone to Athens, leaving the *Kambos* to engulf the city: "With the new irrigation systems they live in Volos in those big apartment buildings by the sea and turn on the computers from here."[31] As these comments suggest, the modern city of cement apartment blocks is itself perceived as a physical symbol of the encroaching of the historyless and culturally deficient Thessalian plain. For their part, people from the *Kambos* often referred to Voliotes as "Austrians" (*Afstriaki*). While the term typically was invoked in a derogatory fashion, as far as I could tell, it did not seem to bother Voliotes, perhaps because it simply confirmed their sense of distinction and air of "Europeanness."[32]

Despite the fact that the nostalgias of the 1930s and 1990s refer to different historical moments and experiences of social and economic change, they nonetheless have often been confused. In the 1987 reprint edition of Trigonis's book, for instance, the author of the new preface claims: "The very old will remember the Volos of then, the old Volos, the Volos that the writer describes." The claim, of course, is preposterous since Trigonis wrote about the Volos of the 1850s and 1860s; however, after quoting lyrics from a romantic song, the author continues: "Yes, that was Volos and that is the Volos we want to remember, all of us who lived it before and in the first years after the war." A slippage between different incarnations of "old Volos" also can be detected in the editorial interventions in Gatsos's republished articles, which have been compiled in book form by the municipal history center. A number of old photographs have been included in the new edition that depict the Volos of the turn of the twentieth century, not the city of the mid-nineteenth century described in Gatsos's text. The inclusion of these photographs suggests the tendency, as Williams observed, for nostalgias to become conflated, while also underlining the fact that in the 1990s Gatsos's essays were of interest as much for the past that he described as the one in which he lived and wrote.

If nostalgia, as many have suggested, is the quintessential "disease" of modernity, then, "old Volos," in its constantly changing guises, will represent at every point in time a simpler form of capitalism and the ideal of a homogenous society: a "village" of common blood. In the wake of contemporary deindustrialization and the emergence of post-Fordist production regimes, the factory-based economy of the 1930s seems to represent a tangible and understandable form of capitalist production sustained by "local" capital. For writers of the 1930s, however, these then new modes of mass production must have seemed inscrutable in comparison to the workings of the Ottoman bazaar and the agricultural economy. Notwithstanding the different references of these nostalgias, they converge in viewing the "native" elites as paragons of civic virtue and in downplaying the presence and contribution of newcomers to the city, not to mention instances of class and ethnic conflict. That the multiple layers of "old Volos" have been homogenized into a chronologically hazy "before" has only redoubled some residents' sense of entitlement and injury in the face of contemporary changes and further enhanced the romantic aura surrounding the city's past.

Nativism, Communism, and the Mountain

Contemporary fascination in Volos and other parts of Greece with local histories of urbanization and industrialization represents a notable break with a long period in which local intellectuals and cultural producers had devoted themselves to celebrating Greece's precapitalist and non-Western cultural practices and forms. During the interwar period, elite Greek cultural producers and critics as well as foreign writers, such as Lawrence Durrell and Henry Miller, had trained their sights on the Greek countryside and seascape, which had recently been "discovered" as a site of undeveloped nature and traditional Greek folkways, not just a landscape of classical ruins.[33] Thus, in Volos, during the interwar period, but much more markedly in the postwar years, the countryside surrounding the city and specifically nearby Mt. Pelion became the center of historical and cultural interest. While writers of romantic diachronic histories had depicted Pelion as the originary homeland of the Voliote elite, in modernist and Marxist frameworks the peninsula would be refigured as a repository of a traditional peasant culture and pristine nature, rapidly being destroyed by "Western" modernization.[34] In some instances, Pelion also would be cast as the wellspring of local radicalism and democratic ideals. This turn away from the city to the countryside was accompanied by the emergence of an invigorated folklore discipline as an important voice in discussions on the past.

In international and Greek historiography, one of the most important developments of the interwar period was the emergence of a Marxist approach to history. Although Greek Marxist historians would reread Greek history through the prism of class struggle and come up with some startling conclusions, they would not fundamentally challenge the diachronic model of Hellenism proposed by romantic national historiography. Ironically, then, as intellectual historian Elli Skopetea has pointed out, ideologically opposed historiographical projects have ended up as strange bedfellows, with Marxist accounts implicitly endorsing Paparrigopoulos's masternarrative of Greek national continuity (1988b: 287).

One of the most important early Greek Marxist historians, Yiannis Kordatos happens to have hailed from the village of Zagora on Mt. Pelion. As a good local son, he wrote, among his many works, a history of his birthplace and the surrounding region: a 1,000-page tome entitled *The History of the Province of Volos and Agia from Antiquity to Today* (1960). This history, which remains the only book about the city written by a historian of national repute, notably was out-of-print in the late 1990s. Writing in demotic, Kordatos, who also had published a well-known critique of the class politics behind the Greek "language problem," reviews the area's history from antiquity until the beginning of the twentieth century. He debunks the assertions of ethnic purity that had been put forth by earlier writers, while bringing peasant experience and progressive political action into the center of historiographical inquiry. Throughout the text he stresses the oppression of common people by the *kotzabasides*, the local Greek elite who collaborated with the Ottomans. He also has particularly sharp words for many of the earlier writers of local history, especially Dimitris Tsopotos, a member of an old land-owning family, who, according to Kordatos, used historiography "to whiten the faces of the *kotzabasides* and in general all the exploiters of working people" (11).

As site of both the Greek uprising against the Ottomans and of the communist-led Resistance during World War II, mountains have accrued a symbolic charge in the modern Greek public culture of history as birthplace of revolutionaries and refuge from foreign colonization and influence.[35] Much of Kordatos's history focuses on Mt. Pelion and the numerous armed struggles against the Ottomans staged there as well as on the activities of important local figures of the "Greek Enlightenment." He also looks to folk songs collected in his natal Pelion village as documents containing evidence for peasant counterhistories. For Kordatos, in striking contrast to contemporary local historians, the "Europeanization" of Greece following Ottoman rule represents a new form of foreign domination. Thus, he laments that with the annexation of Thessaly by the Greek state, "the imitation of so-called European culture, in all the expressions of social life, stopped the further development of folk art on Pelion" (608).

The final section of Kordatos's history, entitled "Awakening," in which he describes liberal and leftist activism in Volos in the early 1900s, has formed the basis for an important strand of contemporary local historical writing. In the early stages of my research, a history professor in Athens told me that I should keep in mind that, by Greek standards, Volos "is not just any city" (*den einai mia tyhaia poli*), before proceeding to underscore the city's progressive political tradition and early labor movement, which she hailed as the city's "endowment" (*proika*). The first Labor Center in Greece was established in Volos in 1908, the same year that the demoticist educator Alexandros Delmouzos opened a progressive girls' school in the city. In 1914, leaders of both institutions were run out of town by local conservatives and prosecuted in the so-called Trial of the Atheists (*Diki ton Atheikon*), undoubtedly one of the key "events" of Voliote history. This incident has served as a foundational narrative of Voliote liberalism. While images of Marx, Christ, and the poet Solomos, a key figure of the demoticist movement, did once hang side-by-side on the walls of the Labor Center, the period in which workers and middle-class reformers were allied against the religious conservatives and old land-owning families was, in fact, extremely brief (Apostolakou 1997). The pictures soon came down as bourgeois reformers distanced themselves from socialism. The frequent reference to the Trial of Atheists as an originary mythology for local progressivism thus served to mute acutal divergences between radical and liberal political agendas in the past and the present.

While the introduction of Marxist approaches would prove significant for developments in historiography, during the interwar period the discipline of history itself started to become less influential in cultural politics as poets, artists, and folklorists took the lead in articulating the "national essence." Unlike Marxist historiography, which continued to be elaborated within a rubric of historical continuity, the literary and artistic "Greekness" (*Ellinikotita*) movement consciously broke with this schema: time and space came to be seen less as a matter of precise chronology or topography, but of broad contrasts (past vs. present, country vs. city). The conception of the past as "tradition" (*paradosi*) led to a blurring of the boundaries between history and folklore (Liakos 1994). Expressing a resistance to Western culture, similar to the negritude movement or *hispanidad*, the Greekness movement promoted an aesthetic nationalism, which compensated for the dashing of Greek irredentist ambitions in 1922 by rooting a transcendent and metaphysical Hellenism to the particular geographical ground of the small Helladic state (Leontis 1995: 91–2). Considered by many scholars to be more of a continuation of demoticism than a true opening to European modernism, the so-called Generation of the Thirties, which elaborated this vision of autochthonous Hellenicity, embraced folk art, vernacular language, and the aesthetics of the Greek landscape (cf. Tziovas 1986, 1989; Layoun 1990; Calotychos 1992; Leontis 1995). Released from the imperative to demonstrate cultural continuity, folklorists at this time would place less emphasis on texts (songs, proverbs, myths) than on material artifacts (woodworking, "naïve" painting, textiles) that testified to a traditional "way of life." With the rise of communism, however, as literary critic Dimitris Tziovas (1989) has noted, the "people" (*laos*) on which the Greekness movement was based became an increasingly politicized category, and tensions began to develop between liberal and radical cultural agendas.

In Volos, many vocal proponents of the Greekness movement identified openly with the Left, politicizing their cultural production in order to critique capitalism and foreign imperialism. Through his lifelong study of the folk art of Pelion as well as his active participation in the public life of the city, the folklorist Kitsos Makris, the primary local exponent of the Greekness movement, generated popular enthusiasm for traditional arts and crafts. Appropriately enough, his first book was a 1939 introduction to the folk artist Theofilos, a key symbol of the Greekness movement on a national level. In the introduction to this book, republished by the municipal history center in 1998, Makris notes:

> It is enough to make a person's heart break when he sees the unique frescoes of the *foustanella*-clad painter being destroyed. A few years ago there were so many frescoes and paintings of Theofilos. But the apartment blocks that are being built in the place of the humble little shops and the ignorance of the locals are stealing from us one by one the remnants of his art. (11)

Writing in demotic, Makris explicitly situates his project within a critique of capitalist modernity, westernization, and consumerism, though he does not write in as strident and explicitly antibourgeois a tone as Kordatos. After the war, Makris, a communist who had fought in the Resistance, actively set about trying to rescue local folk art and architecture from neglect and destruction in the wake of postwar reconstruction. As the head of the National Organization of Greek Handicrafts in Volos from 1964 to 1984 (with the exception of a brief period during the dictatorship when he was dismissed for political reasons), Makris was active in developing the arts and crafts movement in the city by funding traditional craftsmen and sponsoring handicrafts workshops for the public.

Two buildings constructed in Volos in the postwar period reflect the influence of the Greekness movement. The first is Makris's own house. Built shortly after the 1955 earthquake, this neo-Peliorite building, the first of its kind in Volos, symbolically brought the mountain "down" to the city. In doing so, it could be seen as a pointed critique of the modern cement apartment blocks being built at this time. With its slate roof, small courtyard area, and old marble fountain, Makris's house, which was designed by Argiris Filippidis, a well-known neotraditional architect, incorporated folk art, including frescoes and wooden-carved ceilings that Makris had salvaged from ruined tower houses on Pelion.[36] The care with which Makris built and decorated his own house was meant to (and did) serve as a model for others in the community. Decorating one's house with regionally appropriate folk art and even producing one's own traditional crafts became a statement against modernity as well as, of course, its most distinctive gesture. In a similar spirit, a new town hall, designed by Dimitris Pikionis, one of Greece's most famous modernist architects, was built to replace the neoclassical town hall, which had been irreparably damaged in the 1955 earthquake. Also constructed in a neo-Peliorite style, the building boasts at its main entrance a Theofilos fresco, which was recovered from an old store in the Palia district, as well as a series of strident black-and-white woodcuts by the leftist artist Tassos and others working in his style. These images depict scenes from the city's liberal and radical past, such as masses of striking workers and Resistance guerrillas. In the late 1990s, Makris's house, the town hall, and Tassos's didactic engravings as well as the few remaining, dusty stores selling heavy wooden furniture and other folk art products seemed to speak of another time. If the town hall were to be rebuilt again, one suspects that city leaders would opt for something more along neo-neoclassical lines.

As this brief review suggests, contemporary historical writing, with its emphasis on preserving and promoting the city's European aspect rather than its "indigenous" culture, might break with the anti-imperialist arts and crafts movement of the 1970s and 1980s, but has plenty of precedents from which to draw in other moments of local historical production. With its focus on economic development and Europeanization, contemporary local historical writing could be said to return to some of the fundamental concerns of the earliest historical texts about the region. Republication of these works, in turn, not only gave substance to nostalgic representations of the "old city" (especially by treating older texts of local historiography as documents of bourgeois cultivation), but also held important implications for local negotiations of political power. Indeed, as much as academic historians might have wanted to distance themselves from local historiography, in the late 1990s the

Volos municipality, like municipalities all over Greece, was proving exceedingly eager to promote its production.

Reproducing Enterprise: The Municipality and Heirloom History

During the discussion period at the "Local History/National History" event, the mayor of the city at the time, Dimitris Pitsioris, stood up and delivered a passionate defense of the plan to introduce a course on local history into the schools. Notwithstanding his forthright commitment to cultivating local historical con-sciousness, the mayor's comments betrayed a measure of uncertainty about which groups in the city actually felt connected to that history:

> I want to note that the void in knowledge of local history is scary, even given the fact that populations formed in modern cities such as Volos are populations that for the most part are not local populations. They don't have tradition (*paradosi*). You will say to me, what role does that play? It plays some role. When your family comes from a place, you will carry with you, in some way or another, its history. You will hear it. Your parents will tell you about it, your grandparents—something will exist within the house.

Pitsioris, who was elected mayor on a socialist ticket in 1990 and held office until 1998, went on to highlight the heterogeneity of the city's current population, describing various waves of migration to the city, including the large influx of refugees from Turkey in the 1920s and of immigrants from villages and towns of the neighboring Thessalian plain after the war decade of the 1940s. Noting the plethora of cultural organizations that existed in the city, he acknowledged that many resi-dents not only did not identify with Volos but also actively maintained connections to their originary "personal homelands" (*idiaiteres patrides*):

> So there is the problem of how we can compile and continue our local history, which isn't a factor (*stoicheio*) for 50 percent or more of the Volos population today. It is questionable if 50 percent of the population—the so-called Peliorites who came down to Volos—still exist anymore. We have an aggregate of small groups in the city. We live here—this is where we are going to go on living. So we need to know what was here two, three, four and seven thousand years ago. A continuity. It is not just that we *must* know this history, but because it is interesting. It is alive and beautiful.

While the mayor ended on an upbeat note, confident of the inherent value of history (the more the better), his initial tentativeness hinted at the actual contradic-tions and ambiguities involved in assuming that history is an inclusionary discourse or an effective vehicle of civic assimilation. What, for instance, is the point of producing local history under the aegis of the municipality if many people who live in the city do not feel "at home" there? Despite the fact that Volos, like any manu-facturing center has always been composed of a shifting amalgam of populations, the mayor's words make clear that to this day it has not proved easy for newcomers to become locals: one has to trace one's roots to the villages of the nearby Pelion peninsula to be considered a "true Voliote." The municipality's aggressive interventions into local historical production in recent years, including the establishment of a municipal history center and archive, the publication of new historical studies and republication of long out-of-print ones, and the renovation of "historical" buildings, thus, might be viewed less as a means of democratizing that history than of replicating the selective representations of the local past promoted by the city's former industrial class.

Seen within a global context, the fact that history has become integral to the way that the municipality is currently constructing its distinctive character is not surprising. In his study of urban capitalism, David Harvey (1989) has documented the rise of the "entrepreneurial city" in the aftermath of the major global economic crisis of the mid-1970s and ensuing transformations in the circulation of capital. He explains that cities currently jockey among themselves on an international level to enhance their positions as centers of consumption and "control and command functions" (especially of financial and administrative powers). The recuperation of history and community through the rhetoric of heritage has become an essential marketing tool as city officials attempt to sell their cities to investors, consumers, and tourists as well as to attract government redistributions and create new jobs.[37] These efforts are also addressed to the local population, as politicians turn to the past to restore faith in the local economy and bolster civic identity.

In the wake of the city's economic crisis in the 1980s, the municipality of Volos could be said to be engaged in the kind of historical entrepreneurialism described by Harvey. The city leaders have been actively attempting to transform the city's image from that of a "worker's city" (*ergatoupoli*) to that of a city of "culture," oriented around a newly established university and the nearby tourist destinations of Mt. Pelion and the Sporades islands. Through the Municipal Enterprise for Urban Studies, Innovation, and Development (DEMEKAV), set up in 1987, the municipality was effective in the 1990s in securing funds from the European Union for heritage-related projects.[38] In addition to the ongoing renovation of factories and warehouses around the city, there were plans for the creation of a historic zone in the "Old Town" district of *Palia* and the establishment of a museum of industrial heritage. These projects ran parallel to private initiatives, such as the restoration of neoclassical buildings and of the steam engine train on Mt. Pelion.[39] With the establishment of the Municipal Center for Historical Research, Documentation and Archives (DIKI) in 1992, the municipality also became the city's leading publisher of local history and the principal sponsor of the historical *ekdilosi*, a combination lecture, discussion, and celebration, such as the event I have been describing.[40]

Since these gatherings function as much as performances of hierarchies *within* the local historical community as between amateur and academics ones, in sponsoring them the municipal history center implicitly aligns itself with academic history and legitimizes its role as frame and filter of local historical production. Upstaging various community historical and cultural associations, the municipal history center by the end of the 1990s had come to dominate the local historical scene, introducing new themes for local historical research as well as a new format for its production.[41] The novelty of DIKI as an institutional structure and program for local historical production can be best understood if one peeks into the city's historical library where local writers have done much of their research. The "People's Library of the Three Hierarchs" (*Laiki Vivliothiki ton Trion Ierarchon*), located in the city's central downtown area, was established in 1912 by the eponymous Religious-Philological Association of the Three Hierarchs and until recently served as the city's only public library. At the time of my research, a large, glass-fronted, wooden bookcase, full of leather-bound volumes, including rare travelogues, historiographies, and theological and philological studies from the eighteenth and nineteenth centuries, lorded over the small reading room. The library's holdings were listed in unwieldy catalogues and classified according to the date of their acquisition, not by author, title, or even date of publication. In an upstairs lecture room where religious and philological discussions occasionally were held, a large icon was displayed, flanked by oil paintings of some of the association's benefactors. Aside from local schoolchildren who came in to consult the encyclopedia, the principal patrons of the library were amateur local history writers. The tomes of old local newspapers held by the library constitute one of the principal sites in which they hoped to discover traces of the past.

The atmosphere at DIKI could not be more different. The municipal history center was located above a music studio on the top floor of the renovated Spierer warehouse building. Decorated with poster-size photographs of "old Volos" (scenes of the train station, city streets, etc.), the office was an open loft-like space with several computer stations (fig. 2.2.). Bound minutes of the municipal council, which gradually were being entered into a computer database, lined the back wall. Other bookshelves and display cases contained secondary source material on Greek and

Figure 2.2   History on display. Volos Municipal History Center. Photograph by author.

local history, which was being organized so it could be searched online. The main archive was located in the basement and included, along with the core holding of the municipal archives, factory archives, family archives, photographs and slides, and architectural plans. DIKI's two principal staff members, Aigli Dimoglou, the director, and Yiannis Koutis, both in their thirties and with undergraduate degrees in history from Aristotle University in Thessaloniki, approached Voliote history through the prism of academic trends in social and economic history and particularly the research paradigm of the "neohellenic city."

When reflecting on contemporary changes in local history writing, many amateur writers complained to me about what they perceived as the growing commercialization of historical production and the substitution of an honest and genuine passion (*meraki*) with money. I heard of several cases in which published local historians had been approached to write histories on commission. "Every village wants to have a written history," an older local historian once told me: "They consider it a disgrace not to have one—even if it is an unimportant village." Indirectly, these comments seemed to reflect back on the municipal history center and the way that it has contributed to the professionalization and commodification of local historical production. Unlike the city's volunteer-run cultural and historical associations, DIKI has a paid staff and *must* produce historical texts and exhibitions, sometimes at the personal request of the mayor. Clearly, however, the introduction of money into local historical production also has been a boon for many local writers who would not have seen their books in print if municipalities and other cultural organizations had not funded their efforts. Indeed, even though most municipalities, unlike Volos, did not have the resources to sponsor a local history center, they were often willing to publish local writers' books on vanity presses.

While in the past, charismatic figures such as Kitsos Makris spearheaded projects of historical preservation in the city, the public face of DIKI, by contrast, concealed the distinct personalities and intellectual and political trajectories of the people behind it. Articles about the municipal history center in the local newspaper typically were accompanied by photographs displaying neat rows of books, archives, computers, and desks, but no people. One of DIKI's major projects, a history of the city "from the Neolithic to the present day" aims to bring together essays, many by amateur writers, on different aspects of Voliote history. The first attempt to produce a comprehensive diachronic history of the city and region since Kordatos's 1960 classic Marxist analysis, this work will apparently employ the familiar narrative of historical continuity framed around the city-as-subject; however, the shift of production scheme, from the individual historian (with an explicitly antiestablishment agenda) to a collective of writers funded by the municipality, might be seen as indicative of the rise of a new bureaucratic model of history writing.

As suggested by the plans for this comprehensive history, municipal interventions into the field of local historical production have not excluded amateur writers. To the contrary, their research skills, local knowledge, and personal archives often have been drawn on by the DIKI staff, thus leading to the confirmation but also sometimes the transformation of local writers' conceptions of the relevant sources and subjects of local historiography. Testament to a hierarchical but close relationship, the first time I visited DIKI and mentioned that I was interested in talking to amateur local historians, the director drew up a list of fifteen writers' names and phone numbers in a matter of a few minutes. While as far as I could tell few local writers actually made use of DIKI's archives—perhaps not knowing what *to do* with municipal minutes or the archive of a factory—DIKI's definitive break with philological categories of evidence appears to have influenced local writers' ideas about the possible topics of local history. More patently, though, the frequent events sponsored by DIKI on subjects such as local industry, architecture, and local political and intellectual figures contributed to generating popular interest in researching these subjects in the 1990s.[42]

At the same time, DIKI's initiative to compile and display the local historical bibliography demonstrates the degree to which local history has started to seem identical with the history of the municipality itself. Tellingly, the first event organized by DIKI, "Local Self-Administration, Local Development: The Case of Volos" (1993), paid tribute to the city's first and perhaps most "heroic" mayor, Nikolaos Georgiadis. As the mayor who tore down the Ottoman fort and completed an impressive number of public works, Georgiadis embodied the modernizing, European values that the municipality was espousing at the time of my research. With roots in an important village on Pelion, Georgiadis, who was also author, as we have seen, of one of the classic local histories of the region, could be considered the quintessential Voliote bourgeois political reformer. No other figure from the city's past more perfectly brought together municipal and historical rhetoric, blurring the lines between the two. In a preface to a facsimile reprint of Georgiadis's 1903 report of public works, mayor Pitsioris referred to Georgiadis as the first person to have a "vision for the city and be decided on realizing it" (1997: 5).

Bringing a dynamic mayor like Georgiadis back into local public memory is illustrative of the way the municipality was using history to legitimate its newly expanded powers. In the 1980s, as an attempt to offset the disastrous effects of the overcentralization of government in Athens, the socialist PASOK government had introduced the institution of "local self-administration," or *topiki aftodoiikisi*,[43] which granted provincial officials much greater political and economic autonomy over local affairs than they had had in the past. In Volos, the first mayor to run the municipality under this new arrangement was Mihalis Koundouris, who was elected on the ticket of the local left coalition and served as mayor from 1979 to 1990. His administration coincided with the socialist euphoria of the 1980s but also with the economic decline of the city. Some of the municipal interventions of this time, including the installation of Tassos's woodcuts in the town hall, with their celebration of progressive and radical moments in the local past, as well as the granting of the medal of the city to the famous communist poet Yiannis Ritsos, gave official sanction to the vernacular aesthetic associated with leftist politics.

In the 1990s, however, the municipality started to draw its symbols less from the folk and the proletariat than from the elite to turn its attention to the city's bourgeois past. The contributions of municipally minded entrepreneurs to the city's early development started to be looked to as a template for a Europe-oriented and newly entrepreneurial municipality. The restoration of commercial buildings and the installation of municipal services in them, thus, could be said to reflect the municipality's bid to assume the place of industry as agent of prosperity. In his introduction to the 1991 municipal-funded, posthumous publication of Dimitris Tsopotos's *History of Volos*, Pitsioris describes the book as:

> a representative document (*dokoumento endeiktiko*) of the mindset of those who built the New City of Volos and gave it great economic, cultural and urban development in the last decades of the past century and the first ones of ours. Of the people who created, in an improvisational manner, the framework and the prototypes for the idiosyncratic (*idiomorfou*) Voliote bourgeoisie, with its independent code of bourgeois behavior. (7)

The mayor's use of the word "document" to describe Tsopotos's history suggests, as I have discussed above, that the contemporary importance of a text such as this rests less in its account of the past (which the Marxist Kordatos had so maligned) than in its status as a primary source in its own right: as evidence of the sophistication and scholarly pursuits of the "idiosyncratic" Voliote bourgeoisie. In quoting, prefacing, and republishing historical texts such as these as well as renovating old buildings, local government officials folded their contemporary political program into the erudite, optimistic, and compelling visions of the city proposed by former city leaders, historians, and other cultural producers. Through these acts of "reaccentuation," to use Bakhtin's (1986) word, the municipality also signaled its *right* to appropriate, even "inherit," the symbolic capital associated with particular historical figures and monuments as a means to legitimate its own authority.

   In response to the municipality's sudden interest in and confirmation of the significance of the city's industrial past, some descendents of local capitalists were themselves compelled to write local historiography in the 1990s. The idea that "old Volos" is located in a particular series of urban and industrial monuments from neoclassical gravestones and buildings to old factories and railway stations, in turn, could be said to have generated an "heirloom" conception of local history: buildings and monuments are seen as "belonging" to certain families, whose stories are needed to reanimate them in the course of their architectural restoration. Thus, the "factory" often seems to be treated by local writers as a legacy of the bourgeoisie rather than as a highly charged and conflictual social space produced by flows of capital, people, and goods.[44] Eleni Diomidi, the author of a history of her industrialist uncle, for instance, complained to me that one of the city's old tobacco warehouses, known locally as the "Yellow Warehouse" (*Kitrini Apothiki*), had yet to be renovated. (Notably, this warehouse, where executions took place during the Nazi Occupation, is pictured on the cover of the 1985 history of the local wartime Resistance, written by Nitsa Koliou). She explained:

> So twenty people died in there. But then all of Greece is a memorial. They killed everywhere. It was a war. But that building also gave food, money, bread to 20,000 workers. Saturday, when the factory closed and the people came out, do you know what money came into the market? That's how the economy of Volos thrived. Now who produces money? Why should we keep that building a monument to Auschwitz in Volos and not make it a building of joy?

As many critics of the "heritage industry" have noted, the preservation and renovation of factories often leads to their aestheticization and commodification and to the erasure of histories of labor that occurred there (cf. Hewison 1987). In their renovated state, the warehouses and factories seem like ornaments or gifts of the city's industrialists rather than the very foundations of their wealth. By extension, this view of the city as a collection of historical artifacts, instead of as a product of *urbanization* as socioeconomic process, contributes to the territorializing of history I discussed above, making histories of people and places outside the city limits (working-class districts, migrant workers) seem irrelevant to the city's past.[45]

In centering its commemorations on figures of Voliote mayors, industrialists, and intellectuals, the municipality implicitly defined local citizenship, historical agency, economic well-being, and the public good in ways that were hardly disinterested. These interventions often gave the impression that the city's industrial growth was indeed a mere extension of the business acumen of the city's elite classes rather than also the product of the labor of its workers, including populations of "foreigners" and "newcomers" such as immigrants and refugees. In this discourse, capitalist development also appears to be an outgrowth of "local" capital and investment not the result of a complex conjunction of global economic relations and forces. Finally, as "traditions" of "old Volos," philanthropy seems to be a logical substitute for public spending, and entrepreneurialism a basic characteristic of good government. The staff at the municipal history center, of course, hardly sees its work in these terms; to the contrary, they intend their focus on industrial history as a critical corrective to traditional event-centered history and as a potential means to approach history "from below." But the politics of preservationism tend to be ambiguous. While factory renovation projects often begin within the context of leftist social and economic history, local elite and political conservatives can come to embrace them for quite different reasons (Samuel 1994: 288–312).

In the 1990s, the class anxieties of some of Volos's old families and the pragmatic politics of the municipality coincided in producing histories of the city's "industrial revolution" and its bourgeois class. The city's past, however, potentially contains many other kinds of social experience. If we consider local historiography not so much as emerging in a local public sphere but as defining its parameters, it is clear that there have been significant shifts in the social and political backgrounds of those who feel authorized to write local history. While the historical production of amateur writers has been critically shaped and redefined by the municipality's deployment of historical discourse, this "guidance," nonetheless, did not entirely determine the directions in which local historiography has developed.

Newcomers and Other "Others"

Vassilia Yiasirani kept putting off our first meeting. She was busy and, as she told me later, did not have time to arrange her house, so she could receive me properly. So, it was not until a month after my initial phone call that I arrived at her home, a modern two-story apartment building with colorful flowers and vines painted on the wooden balcony doors. Wearing jeans and an Oxford shirt, Yiasirani, with her bright red nails and silver bangles, did not fulfill my stereotypical image of a local historian (i.e., a bespectacled, formal, gray-haired man). Her 1996 *Stories of Life and Death in the Cemetery of Volos*, a book of genealogies of local families buried in the city's cemetery, also had not seemed to me a "typical" local history. While Yiasirani's formation as a writer, her mode of producing and circulating texts, and the documents and monuments she used as sources were not actually unusual, her situation was at just enough of an angle to bring into focus shifts in the categories of people who feel authorized to write local history.

Once the exclusive privilege of educated elite men, local history writing in Volos has become a solidly middle-class activity in which both men and women participate. Yiasirani, who has a degree in archaeology from the University of Thessaloniki, was a grade school teacher, by far the most common profession of local historians. In 1990s Volos, though, writers also included housewives, bank employees, journalists, lawyers, and local businesspeople, the majority, unlike Yiasirani, retired. Yiasirani told me that the idea for her cemetery book had come to her while she was mourning the death of her only sister. After the first shock of her death had passed, Yiasirani began to take notice of the impressive old neoclassical tombs during her daily trips to the cemetery to tend her sister's grave. Over the course of a five-year period, she spent all of her free time at the cemetery measuring, photographing, and studying the monuments. She also scoured church registers, local newspapers, and municipal records for information as well as interviewed the descendants of people buried in the family tombs. Yiasirani told me that she had always felt close to the world of the cemetery, since she grew up nearby and used to watch processions of coffins as she played in the streets. Her research, however, took her for the first time into the homes of the former leading families of the city. With her cemetery book she also, as she put it, "broke into the circle" (*bika ston kiklo*) of local history writers.[46]

Strange and macabre as her decision to write about the history of the cemetery appeared to other local writers with whom I spoke, Yiasirani's subject was, in fact, very much in step with the contemporary paradigm of historical research I described above. Indeed, the municipal cemetery, especially during the period on which she focused (the end of the nineteenth century until 1934) could be seen as the ultimate monument to the "old Volos" of the modernizing elite. During Ottoman rule, people had been buried in cemeteries adjacent to their houses of worship; thus the establishment of a municipal cemetery in Volos, shortly after the incorporation of Thessaly into the Greek state, represented an important symbolic break with the Ottoman social and political order, signaling the adoption of European discourses on state and citizenship.[47] Since Greek Orthodox typically exhume their dead after three years, the grave monuments in the cemetery in Volos, though, only record the deaths of wealthy Voliotes who had the means and ambition to imitate western European burial practices. As a result, Yiasirani's book, which she describes as the "echo of the old Volos" (*o antilalos tou paliou Volou*), reads like a "who's who" of the local elite and, for this reason, has become a handy reference work for other local historians. As in the First Cemetery of Athens, with its replicas of ancient tombstones, many of the grave monuments in the Volos cemetery are neoclassical in style. While not long ago considered by many Greeks, especially those involved in the arts and crafts movement, a symbol of the ideological colonization of Greece by the West, by the 1990s, the neoclassical, as we have seen, had become a positively valued sign of Greek modernity. Yiasirani's cemetery study, thus, formed a telling and timely departure from the more properly "Greek" subject of her first book: Byzantine monasteries on the island of Skyros.

Yiasirani's text first drew my attention because she did *not* write as a spokesman of the particular social group to which she belonged. She had taken the unusual step of writing about the Voliote elite even though she herself was a child of Greek Orthodox refugees from Turkey and thus a relative "newcomer" to the city. For the most part, local histories about Volos still tend to be written by people who consider themselves "true Voliotes" (*veroi Voliotes*) and trace their roots back to Mt. Pelion.[48] In fact, an entire subgroup of local writers is made up of descendants of elite families who write local history as an extension of family history and ground their authority to speak about the local past on their privileged access to family archives.

This legitimating strategy was common in the past as well. In his 1928 newspaper articles about "old Volos," Nikolaos Gatsos notes that his sources were family and friends, who also happened to be the leading figures of local society:

> The aforementioned unforgettable men are the main source of my reminiscences (*anamniseon*) presented here. It is just a shame that when our fathers were living care was not taken to preserve documents (*engrafa*), letters, verified narratives, in order that the tumultuous and tragic history of our fathers during the years of their labor might be more fully known. We also needed a Vlahoyiannis who with zeal and diligence would have preserved some of the sources (*pigas*) of our modern history. (1998: 17)

His tongue-in-cheek reference to the philologist and indefatigable historical collector Vlahoyiannis, who had documented the life stories of the heroes of the Greek War of Independence, presages the contemporary transformation of industrialists into local "heroes" and the records of their commercial enterprises into historical documents. Similarly, for his 1934 *Chronicle of Volos*, Athos Trigonis collected what he calls "little stories (*istorioules*) of old Volos" from "very old Voliotes," who happened to be members of the city's oldest families. More recently, in a slim 1995 biography of her uncle, *Mihalis Kazazis (1850–1938): Pioneer in the Development of Industry in Volos and Thessaly*, Eleni Diomidi also invokes an insider's discourse: she tells her reader that she is relaying stories of her uncle's life and hard work that she had listened to as a child as if they were "fairy tales" (*paramythia*). When Eleni Triandou, daughter of a Voliote merchant, began research for her 1994 *Volos through the Mist of Time*, she simply called on her own friends and family. People gave her materially freely, she told me, because they "knew I wouldn't change anything."

While it might seem odd that Yiasirani chose to write a history that involved her so deeply researching the lives of the local elite, it is no coincidence that she grew up next to the cemetery in which the leading families of the city have been buried. When the cemetery was established at the end of the nineteenth century, it was placed at the edge of the city in an infertile area known as *Xirokambos* (literally, "dry field") where some decades later refugees from Asia Minor, including Yiasirani's family, would be settled. The proximity of Yiasirani's house to the graveyard speaks to her social distance from it: none of her own ancestors have grave monuments there. When Yiasirani began contacting the city's "old families" during the course of her research, she initially was met with suspicion. She clearly was not a member of their community and there was little reason to trust her. Thinking, further, that she was an agent of the cemetery involved in the campaign to have it moved to a new location (which would lead to the break up of family tombs), a group of the families even hired a lawyer to stop her research. According to Yiasirani, this blew over quickly, and she soon became friendly with her informants. "It really was not difficult to talk to those women," she told me. "Deep down what they want is to talk about their families and everything they once were." Although she told me that she does not have a particular interest in the history of the ethnic Greek presence in Anatolia or of her neighborhood, Nea Ionia, she recently agreed to contribute some articles to the local newspaper about the genealogies of "important" local refugee families. After the publication of these articles, she told me that her informants from the cemetery book congratulated her for finally writing about her "own."

Since 1990, the history of the city's various ethnic and religious "Others" has, in fact, started to be produced. Written exclusively by people who identify as members of particular "minority" communities, these histories typically describe the contribution of that group to Voliote history. After demonstrating the given community's "Greekness," they go on to highlight certain positive aspects of the group's cultural difference. Issues of class conflict—or identification—with the "locals" tend to be downplayed. Thus, in his 1994 *The Israelite Community of Volos*, Rafael Frezis, a local businessman and head of the Jewish community in Volos, plots the history of Voliote Jews within a diachronic narrative of Hellenism. His history begins with a reference to ancient epigraphs that attest to an age-old Jewish presence in the area and is followed by a discussion of the development of the "New City" of Volos as a joint creation of Jewish and Greek merchants. On the urging of his editor, he included, despite his own reservations, a final section describing the "exotic" rites of Judaism.

Similarly, in his 1994 *Chronicle of Nea Ionia*, Dimitris Konstandaras narrates the history of the settlement of Asia Minor refugees in the city as a much-needed appendix to the history of Volos. Talking to me at his house one day, he pulled down Tsopotos's *History of Volos* from a shelf lined with encyclopedias and history books. Pointing to the few sentences in which Tsopotos refers to the refugees' arrival and presence in Volos, he told me that it was this erasure from the historical record that had motivated him to undertake his research: "I wanted to find the roots, how Nea Ionia came to be, when the first houses were built, when the first people came, when it got the name Nea Ionia, when the Evangelistria [the community's main church] and the first schools were built." Although it includes an account of the 1936 arson of refugee-owned shops by local Voliotes, his book focuses primarily on the "originary" history of the refugee neighborhood and not on antagonisms between refugees and locals. For her part, the local writer Eleni Kartsagouli did not hesitate to remind people in private and public about local racism against the refugees; however, she chose not to *write* about these unpleasant memories. As indicated by the title of her 1995 book, *There Where the Roses Had No Thorns*, she narrates the "good life" of the refugees in Anatolia before they came to Volos. Notably, these two books about Nea Ionia focused exclusively on the neighborhood's refugee identity not its important role in left-wing wartime radicalism or its working-class history. Indeed, despite the interest in industrial history in 1990s Volos, it is striking that there were no attempts made by amateur historians to write a history of labor or collect testimonies from workers.

On many occasions, amateur historians told me that they felt they should refrain from passing judgment on the past and using history to promote particular political agendas. Although almost every author told me that the 1960 history of the region written by the Marxist historian Yiannis Kordatos was the most important book in their libraries, they also almost always pointed out in the same breath that the book had "weaknesses," or that Kordatos was a "Marxist and made a lot of generalizations," or that "he sees things one-sided, as all about class struggle." In these conversations, Nitsa Koliou's name often came up as an example of a local writer "with politics." However, Koliou herself, who happens to be a "true Voliote" with Pelion roots but to come from a working-class background, categorically rejected the term "political" to refer to her work. One day I asked her about her 1988 *Roots of the Worker's Movement and the 'Worker' of Volos*, which discusses the establishment of the city's Labor Center and labor newspaper:

> P: You were interested in these subjects—
> K: —of course.
> P: —from a political point of view?
> K: No, not political. I don't put politics before anything. I put it at the end. In other words, when I write, when I search, I am not at all interested in politics. For instance, with the book on the Resistance, some people might have told me: "You know so-and-so later moved to the Right." And I would say, "I am not interested in that at all. I am interested in what happened in the Occupation. Since during the Occupation that person fought for independence (*apeleftherosi*), for me he is respectable (*sevastos*). Now what he did afterwards, God bless him (*me geia kai hara tou*). He switched over to another legal party. He didn't pass into some illegality (*paranomia*) or to the *junta*, in which case you might say, I am not going to deal with him at all.

Like most local writers, Koliou believed that historical truth is compromised if writers expose their politics (in the sense of *party* politics). Nonetheless, her choice of subjects (the Labor Center, the history of the Resistance, etc.), with their patent connection to radical political movements of the past, differs strikingly from the conservatism of many of the city's other amateur local historians.

Given this context, the fact that many women were writing local history in Volos also cannot be assumed to signal a particularly feminist orientation in historical research or to constitute a significant challenge to the gender hierarchies involved in historical production itself. While the opportunity for women to write local history increased dramatically in the 1990s, most women history writers whom I met were unmarried, divorced, or financially well-off. The last group usually had full-time maids at home and wrote history as an extension of other "civic" activities, such as giving public lectures about their travels. Koliou's route into writing, by contrast, was much less easy. She did not have the money to go to college, so after high school she took a job setting type at a newspaper, which soon led to an opportunity to write. At the end of one of our first conversations, she noted: "Well, that's a little bit of my story—a story that has meant the surrender (*apallotriosi*) of everything. My dear departed mother used to say that I married the *Tahydromos* [the newspaper where she worked]." Yiasirani, who was teaching, married, and taking care of two teenage children when she took up history writing, also had to make significant personal sacrifices to pursue her research. For her, history proved a life-changing step into the public sphere:

> When I got married in 1977, I would not have imagined at all—not at all—that I would have a life outside the house. But after 1990, 1991, everything changed. I couldn't write history before. I might have had it inside me, but I couldn't do anything. When I married, I disappeared. I was shut up inside here. I raised the kids and I raised them well. That's what I wanted. But now I desire my writing. Other people look at me and they say, why bother (*den variesai*). Why are you doing all that work now, running around to people and archives? Haven't you done enough? No, I don't feel that way at all. I stay up every night until two or three in the morning.

During our conversations, Yiasirani's frequent references to housekeeping (how she used to like it, how she could not be bothered with it now, how she still had to take care of the house, etc.) brought into relief how gender and class asymmetries continue to delimit *who* produces historical knowledge.

The life experiences of women local historians, however, could not be said to have led to a problematizing of the gendered dimensions of social relations in the past or inspired a bluntly politicized history of women's experience. In her history of women's education, *Souvenir of Girls' Education*, which focuses on the period between 1900 and 1930, Koliou is quick to deny that any "feminist intentions" guided her choice of subject matter; as she writes in the introduction: "It is worthwhile to present the general indifference and attitude of Society and the view of parents about a fundamental subject, without that meaning that we arrive at feminist sermons and analyses of [social] Movements, without meaning that we condemn them" (1997: 8).

In local historical writing, one of the most common strategies for addressing controversial issues is simply leaving them out. Unlike most academic historians, local writers live in the community about which they write and socialize with many of their informants and descendants of the people about whom they write; many authors pointed to this intimacy as justification for their reticence about certain subjects. Yiasirani, for instance, told me again and again how bad she felt about compromising historical accuracy in her book; however, she admitted that upon request of the families she interviewed, she frequently silenced "family secrets" (illegitimate children, suicides, etc.). In my conversation with Frezis, he told me that even though he felt there was not a particularly bad history of racism against Jews in Volos, he nonetheless did not feel comfortable writing about everyday incidents of racism in the past. By switching midway through his book on Asia Minor refugees from a chronological narrative to a thematic one, and also as a result of relying solely on written sources, Konstandaras bypassed the subject of the war by default. When I asked him about this, he told me:

> Nea Ionia had lots of people in the communist party and the democratic parties generally; in Volos, they considered us a small Moscow . . . I wanted to write their names so that I could honor them (*Ithela na tous grapso eponyma yia na tous timiso*). . . . The truth is that I began to collect information. One man would tell me

one thing. Then another would tell me something else. But I saw that most times there was a contradiction between what they told me and I didn't have any written sources on which to depend. Oral sources didn't give me what I needed and so as to not displease anyone and so that no one would say, you wrote his name, why not mine? I just left it vague, I'm afraid.

In the 500-page local history he wrote about his Peliorite village, Kostas Liapis told me that he took a "neutral" stance in his description of the Civil War:

> There were fewer reactions than I expected. But one woman called me and told me that she would sue me because I slandered the memory of her father, who had killed an *andartis* (left-wing guerrilla). Her father had slaughtered him in the town square. She wanted me to write that. I knew about the incident. First off, it wasn't true. I saw it myself as a twelve-year old. It has stayed in my soul as an open wound . . . it wasn't her father who killed him. Her father came half an hour later. He just cut off his head with an ax. She wanted me to write that, but I respected the memory of her father.

He told me of another friend who wanted to write a history of his village, but kept putting off writing because he could not confront the horrible things that had happened there during the war years. When I asked Koliou why she did not write about the Civil War after finishing her research on the local resistance movement, she waffled in her response. She told me that she had thought about doing it, but then got caught up with other things. She also said that she expected that someone else would have done it by now. More than anything, she worried about the pain of reopening old wounds. She told me about a boy going to his mother after her book on the Resistance was published and proclaiming his discovery: "Grandfather was a traitor!"

Since authors do not ground their authority to write on academic credentials but on their intimacy to the subject matter of their histories, the fact of their writing speaks of a historical moment in which their personal, family, and neighborhood histories have acquired historical significance. Notwithstanding the heavy hand of municipal and elite interests, the liberal expansion of the public sphere has widened the local community described by local history, but hardly has led to a radical questioning of historical exclusions or an exposure of the social and political conflicts in the city's past. The blind spots of local historiography, however, cannot be ascribed entirely to the social backgrounds and politics of its writers or to a problem of access that could be remedied simply by "giving voice." In part, I contend, these silences have been produced and naturalized by the conventions of the genre of local historiography itself as well as by prevailing common sense about how new artifacts and documents should be incorporated into historical discourse.

Domestic/Scriptural Spaces: Enacting Historical Ownership

Just as monuments in their guise as public heirlooms connect personal histories with public ones, so too does the home serve as a site to assert the place of personal or family stories in national and community histories. This intertwining of home and history is captured in the phrase, "my house is a museum," which next to "I am not an historian" was by far the most common statement I heard when I crossed the threshold of writers' homes. In his study of the "historical constructivism" of upper-class Athenians, James Faubion (1993a) has demonstrated the importance of interior decorating as an element of "self-formation" through which subjects assert their interpretations of national historical narratives. While their living-room historical displays might not have involved the eclectic bricolage of different periods of the Hellenic past that Faubion has described in the homes of the Athenian elite, Voliote history writers were equally engaged in arranging these kinds of domestic exhibits. Although in other cases I will consider in this book the home as symbol of personal or family history and repository of private archives was used to construct alternative histories, in the case of local historians I found that home archives and living-room historical displays served primarily as a vehicle through which to inhabit dominant narratives and weave individual histories into them. Storing documents and display-ing historical objects in their houses offered local historians a way of demonstrating their sense of possessing and being possessed by the past as well as of asserting the authority to speak about it. The assumptions about the nature of historical docu-ments and objects that underlie these projects of home decorating, thus, are not inci-dental to our discussion but linked to a fundamental orientation toward history as patrimony.

Susan Stewart's (1993) discussion of souvenirs might provide a starting point for thinking about the materials gathered in these home displays and archives. Like the souvenir, the historical object represents a metonym of a particular historical period and cultural group. As a miniature of a larger whole, it can be appropriated and possessed by an individual or family and transmitted as a piece of property. Its status as a material object is integral to the longing it inspires in its owner; by establishing a sense of unbridgeable distance, the historical artifact, like the souvenir, functions to "authenticate a past or otherwise remote experience and, at the same time, to discredit the present," which is "too impersonal, too looming, or too alienating" in comparison to direct contact with the historical object and its putative reference (139). Finally, like the souvenir, the historical artifact remains incomplete without the supplemental narrative of its owner. Rather than simply evidence to be cited in a historical account, then, historical documents often seem to be that which motivates the act of writing. As tangible objects, they also provide authors a medium through which to enact "ownership" of the past through the ritual of affixing a signature.

Although many local writers called their house a "museum," the comment actually referred to two quite different situations: an old house full of inherited things or a relatively new apartment or house decorated with antiques or folk art. In the first case, the person would self-identify as a "real Voliote" or an "old Voliote." Having succeeded in holding on to old things that have been in the family for generations (a house, photograph collections, furniture, paintings, letters), of course, is fundamental to claiming that identity in the first place. As Benjamin has noted, inheritance itself is so often the basis for collecting: "a collector's attitude toward his possessions stems from an owner's feeling of responsibility toward his property" (66). To the extent that a particular family history is perceived as integral to the city's history, the family house becomes de facto a "museum" and its contents potential pieces of historical evidence. When I arrived at Eleni Diomidi's house in the city center, she ushered me into a small living room cluttered with doily-covered tables. Without any prompting on my part, she told me that the velvet-upholstered couch and chairs, hand-stenciled along the wood with a Greek key design and acanthus pattern, were a hundred years old and had belonged to her uncle, the local industrialist about whom she has written. Oil paintings in muted colors, including one of the Peliorite town, Makrinitsa, hung on the walls. (In the homes of "real Voliotes," I found that an oil painting of a Peliorite tower house, with its distinctive slate gray roof, was a must.) Catching my glance toward the paintings, she hastened to inform me that they were the work of her brother, who had studied in Germany; she then handed me a copy of *Thessalian Painting 1500–1980* (Voyiatzis 1980), opened to a section on her brother. When I asked Diomidi how she came to write the biography of her uncle, she explained:

> I had a lot of . . . mementos (*enthymia*). Let's call them mementos. From the Chamber of Commerce, which said how much money he made. And photographs. I knew his life. I was attached to that factory and to my uncle. I thought that the information I had could help a person who was undertaking a history of Volos. Not just to say here we are, but to have documents (*dokoumenta*). And the documents are letters, papers (*engrafa*): those are the documents.

This notion that the personal papers of the city's elite families were, by definition, "documents" of the city's history echoed the assumptions of earlier writers of local history. In his 1933 essay "The History of the Founding of Volos," Tsopotos, for instance, used 300 letters exchanged between his father in Istanbul and his brother and other merchants in Volos to reconstruct the history of trade in the city between 1840 and 1841. In a footnote, he explains that he took these letters, which he had found in an "old, worn book," and "deposited [them] at the Archive of the Historical and Ethnological Society of Athens."

While the personal records of the city's leading families might always have the potential to be read as documents of local history, the degree to which people offer up these materials to public scrutiny varies, depending on the historical moment and the prevailing historical paradigm. Diomidi, for instance, appears to be so used to being interviewed about her family's history that she commented on the fact that I did not immediately bring out a tape recorder to record our conversation. Over the course of our meeting, she also enumerated for me the various people, prominent in both local and national historical circles, who had come to speak to her about her uncle: Koliou, gathering information for her book on the local history of girls' education; Aigli Dimoglou, the director of DIKI, looking for information for a study of the city's industrial past; Manolis Haritatos, the director of the Athens-based Greek Literary and Historical Archives (ELIA), interested in buying her old books; and the historian Vassilis Panagiotopoulos, then director of the Institute for Neohellenic Research at the National Hellenic Research Foundation in Athens, hoping to find out information about her industrialist uncle. According to Diomidi, she told Panagiotopoulos: "Leave it to me to write about him myself!"

Local elites often implied to me that the respect and care they lavished on preserving records of their family histories could be a model for historical preservation more generally. Militsa Karathanou, a descendant of an old Voliote family who spearheaded the local campaign to restore the Pelion steam train, proposed that preservation be seen as a kind of "recycling," not unlike her own strategies for reusing historical objects she had inherited. As an example, she showed me an antique armoire she had transformed into a china display cabinet by replacing wooden panels with glass ones. Similarly, she suggested, outmoded forms of transportation, such as the steam train or the little boats that once used to ferry people across the bay, could be turned into tourist rides. Her family photograph album also seemed to carry a didactic message about preservationism. Tracing her roots back to a Peliorite village as well as to some important intellectual figures of the region, the album interweaves family photographs and other memorabilia with short texts summarizing key events of local and national history. While Karathanou told me that she felt people in Volos were starting to develop sensitivity to history in recent years, she regretted that so much of the city's modern history already had been "lost." In addition to the destruction of buildings, she noted that many collections of furniture, paintings, and other objects once belonging to "important" Voliote families had been broken up and sold off. "Looking around, sometimes you'd say that Volos just fell from the sky today," she noted. "That it doesn't have a past."

For people who made no claim to Voliote heritage and who lived in houses they had bought or built themselves, the home also was a space for the projection of their relation to local and national historical narratives. Rather than bringing personal history into the public realm, however, their home displays principally served to "bring home" a public discourse on national culture and heritage. Reflecting the influence of the arts and crafts movement, heavy rough-hewn wooden furniture, colorful patterned rugs, textiles, and other Greek (neo)traditional crafts decorated these writers' homes, not the European-style antique furniture preferred by "old Voliote" families. Local writer Kostas Liapis, who hailed from Pelion but had lived many years in Volos, invited me to the neo-Peliorite home he had built for his retirement. Located in a Pelion town near Volos, the house boasted an Ottoman-style sitting room with carved wooden ceilings; the walls were hung with several oil paintings of Pelion tower houses. "Nothing here is new," he told me, "and all the designs are authentic." In this sort of home, then, traditional not aristocratic Pelion set the tone, as suggested also by the kind of coffee and cakes usually served there: sweet cups of Turkish coffee and local candied preserves brought out by writers' wives on trays with lace doilies, rather than the filter coffee and layer cakes that were often proffered at the homes of "old Voliotes."

The houses of local writers with roots in Asia Minor, on the other hand, typically lacked a reference to Pelion entirely and projected the "Eastern" (*Anatolitiko*) dimension of Greek folk culture. It seemed that every inch of Yiasirani's house, which her husband referred to a bit sarcastically as an exhibition space (*ekthesiakos horos*), was covered with some sort of handicraft, traditional object, or natural artifact, ranging from bronze plates, Byzantine icons, and swords to wood carvings, big pieces of driftwood, and brightly-colored textiles. Display cases flanking one wall of the living room held hookahs, bronze Turkish coffee cups, and painted ceramic plates. The focal point of the living room was a large fireplace around which heavy wooden-carved chairs, kilim rugs, and stools had been arranged. Before she began writing, Yiasirani told me that she had spent much of her free time making craft items to decorate her house as well as painting floral designs on the interior and exterior walls. Eleni Kartsagouli, the writer of the book about local Asia Minor refugees, had decorated the living room of her apartment in Nea Ionia with hard-backed wooden chairs engraved with the double-headed eagle of Byzantium and wood carvings she had made herself. She told me that she kept pomegranates on her coffee table to remind her of her mother and a special Anatolian custom involving the fruit. On one wall, metal ornamental wedding belts and a relative's fez were pinned against a bright fabric, while on another family photographs were displayed beside a panoramic image of a Turkish coastal city.

Books also occupied a prominent place in these home displays. Although some writers kept their books in the living room, most had created a separate office space within their homes to store them; books, however, often overflowed into other rooms (see fig. 2.3). Koliou was the only local writer I met who kept an office outside the home where she would go punctually in the mornings. In her case, though, writing local history had not developed out of her personal collecting, craft making, or family legacy, but from her career as a journalist. She had turned her work into a hobby rather than vice versa. This was reflected in the décor of her office: heavy antique wooden office furniture and sober wall decorations, such as old advertising posters for Voliote tobacco companies. Most writers with whom I spoke also preserved and organized their own writings as carefully as the various documents, photographs, and notes they had gathered in the course of their research, underlining the fact these were

Figure 2.3 Bedroom library. Vassilia Yiasirani at home. Photograph by author.

among their most precious possessions. As Rey Chow (2001) notes, apropos of Benjamin's observation that writing books is considered one of the most "praisewor-thy" methods of acquiring them, ownership, collecting, and writer's self-identity are inextricably bound together in these cherished tokens. For local writers, I also found that books, not scholarly articles, were considered the basic unit of historical pro-duction, perhaps because of their more substantial physical presence. Despite the easier access to publication afforded by vanity presses than by scholarly journals, I was told by one local historian that a woman with a doctorate in history who had published several articles on local history could not be considered a "writer" because she did not have a book. Many writers, in fact, treated their books as material objects in their own right by framing their front covers, hanging them on the walls of their home offices, and sometimes even binding them in hardcover or leather.

In the case of "real Voliotes," the status of the home as personal archive legitimated their right to speak about the local past while, at the same time, demon-strating the importance of their family's history to that past. For them, writing local history represented a calculated exposure of the family living room and the contents of their desk drawers. For other writers, the construction of personal archives and historical displays in the home enabled them to domesticate public historical narratives and bring family history in line with them. In both cases, though, the materiality of historical artifacts and the urge to possess them predominated. For many writers it also seemed that a period, often lasting several years, of arranging his-torical objects in their homes served as a first step, a kind of apprenticeship, which preceded historical research proper. In fact, one might speak of a continuum in which the writing of local history represented simply one further step in making public a painstakingly gathered and organized cache of documents and objects.

Framing Documents: Newspaper and Photograph Histories

Although contemporary local historians approach documents and artifacts with the same kind of reverence as historical collectors of the previous century, new thematic interests have led to the incorporation of novel categories of evidence in local historical production. Two of the most common and popular sources for 1990s local history, for instance, were old photographs and local newspapers. These sources have become newly available to researchers in part because of the advent of new technologies of document reproduction. The bias against "creating documents" (through oral testimony, for instance) implicitly naturalizes the recovery of these already "existing" (and hence "objective") sources as part of the ongoing process by which the documentary base of local history has expanded. The incorporation of new sources such as these, in turn, has played an important role in setting in motion shifts in historical narratives and subjectivities. Thus, even though newspapers and photographs were ostensibly being drawn on by local historians to "illustrate" histories of urban life focused on the bourgeois classes, the reverse might in fact be the case. In other words, one reason that the history of the city is being written about the local elite is because it is being composed from the quintessential artifacts of bourgeois culture: the newspaper and the photograph.

In his study of popular historical culture, *Theatres of Memory* (1994), Raphael Samuel notes that a market for old photographs began to develop in England in the 1960s, at the same time that the technology for their reproduction became widely available. In the 1970s, the archives of forgotten local photographers and the photographic collections of local libraries began to be "discovered," leading to the publication of photographic albums depicting the history of particular villages, towns, and neighborhoods. As photographs became incorporated into historical research, though, they were not, as Samuel observes, treated with the same rigor as other historical documents: "we do not have a way, as we would when making use of a manuscript or printed source, of putting quotation marks, metaphorically speaking, around old photographs; nor, even if we are using them to pursue an argument, of footnoting and referencing them" (329). Old photographs used in historical works tend to be accompanied by a credit (i.e., "courtesy of the archive of . . .") rather than information about the photographer and the context in which the photograph was taken. While genre analysis, which would identify the ideological as well as imaginative constructs underlying particular images, also is necessary for the interpretation of photographs, it is rarely provided, even by professional historians. This is not surprising, though, since the authenticating power of photographs lies precisely in their seeming ability to bring the viewer directly in touch with an unmediated past: "Ideally, the photograph, if it is well chosen, should—like oral testimony or, for that matter, the archive document—speak itself" (328).

In Volos, the interest in old photographs began to develop in the 1980s, but it was not until the 1990s that public exhibitions of old photographs, the use of photographs as illustrations in historical texts, and the production of coffee table books centered on old photographs (*lefkomata*) became common.[49] Testament to the novelty of photographs as historical evidence, Maroula Kliafa, in the introduction to her 1983 *Thessaly, 1881–1981*, the first book of old photographs published in the region, explains that she had searched everywhere for photographs: "the old chests of relatives and friends, in old yellowed albums, in the archives of old photographers, collectors, collections, organizations, as well as in museums and libraries. In my research I discovered how hopelessly poor is the photographic material held by our museums and libraries" (7). By the 1990s, though, old photographs—and the deep emotion generated by handling them—were inspiring local people to compile their own photographic archives and even to become historical writers themselves. In many contemporary local histories, old black-and-white photographs are employed simply to evoke a vague sense of a past time. When I asked Yiasirani why she put an old photograph (without a caption) on the back cover of her book, she told me: "It is an old family picture from an excursion to Tsagarada [Pelion]. I liked it because it shows the dresses, the clothes, the hats, the way the people sat. I wanted to show the period." Her book includes many photographs, primarily family and individual portraits and pictures of excursions, which taken together could be said to compose a collective family album of the Voliote elite.

The construction of local historiography around old photographs means that the world as seen through bourgeois eyes has come to represent the local past as a whole.

Eleni Triandou's 1994 *Volos Through the Mist of Time*, a nostalgic look at "old Volos," can be seen as an elongated caption on a series of photographs of the city's elite and their monuments: important people, factories, banks, schools, and private homes. The few comments she makes about the working classes concentrate on quaint figures, including carriage drivers, shoeshine boys, and porters: just the kind of workers "visible" to a young girl from a wealthy family. Their images are sketched since no photographs of them apparently were available. DIKI's (1999) *Volos: One Century* attempts to counterbalance this emphasis on the bourgeoisie by including pictures of workers in Volos factories. However, these are images of workers taken by their employers. As Samuel notes in the case of Victorian-era industrial photography, employers' photographs of workers tend to make "backbreaking tasks appear as honest toil" (324) and hide degrading and exploitative aspects of labor behind representations of its nobility.

Photographs in local histories not only represent the world through the eyes of the bourgeoisie because this class had greater access to photographic technology but also because the very idea of the photograph is linked to bourgeois social values and the peculiar formality of "posing" a body before a lens, which Barthes has identified as a key feature of the experience of being photographed (1981: 79). In addition, the thematic categories of photographs (family portraits, school pictures, excursion snapshots, pictures of cultural events) themselves reflect bourgeois investments in family, education, leisure, and culture. Koliou's 1997 *Souvenir of Girls' Education*, for instance, which treats the history of private girls' schools in the city and the surrounding region between 1900 and 1930, is largely composed of school photographs as well as pictures of handiwork displays, excursions, and plays. At another point in time, the stiff poses of the girls, their "European" affect, the restagings of classical dramas, and the home economics lessons depicted in these photographs might have been seen not as a touchstone for nostalgia but as evidence of self-colonization. However, in "period dress," as Samuel has written of Victorian-era British photographs, a stuffiness and commercialism once the target of intense public criticism can suddenly become appealing (324). In terms of Koliou's writing career, the great political distance between her 1997 book on "girls' education" and her 1985 *Unknown Aspects of Occupation and Resistance 1941–4* probably cannot be explained in terms of an ideological change of heart; rather, her recent choice of subject matter suggests the degree to which the paradigm shift in local historical narratives I have been describing has been driven by the "obviousness" of the evidence itself.

Another popular new genre of local historical writing is history "as it was recorded in the press of the day" (*opos apotypothike ston typo tis epochis*). As suggested by the fac-simile reproduction of newspaper excerpts on recent book covers—ragged scissor snips attesting to the "context" from which the articles have been shorn—newspapers are being treated much like photographs: namely, as tactile, visual, not just referential, artifacts. While the importance amateur writers typically accorded to maintaining the integrity of written sources has been carried over to their treatment of visual evidence, in turn, the new emphasis on visuality in history has led to an aestheticization of written documents as objects not only to be held but also to be *seen*.[50] Newspaper local histories in the 1990s typically took the form either of a history *of* the local press or, more commonly, a "glance" at local history as gleaned from reading various "interesting" articles.[51] Leafing through yellowed newspapers, like holding old photographs, is another way in which historical writers feel they have made "direct" contact with the past. To research his *Chronicle of Nea Ionia*, Konstandaras, for instance, told me that he read through old local newspapers "page-by-page" (*fyllo-fyllo*), dictating into a tape recorder any article that mentioned Nea Ionia. At home, he then played back the tape and retranscribed his dictation. In his book, he used italic typeface to mark those passages that were "direct" quotations from the newspaper. From the perspective of historicist ideology, this elaborate chain of reported speech supported by various forms of technological mediation (tape recording, handwriting, printing) involved no change, or "play" in the Derridean (1978) sense: the signifier and the signified were believed to remain identical. Given this profound faith in the metaphysics of the sign, historical documentation, as a process of domesticating the archival origin and bringing it home through links of embodied transcription, could be said to constitute a deeply moving, sensual experience for practitioners.[52]

Like the photograph, the press was also a key technological resource of bourgeois modernity. Rather than just a source on the past, the newspaper, as Benedict Anderson (1983) has famously argued, played a central role, along with the novel, in forging a sense of belonging to a national community (1983: 35). By reading the newspaper each morning, a group of strangers could imagine themselves as fellow citizens interacting in a public sphere. Despite the sense of totality conveyed by the narration of a multiplicity of different, simultaneously transpiring events, the newspaper, of course, presents only a selective vision of social life. In using local newspapers as the principal source for his history, Konstandaras, thus, ironically, can be said to have written a history of refugee settlement *as seen by* the "native" Voliotes. He did not interview many people for his book, he explained to me, because: "I was burning with the idea of finding sources, written sources." As a result, the only time we hear the voice of the refugees is in a "thank-you letter" signed by the "quarantined refugees in the New Settlement" (*apokleismenoi prosfyges en to Neo Synoikismo*). This letter, entitled "We Thank Them," was written in 1924 when the refugees were moved to their new settlement (the future Nea Ionia) after a typhoid epidemic had spread through the warehouses and tents where they were staying. Although Konstandaras told me that he included this article—and reproduced it in facsimile on the back cover of his book—because it provided proof of the precise moment Nea Ionia was founded, other readings are possible. For one, the text demonstrates with stunning clarity how the founding of the new refugee settlement was catalyzed by locals' fear of the refugees' diseased bodies, which they wanted to expel as quickly as possible from the city center. Second, the article depicts the voice of the refugees in the only way that locals wanted to hear it at that time: grateful. By implicitly appropriating this voice himself, Konstandaras adopts a conciliatory stance toward the history of relations between locals and refugees, something that several readers of the book mentioned to me.

Given a view of historical sources as "found objects," it is unsurprising that despite this openness to new kinds of evidence, local writers were wary of oral sources they themselves might have had a hand in producing. The repression of orality from local historical texts and the reverence for the written word and material artifact does not just reflect the guiding positivism of local historical writing but also the broader culture of textuality in which many local writers have been inculcated through their education and occupational background (i.e., teacher, bank employee, civil servant). Some writers, for instance, were quite critical of Koliou's extensive use of testimonies in her history of the Resistance. One writer, for instance, complained that she just "lets each person speak and say whatever they think is true, put forth his own personal ideology." Koliou's openness not only to using oral sources but also to presenting large extracts from transcribed testimonies might be attributed, however, to her work experience as a journalist. Most of the writers with whom I spoke did use interviews (both formal and informal) in the course of their research, though many said that they used oral sources only in a supplementary way. Oral sources, they told me, should not stand alone and multiple interviews were usually necessary to "cross-check" (*diastavrosi*) a particular piece of information. Some writers got around the "problem" posed by unreliable oral testimony by writing two books: a history and a volume of "stories." In addition to his *Chronicle of Nea Ionia*, Konstandaras, for instance, has published a slim volume entitled *True Asia Minor Stories*, based on "tales" told to him by his mother and his neighbors.

For local writers, then, the idea of creating an "oral archive" was not a serious consideration. Audiocassettes of interviews were rarely treated as an important component of personal archives. Koliou told me that once she transcribes relevant excerpts from recorded testimonies, she tapes over them with new interviews. In most cases, writers did not view the narrative part of oral testimonies as nearly as important as the information they contained. Yiasirani spoke with many descendants of people buried in the municipal cemetery, but she usually did not record the conversations; in footnotes in her book, she has simply attributed certain "facts" to particular informants. Exceptions to this use of oral testimony were memory texts about Greek Anatolia, a common genre that runs alongside local historiography, which I will consider in detail in the following chapter. Kartsagouli's (1995) *There Where the Roses Had No Thorns*, for instance, is almost entirely based on oral testimonies collected from her Nea Ionia neighbors, who had come to Greece as refugees. In this case, though, the value of the narratives lies as much in how they are narrated as in what is said. Furthermore, as living witnesses of a lost world, the informants (as bodily presences) tend to be treated as key pieces of evidence in their own right, as testified by the photographs of informants included in Kartsagouli's book and others like it.

Since local historians began not so much with a question as with evidence, they rarely sought for what was "missing" and instead employed oral sources in a circumscribed way. However, in making liberal use of "material" evidence, such as newspapers and photographs, and treating them as transparent transcriptions of the past, writers, wittingly or unwittingly, ended up presenting a vision of local history as "framed" by these discourses. Interestingly, since new technologies have made the modes of representation employed by newspapers and photographs and the networks of communication and visual landscapes they produce seem incredibly dated, the nostalgia of newspaper and photograph histories often appears directed not only toward the past depicted by these images and texts (i.e., the "old Volos" of the industrialist class) but also toward the media themselves: something that is striking, for instance, in the popularity of old newsprint and photographs as visuals for book covers.[53] Document-based histories, of course, are always to some extent metacommentaries on forms of representation, technologies of communication, and archival practices that shaped a previous documentary order. As assemblages of the discarded media of modernity, then, 1990s newspaper and photograph-based local histories could be said to express a malaise with the ways that new technologies are re-creating locality, community, and even reference itself and, in this sense, might be understood as a response of sorts to the contemporary "postmodern" moment.

The Ghost of History Past

Theoretical pronouncements about the proper subjects and methods of historical research, use of expert jargons, the issuing of credentials and titles, and the vetting of historical scholarship all can be seen as disciplinary gatekeeping mechanisms that contribute to naturalizing distinctions between amateur and professional spheres of historical production. In opening this chapter by drawing attention to some of these practices, my aim was neither to argue for the "democratization" of historical scholarship nor to deny significant differences among historical discourses currently circulating in Greek society. Rather, I wanted to suggest the degree to which historical professionalism and standards of academic scholarship have been constructed in opposition to amateur work, making professionalism, in Bonnie Smith's words, "a relationship dependent on discredited voices and devalued narratives" (1998: 10). Furthermore, in this chapter I have attempted to show how the rejection of amateur historical writing on the basis of epistemological criteria prematurely closes down some important avenues of reflection on historical production more generally.

For one, the figure of the amateur local historian raises the specter of academic history's not so distant past, forcing a confrontation with the discipline's historicist legacy. Amateur historical practice forces professional historians to face the "archivist within" and acknowledge the importance of "lowly" aspects of their trade: the routine copying of documents, the desire to possess and order physical remnants of the past, and the thrill of tactile contact with old papers and things. While these archival practices ostensibly precede the vaunted historical analysis, they might instead be said to *haunt* it. In 1990s Greece, the persona of the *istoriodifis*, the historical researcher and collector, also brought into view the identity crisis some historians have been experiencing concerning the place of the political in historical practice. A quarter century after the end of the dictatorship, with the adoption of leftist historical agendas by many university history programs and research centers, increasing careerism in the field, and critical theory's assault on empiricism, some historical practitioners are stranded at an existential crossroads. Is making archives a career dead end or still the most important of political gestures, or both? In the context of modern Greek political history, the subject position occupied by the *istoriodifis*, as both positivist and amateur, is more ambiguous than initially appears to be the case. Even though working outside the university or some other institutional framework nominally undermines the credibility of historical scholarship, this independence, particularly in politically repressive periods, has guaranteed an intellectual freedom that authenticates that research. Similarly, while the making of archives might seem like drudgework lacking intellectual content, it has at various moments in time seemed the most radical and purposeful kind of historical labor. Indeed, some might say that archival activism is simply the structural condition of modern Greek historical studies, given its marginal place in the political force field of national and global historical scholarship. Furthermore, the state's assault on the memory of the Left, witnessed by the 1989 burning of the security files, means the pressure to "rescue" endangered documents and register "irreplaceable" testimonies has not let up even, as I will discuss in chapter 4, in the post–Cold War era. As a result, the habitual denigration of the *istoriodifis* by academics, although an unsatisfying appraisal of amateur practice, might always have something important to tell us about the political objectives and theoretical trends of *scholarly* historical production.

Practices of documentation based on principles of historical positivism also should not be dismissed casually as mere "survivals" of an earlier period of historical practice or as a "burden" that can be managed by mechanisms of scholarly evaluation. There is more at stake here than keeping academic history rigorous and pure. At the time of my research, the "textualized archives" and "source books" of local historians were bringing new evidence into the flow of historical semeiosis at a tremendous pace, simultaneously stripping it of signs of its social production as well as of the many contexts through which it had passed in the course of its sociotechnological mediation. The assumption that historical evidence should assume a *material* form, as history's "building blocks," also led to the privileging of certain kinds of evidence (written texts, photographs, buildings, etc.) while discrediting the "creation" of new sources (through oral testimony, for instance). As a result, in the name of objectivity, the differential access that various social groups had to creating and maintaining physical signs of their former presence and importance was continually left unquestioned.

Seen from an ethnographic perspective, the production of local historiography, thus, illuminates ongoing assertions of political legitimacy and class distinction. While the democratization of the public sphere in the years following the dictatorship has allowed for a more diverse vision of the local past to be represented, it has not led to a fundamental questioning of local history's exclusions and silences. To a large extent, the class interests of the local Volos elite and the pragmatic goals of the municipality have coincided in the production and reproduction of a reverent discourse on the city's modernizing elite, whose business ventures appear not to have conflicted with progressive politics but, to the contrary, to have "trickled down" more effectively for the public benefit than national government spending. Making personal archives for local history, as a result, more often seemed to act as a means to *expand* the local historical record than to challenge its categories, as documentary assemblages composed by local historical producers in their living rooms and in the pages of their texts connected personal and family histories to dominant narratives of capitalist progress and local belonging. As chains of citations passed through the bodies of historical writers during the manual labor of research (flipping through old newspapers, copying over documents, rereading notes), the archival "origin" was internalized in visceral and persuasive ways. To the extent that the fetish of the document confirmed a vision of history as possession and ever-accumulating "hoard," these historical practices asserted a powerful sense of owning and being owned by the past.

Finally, a close examination of contemporary local historical production rather than its usual summary castigation exposed some of the anxieties generated by the profound transformations in citizenship, political ideology, and capitalist production that occurred in the final decade of the twentieth century. Posing a sharp break with the anti-Western, antimodernizing rhetoric of the arts and crafts movement of the socialist Eighties, the 1990s fascination with the history of the bourgeoisie—and the political rationality and "European" cultural tastes they promoted—appeared to reflect a number of contemporaneous political shifts: namely, the deflation of energies surrounding the Left in its opposition to the dictatorship, the ideological depolarization of Greek society in the post–Cold War period, and the emergence of a discourse of modernization (*eksynchronismos*) on the part of second-generation socialists. The nostalgia for origins evidenced in the outpouring of local history writing also could be said to constitute a defensive discourse on citizenship in the face of the new migration to Greece and a generalized fear of the economic and technological future following the collapse of the local manufacturing base and the emergence of post-Fordist production regimes.

Unlike the other genres of historical writing I treat in this book, local historiography never seems to have to explain its raison d'être. Yet, as I have attempted to demonstrate, the routinized documentary practices and textual conventions associated with this genre as much as the social backgrounds and ideological agendas of its writers and sponsors contributed to effacing the presence and contribution of "newcomers" in narratives of the city's development. The intertexuality that both enables and is enabled by the stability of local historiography as genre confirmed the impression that the city forms an ontological unity, a "character-in-development," despite the many experiences of social crisis, dislocation, and outright conflict that have threatened to tear apart the coherence of stories about the city's "life." The sheer volume of local historical output also appears to demonstrate the "obvious" point that time *takes place:* namely, that the past must be localized (and nationalized) in order to be told in collective terms. Despite the fact that it seems that anybody in Greece today could write local history, a genre that has long ceased to be taken seriously by the intellectual elite, in reality, this is not the case. To write in the name of the community requires not only mastery of certain discursive tools and access to some institutional power—these days, admittedly, not so out of reach—but also a sense of being *at home* that is hardly a given.

Chapter 3

Witnesses to Witnessing:
Records of Research at an Archive of
Refugee Testimony

With its clear "before" and "after" graphically captured in grainy black-and-white photographs and film footage of Izmir (Gr. Smyrna) in flames, the 1922 "Asia Minor Catastrophe" (*Mikrasiatiki Katastrofi*), as it is usually called in Greek, presents itself as the quintessential event of modern Greek history. In 1919, Greek troops had invaded Asia Minor with the aim of fulfilling the nation's so-called *Megali Idea*, or "Great Idea,"[1] to expand its territory and population by "redeeming" the lands and peoples of a historic Greek Empire. Three years later, Turkish armies under the command of Mustafa Kemal, who later took the name Atatürk, would decisively rout Greek forces, sparking the mass exodus of the ethnic Greek communities of Asia Minor[2] and precipitating the final collapse of the Ottoman Empire. Following these dramatic events, the 1923 Treaty of Lausanne stipulated a compulsory population exchange—the first in modern history—between Greece and the newly established Turkish republic.[3] In reality, though, the treaty described and ratified, rather than set in motion, a massive population movement that, for the most part, had already taken place in violent and chaotic circumstances.[4] Ultimately, as a result of the "Catastrophe," at least one and a half million Greek Orthodox and 400,000 Muslims were expelled from their homes and resettled in Greece and Turkey, respectively.

The influx of refugees proved such an important catalyst for Greece's economic and demographic development and so transformed the political and cultural life of the country that many scholars consider 1922, not 1832, the real date on which the modern Greek nation was established. Yet, if the Asia Minor Expedition of May 1919 can be considered Greece's first act as a modern nation (i.e., as a state with colonial ambitions and originary homelands outside its borders), then in its failure, as Stathis Gourgouris suggests, "*modern* Greece has become by 1923 a euphemism and its modernity counterfeit money" (1996: 146–7).

Despite its humiliating conclusion, however, the "Catastrophe," *historiographically* speaking, has proved a much easier story to narrate than other experiences of jarring dislocation, violent conflict, and seemingly irrecoverable loss that have occurred over the course of contemporary Greek history. Immediately after the "Catastrophe," a story about it found its way into the final paragraphs of Greek school history textbooks and has never been absent since.[5] While as a means of attaining "ethnoreligious cum national homogeneity," the population exchange would prove, in Mary Layoun's words, "a violently wrought utopian—or dystopian—project" (2001: 21), it could be viewed in *retrospect* as instrumental to national redemption. With the arrival of the refugees, "Greeks" finally had been "congregated" if not in a vast empire, at least within the borders of a "compact and homogenous nation" (Cunliffe-Owen 1927, cited in Pentzopoulos 1962: 123).[6]

The "Catastrophe," furthermore, has been central to fundamental shifts in conceptions of historical subjectivity in modern Greek society. Just as World War II proved the world historical event that impelled the emergence of theories of memory, trauma, and witnessing on a global scale (cf. Langer 1991; Felman and Laub 1992; LaCapra 1998; Agamben 1999), the "Asia Minor Catastrophe" represented a watershed in the development of Greek testimonial discourse and practices of civic commemoration as well as of photographic and filmic reportage of war and human disaster. Although it might be argued that a generalized sense of the self as a historical actor emerges in Greek society in the context of leftist ideology and mass participation in the World War II Resistance, discourses on the "Catastrophe" were the first to envision the ordinary person, and specifically the *victim*, as witness to history. A dominant theme of Greek literature both before and after World War II, the "Catastrophe" galvanized the development of first-person testimony as a central narrative form in modern Greek literature and later in popular historical writing.[7] The "Catastrophe," thus, could be said not so much to have provided yet another subject for historical elaboration in the continuous, unfolding chronicle of the Greek nation, as to have created the potential to shatter historicist definitions of history as progress and victory and to transform established genres of historical writing.

Shortly after the population exchange was agreed upon in Lausanne, Melpo Logotheti-Merlier (1890–1979), a cosmopolitan Greek aristocrat, began a project of historical re-collection devoted to documenting the life of Greek Orthodox populations in Asia Minor as well as, importantly, the refugee crisis itself. Merlier had been trained in ethnomusicology in Paris, and the idea for the Center for Asia Minor Studies (*Kentro Mikrasiatikon Spoudon*, also known as CAMS) grew organically and ambitiously out of a pilot folk song collecting project she had undertaken in 1930 using the most advanced recording technology of the day.[8] It did not take long, though, before refugees were being asked not to sing, but to *talk*, and describe the physical and built landscape, social life, ethnic relations, and religious practices of their native homelands as well as to narrate in the first person the circumstances of their flight from Asia Minor. These testimonies were referred to as stories of "Exodus," consciously invoking Biblical themes of martyrdom, but also of redemption and transcendence.[9] By the time the fieldwork came to a close, the center's "Archive of Oral Tradition" (*Archeio Proforikis Paradosis*) held over 145,000 manuscript pages of data about the history and culture of the former Greek Orthodox populations of Asia Minor and the liminal moment of their transformation into "refugees." The material was collected from over five thousand refugees, who were interviewed by Center researchers from the early 1930s until the early 1970s.

On one level, this chapter considers the role the creation and ongoing use of this archive has played in forming and reforming cultural memory about the Greek Anatolian past and the refugee experience. As might be expected, the representation of the "Catastrophe" in Greek public discourse has undergone numerous transformations over the course of the twentieth century. At first, as Effi Gazi (n.d.) has shown, the refugees and their former homelands were hardly at the center of the story, as public attention focused on the debacle of the Greek army's defeat: *this* was the catastrophe. In the wake of the army coup following the military withdrawal, the Greek prime minister, his cabinet ministers, and the general who had served as commander-in-chief of the Asia Minor Campaign were brought to trial and found guilty; six of the eight who stood trial were summarily executed. In this general climate of acrimony and recrimination with roots in sharp social and economic tensions and political rivalries predating the Greco-Turkish War of 1919, a spate of texts were published enumerating the causes for defeat and fingering the parties to blame.[10] Attention was focused on the responsibilities of key actors in the domestic political arena as well as among Greece's European allies, who were accused of having betrayed and abandoned Hellas in its hour of need. Notably, an intractabile Greek-Turkish enmity was not yet seen as the ultimate cause of the crisis.

Meanwhile the new social rifts created by the settlement of the refugees, who had increased the Greek population by almost a quarter, had not made the events of 1922 seem like *shared* history. The distinct cultural and linguistic features of the refugees turned them into easy targets for nativist ire, and their "Greekness" was often challenged, as reflected in the derogatory epithets commonly directed at them by "natives," such as "Turkish seed" (*tourkosporoi*) or "baptized in yogurt" (*yiaourtovaftismenoi*) (Mavrogordatos 1983: 194). Competition for land and work as well as the new refugee voters' overwhelmingly one-sided support for the liberal politician Venizelos further contributed to "native" Greeks' antagonism toward them. It was not until well after the end of World War II that the refugees replaced the politicians and generals as the central figures of this event and that academic discourse, following a broader turn from political and military history to social history and social anthropology, would begin to address the refugee settlement process and the multiplicity of Greek ethnic*ities* that the refugees' arrival had revealed (cf. Pentzopoulos 1962; Mavrogordatos 1983; Hirschon 1998[1989]).

This shift in focus from the architects of war to war's civilian victims could be said to parallel the turn from *prosecuting* Nazi leaders to *listening* to Holocaust survivors in discourses on World War II. While lawyers in the 1945 Nuremberg Trial had made their case almost entirely on the basis of written documents, the emotional Eichmann trial seventeen years later relied heavily on eyewitness oral testimony given primarily by Holocaust survivors—"a 'tragic multitude' of sufferers," in Arendt's words (1963: 209). These witnesses were not called forth to provide specific evidence about Eichmann's crimes but to convey in emotional and affective terms the horror of the Holocaust. Ultimately, the Eichmann trial would have an enormous impact in normalizing the concept, so familiar today, of the individual survivor as "existential witness, man of memory who embodies the past and demonstrates that it is present still" (Wieviorka 1999: 133–7). As Shoshana Felman has argued, the central difference between the Nuremberg and Eichmann trials lay in the shift from viewing "murderous political regimes and their aggressive warfare as the center of the trial and the center of what constitutes a monumental history" to seeing *victims* as providing history's monumental dimensions and their suffering as the grounds for historical authority (2002: 106–30).

In the case of the "Asia Minor Catastrophe," the transformation of the refugee from "vermin" to "victim" could only occur when tensions between native and refugee were overwritten by a new social and political polarization: this time between Right and Left during the war years of the 1940s. A public discourse on the so-called lost homelands (*hamenes patrides*) of Anatolia would finally emerge in the 1960s, but by then the "Catastrophe" had been recast as an archetypal story of *national* loss that opposed "Greek victims," stripped of undesirable signs of linguistic and cultural difference, to "Turkish subjugators."[11] This narrative would be powerfully reinforced by the 1955 Istanbul riots and the expulsion of ethnic Greeks from that city and then even more profoundly by the 1974 Turkish invasion of Cyprus and the subsequent refugee crisis. Since 1989, in the context of a new upsurge of nationalism as well as a climate of ethnic self-discovery, an extensive memory industry continues to proliferate around the commemoration of Greek Anatolia and the refugee experience.

In 1930, when Merlier began her project of folk song and folklore collection centered on Asia Minor refugees, however, much of Greek society would just as soon have *forgotten* the cultural history of Asia Minor Hellenism, which had formed the political and emotional justification for the failed campaign.[12] Indeed, as Merlier often complained in the aftermath of the "Catastrophe," the Greek state would make no investment in documenting the history and culture of this now "lost" Greek territory, while efforts to do so by intellectuals among the refugees were narrowly focused on specific personal homelands, rather than Asia Minor as a whole (M. Merlier 1948: 13–14). From the outset, then, Merlier's intentions, unlike those of the local historians I discussed in the previous chapter, were explicitly reformist: she did not so much expect her personal archive to *supplement* an existing historical record as to *transform* official and popular historical narratives that did not—at least yet—have a place for the stories she wanted to tell. In claiming to be a *Greek* archive, the Center for Asia Minor Studies, in turn, could be said to have occupied but also created a new kind of postcolonial intellectual space in the wake of the Ottoman Empire's collapse and the deflation of Greek irredentism. In the eyes of some, however, this effort was more akin to a European-style Orientalist project, a neocolonial enterprise conducted only nominally under a Greek flag. Between 1948 when the center was formally established and 1962 when the Greek state took over its funding, the center's activities, in fact, were sponsored by the French state and, tellingly, its archive was housed in the French Institute of Athens where Merlier's husband, Octave Merlier, an enthusiastic supporter of the center's work, was director for many years.[13] Since the center was not under the Greek state's jurisdiction during the politically repressive postwar years, it would also end up playing a special role within the Greek political and intellectual landscape, serving as a haven for educated leftists who had been barred from working in the civil service.

Reform of cultural memory usually cannot proceed without reform of memory work itself. In addition to disputing the thematic priorities of national history, the center posed its research methods as an alternative to the positivism of academic history and folklore. While Merlier tended to overstate the innovativeness of the research and overlook its methodological eclecticism, the center can be credited with introducing into the culture of Greek historical scholarship new technologies of documentation involving voice recording and photography as well as, as I have already suggested, a new conception of historical truth grounded in the experience and testimony of individual witnesses. In handpicking Greek and foreign academic experts to consult on the center's work and participate in special tutorials (*frontistiria*) and in drawing inspiration from the textual innovations of Greek modernist writers, Merlier appeared to have been attempting not so much to meet the standards of the intellectually and politically conservative Greek academy as to surpass them. Nonetheless, hierarchies of scholarship bound up with gender identities, geopolitical relations, and institutional status as well as the fact that the center's informants were destitute and illiterate Greeks have affected the degree to which this project has been viewed as "serious" even to this day.

Archives of "oral" testimony, unlike those composed from (apparently) preexisting documents, are always fictions of a kind: they require the imagining of the documents from which they will be composed. Since the process of making new documents in the name of history cannot but be a fraught and risky operation, it is little wonder that the manufacture of the center's archive entailed the production of a parallel discourse by its makers, detailing their intentions and methods and vouching for researchers' integrity and discipline. The center's archive thus is fiercely reflexive, rife with discussion *about* archiving. An array of "secondary" texts record the ongoing debates about how to do research, the particular conditions in which the data was collected, and the changing categories in which it ultimately was archived. In these writings about the everyday business of memory work, the manifold social tensions and epistemological contradictions involved in inscribing "refugee memory" are exposed.

Just as finding a way into an archive requires, but also enhances, an understanding of the political climate and intellectual frameworks within which it took shape, reflection on how people use archives at particular points in time sheds light on the current historical moment and new conceptions of historical knowledge and practice. Against the backdrop of contemporary rereadings of the archive's materials, then, I undertake a historical ethnography of the center's practices of documentation and archiving, focused on the 1950s and 1960s when the bulk of the interviews were conducted. I base my observations on conversations with current and former staff as well as on my reading of three kinds of texts produced in the course of composing the archive: Merlier's letters, the field reports of the researchers, and brief biographies written about the informants. Each of these texts defines different "people" in the archive: Merlier, the master Archivist and first reader; the researchers, in their dual role as scribe and witness to witnessing; and the refugee informants, as survivors, eyewitnesses, and "living proof" of the former Greek presence in Anatolia.[14]

Rather than a dead, sepulchral space in which only historians seek the past, the archive in this view emerges as a busy crossroads, intersected over the course of time by the diverse trajectories of researchers, archivists, secretaries, informants, and donors. As a result, the process of making this archive could be said to have actively contributed to reconfiguring boundaries of class, ethnicity, and citizenship in early postwar Greek society. Furthermore, in casting Asia Minor refugees as "speaking subjects" of their own history and questioning the adequacy of established categories of historical writing and knowledge to articulate an overwhelming experience of mass dislocation, this project introduced the problematic of witnessing, testimony, and trauma into modern Greek historical studies in a prescient manner, even if the consequences of such a gesture were not, and perhaps could not be, adequately addressed.

Reading in the Archive Today

In Melpo Merlier's day, the Center for Asia Minor Studies was located in Kolonaki, in the heart of Athens' highbrow cultural and intellectual life.[15] Perpetually understaffed and underfinanced in relation to its goals, it formed a hub of activity as researchers shuttled between deskwork and fieldwork as well as, for many, their regular jobs at the French Institute.[16] The messianic goal of "salvaging" the record of Greek Orthodox life in Asia Minor before the deaths of the last informants added a sense of urgency to daily operations. At the time of my research, the center, with its tiny staff, was housed in a large historic building on a pedestrian street in Plaka, Athens's old town and principal tourist zone. With its more modest research objectives and equally shaky finances, the center was a peaceful place cut off from the public life of the city, if not from contemporary developments in Greek and international historiography.

The center's small reading room was located on the top floor of the building, up a flight of handsome wooden stairs. The metal cabinets flanking the back wall of the reading room "contained" the Anatolian province of Cappadocia in row upon row of bulging manila envelopes with small, neatly folded pages (fig. 3.1). On one wall hung bronze medallions of two refugees who had volunteered their services in translating documents from Ottoman Turkish and had been called affectionately "Fathers" (*Pateres*). Other walls of the cavernous building were decorated with poster-size black-and-white photographs, some depicting landscapes and monuments in Asia Minor and others Greek school or musical groups shortly before the "Catastrophe." Like photographs of Jewish life prior to the Holocaust, these images cannot but elicit a sentimental reaction from the viewer, who knows that shortly after they were taken the people depicted in them would lose that world and their place in it forever (cf. Hirsch 1997: 20). Downstairs from the reading room, Merlier's and her husband's heavy wooden desks, assorted memorabilia, and vast personal archives slumbered, enshrined in silence. Photographs of prominent political figures, such as Charles de Gaulle and the Greek prime minister Eleftherios Venizelos, as well as writers, such as Penelope Delta and Angelos Sikelianos, attested to the Merliers' membership in an elite circle of cosmopolitan liberals.

Like most first-time visitors to the center, I was introduced to its collections through *The Last Hellenism of Asia Minor* (O. Merlier 1974), the catalogue for the center's major 1974 exhibition and a detailed summary of the progress of its research. The outside cover, with its striking photograph of a minaret casting a

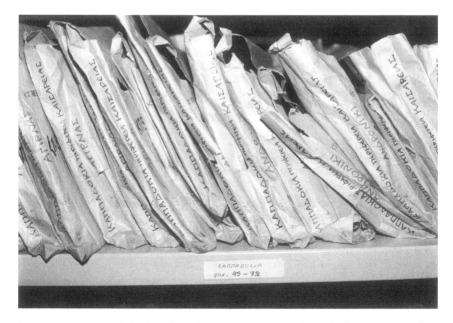

Figure 3.1   Cappadocia in the archives (Center for Asia Minor Studies). Photograph by author.

shadow on a neighboring Orthodox church, announces the center's embrace of religious diversity and focus on interethnic relations. Inside, one cannot help but be struck by the numbers. Progress was accounted for in manuscript pages: material collected on each Greek settlement is totaled and tabulated down to the very last fraction: 2,163 Greek settlements, 1,375 studied, 5,000 informants, 145,000 pages of data. Although many days I would be the only person working there, over time I saw a varied cast of figures move through this space: people of Asia Minor ancestry working on histories of their region or city of origin; local historians from other parts of Greece looking for information about refugees who had settled in their towns; Turkish researchers and history buffs who in recent years have become interested in the former Greek populations of Asia Minor; and other graduate students and academics working on currently popular topics, such as cultural life and ethnic consciousness in the Ottoman Empire. Once I even met a man who was trying to locate information his grandparents had provided to center researchers decades before. While some visitors worked with materials from the oral archive, many used the center's other resources: its extensive library of books about Asia Minor and modern Greek history, European travelogues, registers from former Greek communities of Asia Minor, Karamanli texts (i.e., Turkish books printed in the Greek alphabet), or the photograph and folk song archives.

On one of my first visits to the center, I met Ioanna Petropoulou, a center researcher, historian, and expert on the Anatolian province of Cappadocia. Her writings about Merlier's intellectual formation and the ideological ramifications of her project have helped dispel the aura that had long shielded "Melpo Merlier's Center" from critical scrutiny (1995, 1996, 1997, 1998). Petropoulou quickly became the interlocutor to whom I presented my early impressions of the personalities and politics of the different people—researchers, key informants, and, of course, Merlier herself—whom I encountered as I read in the archive. Petropoulou belonged to a second generation of center "collaborators" (*synergates*), as they were called, who did not conduct fieldwork with refugees. In Merlier's day, ambitious young college graduates had used the center as a steppingstone to graduate study abroad, often in France; by contrast, Petropoulou, like the rest of the staff at the time I conducted my research, had done graduate work before being hired at the center. During the military dictatorship, Petropoulou had studied with the Greek intellectual historian Konstandinos Dimaras at the Institute of Modern Greek Studies at the Sorbonne.

When she returned to Greece following the regime change and started working at the center in 1977 under its new director, Fotis Apostolopoulos, Petropoulou told me that she was disheartened by what she found.[17] The center appeared to be a microcosm of a parochial Greek society just emerging from the conservatism of the dictatorship era. The resistance she met from other staff members when she began cataloguing the library using the Latin alphabet (in order to integrate foreign language books) reflected the reigning provincialism. Despite scholarly aspirations, the center's research with its patchwork of methodologies and unrealistic goals seemed hopelessly amateur to her. Most importantly, the purpose of the center itself was no longer clear: the "cosmogonic" phase (as the center's former secretary Maria Asvesti described it to me) of fieldwork in the 1950s and 1960s had drawn to an inconclusive close. Merlier herself had died in 1979 after a long illness and to a professionally trained historian, the "documents" that had been painstakingly created and archived could not but look like the product of a vanity project that had run its course. Although Petropoulou told me that she initially had no higher regard for the center's archive than she did for its prim social world, after many years of rummaging through it in the course of her daily work, she admitted that she had come to see beyond Merlier's imposing figure and appreciate its holdings in new ways.

Petropoulou's office was located directly behind the reading room, a whole wall of which was filled with local histories, autobiographies, journals, coffee-table books, and other publications about Greek Anatolia, many published by refugees, their descendents, or the plethora of Asia Minor associations spread throughout Greece.[18] Petropoulou told me that most of the amateur historians who used the center's archive and library never believed that she was not of refugee origin and yet had chosen to research "their" past. This surprise could be ascribed as much to the unusual position the center occupies among a constellation of local and national groups and organizations producing discourse about "lost homelands" of Asia Minor as to the role those discourses play as a source of ethnic pride and vehicle of cultural pedagogy. In contemporary Greek society, countless books, documentaries, dance and music performances, historical events, ethnic restaurants, and traditional craft products converge in celebrating the Anatolian past, decrying Turkish persecution, and mourning Greek suffering. Merlier's fear that this history might be forgotten and the plight of the refugees left unrecorded has not been borne out.

To the contrary, an elaborate, even strident, discourse on "lost homelands" has taken shape, centered not so much on defending the "Greekness" of Asia Minor

Greeks (against earlier accusations of their "Turkishness") as on projecting an image of them as "Greeker" than (and superior to) Helladic Greeks. In this rhetoric, the Anatolian Greeks' cultural sophistication, business savvy, and first-class "European" education are overrepresented through a focus on the elites among the former ethnic Greeks of the Ottoman Empire.[19] At the same time, "rags-to-riches" tales of refugee success and assimilation in Greek society have worked not only to isolate the experience of Asia Minor Greeks from general histories of class formation and labor relations, a point on which I touched in the previous chapter, but also to foreclose a comparison of the Greek refugee experience with that of other refugees and displaced peoples (e.g., migrants, exiles) around the globe as well as in Greece. Furthermore, a centering of narratives of refugee experience on the figure of the Greek victim, especially the "Asia Minor mother," a popular subject for melodramatic memorial statues, has served to downplay, or simply efface, certain disturbing aspects of the events of 1922, such as the colonial ambitions of the invading Greek army in Asia Minor or the suffering of Turkish Muslim refugees displaced from their Greek homelands.[20] Finally, the sheer abundance of discourse produced about "lost homelands" of Anatolia and the refugee crisis have contributed to making "memory" itself, as hallmark of an inalienable cultural essence, seem a unique possession of people of Asia Minor heritage.[21]

Since the end of the Cold War and especially in the context of the bloody disintegration of Yugoslavia, many Balkan writers, musicians, scholars, and other cultural critics and producers have been turning in a quite different spirit to the history of the Ottoman Empire, both prior to and during its traumatic dismantling. By illuminating the linguistic, religious, and ethnic diversity of the Ottoman past, they hope to promote an indigenous ethic of multiculturalism. In this reformist rubric, the center's archive presents itself as a prime site in which counternarratives to dominant conceptions of the Greek Anatolian past and refugee experience might be located. For one, the bulk of the center's research was focused on remote regions, such as Cappadocia and Pontos, and on "traditional" peasant life rather than on the cosmopolitan culture of more Europeanized commercial centers. Researchers also were instructed to seek out refugees who had lived humble lives in Asia Minor and were marginalized in contemporary Greek society, not their well-heeled and educated compatriots. Finally, in a context of heightened nationalism and strained Greek–Turkish relations, the researchers were meant to gather testimonies from non-Greek speakers among the refugees—to the extent that this was possible given that few researchers themselves knew Turkish or dialects of Greek, such as Pontic.

Merlier herself had hoped that the center's research would further the cause of Greek-Turkish reconciliation. In a letter to a researcher written on July 5, 1967 from Aix-en-Provence, Merlier nostalgically recalls a center-sponsored journey to Cappadocia:

> Remember, my dear Mr. Andreadis, our missions in Cappadocia, your stay in Halvadere, "our Turkish cousins," Mamout and Giaour-Ali, and little Nil, who asked you "if we see the same stars in Greece" and cried out after your affirmative response, "Therefore, my uncle, we are not so separated, since we see the same stars!" When will the roads open, my dear Mr. Andreadis, so that we can go again.

Given Merlier's desire to locate a past with which to imagine a more tolerant future, one can understand the center's focus on a place like Cappadocia. Smyrna (Izmir) might have been the heart of the Greek presence in Asia Minor, but its horrific burning would always bring to mind Turkish violence and a scene of final closure. Cappadocia, on the other hand, offered the possibility for better memories: the Greek Orthodox populations of this central Anatolian province had not been forcibly expelled but "exchanged" according to the terms of the Lausanne Convention.

Rather than document Turkish violence against Greeks, then, Merlier pushed her researchers to find (and perhaps even fabricate) signs of harmonious interethnic relations in the stories their informants narrated.[22] In a letter from July 23, 1962, for instance, Merlier notes her pleasure in finding a "multicultural" proverb among the materials gathered by the researchers; she writes:

> It is so nice that I recopy it so that all the researchers can enjoy it: "With the Turkish language one sings. With the Greek one prays. With the Russian one tells folk tales." The proverb is Turkish. The informant heard it in Russia from Turkish-speaking Pontians. It is the first time that we have evidence of the cohabitation of the three peoples; it is very interesting. Maybe we also can find some narratives.

Former researcher Christos Samouilidis described to me the pressure that was put on researchers to "find some narratives" that confirmed Merlier's hopeful vision:

> She did not want material that would show the violence of the Turks. As much as she could, she tried to take a neutral stance. In fact, she really wanted material to come out that the Turks were good. So we tried to find material and testimony that showed that the Turks were good people. Whoever discovered such material in testimonies—Merlier would be enthusiastic. In this respect researchers could stress certain things or even make up reports to please Merlier.[23]

At the center, contemporary researchers seeking signs of interethnic communion and cooperation in the Ottoman past, thus, are often surprised to find their desires reciprocated by those of an earlier generation of memory workers and, above all, by Merlier herself, whose transference is imprinted on the archive's documents and categories.[24] Although Merlier's fascination with cultural syncretism, which derives from the philological study of "survivals" and other "curious" phenomena, did not extend to issues of subjectivity and power relations, the center's record of the ethnically mixed and blurred resonates surprisingly well with contemporary theoretical interests in diaspora and cultural hybridity.[25]

Aside from its appeal as a resource for writing antinationalist histories, the center's archive has also recently attracted the attention of scholars of the refugee phenomenon, who look back at this first compulsory population exchange as an important precedent for "ethnic cleansing" later in the twentieth century and, thus, as a key site to critique the politics of national supremacy as well as to assess the long-term effects of violent population displacements (Layoun 2001: 17). As anthropologist Liisa Malkki has noted: "It is precisely the interstitial position of refugees in the system of nation-states that makes their lives uniquely clarifying and enabling for the anthropological rethinking of nationness, of statelessness, and of the interconnections between historical memory and national consciousness" (1995a: 1).

Although the center was established for the purpose of studying life "over there" in the past, materials recorded for other, mostly bureaucratic, purposes have started to be read against the grain by scholars seeking information about the refugee experience. Such information can be found, for instance, in the "Archive of Current Settlement of Asia Minor Refugees," whose original purpose was to keep track of the whereabouts of potential refugee-informants from different places in Asia Minor not to describe the new communities formed by refugees in Greek society. Indicative of the ways that the center's staff has been rereading its own archive and bringing formerly unstudied parts to public attention is the volume *Refugee Greece: Photographs from the Archive of the Center for Asia Minor Studies* (Yiannacopoulos 1992), which is largely based on the center's collection of photographs of refugees and refugee settlements. Similarly, Petropoulou (1997) found herself drawn to examining the center's fragmentary data on settlement in order to question currently dominant mythologies of the cultural and linguistic "Greekness" of the refugees and the tenaciousness of their adherence to the cultural practices of their homelands.[26]

Finally, with the recent development of scholarly interest in oral history and memory among Greek academics, the present staff at the center increasingly finds itself being called on to speak about what is often referred to as Greece's "oldest and largest collection of oral history" (Kitromilides 1987: 22; cf. Yiannacopoulos 1993; Petropoulou 1998). While the center's oral archive might have seemed like an embarrassment a short time ago, these days it is hailed for its distinctive contribution to Greek historical scholarship. The center's project actually does not represent the first attempt on a national level to document eyewitness testimony. Famously, in the early 1900s Yiannis Vlahoyiannis, who would later direct the General State Archives, had published the life stories of generals of the 1821 War of Independence, including the biography of Karaiskakis (1903) and the memoirs of Makriyiannis (1907). Later, in the early 1930s Penelope Delta, the acclaimed children's book writer and Merlier's personal friend, had transcribed the testimony of several *Makedonomahoi*, guerrillas of the so-called Macedonian Struggle of 1912–13, which led to Greece's annexation of Macedonia (Delta 1959–60). In these cases, though, the subjects called on to give testimony were aware of themselves as historical actors—"great men"—who had not simply participated in, but *created*, national history. The major innovation of the center's project, thus, lay in claiming the testimony of victims, rather than heroes, as historically important.

Given the preoccupation of Greek novelists with the theme of the "Catastrophe" and the narrative form of testimony, it is not surprising, however, that the first attempt to gather oral historical testimony from "ordinary" people focused on the Asia Minor refugee. Merlier had brought into the center's fold some of the most renowned Greek writers of her day, many of whom were personal friends.[27] Another important context for the center, then, was the so-called Generation of the Thirties, a movement of Greek literary and cultural "modernism," in which many refugee intellectuals were prominent.[28] While for many academic historians the dubiousness of Merlier's work stems precisely from its literary "excesses," I believe that this turn to literature—and the breaking of the borders between personal and public knowledges, prose and poetry, it entailed—opened radical new possibilities for historical research and writing, which Merlier, in fact, did not *fully* exploit.

Notwithstanding the novelty of the center's research, its identification as an "oral *history*" project is anachronistic, or at least uninformative about how voice entered this project. Merlier herself always spoke of "oral *tradition*" (*proforiki paradosi*), reflecting the fact that she came to history from orality, not vice versa. Merlier's initial interest in the "voice of the folk" can be traced back to a common agenda of bourgeois elites, who championed the demotic language in Greece's highly politicized language debates as well as to a well-established tradition of folk song collection (Petropoulou 1998: 123; cf. Kyriakidou-Nestoros 1978; Herzfeld 1986; Politis 1984). On the other hand, the research conducted at the center could be said to pose a radical break with these earlier conceptions of orality, reflecting Merlier's early introduction to and use of new technologies of voice recording. In 1929, in his capacity as director of the Musée de la Parole in Paris, Hubert Pernot had proposed to Merlier that they undertake the documentation of Greek folk songs. In 1930 and 1931, using the most up-to-date recording technology from La Maison Pathé, they would succeed in taping a remarkable 220 records.[29]

While the research conducted by the center would implicitly rely on the philological category of the song as template for informant discourse, the memory of voice-recording technology would always haunt the project. Indeed, the shift from thinking about the refugees' discourse in terms of song (i.e., meaning) to sound (i.e., noise) risked freeing the witness to *speak on* in a way that would constantly threaten to overrun the archival categories Merlier was intent on setting in place (cf. Kittler 1999). While voice recording also would be central in the development of oral history, we probably should not only look within the confines of intellectual history to see where the technologies of documentation used (or imagined) in the center's project "came from." As refugees (and not refugees-restored-to-the-folk), the center's informants had already become subjects of a radically new apparatus of knowledge collection and representation. New bureaucracies of managing displaced people and a new reportage of disaster, thus, also can be seen as underlying the center's use of technologies of voice recording, photography, and typewriting.[30]

At the same time, the foundational place occupied by philological folklore in this project cannot be ignored. Although Merlier began her ethnomusicological research with the intention of collecting songs from all over Greece, she soon decided to focus her efforts on those of refugees from Asia Minor, whose cultural traditions were particularly vulnerable to loss or transformation. It was the refugees' unprecedented dislocation and resettlement that pushed them from the static eternity of the folk into Time, and pushed Merlier to the study of folklore and history.[31] Seeking a new culture concept for her project, Merlier initially turned "back" to the Greek folklore establishment, opting to adapt its questionnaires and archival practices to the center's research.[32] While later in her career Merlier would definitively forsake folklore for ethnology and geographical history, the discipline nonetheless left a strong imprint on the research.

If, as Derrida suggests, "archivization produces as much as it records the event," with the technological structure of the "*archiving* archive" determining the "structure of the *archivable* content" (1996: 17), technologies and genres of documentation must be seen as crucial elements shaping what can ultimately be re-collected and archived. It is not insignificant, then, that researchers would end up employing a model of documentation based on the philological methods of the Greek folklore discipline not those of the ethnomusicology Merlier had studied in Paris: namely, "pen-and-paper" transcription rather than voice recording. Researchers would be asked to act *like* tape recorders during interviews, but they would not actually use them. Similarly, Merlier expected to "see" the refugees and their poor living quarters, but photographs were only taken occasionally. Thus, even though participant-observation methodologies based on this ethic of realist and real-time documentation were well established in postwar Anglo-American anthropology, the center's researchers, like nineteenth-century folklorists, were sent to the field to elicit quantifiable units of data from informants whom they interviewed with questionnaires (cf. Kyriakidou-Nestoros 1978: 95). To make matters even more complex, Merlier's true intellectual passion was geography and over time, she seemed to have hoped that the center's research might amount to a Braudelian history of Asia Minor Hellenism in the *longue durée* (Petropolou 1998). As a result, refugee memory was not just conceived as a conduit to a moving testimonial and a repository of folk culture but also as a source of topographical knowledge.

Even though Merlier saw the center's research as evolving alongside European history and ethnology, in reality a variety of methodologies culled from folklore, ethnomusicology, geographical history, and literary modernism but also from practices of social reportage and bureaucratic refugee management converged on—and quite often clashed over—the words of the refugee-informants. In introducing personal narrative into a project of ethnological and geographical fact-gathering, Merlier established a chronic tension at the heart of the archive between the authority of refugees' voice and the exigencies of "objective" documentation.

This unorthodox state of affairs seems to reflect the fact that the center was located not only on the intellectual margin of Europe but also on its geographic one—the Balkans. The collapse of the Ottoman Empire and the rough installation of the nation-form in Turkey (as well as its "finalization" in Greece) had made this region an early witness to the violence of genocidal politics. The collective trauma of World War II and the Holocaust would definitively usher in the "age of testimony" (Felman and Laub 1992: 5) and indeed most of the center's research, especially the collection of "Exodus" testimonies, took place in the aftermath of a second experience of tremendous violence, death, and suffering. The center's early identification of victims as historical witnesses, nonetheless, was rather remarkable. Instead of a failure of scholarship, the center's theoretical and methodological bricolage, thus, might best be understood as an artifact of the struggle to find a language with which to speak about what was then a newly emergent global subject: the refugee.[33]

Diaspora, Maps, Letters: Making a Home in Hellenism

Wherever I travel Greece wounds me.

—G. Seferis

When I first started looking into the history of the center, it was pointed out to me that Merlier never brought to a satisfying conclusion this grand project that had lasted over forty years. With the exception of an unremarkable article on Cappadocia, she never actually *wrote* anything about Asia Minor. Part of her unfinished dissertation on Greek folk songs lies filed among her personal diaries and diplomas from piano study, accompanied by a sad little note in French: "Cast a glance July 20, 1952. What melancholy. So much work without being able to finish it."

Yet, despite this apparent failure to write, her prolific letters, notes, and multiple "introductions" (1935a, b, 1948, 1951) to the work of the center have spread their calligraphic trails throughout the archive.[34] Indeed, if one seeks a voice in the center's materials, it is certainly much easier to get a sense of hers than that of any individual refugee. While Merlier's personal archive of letters and notes might be seen as an extension or supplement to the center's archives, another view is that the center itself constitutes an extension of her personal archive. Rather than a mere byproduct of research, her writings about research, such as her copious "work letters" (*grammata ergasias*), might be treated as documents as in their own right, in which Merlier attempted to compose the gaps and contradictions between territories and temporalities, amateur and professional scholarships, and imaginative and empirical observation as well as between her personal life and modern Greek history. That Merlier only seemed able to resolve these tensions in letters pointedly exposes the fault lines of class and gender running through this project and the incompatible discourses of credibility, authority, and respectability governing the archive's production.

Consider the following letter. It is September 1956 and Merlier sits in a café in Geneva studying a map of Pontos, a region along the coast of the Black Sea. Merlier usually spent at least half of the year, and sometimes longer, in Geneva or in later years in Aix-en-Provence, where her husband Octave taught modern Greek at the university. The map had been sent to her by the center's two cartographers, whom she refers to proudly, if grandiosely, as the "Cartographic Department." With the maps spread before her, she writes:

> My dear, missed researchers of the Cartographic Department,
>
> I am in Bel D'Or, opposite my hotel, where I came to take two coffees, one after the other, to settle my spirits, which are not first-rate. I took with me a lot of work, because I came at 8:30, just after I ate.
>
> I am here a little like at home. On the couch where I sit, right and left, I spread out my papers in stacks on stacks: letters from Aglaia [Ayioutanti, the assistant director, who essentially ran the center in Merlier's absence]; my letters for the "centerites" [i.e., the researchers]; map drafts. On the table, pencils, pencil sharpeners, paper clips. My neighbors here, both near and far, are scandalized looking at all these implements. Their curiosity, however, reached its zenith when, having unfolded the sketch of Yesil Irmak on my table, I studied the memo from the Cartographic Department and followed it on the map draft. I was quite lost in my thoughts about southern Pontos. When I raised my head, ten eyes from three tables were looking at me with sympathy and sweetness. I smiled at them gratefully and continued.
>
> You might ask—Is this a beginning for a work letter to be typed? I also thought of this. But I think it is. Is it right for one always to separate work from life? Then, how would you know, my dear Cartography Department, the sympathy that your maps call forth?[35]

The scene Merlier paints here, like those in which she describes buffet tables laden with papers, suggests the genteel form her academic research took as well as the thin line that separated a "work letter to be typed" from a personal (i.e., handwritten) one.[36] The question might not be if it was "right" to "separate work from life," but if it was possible for Merlier. As she notes in another letter from Geneva, dated July 5, 1963: "Our uprooting from Aix, especially for Octave, who lives there permanently now, but also for me, was laborious and took us a lot of time. Trahia, Kilikia travels with me, as did the center's papers, and they all arrived well."[37] These offhand comments also underscore the tenuousness of Merlier's sense of belonging anywhere, except perhaps in the place created in the ongoing work of the center: reading research reports, poring over maps, writing letters, and reconstructing Anatolia in her mind's eye.

It is not surprising that Merlier was most at home with herself as a writer when she wrote letters. Aside from their association with elite women's schooling and communication, letters themselves in their circulation enact diasporic networks. As a genre, the letter also offered Merlier the possibility of bringing together disparate temporalities and geographies, allowing her to be many people at once: Swiss café lounger, director of an archive in Athens, and even a Pontic time-traveler—in short, a certain kind of cosmopolitan Greek. As in the travel diary, the letter's almost formulaic invocation of the scene "as I write" creates a space in which a narrator can move and speak (Hassam 1990: 34–5). As a key technology of diaspora living or "dwelling-in-travel" (Clifford 1994), letter writing delineates a "here" and "now" in which Merlier can feel "a little like at home." Svetlana Boym (1998) has coined the term "diasporic intimacy" to describe the "fragile coziness of a foreign home." This notion of diaspora as a site of intimacy and furtive pleasure, not just melancholy, is useful for reading Merlier's letter. Her encampment in the café with reports, papers, letters, paper clips, and pencils forms a fragile residence. A certain pleasure lies in erecting it in such an anomalous space.

Merlier's fascination with the refugees' situation might have had something to do with the fact that she herself was a kind of a refugee. Born in Xanthi (Thrace) in 1890, she graduated from the elite Zappeion Academy in Istanbul and studied music and ethnomusicology in Dresden, Geneva, Vienna, and Paris, where between 1920 and 1925 she taught Modern Greek at the Sorbonne. Merlier belonged to a cosmopolitan Greek world in which Alexandria, Izmir, and Istanbul were more important Greek urban centers than Athens and in which being Greek was not coeval with citizenship within the narrow confines of the Greek state. The events of 1922, however, shattered this world of diasporic Hellenism, forcing Merlier, like the refugees, to find a new way to define home and her Greek identity. As literary critic Vangelis Calotychos has noted: "the refugee Anatolians in Greece in the 1920s had to conceive of themselves in a way most uncustomary for them: either in reference to a 'home' that was irretrievably somewhere else (a territory elsewhere—Anatolia) or to their current estranging land, the Helladic state" (1992: 41).[38]

Merlier's projection of an imagined "there" into the space of Asia Minor also can be better understood if we situate her project alongside other modernist cultural works whose defining context was the shrinking of Hellenism after 1922. Intellectually and spiritually restless, writers of refugee background, as Calotychos points out, came to refigure the Aegean as a gateway to an expansive Greek "East," though one now rid of its Turkish elements. In this new symbolic geography, Athens, like a colonial metropole, became a site from which to embark on a journey from modernity back to the rejuvenating, primeval, natural world embodied in the open horizon of a limitless (and borderless) Greek sea (42–3).

Despite Merlier's avowed interest in putting the Turks back in the picture (a standard category of the center's questionnaires was "Relations between Greeks and Turks"), these trends in literary and artistic production can explain why she chose to focus the center's research on the exotic "Eastern" peoples of Cappadocia rather than on the more familiar—and more clearly "Greek"—populations of northwestern and western Asia Minor.[39] Cappodocia represented a Greekness that was both the most *tenuous* (most Orthodox populations were Turkish-speaking and shared the same cultural practices as the local Muslims) and the most *authentic* (since the late nineteenth century and beginning of the twentieth, Greek intellectuals had started to think of Cappadocia as the original homeland of the Greek race).[40] The map of Asia Minor described in Merlier's letter to the center's cartographers, thus, might be seen as opening up a chronotope of a lost Eastern homeland that in moments of historical reflection and reverie allowed her to join her adoptive home in western Europe to her parochial one in Greece. In this vision, Athens would constitute a central, though not exclusive, point of reference.

While the center's work ostensibly aimed to reconstruct the map of Greek Anatolia as a supplement to that of the Greek state, the process of making the archive, in fact, enacted new geopolitical relationships in which the imagined *topos* of Asia Minor was reinscribed *within* a transformed map of Greece. When a particular village or town could not be "reconstructed" because of a lack of informants in Athens, field research in the provinces was often initiated if funds permitted. In a letter to a researcher, Merlier notes:

> This isn't the first time that I observe that researchers' material would be valuable from another standpoint, because it shows how our beloved *Mikrasiates* [i.e., people from Asia Minor] live here, in various parts of Greece. From now on, next to the open map of Asia Minor, I should have open a map of Greece when I read reports from your missions.[41]

These parallel cartographies would, in turn, confirm the growing concentration of the country's economic, political, and cultural life in Athens during postwar reconstruction. Even with a wave of internal migration to Athens during and after the war, Thessaloniki and the northern Greek provinces remained the true centers of the refugee population. Reflecting trends in Greek society in general, then, the location of the center in Athens demonstrates how the rest of the country was being reimagined as "provinces" for "pioneering" Athenians.

At the same time, the research conducted at the center represented an attempt to reposition Athens in "Europe." Merlier's loaded movements between Athens and various European cities held for her a significance far beyond that of settling her existential problems. In her role as both messenger and diplomat, she saw her journeys as symbolically inscribing modern Greek history—and historiography—within a European archive. In this ongoing job of promoting Hellenism abroad, Merlier had to propose a vision that Europeans could gaze on with "sympathy and sweetness." In a letter dated June 14, 1962 written in Aix-en-Provence, Merlier describes to her researchers a presentation she had recently given. Again the maps were spread out, but this time in the small hall of a hotel. Merlier explains that the audience was impressed not only by the amount of material but also by its orderliness: "They admired April's Work Chart, they admired the writing, the order, the organization." Perhaps conscious that the researchers in Athens might not be entirely convinced by the methods she was advancing at the center, she reports: "they immediately understood and praised the fact that 'folklore' does not play a leading part . . . they felt and said on their own 'It is a resurrection.' "[42] In this letter, the map is not so much a trap door through which Merlier can escape, but along with the charts and neat reports, a mirror reflecting research that meets French criteria. The praise of her audience and their spontaneous exclamations of surprise that this was "not folklore" are signs that the center's research had attained standards of scholarship these onlookers hardly had expected from a backwater place such as Greece.

If Merlier was bringing "Greece" to France, she also perceived herself as bringing "France" to Greece, overleaping the local academic establishment by introducing new theories, technologies, and, as often as she could, experts from metropolitan Europe. In locating the center in Athens (and not, for instance, in Paris), Merlier made a bold gesture. So long an *object* of study by the West, Greece would now take on a large-scale Orientalist project of its own. Indeed, there is a distinctly colonial feel to the terms used to describe the field work ("missions," "campaigns," "voyages"). In a letter to a researcher about to set out on a center-sponsored research trips to Turkey, Merlier, for instance, muses: "September, the month of missions (*apostoles*). And you will go to Enehil, imagine: Athens-Enehil. Taurus Express."[43] Significantly, the basic cartographic unit used in the center's research was that of the seventeen ancient Roman provinces (with their Greek names), not the Turkish administrative or Orthodox ecclesiastical ones. Settlements were identified according to ethnic Greek toponyms, even if these had never been used in political administration (1948: 14–17).[44] Refugees were treated—and classified—as representatives of their place and because of the emphasis on geography were routinely asked to describe and even physically sketch the topography of their villages and towns. The center's explicit aim was to "resurrect" the homelands of the refugees, and Merlier would often remind her researchers that they were the "builders" of these settlements, transplanting them onto Greek "ground" with the raw material of the informants' narratives.[45] As a result, the emphasis on mapping at the center recalls not only European colonial surveys, but also Greek irredentist cartography of the late nineteenth and early twentieth centuries.[46]

Yet, if scholarship precedes and follows conquest, what can we make of the recording of the Greek presence in Asia Minor *after* Greek dreams of colonial expansion in the region had been forever thwarted (Kitromilides 1987: 29)? The archive's ostensible resemblance to an Orientalist knowledge project is not only belied by the timing of its construction but also by the fact that it was set up on the basis of personal initiative and without the support of the Greek state. Unlike the British India survey through which, as Thomas Richards explains, "imagined epistemology would intervene to shape political definition of territory" so that "what began as utopian fictions of knowledge . . . often ended up as territory" (1993: 16), the center's research would have no bearing on the world map. The founding of the center's archive in Greece post-1922 thus might be described as an attempt to incorporate a greater Hellenism—the failed, but now re-collected "Great Idea" of territorial expansion—within the Greek national narrative, a "recuperation" of the military debacle on an ideological level (Petropoulou 1996: 416). The question remains, however, what kind of politics such a recuperation might have. Despite the center's liberal agenda, the use of the word "Exodus" to describe the refugees' testi- monies and the frequent evocation of the word "resurrection" introduced a note of ecstatic nationalism to the center's "campaign." On the other hand, remembering origins outside the borders of the state at a crucial moment of its consolidation and homogenization might be seen as heretical to the national project. The symbolic "repatriation" of Anatolian Greeks within the perimeters of the Helladic state thus could be said to hold an ambiguous meaning: both accelerating the nation's assimilation of this population and, at the same time, undermining it by "refiling" the refugees within the pre-1922 categories of a diasporic Greek world.

Analogies to a colonial archive also falter when we consider the status of the archive as monument to state power. Rather than an imposing nexus of power/knowledge, the center's archive and its vaunted order more often seem like an expression of Merlier's personal fastidiousness and sense of etiquette, reflected in such things as her fussiness about penmanship, ban on the use of ballpoint pens (fountain pens only), sending of Christmas cards to the refugees, and pencilled-in grammatical corrections to the researchers' fieldnotes. As suggested by the emphasis on elegant penmanship, the trumpeted model of impersonal, bureaucratic research, processed mechanically through typewriting, photography, and an ethic, if not literal use, of sound recording, was always being subtly, and not so subtly, undermined by an older communication network.

As a result, in everyday practices of archiving, new technologies of documentation associated with the rise of mass culture global modernity often met resistance from that of (good) handwriting, as legacy of high bourgeois European society and as per- sonalizing autograph of the soul (cf. Kittler 1990, 1999). The fact that Merlier's soci- ety "lady" friends were the center's volunteer typists can be seen as a characteristic example not only of the intertwining of diverse media technologies and social worlds in the archive but also of the degree to which at times the project as a whole took on the tenor of a "civilizing" mission. In the tutorials held to discuss the progress of the work, Merlier always would play the role of impeccable hostess serving French (i.e., filtered) coffee and, if refugee informants attended, Eastern sweets such as *ekmek kataifi*. Ultimately, Merlier seemed to treat the archive much like a home that needed to be impeccably presentable ("I will be so happy to see our Archives put in order; they will already be unrecognizable after the first housekeeping (*noikokyrema*) that you will have done to them," she wrote from Aix-en-Provence in 1967).[47]

For Merlier, the conjunction of "work" and "letter," like that of "personal" and "archive," appeared to create the possibility to overcome a narrowness in how identity as well as scholarship are often defined. As material circuits and imagined places, work letters enabled her to weave her personal history back into Hellenism through the mediating figures of a "resurrected" Anatolia and a rapidly modernizing Athens. Letter writing, which can be seen as the *modus vivendi* of any diaspora intellectual, exemplified her dual role as purveyor of cosmopolitan knowledge (in Greece) and of exotic fieldwork goods (in France). In letters, Merlier could also speculate about the future, not just dwell on the past, thus opening a space for fantasy in which she could assume her role as dreamer of the archive.

Yet, as Merlier herself seemed aware, the fact that the center had been independently established could make its work seem irrelevant to scholarship and easy to dismiss as the amateur pastime of an educated "lady of leisure." As opposed to the purposive gathering of data necessary for the epic expansion of the nation, "picking up the pieces" of a refugee crisis might be rated a typically "womanly" act of charity and philanthropy. To critics, Merlier's earnest commitment could be viewed as the selfish satisfaction of a whim, her turn to narrative an extension of women's pleasure reading, her diplomacy mere resort hopping and her center a classroom she built so she could play professor. The determination to call her letters *work* as well as to do work in spaces of leisure seems to manifest her own concerns about how to define her labors in the absence of "accrediting" institutional structures. It also might reflect an anxiety, based in her class and gender, about *having* work in the first place: "Is it right to always separate work from life?" This uncertainty, of course, should not be reduced to psychology, but might instead be seen as indicative of the place of gender in shaping hierarchies of scholarship. As Bonnie Smith has cautioned, only the "interlacing" of men's and women's historical writing reveals the extent to which professionals have "constructed their standards of excellence by differentiating themselves from a low, unworthy, and trivial 'other,' " so often embodied in the woman historian as "obsessive" amateur and "vain" scribbler (1998: 9).

Although letters connect worlds, they also mark distance and signal absence. Rather than broaching dialogue, they can conceal solipsism. Merlier invested her soul in redefining Hellenism, but the locals might not have cared. In a letter to the researcher Christos Samouilidis, dated April 6, 1966, Merlier wrote from Aix-en-Provence:

> It is seven o'clock, night falls and an ashy blue-colored mist surrounds the small city. I think of violet-crowned Athens, as her old eulogists used to call her. In Macedonia I imagine other colors would rule, more generous, or no? Thus, one glance out from the large balcony door takes one out of work, to which I do return . . .[48]

If the imaginary map of Asia Minor that drives the construction of the archive promises to reunite the diverse populations, homelands, and histories of Hellenism(s), something as simple as the weather can expose the tenuousness of these desired connections. In her letters, peppered with French words and terms, Merlier offered the researchers glimpses into elite spaces of sociality and intimate scenes of intellectual pleasure and conversation. Her lifestyle contrasted sharply with the petit bourgeois existence of the researchers, who struggled to get by on their small salaries in the difficult postwar years, not to mention with the hard and marginal lives of most of the center's refugee-informants.

Reflecting the tendency to read intellectual history from the top–down—or, as Nicholas Dirks has pointed out, to seek in the archive the "originary voice of an author or the guiding presence of a master orientalist" (1993: 308)—the history of the center has only been viewed through the prism of Merlier's persona and her programmatic writings about the research (cf. Kitromilides 1987; Yiannacopoulos 1993; Petropoulou 1996, 1998). The field reports of the researchers have never been systematically examined.[49] Merlier had many opinions about how the research was being conducted and as both employer and first reader she did have considerable control over the tone and content of the material collected. Yet, she herself did not do the fieldwork: she learned about the refugees, their past and their present, by reading about them.

City, Buses, Fieldnotes: Memory Work in Post–Civil War Athens

Why do some people, including myself, enjoy in certain novels, biographies, and historical works the representation of the "daily life" of an epoch, of a character? Why this curiosity about petty details: schedules, habits, meals, lodging, clothing, etc.? Is it the hallucinatory relish of "reality" (the very materiality of "that once existed")? And is it not the fantasy itself which invokes the "detail," the tiny private scene, in which I can easily take my place?

—R. Barthes, *The Pleasure of the Text*

Who, after all, were the "footsoldiers" of the center? While the personal histories of Merlier and the refugees have been carefully documented, the center's archives actually contain little information about the "collaborators" (*synergates*). The few biographies of the original researchers that have been recorded focus exclusively on their academic credentials and scholarly accomplishments. Yet, one of the first pieces of local folklore I learned at the center was that it had been a haven for communists in the post–Civil War period. Even though many researchers had university degrees in philology, they were barred from working in public schools or other civil service jobs because of the anticommunist politics of the postwar Greek state. As a private institute, the center, though, could hire people with a "checkered" past and indeed a great many of the former researchers, I learned, had been politically active on the Left. Several had been jailed or exiled before or after working at the center or had had close relatives executed for political reasons during the war years of the 1940s.[50]

Although the intellectual roots of the center's project lie in the interwar period, the bulk of the research was conducted after World War II, after the Holocaust, and after the Greek Civil War.[51] As a result, pressing questions arise about how overlapping experiences of traumatic loss were experienced and, specifically, how memories of Asia Minor and the "Catastrophe" might have been reworked, but also reenacted, after the war, haunting survivors perhaps not as knowledge to be passed on, but as experience profoundly *unknown* and unavailable. The fieldwork reports (*deltia metavasis*), which researchers were required to submit with their data and which have been filed permanently alongside them, however, show how researchers systematically avoided addressing recent political events that in many cases impinged so directly on their own lives. In describing the successful "recovery" of the Anatolian past at the edges of postwar Athens, these reports instead demonstrate how practices of collective remembering can entail and even promote forgetting: in this case, the selective emphasis on ethnic origins became a means of effacing personal political pasts and class histories.

Christos Samouilidis, one of the last living center researchers as well as one of the most productive (he estimates that he interviewed 1,500 refugees), greeted me at the door of his apartment in the northern Athenian suburb of Halandri on a sunny February day in 1999. A bit over seventy, with curly hair and taut skin, Samouilidis was wearing an Oxford shirt with a pen tucked in the breast pocket. He sat me down on a couch across from a striking black-and-white photograph of his parents as a young couple in Pontos. A computer covered by a piece of green felt was set up on the dining room table, and his books, bound in matching ecru-colored leather, were neatly lined up on a nearby bookshelf. He has written over twenty of them, including volumes of poetry, historical novels, folklore studies, and historical monographs. Most deal with subjects related to his personal history: Pontos, the homeland of his parents; his hometown, Kilkis in Macedonia, which was largely settled by Pontic refugees; the wartime Resistance in which he participated; and his subsequent political imprisonment on the island of Makronisos.

Even though, unlike most of the center researchers, Samouilidis was of refugee origin, he told me that he did not begin working at the center out of a particular desire to discover his "roots":

P: Were you interested in the subject of Pontos from a young age?

S: No, I have to admit. My interests were literary. Before I finished high school I had decided that I wanted to become a writer. I studied philology. . . . But I had some political adventures . . .

P: You had been exiled?

S: Yes. At Makronisos [in 1949]. I went through a court martial. I was a leftist and this played a role in my not being able to get an appointment (*dioristo*) in a school when I finished my degree. No one could who had in their file that they had been in the Resistance.

P: What was it like talking to the refugees after the second trauma of the war?

S: Of the war *and* the Civil War. Many refugees had come from the provinces to Athens after the war. We talked about these things, but we did not put it in the material, not even in the field reports. We didn't touch politics. We had a good relationship with the refugees, though, because we had the same ideology: populist. When we started to talk about their homelands, they felt good. We were talking about a peaceful time when they, too, had a life that was settled (*stromeni*) and nice. In their biographies, things about the war came out—but very rushed. It was still fresh. We didn't know it had any value. Another center should have written about their life in Greece. But for us the goal was Asia Minor.

P: Do you think the experience of the research was different for you than for the others who were not from a refugee background?

S: The center was really a solution for my problems in earning a living. As I said, I couldn't work in a school. It wasn't that I had adored Pontians or was fascinated by the origins of my parents. No. I had another goal: modern Greek poetry. The other researchers were mostly natives (*dopioi*) from Crete, Volos, and other places. But that didn't separate us. In the final analysis, when I joined the center, I, too, worked in the capacity of my expertise. It wasn't significant that I was Pontian and knew the Pontic dialect. I was a part of Greek life, modern Greek life. Of course, once I was at the center, the subject really grabbed me. I was charmed. It was another world and if you enter into that Eastern world, an Eastern Greekness (*Ellenismos anatolitikos*), with its other characteristics and other experiences, you can't help but be seized by it.[52]

As Samouilidis's comments suggest, he had not been drawn to research Asia Minor as an "ethnic" Greek. Rather, the work at the center had led him to see his and his family's past from the outside: as a charmed, but aloof observer, comfortable enough in his position in mainstream Greek society to look "back" ("I was a part of Greek life, modern Greek life").

For other researchers and for Merlier herself, by contrast, the refugees significantly complicated their conceptions of Greekness. In the mid-1930s, Merlier had written with excitement about the "panhellenic mosaic" she had seen one day in the vegetable market in Thessaloniki:

Turkish, the strangest dialects from Asia Minor, the dialects of Macedonia, of Thrace, lastly, common demotic, the way they sounded all together, mixed together, strange even to Greek hearing, mother tongues of Thracian and Asia Minor Hellenism, one could not look on the miniature panhellenic mosaic, which I saw that morning in the market of the Macedonian capital, without emotion. (1935b; cited in Petropoulou 1998: 131)

In contrast to the logic of the population exchange, which had been premised on the assumption that Greeks of the former Ottoman Empire and the Greek state were the "same," Merlier was intent on bringing to the fore Greek linguistic and cultural heterogeneity. From her perspective, the "Catastrophe," in leading to the installment of all these exotic ethnics at the heart of Greek cities, had created an unprecedented opportunity for ethnology.[53] Her mission would be to encourage "native" Greeks to approach this "mosaic" with liberal tolerance and ethnographic curiosity rather than with the discrimination, rejection, and indifference that typified initial reactions to the refugees' presence. Indeed, for many researchers of nonrefugee origin, the decision to work at the center did seem to have been motivated, at least in part, by a desire to counter negative stereotypes of a stigmatized population with whom they previously may have come into contact only in highly asymmetrical class relationships (as domestic servants, day laborers, etc.).[54]

Samouilidis' comments also make clear that the center's project explicitly was *not* about politics. It was too soon—things were "too fresh," according to Samouilidis—to address the traumatic events of the war years. On the side of both researcher and informant, conversations about Anatolia represented an exercise in imaginative displacement to a time, unlike the present, when life was peaceful. Visiting the refugee quarters, however, was not always such an easy matter during a period of intense government surveillance. As the center's retired longtime secretary, Maria Asvesti, told me:

People were very tense. It wasn't easy to knock on the door and explain what you wanted. People didn't open the door easily. The researchers came into contact with houses that had people who were in exile, who were in jail. If you went to a house and heard "my husband is in exile or he is in jail because of anticommunism," you froze up (*koubosouna*). You didn't know if you would go again. The researchers would become scared for themselves afterwards, you understand.[55]

Although the center was protected from government interference because of its connections with the French Institute, the researchers were issued special identification cards to gain the trust of the refugees themselves. Seminar minutes from 1957 report:

> It was decided . . . to supply the researchers with a certificate, which would show their official status, so that they can easily circulate in the [refugee] settlements (*synoikismous*), and dispel any chance suspicions that they encounter from new informants, who often think they are tax collectors (*foratzides*).[56]

In this charged political climate, the office at the center was also a place where people had to watch what they said. Both before and after she was sent into exile (1948–52), researcher Kaiti Reppa-Kritsiki told me that she was involved in underground communist activities, but she never shared this information with her co-workers.[57]

The field reports of the researchers, in turn, repressed the political character of the refugee neighborhoods (some of which were known locally as "little Moscows") by depicting them as spaces of cultural difference and precapitalist social life. The myriad little journeys researchers traced through the streets of the city to reach refugee quarters thus could be seen as marking out distinct zones of alterity in which ethnic identity, rather than class or political affiliation, predominated. As a result, in field-notes, refugee neighborhoods, such as Kokkinia, Kallithea, Moschato, Nea Smyrni, and Nea Philadelphia as well as specific areas such as Armenika (Armenian area) or Palia Sfageia (Old Slaughterhouses), were represented as gateways into a mysterious "Eastern" world even by researchers who lived quite nearby.

In this report from her first data-collecting expedition in 1949, Tatiana Gritsi-Milliex, who later became a well-known Greek novelist, seems to have found what she had been expecting:

> It is the first time that I go to collect data and I am anxious. Will I succeed in understanding what they say? Will I ask the right questions?
>
> I go down to Kallithea where my mother, who has a list of Pontians, lives. I explain to her what I want and she takes me to the Palia Sfageia to my first Pontian . . . They take me to his house. Inside the wooden shack, with its shining clean beds and throw rugs, I come into contact for the first time with residents of Pontos. Two or three times expelled from their homes (*topous*), still clearly bearing the marks of their last catastrophe, when the Germans burned this same settlement where they reside—They haven't lost their courage, and when I explain—doubly moved—what I want, their eyes come to life, their talk becomes clear, they seek all at once to tell me something. Their desire is hidden and great that their fatherland is not lost, and will live, even if only inside books. I leave choked up.[58]

This research encounter is successful because it strikes the appropriate sentimental register: she is almost moved to tears. The refugees, for their part, despite the catastrophic events of the recent war still keep Asia Minor as a life-reviving secret. They confirm the value of the center's project of making Asia Minor live "if only inside books."

While all roads might lead to the center of Athens, finding one's way from the city center to the refugee neighborhoods turns out to have been more difficult. The researchers describe various combinations of buses, trams, and walking required to get to their destinations. When they arrived in a new neighborhood they often wandered around haphazardly ("I went for the first time to Nea Ionia. I didn't know where to get off [the bus] and how to orient myself"[59]). Sometimes it is only after entrance to a "backstage" area—a courtyard, the interior of a home—that the researchers feel they have come into contact with the "authentic" Asia Minor. Consider a report written by Eleni Gazi of her meeting with Penelope Baloglou:

> Skouze street, where Baloglou lives, is a pretty street with old aristocratic Piraeus houses. The number twenty-eight, however, of the same street is above a very old door, which leads to a big courtyard and around which in a row, door-to-door, are squalid residences. . . . The image that opens before me, as I wait for Penelope Baloglou, is reminiscent of scenes from the Neo-realist Cinema. Clothes spread out on lines; dirty, weak children who run around and hit each other; and one or two men, who prepare the cutting of the onions for the famous *souvlaki*, which will be sold from carts on the streets. Such squalidness! But so it is; in a few minutes Mrs. Penelope Baloglou comes and takes me to her room. Poor, small, semi-basement, but well-kept and cute.[60]

In this passage, we see that "Asia Minor" is just behind a door on a "respectable" street. Imitating a neorealist cinematographer, the researcher scopes the courtyard for Merlier's benefit. The scene presents itself to her only as a simulation of itself: it is *too* real to be real. Its difference corresponds to her stereotype: it looks like the kind of place from which the *souvlaki* carts with their tasty Eastern foods might come. However, the predictable shock occasioned by the disconcerting juxtaposition of the "old aristocratic houses" and the "squalid" courtyard might lead to disgust and pity if another door did not lead to her informant's dignified and neat room. Due to the reputation of Asia Minor refugees for maintaining "spotless slums" (Hirschon 1998: 3–4), researchers *expected* to find a sparkling interior that would sanitize their contact with the urban poor.

Occasionally, objects found in these interiors "materialized" their inhabitants' cultural difference. Ermolaos Andreadis, himself a refugee from Gelveri (Karvali) in Cappadocia and a Turkish speaker, notes:

> This afternoon I went to the informant Thomas Milkoglou, in the community of Vyronas, to take down his "Exodus" from Kaisareia [Kayseri]. His wife opened the door. He himself was sleeping. I waited for him in the living room. I was impressed by the beautiful Cappadocian rugs and kilims spread on the floor, in a variety of colorful combinations and patterns. Despite the passage of time, the colors had kept their initial freshness. What Cappadocian, what Anatolian house, doesn't have such rugs and kilims! And even in the poorest shacks of the community you will find such things. Who is going to take up the subject of folk art?[61]

Again, a beautiful interior compensates for a miserable exterior, while the bourgeois fetish for interior decorating translates itself into curiosity about the exotic "folk art" showcased in these humble homes.[62]

In the fieldnotes, movement into refugee space also was imagined as a kind of time travel to a rural world still embedded in the modernizing city. Although peasants from remote Cappadocia had been transformed into members of the urban proletariat living in shanties a few kilometers from downtown Athens, memory work would restore them to their Anatolian villages and traditional occupations. In 1955, the researcher Hara Lioudaki on an expedition to Kokkinia noted:

> In the meantime it had gotten dark. Women of the neighborhood, some with pails, other with tin canisters, and another with a clay jug (*stamna*) gathered to draw water. The informant had a tap in her courtyard and she sold water to her neighbors. They had just gotten off work and had come over all at once.[63]

This scene reads like a page out of a village ethnography: one woman even carries a clay jug to the tap. The difference here, of course, is that the women have probably just gotten off work at a factory, and the water is not flowing freely from a village spring, but is for sale. Nonetheless, for modern Athenians the courtyard of the refugee house seemed to hold out to the possibility of escape into a precapitalist world despite the fact that capitalism itself, of course, produces such zones of social segregation and economic depravation from *within* the urbanization process.[64]

As much as researchers deplored the poverty of these districts, their gradual erasure could be occasion for regret. In 1964, Samouilidis found himself looking for an old informant of the center in "the shacks of Koukaki." The residents of this area, however, did not remember that such a settlement had ever existed. He finally found a shoemaker who recalled the shacks, but told him that they had all been torn down with the exception of a few along the shores of the cemented-over Ilissos river. Samouilidis notes with disgust:

> I crossed the bridge which joins Koukaki with Kallithea and I advanced alongside the "river." . . . The high banks of the capital's little river have been built up with reinforced concrete, the dirty water runs along a cement-covered "bed" and "burbles" slowly in the midst of the urban noise of the city and of the buses which pass on the opposite bank.[65]

When he arrives at the shacks, the people living there also have never heard of the person he is seeking and assure him that they have no neighbors who are refugees. By referring derisively to refugees as *pro-sfinges* instead of *prosfyges*, punning on the word for "wasp" (*sfika*), they make clear, furthermore, that they consider them to be "pests." In the context of the cementing of Athens, the remaining (or remembered) refugee districts seem like lost oases of civility.

Although Merlier's intention in setting up the archive was to reform cultural memory, the center's research could be said to have prepared the ground for the nationalistic discourse on Greek Anatolian ethnicity that emerged in postwar Greek public culture. The fieldnotes—both as content and practice—demonstrate how the research contributed to institutionalizing the "refugee quarter" as a space of memory work by territorializing ethnicity and ethnicizing territory. In turn, the refugee districts served as zones of mysterious cultural difference and rural community to which the researchers, consciously or unconsciously, juxtaposed their own modernity and normative Greekness. In discovering these worlds in post–Civil War Athens, the researchers overwrote recent and ongoing political and class conflicts while, at the same time, suppressing their own political pasts. Even though researchers in their fieldnotes were called on to be witnesses *to witnessing*, their research was not conceived as a dialogue in which they could acknowledge their "interchangeability" (Felman and Laub 1992) with the refugee-witnesses; to the contrary, researchers were meant to extract testimony and knowledge of the Asia Minor past from the refugees as if it were a monologue that was entrusted to them to transcribe and translate accurately. Given the common ground that researchers and informants shared because of their recent political experiences, however, it is not impossible that at the edges of the center's structured data collection such mutual recognition did occur.

Scribing: The Labor and Language of History

While Merlier perceived herself as the Archive's solitary author (or its author in the final instance), she seemed to have looked upon the researchers as replaceable members of a team, accountable to a bureaucratic order. They would do the dirty work of collecting the primary data from the refugees, which she then hoped famous authors and academics would transform into polished literary products.[66] As a result, Merlier often moved researchers from one area of research to another and in general seems to have tried to prevent them from working on any one subject long enough to develop a specialty. Researchers' work formed pieces of a puzzle they were not meant to synthesize.

Since the bourgeois fascination with vernacular language that underlies the center's project was based on a dialectic between the *oral discourse* of the "folk" and the *final written text* of the literary author, it is unsurprising that the researchers' "intermediary" work of transcribing easily slips from view, especially given that scribing and authoring were carried out by different people—or, rather, made different "people." A focus on archiving, however, brings to the fore these seemingly mundane practices of documentation, showing them to be highly consequential for the formation of social subjectivities.

As Ann Stoler (2002b) has pointed out in her study of Dutch colonial archives, reading archives *along*, rather than against, their grain can provide insight into the emotional economy of the particular political regimes that produced them as well as illuminate ethnic and racial hierarchies on which they were founded. In colonial Indonesia, for instance, "mixed blood" Indonesian-Dutch clerks were barred from promotion since they were seen as incapable of doing any more complicated task than copying. Dutch colonial agents, on the other hand, learned a quite different part in the colonial drama by being trained through bureaucratic report-writing to affect the appropriate degree of compassion and contempt for the "natives." Similarly, center researchers, in casting themselves in their fieldnotes as "dutiful scribes" and "sensitive listeners," defined a historically new subject position in the Greek culture of historical production: namely, that of the professional, middle-class "memory worker."

As both a disciplined routine of scholarship as well as a formulaic scene of writing, the researchers' fieldnotes were self-consciously constructed as pleasurable stories addressed to Merlier as the archive's first reader. They were intended to satisfy her desire to "see" and "hear" the refugees and be moved by their stories, their strangeness, and their problems. Rather than hiding behind a mask of detached objectivity, Merlier encouraged the researchers to foreground research *as experience* when writing their fieldnotes (cf. Scott 1992).

It might be helpful at this point to reverse Natalie Davis's (1987) felicitous phrase "fiction in the archives" and speak of the "archive as fiction." Indeed, the researchers' fieldnotes, like Merlier's "work letters," the refugees' stories of their "Exodus," and the informant biographies, all can be seen as artifacts of Merlier's attempt to reform historical scholarship through narrative. In a presentation given at a seminar in 1959, she noted:

> Don't think that scholarship, which also has wings, has to be colorless and dry. As material, I also regard whatever you write—fieldwork reports, informant reports, travelogues—and in those I sometimes find your best, truest self. Don't forget that those, too, will remain, framing the oral tradition, enfolding the roads that you took to find it, the pains you endured to save it. And next to it will remain your names, my dear researchers, which will testify to our campaign, which a handful of people attempted out of love for the last Hellenism of Asia Minor.[67]

This "framing" and "enfolding" of the data with personal stories, however, created an odd schizophrenia in the archive as one layer of texts focusing on the subjective experience of witnesses—whether to trauma or to witnessing itself—runs parallel to another that presents disembodied bits of social knowledge concerning customs, topography, and local history. While to some extent Merlier posed the story *against* the document, she simultaneously insisted that these narratives of research be treated *as* documents and be carefully preserved in the archive. Indeed, even her "work letters" have been typed up, numbered, and bound.

Since the fieldwork reports were first-person narratives, in order to write them the researchers had to create personas for themselves distinct from those of the refugees, on the one hand, and Merlier, on the other. In these tales, defining the *work* of memory would be essential to establishing the legitimacy of a new kind of historical producer: the professional scribe. Some photographs capture both the poignancy and oddness of researchers' meetings with the refugees: the researcher in a suit or a nice dress speaking to an old man in tattered pajamas or an old woman with a black headscarf (see fig. 3.2). Refugee homes, which often had working gardens attached to them, were sites of intense household production, and researchers would often come upon informants at the most inconvenient moments to ask them to "remember" for them. While often flattered by these visits, informants could also be preoccupied with childcare, cooking, housekeeping, gardening, and miscellaneous crisis management. Aglaia Loukopoulou describes going to Drosia, a neighborhood far north of Athens, and finding the wife of an informant washing wool for quilts. Not in as "good spirits" (*kefati*) as the previous time they met, the woman informs her that her husband will not be back until late. Upset because she had traveled so far, the researcher speaks with the man's daughter, only to find out that he is actually on his way home. Realizing that the woman's initial curtness had to do with the fact

Figure 3.2   Christos Samouilidis conducting research. Date of photograph and photographer unknown. Collection, Center for Asia Minor Studies.

that she did not have time to stop working to talk to her, the researcher volunteers to help her by drawing water from the well: an offer the woman accepts. In remarking on this incident, the researcher depicts herself as sensitive to class differences and eager to erase them.

Researchers, by contrast, usually drew a sharp line between themselves and businessmen refugees. The bias against the business classes, of course, was built into the research agenda as commercial centers with a large Greek presence were last on the center's list of priorities. Thus, Merlier is enraged when material comes back on Ankara with only bourgeois sources; she remarks sarcastically:

> The material that was collected shows a bourgeois Ankara: educated people, rich, well-traveled. In this respect Mrs. Mastoridou stands out. Born in 1902, a twelve-year old when World War I broke out, the Greek schools had closed. Deft at handiwork, she perfected it with the Catholic nuns. Thus during these unlucky years she crocheted and sewed. . . . In the material on Ankara the folk do not appear at all. . . . Sofoula [the researcher] might have found people of the folk in the provinces; three, three and half thousand Greeks could not have all been bourgeois.[68]

Unsurprisingly, then, offices were seen as the least promising location to conduct fieldwork. Eleni Karatza, for instance, describes a visit to Haralambos Mouratoglou, who owned a medium-sized wood factory in Piraeus. As she waits in the office inside the factory, she becomes skeptical of how helpful he will be:

> Everything smelled *business* and I began to doubt if I would get a response. Finally Mihalis Mouratoglou, the son of the informant, came . . . I gave him the circular from

the center. He read it with great attention and quite the opposite of what I expected he showed great interest. In a little while his father came and we sat together until 8:15 although usually the store closes at 6:30.[69]

Sofia Dondolinou reports a similar encounter with the businessman Vassilis Mouratoglou:

> He was pleased as a small child who remembers a past life and he did not hurry at all to close the door of memory that the center had opened for him. So I let him talk and sketch his neighborhood and the courtyard of the church of Agios Nikolaos, of the Metropolitan of Kaisareia. . . . He wants in every way to help us and for the Kaisareian merchant this interest is rare. The stores have closed and Mouratoglou, who for my sake had stopped his work for hours, does not show any rush to leave.[70]

It is not only Mouratoglou's interest in talking about his Asia Minor past but also his selflessness that strike her as remarkable. Rather than a heartless businessman only out for his own profit and unsentimental about the past, Mouratoglou stops his work for her and does not seem to be in any "rush to leave" or "shut the door of memory." The issue of time is central here. While it was assumed that businessmen would not have time to waste on heritage, it was expected that lower-class informants, especially women, would *make time*.

Upon entering refugee quarters and homes, the researchers anticipated encountering "traditional" patterns of social interaction. They assumed, for one, that the refugee districts constituted close-knit and neighborly communities. Aglaia Loukopoulou, for instance, describes a fieldwork foray to Kallithea in 1956; since she does not know the exact address of the informant, she asks at a nearby kiosk: "They didn't know such a name, though, and they sent me on to a neighboring tailor shop, which was owned by Pontians." Since at the shop they do not know either, they ask on her behalf at a café across the way. Again she has no luck and begins wandering the streets, becoming increasingly desperate:

> An old woman was sitting outside a door. I start a conversation with her. Maybe something will come of it. Yes, she knew a woman from the villages of Trapezounda [Trabzon] and she could take me there right away. How obliging and good are the people of the folk![71]

Researchers also expected that despite their poverty, the refugees would be hospitable and welcome them into their homes, something which in fact often happened. Thanassis Kostakis describes going to Perama on an August day in 1939 to interview a refugee from Cappadocia. He had arrived at eight in the morning only to find out that the informant had left the house at five. He sat with the informant's wife until the man returned, laden down with figs: "We sat and talked (*ta eipame*). At midday, we ate together under a pine tree, we slept and parted in the afternoon."[72]

Although researchers idealized the legendary hospitality of the Anatolian Greeks, turning a conversation about the past into historical research necessarily interrupted many of the traditional practices by which a stranger would be welcomed into a house. It seems that many informants were uncomfortable when researchers, after they had drunk their coffee and eaten a sweet, wanted to start formal questioning. As one researcher complained:

> Practically one hour had passed and with the back-and-forth about various family matters, which Mrs. Anastasia tells me; the work still hadn't begun and my watch showed 6:05. But how can you stop her when she narrates a life full of pain, toil and struggle, and she thinks that you are a hope maybe to help her. On her own, though, at some point she tells me to take out my paper and we begin work. . . . But Mrs. Anastasia gets up for various tasks around the house and in the meantime she loses her thought and has to start again.[73]

Her unbridled outpouring as she "narrates a life full of pain, toil and struggle" is cut short by the researcher's watch and her anxiety to begin work.

In a similar incident, the researcher reports an informant's resistance to submitting to the discipline of remembering:

> I can't, I can't today, she said with effort, but nevertheless she said it. She is a very polite person and it was an effort to refuse. "I'm tired, I'm sick, I have a headache," she added more softly. She opened her drawer and took a pill for her headache. "OK, since you can't work; we won't work today." I closed my notebook and started to talk with her again, about the work, but without writing. I asked her about her village, Rision. She told me all she knew. "Now *that* I would like to write," I said, "We have to be able to make other people understand what Rision is." "Ah, now my headache is gone, write it."[74]

While one can only conjecture how these women spoke about their past in everyday life, one can be sure they did not speak of it *this* way. The frame for conversation imposed by the researchers' questions must have been off-putting and intimidating for some informants. Despite the fact that in these interactions the refugee informants were being recognized (positively) in terms of their former identities, they might not necessarily have seen the center's documentary practices as of an entirely different order than those they had encountered at bureaucratic agencies during the course of their resettlement.[75]

Encounters between researcher and informant, thus, both depended on and exploited practices and idioms of hospitality. Over the course of the research, some informants seemed to have hoped and even expected that real friendships were being formed. Refugees would sometimes cook special meals for the researchers, only to be disappointed if they did not show up. Alexandros Ioakemenidis, for instance, developed a warm relationship with some Pontian informants in Patissia. He notes: "With my frequent visits I have become for them like a relative. For that reason, every time I come they make sure to take care of me better. Anna's sister starts boiling a plum compost to give to me later."[76] They complain another day when he does not come and they have prepared special meat pies (*piroski*) for him.

Unsurprisingly, the researchers ended up speaking most often with lonely old women, who had time on their hands and were always home. One woman even promised to keep remembering in order to bring "her" researcher back:

> Every night . . . when I lay down to sleep I sit there thinking what else to remember so I can tell you and each time I remember something else and I talk about it with my

brother and I wait for you to come. "In one afternoon or two can you remember and talk about a whole life and a land so big?"

The researcher adds: "Elisabet is right! All of this she tells me with her strange Greek, which one struggles to understand." When she leaves, Elisabet accompanies her to the bus and says good-bye with "the entreaty that I go at least one time a week to her house. 'Every time I will remember something to tell you,' she said."[77]

While for many informants talking about their homelands was a pleasurable experience, others seemed to have felt that these conversations were not a fair exchange. One informant is hesitant to sing songs for the researchers because he had been interviewed once before: "They came from 'Music Magazine' in just the same way. I sang for them so they could write the songs down and they didn't even bring them for me to see."[78] Information, thus, could not always be acquired without a price. In order to get a particular informant to speak with her, Eleni Gazi finds she must buy one of the "American Dresses" the woman is selling. Other informants waited eagerly for the little gifts that the researchers would bring: some coffee, sweets. Aglaia Loukopoulou reports that her informant in Moschato is happy to see her, but also angry that it has been two months since she last visited:

> She gave me a regular interrogation, "where was I and what was I doing." Some friendship and intimacy has developed between us. Besides the old lady waits for me for some other reason. She has become like a small child and any little treat (*filema*) that I bring her now and again gives her great happiness. With what emotion she hides it in her pocket.[79]

While researchers might patronizingly report their informants' "childlike" glee at their visits and little gifts, sometimes a more demanding voice breaks through from refugees who hoped for more than a "treat" from their well-connected friends. A researcher notes these comments made by an informant:

> We have talked about most everything (*ta pio polla ta eipame*). Now we are starting to forget. Mrs. Merlier did good for our homelands, now she should do good for us. Something she should take care of, if she can, is to give us a house; living here paying rent, we just can't make it. Write down the number of the application we have submitted and give it to her. With a phone call she could save us.[80]

In reporting an incident like this, the researcher expresses her sensitivity to the superfluity, even inappropriateness, of academic inquiry given the chronic problems faced by many of the center's informants. She also signals her willingness to use fieldnotes as a medium to transmit the refugee's demand directly to Merlier ("now she should do good for us").

As the refugees seemed keenly aware, writing was the only way that all this "idle talk" could be turned into "memory work." The researcher Ioakemenidis, for instance, describes the intensity with which he writes: "Tirelessly and quickly I 'suck' my notepad with my pencil, filling it with short notes. I have made up my own stenography. Thus I can keep up with the informant as she speaks."[81] By switching from small talk to writing, the researchers established the lines of social distinction that separated them from their informants. Researchers' practices of documentation not only transcribed speech into writing, but also translated foreign idioms into demotic Greek. Even though Merlier wanted to hear stories straight from the mouths of the informants, she discouraged researchers from taking down whole texts in dialect, instead suggesting that they quote a few characteristic words or phrases.[82] In a heated seminar meeting in 1958, the editor of the first volume of "Exodus" narratives remarked that the intervention of the researchers into the testimonies was sometimes so great that he could tell which philologists had "written" which texts.[83]

Even though Merlier embraced a modernist conception of the truth of experience, she continued to maintain a positivist's fetish of the document. The everyday business of making memory thus seems to have led to frequent disagreements over the relationship between the document as knowledge statement and testimony as emotive linguistic performance, a subject that also came up in my discussion with former researcher Christos Samouilidis:

P: Merlier seemed to put a lot of emphasis on descriptive writing. She seemed to want to see and hear the people.

S: Indeed, she wanted things like they were taperecorded. She wanted the material that we collected to be "the narrative of the informant" and not a summary of our own and a documentation of the points they gave us. The material should be rendered in the words of the informant. With his language. His style. And we really did seek out these kinds of narratives. In fact, Turkish speakers who knew little Greek had a style (*ifos*) in their narrating, a real charm. They described things in their own way, with their own language. It was a lively, convincing narrative—the live voice of a *Mikrasiatis*. Whenever we succeeded in finding one of these [narratives] we were happy. But the work did not proceed this way. These narratives didn't give you much—just the least bit of "juice." Ten pages might have only three lines that were useful for folklore, for science. But these texts—this chaotic material—went into the archive all the same.

P: What exactly was the procedure for collecting material?

S: The first phase was primitive. You acted like a tape recorder. A simple person doesn't separate the themes that he tells you. Whatever comes to him he says spontaneously. Some researchers who were not philologists presented the material like this and Merlier would be happy. In fact, she pointed to these as models, in the highest category. She hated us philologists and always wanted to put us down. That material has value as a document, as a testimony. It has literary and maybe sociological value. But it doesn't have value either for history or folklore because it doesn't exhaust its subject, it doesn't answer to questions. You have to use the informant. He is the possessor of the events of his life, but he is not the possessor of the things he must tell you. You must ask him. Like you are doing to me!

P: (chuckle)

S: So that is the first group, the primitive one. The second group took the questionnaire and then cut the material into pieces (*ta ekovan kommatia*), so it seemed that they had gathered the material by topic. But this happened afterwards. You saw what subjects came up and you attached the appropriate subject title. And the third way—and there were only about two or three of us who did it this way, we began with the questionnaire to collect the specific folklore information. We asked specifically and they responded specifically. If they started a narration, we were happy, but once they finished we stopped them to go on to the next subject. In this way we collected material that was already categorized and was easy to separate into subjects.

As Samouilidis' comments suggest, transcribing oral discourse during the course of research and transforming it into an *archivable*, written document always threatened to unravel the center's archive from the inside, revealing its epistemological contradictions and incompatible methodological frameworks ("ten pages might have only three lines that were useful for folklore, for science," "chaotic material," "it doesn't exhaust its subjects," "it doesn't answer to questions"). "Acting like a tape recorder" might have been appropriate for discourse units with a fixed form (i.e., songs, proverbs, folk tales) or for those that did not need to have a fixed form (i.e., testimonies); however, spontaneous discourse with no clear beginning and end was difficult to regiment to the logic of a questionnaire and to the categories of the center's archive. In *handwriting* transcriptions, the researchers—no matter how much they "sucked" on their notepads—ended up filtering refugee discourse through other texts and stories, often literary ones, which they had in their heads. In the final analysis, though, the fact that researchers were called on to act *like* tape recorders and yet not use them probably assured the result Merlier was looking for better than if they *had* used them. Indeed, the orality that Merlier had in mind could not be the product of actual recording practice, but only a sophisticated literary effect—not to be mistaken with a clumsy philological imitation of it immediately visible to an editor's eye.

Samoulidis's castigation of the "primitive," mimetic approach to informant discourse, which Merlier put in the "highest category," not only reveals the tensions created by the irreconcilable philosophies of history and technologies of documentation underlying the center's archiving process but also hints at the gender and class politics complexly entangled in conflicts over the proper methods and products of the research. Given how Samouilidis described his approach to interviewing, it is not surprising that, as he told me, he fought with Merlier all the time and that she considered him the center's "black sheep" ("She hated us philologists"). For Samouilidis, a child of refugees, knowledge of scholarly procedure represented a badge of class advancement, while for Merlier and some of her researchers, dispensing with philology reflected their class *privilege*. Throughout our conversation, Samouilidis highlighted, rather scornfully, what he perceived as the essentially literary dimension of the center's project and seemed convinced that Merlier would have made a better novelist than historian. He reminded me several times that Merlier did not have the credentials to do this kind of work: she had studied music, not history, and in his opinion was not a true scholar (*epistimonas*). In retrospect, though, the center's embrace of literature appears to be precisely that which is responsible for the innovative dimensions of its materials. If Merlier had been truer either to Greek philological folklore and history, with their roots in nineteenth-century historicism, or to the positivism of the then-new French geographical history, the center's archive surely would not command the interest it did at the time of my research.

While many researchers did not accept the division of labor at the center (even center secretary Maria Asvesti would go on to write her own book about Asia Minor), this project marked the end of the monopoly of the Greek high bourgeoisie on practices of historical re-collection and the emergence of the efficient, educated, and modestly salaried middle-class memory worker. As can be seen in researcher fieldnotes, this white-collar work of listening and scribing was defined in contrast to the manual labor of the working-class refugees and the entrepreneurialism of businessman refugees as well as to Merlier's elite reading and writing practices and the volunteer typing and secretarial work of her upper-class lady friends. Nonetheless, the details of scribing remain largely invisible in the archival record; notably, as opposed to Merlier's letters, the field reports of the researchers never depict their actual "scenes of writing": the petit bourgeois Athenian homes where the researchers would write up their notes after a day on the streets.

As artifacts of professional discipline and sympathy, the researchers' fieldnotes also attest to the tensions involved in transforming a space of dialogue into a site of historical labor and in transliterating and translating foreign idioms into a "standard" written Greek punctuated with a few exotic terms. Failed encounters are so often recorded in the fieldnotes because these reports doubled as timecards in which the researchers accounted for their yield of data. The failures also provided the researchers with opportunities to paint touching scenes that demonstrated their sympathy for the refugees' pitiable condition: a condition that was so often "beyond words." But the refugees' silence and refusals might be read in yet another way: as a commentary on the peculiar violence and imposition of memory work itself as well as on the unexamined possibility that the refugees might not have anything to *say*.

Memory, Voice, Biography: Refugee as Witness

> *Triandafyllidi, Evmorfili.* Evmorfili Triandafyllidi was born in Tripolis [Pontos]. As she told me, she is 82 years old. She is illiterate and speaks only the Pontic dialect. She lived mainly in Tripolis. Around 1909 she went to Russia, from where she left in 1919 for Greece. Most of her relatives from Tripolis were lost. She is a willing, but not at all good informant. She doesn't have memory and it is difficult to communicate with her. She lives with her son-in-law. Two of her sons were killed in the *Dekemvriana*. She lives in a tent opposite no. 192 on Kallirois St., in the Sfageia district (Ano Petralona). Tram Kallithea, Karayianni stop.[84]

This spare summary of a shattered life was documented by a researcher in 1957. Resonant with allusions to the city's intimate memories and places, it dashes a brush-stroke across a city emerging from the devastation of the war years. It also shines a light on one of its most marginal residents. Its keywords open up traumatic moments in modern Greek history. *Petralona*, one of the many refugee communities that sprouted up on the edges of the city. The *Pontic* Greeks, an ethnic group that suffered an especially tragic fate, marked by multiple dislocations, purges, and forced movements both prior to and after the "Catastrophe."[85] The *Dekemvriana*, or "December Days," the bitter streetfighting in Athens in 1944 that pitted Greek police, former Nazi collaborationists, and British troops against members of the communist-led resistance movement: the opening moves of the Civil War.

Filed as an "Informant Report," this document and the failure it records reveal in miniature how the center's project sought to transform the individual informant into a historical subject—and specifically a "refugee"—possessed of a unique life story and memories that could be expressed and transmitted despite the ordeal endured in coming to Greece as well as the second and for some even more definitive trauma of World War II and the ensuing Civil War. In this final section, I consider how the production of these informant reports contributed to institutionalizing the individual refugee as witness to a collective history and the "Asia Minor Catastrophe" as subject *par excellence* for Greek memory work. This identification process, I also argue, exposes some of the repressed links between history and bureaucracy as national(izing) discourses and "social welfare" projects.

The informant report, which developed out of Merlier's early research on folk songs, was a characteristic product of the center's experimentation with methodologies. In a 1935 essay about the Musical Folklore Archive, Merlier explains that it would be ridiculous to claim that a singer who is Pontian or Cappadocian comes from Attica or Macedonia if he or she has only been in Greece since 1922 or 1924. Merlier thus decided that a special record, including a photograph and a short biographical note, accompanied by a few remarks about the "personality of the subject," should be created for each singer. She gives the example of the seventy-nine-year-old Eleni Spirou, whose photograph is annotated with the following comments: "She lives in Piraeus (*Neos Kosmos*), exchanged 1922, photographed 1930, she sang two songs, her husband is a sailor. The woman is charming (*haritomeni*), with lots of life and spirit. She only speaks her dialect" (1935a: 18–20).

As brief as this note is, in centering so much attention on the individual informant, it indicates the beginning of a fundamental break with the documentation practices of folklore. Even contemporary research on refugees, as Malkki has argued, continues to be guided by an implicit functionalist logic that assumes that displacement represents an "anomaly in the life of an otherwise 'whole,' stable, sedentary society" (1995b: 508). While the folk "at home," the traditional subjects of folklore study, are not thought to have unique biographies, the displaced, by contrast, are presumed to have an extensive story to tell about their lives. Furthermore, as living "tokens" of a lost world and survivors of a dramatic experience, refugees—their bodies, their worn faces, and sad clothes—are treated as evidence in their own right. This desire to *show* the refugee (and later the refugee shacks and settlements) exemplifies the voyeurism of misery associated with the technology of the photograph and its historical development as a tool for recording the horrors of war and its "human face" (Sontag 2003). Notably, it was the "Asia Minor Catastrophe" more generally that had provided the impetus for the introduction of new film technologies to Greece and the development of social reportage photography.[86]

It might not be an exaggeration to say that it was the difficulty of doing these "simple" biographical sketches that drove Merlier to launch a systematic investigation of the culture and history of Greek Anatolia using refugee testimony as a key source. In the everyday work of the center, informant reports would become an integral part of the research routine. Based on the prototype Merlier initially proposed, these reports included significantly more biographical information; photographic portraits, however, were reserved for a small number of refugees and taken on an occasional basis (see figs. 3.3 and 3.4). As in the case of sound recording, so too with photography: newer technologies of documentation were replaced during the course of research by the cheaper, more familiar mimetic technology of writing while, at

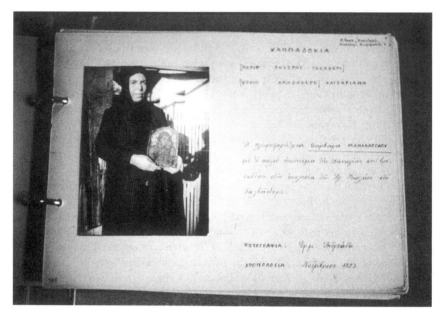

Figure 3.3   Refugee and/as relic. Varvara Manaioglou, from Cappadocia to Kaisariani. Photograph taken in 1953 by Ermolaos Andreadis. Collection, Center for Asia Minor Studies.

the same time, researchers were pressed to intensify the reality-effect of writing in imitation of these other technologies. Although the informant reports have now been permanently archived with the data, while research was still going on they were kept in a working file in the center's office. Since fieldwork was considered a replicable experiment, researchers were supposed to check old informant reports to get names and addresses of informants, especially of "reliable" or "juicy" ones. This is why Evmorfili's "address" and directions to her tent are noted. Since the reports taken together served as a kind of collective address book, they were often updated with new addresses or information about refugees' deaths.

As I have already suggested, the making of these reports resembled countless other bureaucratic procedures through which refugees had already passed in the process of establishing their citizenship and residence in Greece. In *The Memory of the Modern* (1996), Matt Matsuda has described how in turn-of-the-twentieth-century France the "memory of the state" was produced through the creation of police files on vagabonds and criminals that included photographs, body measurements, and other physical descriptions of them. The state sought to "identify" these mobile populations because, as Matsuda argues, their rootlessness posed a threat to French identity and its tenets of stable family, community, and work life. Although automatically granted Greek citizenship upon arrival, refugees were initially perceived as problematic citizens whose cultural difference, lack of a fixed home, and disconnection from local communities were potentially threatening to the social order. Indeed, for the first five years following the "Catastrophe," groups of refugees traveled restlessly around the country trying to decide on the best place to live (Yiannacopoulos 1992: 32). During the course of their resettlement, as their cases

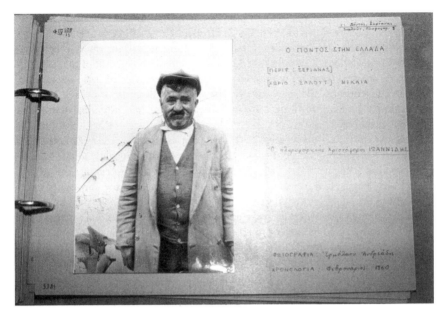

Figure 3.4 Pontos in Greece. Christoforos Ioannidis. Photograph taken in 1960 by Ermolaos Andreadis. Collection, Center for Asia Minor Studies.

were handled by various agencies and state functionaries, the refugees were gradually incorporated into the Greek state system. Many also would adopt Hellenized versions of their names, chosen either for the sake of grammatical correctness (i.e., adding a terminal -s, as in *Topali*-s) or to replace common Turkish suffixes with Greek ones (i.e., from -*oglou* or -*li* to -*idis* or -*adis*). The center's informant reports thus could be seen as yet another tool of location that "translates" people such as Evmorfili and connects them to mainstream Greek life. On the other hand, in "returning" the refugees to their original homelands, the center, in effect, composed a counterregistry and alternative data bank that troubled the smooth incorporation of this population into the taxonomies of Helladic-based Greekness.

For Merlier, the informant reports, as miniature biographies, represented yet another genre of documentation that challenged the anonymity of traditional folklore and historical discourse. In a letter from Geneva, dated September 19, 1956, Merlier tells her researchers:

> I would so much like it if we had some spontaneous "Monuments of the Word" (*Mnimeia Logou*) as I call them—a narration about the Village, a memory of life there, happy or sad, an Exodus. Those pages, which exist and stand out in our material, are the very soul of our populations, much more than the established customs, such as "Monuments of the Word," the products of the anonymous folk imagination and sensibility, much traveled, as we know, so we are not always able to define their origin.[87]

"Monuments of the Word," a standard category of Greek folklore scholarship, included formulaic verbal materials such as songs, proverbs, ritual sayings, myths, tales, and legends, which, like ancient ruins, were thought to have "survived" into the present (Kyriakidou-Nestoros 1978: 66–7; Herzfeld 1986: 10, 113–17). As Merlier's comments suggest, she does not entirely reject this category (or many other ones borrowed from folklore), nor does she forsake the Herderian pursuit of the "soul" of culture. As in the "Exodus" narratives, though, the emphasis on the spontaneous over the conventional, the personal over the communal, and the unique over the representative marks a protean, but conflicted, turn to the individual witness as historical authority.

This extension of personality and "life stories" to the refugees ostensibly constituted a critique not only of folklore but also of the cold rationality of state bureaucracy and its documentary practices. However, given that the products of the center's research were not at all in the hands of the refugees (or, at least, of the uneducated ones) and the relationship of informant to researcher did not entail true solidarity, but rather a kind of "charity," this personalizing of the refugee could be seen as replicating a *characteristic* dimension of bureaucracy in its encounter with the poor and working class.[88] Carolyn Steedman, for instance, has explained that with the growth of the administrative state in England from the seventeenth century on, the poor were constantly made to tell their story to courts and philanthropic organizations as they sought sympathy, mercy, and assistance. In these "enforced narratives of the self" (2001: 54), the poor were called on to narrate, usually orally, basic facts of their life (birth, work experience, marriages, children, criminal record) as well as to provide an accounting of their previous dealings with agencies responsible for managing the problems and claims of the poor; sometimes philanthropic organizations only gave out dole in exchange for a personal narrative. As a continuation of this logic, she notes, letters of recommendation for servants in the eighteenth and nineteenth centuries focused on the "character" of the working-class applicant. Similarly, the center's informant reports dwell on the refugees' personalities, which are described with a wide array of terms, such as bad-tempered (*dystropos*), likeable (*sympathitikos*), willing, smart, cheerful (*yelastos*), chatterbox (*polylogas*), serious, tired, sick, positive, egocentric, worried, and stubborn (*epimonos*). These brief portraits, thus, give us some idea of the stereotypes researchers had about the "folk" as well as the criteria they held for good informants.

As a *bad* informant, then, Evmorfili's case raises several questions about these routine acts of identification. For one, is she even a "Pontian"? Is her Anatolian past alive in her memory after her ten-year sojourn in Russia and her many years in Greece? Was this home, where she appears to have been a victim of harassment and ethnic purges, a place that she remembered with fondness, a place where she felt comfortable and "at home"? Hirschon (1998) describes how refugees as well as their children and grandchildren often sought to distinguish themselves from autochthonous Greeks by referring to themselves either as refugees (*prosfyges*), when claiming a history of suffering and displacement, or as *Mikrasiates* (people from Asia Minor), when stressing their distinct cultural heritage. On the one hand, reaching out to Evmorfili as a *Pontian* valorized an identity that had made her a victim of racism and discrimination in the past. On the other hand, much must have conspired to make Evmorfili think of herself primarily as a *refugee*. Ongoing problems with refugee compensation and housing plagued many families for decades after their arrival in

Greece, relegating them, like Evmorfili, to sordid living conditions.[89] It was 1957, thirty-five years after the "Catastrophe," and she was living in a tent. If the researcher had asked her about her experiences of trying to get compensation for lost property or in dealing with her current housing situation might she have had more to say?

But what if neither the label of refugee nor *Mikrasiatis* fit? After the deaths of her sons in the war, how could Evmorfili remember Pontos? When she returned to Greece from France in 1945, Merlier herself wondered whether it would be possible to write about Asia Minor after World War II and the Holocaust. She realized that she must weigh the tragedy of the population exchange against so much new suffering:

> When the Asia Minor disaster (*halasmos*) took place it was, even on a global scale, an unprecedented event. Since World War II, population movements, enslavement, genocide, and the annihilation of millions of people from the earth have cast into oblivion the Asia Minor tragedy. With one difference though. In world history, not just Greek, Asia Minor occupies a privileged place. Everything about its geography, history, modern folk culture in the broadest sense interests and moves first, of course, Hellenism but also world thought. (1948: 24–5)

This is an interesting passage because it reveals a characteristic slippage: is it the *tragedy* of the refugee crisis that defines the center's project or the *glories* to be unearthed in the Greek Anatolian past? Is it the *testimonies* of the sufferers or the *documents* of "geography, history, and modern folk culture" that make the center's research timely, important, and globally relevant? Merlier, at first, highlights the former, but ultimately privileges the latter; she thus loses the opportunity, taken up by some Greek novelists, to draw out links between these different historical experiences of genocide and refugee crisis as well as to assert the significance of the "Catastrophe" as *precedent*.[90] In deciding not to address this second period of traumatic loss and dislocation, Merlier also will not consider its effect on the center's informants, except in a purely practical way: "How many, I wonder, of the refugees fell in the Albanian mountains, how many died from bombardments, how many were killed as hostages, how many died in the Resistance? Out of our informants how many, when we call them, will respond 'here'?" (10).

In Evmorfili's case, though, it is hard to ignore the fact that she is a recent victim of war. Other informant reports provide similar glimpses of devastating wartime losses: "During the Occupation he lost one child. The youngest of his three daughters, an angel of twelve, who died in the winter of 1942 from hunger."[91] One might also ask whether political orientation had not come to overshadow refugee background for the many refugees and their children who had participated in the communist-led resistance movement.[92] The reference to the *Dekemvriana* in Evmorfili's brief biography leads one to assume that her sons, like many of refugee origin, especially in the cities, were communists or, at least, participants in the Resistance. In field reports, one also finds signs that the war and the ideological battles of the day were foremost on people's minds. For instance, one researcher comments on meeting a man from Pontos who had chosen to write short stories about the contrast between rich and poor in Athens and not about his homeland. In a report filed in one of Merlier's personal dossiers, another researcher describes an unsuccessful journey to the provinces to collect information about Pontos. One woman had pulled a dried-out weed from the ground and, showing him the roots, commented: "From the seed you can get everything, but from the roots you ask everything. How can I know anymore? I got old, *yiavroum* (Turkish for "my child"). I got old! I don't remember anymore." On the way back, by way of apology for the disappointing fieldwork, the guide tells the researcher about the horrible things that local people had experienced during the Occupation and the Civil War.

Evmorfili's silence brings up a final question: Can she even turn her memories into narratives? While she is *willing* to help, she is not *able* to remember (she has "no memory," she is "not at all a good informant"). Is her past narratable and, if not, what can be made of her silence? In expecting historical testimony to be as available and as "spontaneous" and "spirited" as an oft-repeated folk tale or folk song, the researchers assumed that their informants had a way of talking about themselves as historical actors and that the multiple traumatic events they had experienced could be composed into a referential account of "what happened." By constructing the refugee as a "person with a story," the center's research implicitly was based on a notion that victims of trauma possess, rather than are *possessed by*, their experience (Caruth 1996: 7).

Furthermore, the extent to which historical inquiry in its eerie similarity to bureaucratic modes of extracting information and labeling persons also might trigger a repetition of past trauma, rather than "open the door" to memory and provide an escape to a nostalgic past, does not appear to have been considered as a risk or ethical dilemma by center researchers.[93] But Evmorfili is not alone in her speechlessness. Many reports describe inadequate informants:

> Sofia Karfoulou is an old informant of our Center. She doesn't seem to know many things, or probably she has forgotten, as she says.[94]

> Maria Palitsoglou. As an informant she doesn't have much to offer. It is difficult to make her speak. I don't know anything, the others told you about it, she tells me constantly . . .[95]

> Prodromos Mezoglou. Because he lived days of horror, as his family says, he is not quite right in the head. When you think he is well, the same moment he gives signs of unbalance. No one therefore can depend on his information.[96]

Sometimes the informants speak, but they are not naturally gifted storytellers. Ermolaos Andreadis notes his disappointment when an informant does not tell him a good "Exodus" story: "Our always cordial and willing informant was somewhat out of sorts today, taciturn and reserved. For this reason his Exodus, I think, did not come out as I would have liked, juicy and descriptive."[97] In the contemporary outpouring of research on memory in colonial and postcolonial studies, memory, as Ann Stoler and Karen Strassler (2000) have pointed out, tends to be imagined according to a "hydraulic model," in which it is assumed that memories are "housed as discrete stories awaiting an audience" and are available to be "tapped" by sympathetic researchers whenever they happen to show up. Stoler and Strassler question whether such fully formed alternative historical narratives circulate so readily among subalterns, who are often lacking scripts, audiences, and, above all, the authority to craft them.

Merlier and the center's staff, of course, were not looking for a counterhistory or for subaltern knowledge; for them, oral testimony would complement, not dispute, written documents. As might be expected, though, uneducated refugees often did not consider themselves appropriate informants and tended to defer to the authority of educated members of their communities. Eleni Gazi, for instance, mentions meeting a "very willing" and "cheerful" woman from Sinasos in Cappadocia while doing research about another area. The woman asks her if she knows Rizos, a local historian and key informant of the center. "For us," she said, "you don't need to run around and ask. Rizos has written it all!"[98] This comment has perhaps been recorded by the researcher because she thinks it is humorous; the woman does not know that the center's goal was to speak to the uneducated, poor refugees and that refugee scholars were assumed to be bad informants. In particular, their use of the high register of Greek (*katharevousa*) rather than local dialect was considered to render their testimony cold and inauthentic. Merlier once complained:

> In the particular instance of Denizgiren, even though it seems that Mr. Kondozoglou—himself a teacher, priest and son of a priest—knows a lot of things, I can't say that in him the village is brought back to life. With such *katharevousa*, with *eisichthi* and *proichthi* [archaicized verb forms], and with the "*kodones* [a formal word for 'bells'] of the church," how can we hear the bells of the church striking? Mr. Kondozoglou speaks like a book and resurrection needs the warm and live speech of a person.[99]

People who "speak like a book," it was assumed, should not be informants; they should write books themselves (just as those who *can* speak should not write, a matter I take up in my final case study). When Merlier realized that the center would never have enough time to gather material about every Greek community in Asia Minor, researchers, in fact, were told to bring notebooks to the educated refugees and encourage them to write manuscripts about their villages and towns following a questionnaire provided by the center.[100]

In practice, however, it also turned out to be a much easier matter to *speak* with the educated refugees. They might not have provided the "warm and live speech" needed for "resurrection," but they respected scholarship and were willing to submit to the discipline of research. While someone like Evmorfili would have been visited by researchers one time, educated male refugees, such as the priest Papathodoros from Farasa in Cappadocia, were consulted over and over and ended up serving as de facto gatekeepers of local memory. Researcher Aglaia Loukopoulou, for instance, arranged semiregular meetings with Papathodoros at his house. The children off at school, she would work with him at a desk while his wife sat patiently in the corner, only now and then adding an appropriate comment. Of one visit, she notes: "I found him waiting for me in the little garden and we started work immediately. His wife sat near us and listened to us while crocheting."[101] In addition to speaking the language of scholarship, these refugees also spoke a form of Greek the researchers understood. Despite the desire to hear about the experiences of non-Greek speakers, in reality, this proved difficult for most of the researchers, with the exception of the few who were of refugee origin themselves and knew Turkish or Greek dialects of Asia Minor. At least one of the reasons that researchers found it "difficult to communicate" with Evmorfili was that she only spoke Pontic dialect.

While for the most part refugees ascribed their silence to a lack of memory, there are a few occasions on which they were reported as being skeptical about the point of historical research. Sofia Dondolinou, for instance, describes meeting a refugee from Aivali while she was interviewing another man:

> Inside the shop . . . Uncle Dimitris from Aivali works, nailing together benches for the shop's textiles. He hears the conversation and asks, full of curiosity, why we are collecting all of this. He is given to the study of Holy Scriptures and he understands "world history," as he says. Why is the Greek history of Asia Minor needed? I explain to him and ask him to fill out a questionnaire on "colonies."[102]

The researcher registers this informant's doubts about the "truths" secular history can reveal, but goes ahead and plies him with a questionnaire anyway.

The ultimate rejection of history is the refusal to identify with (and through) a *nationalized* past. As Daniel has suggested, when the question of the nation enters into studies on refugees or exiles, there always appears to be a "tacit agenda of restoring to the nation and the displaced national what they have lost and also restoring them to the ideal of the nation-state itself as if it were an ontological fact, given and irrevocable" (1997: 310–11). This tendency is further compounded by the fact that researchers usually end up working with "self-selected" informants who themselves are firmly committed to nation-centered politics. As a result, as Daniel notes: "What goes unnoticed are those displaced persons who have opted out of the project of the nation—any and every nation" (311). Indeed, while the center's work attempted to broaden the referent of "Greek" by documenting the multiplicity of Greek ethnicities, the terms "Greek" and "Hellenism" were always paramount in the research and never under negotiation.

Thus, only in incidental silences, noted mostly to evoke sentiment or justify a lack of fieldwork "goods," can we isolate moments when this project of historical re-collection appeared to run up against resistance to its practices of cultural translation and discursive appropriation. Consider, for instance, this scene described in a fieldwork report. On a hot day in July 1956, researcher Eleni Gazi had gone to interview Yiannis Holetsidis, a barber from Trapezounda (Trabzon). Since his shop had become unbearably hot, he was sitting across the street in the shade with some other men:

> As we talk we hear next to us a slow song [for circle dancing]. The old man who had been reading the paper was also Pontian from Kerasounda and accompanied our talk, participating also with a Turkish song from his homeland. Except for the song, however, he was not willing to say even one word. Neither would he say his name— nor let the others say his name—nor did he want to talk.[103]

Seen as a performative utterance rather than a denotative statement, the man's singing troubles the presumption that refugees' oral discourse could always be transformed into an artifact of historical knowledge relating to a distinctly Greek past. First, by singing: while Merlier's research began with music, her training led her to view songs as "tokens" of Anatolia that the refugees had brought along with them as they did icons, community registers, and front-door keys. By contrast, sing*ing*, as transformable social performance and renewable mode of remembrance, cannot be so easily reified and concretized, rooted to distinct national spaces and languages, and reduced to a logic of "before" and "after." Second, through language: despite the center's interest in linguistic diversity and oral discourse, the ultimate goal of research was to record refugee memories in demotic Greek as well as in writing. The old man's Turkish song, by contrast, hangs in the air as a denial to render an alien world into an understandable idiom of cultural difference or to "settle" his memories in Greece. Lastly, by name: he will not give his name or leave a trace, nor will he identify himself within the maps and histories of Hellenism the center was constructing. Were there others like him whose stories would not be inscribed because they could not commit to "Greece"?[104]

The record of the center's research gives a sense of how assumptions concerning the poor and their innate storytelling capacities, the ease with which traumatic experience can be narrativized, and the suitability of the biological individual as witness to a collective history did not always, or even often, correspond with the realities the researchers confronted in the field. At the same time, transforming the social space formed by hospitality and dialogue into one of structured memory work, this research occulted other modes, idioms, and practices of remembering—or not remembering, not telling. Although considered a purely practical matter by the researchers, locating the refugees within the physical space of the nation and on imagined memory maps of Anatolia demonstrated how history, like bureaucracy, clamps down on people's shifting and overlapping "residences" in diverse languages, communities, and experiences of suffering. Through the tiny window opened by these refusals and silences, however, we glimpse, if only in a fragmented way, traces of truly lost lives, which could not be divided, packed up, and borne across the Aegean for redemption.

Archival Reflexiveness

While doing research for this case study, several Greek historians told me outright that the center's "Archive of Oral Tradition" was not a "real" archive and that I should be careful about using it as the basis for making any general observations about archives. Yet another instance of the vigilant boundary maintenance of the historical profession, this rebuke only confirmed for me how threatening, but for my purposes how illuminating, the center's project has proved to established notions of historical knowledge and documentary practice in Greek historical studies. The reasons that the archive would be approached skeptically by professional historians are clear enough. For one, it was constructed from proactively produced "oral documents" rather than from the "natural" accumulation of state, corporate, or family papers. Second, it was directed by a dilettantish, would-be scholar. As I suggested in this chapter, however, in raising pressing questions about the relationship of archives to the state, citizenship, and bureaucracy, this "personal" and "oral" archive hardly proved irrelevant to discussions of public archives.

For one, "reconstituting" the lands and peoples of Asia Minor through historical scholarship could be seen as an ironic commentary (though it was certainly not intended as such) on the state's aborted territorial expansion as well as on the restrictive categories through which national identity would be defined in an ethnically "homogenized" Greek state. By creating a virtual census of Anatolian Greeks, reinscribing them in the imagined cartographies of their remembered homelands, and reinstating their severed social relationships with Turks and other non-Greek ethnic groups, the center's archive could be seen as insisting on the noncoincidence of Greek citizenship and Greek nationality. Thus, at the end of the 1990s, a moment of profound reckoning for the nation-state form in the Balkans, the center's oral archive has been (re)viewed by its archivists and others as a potential counterpoint to mainstream Greek nationalism and statist historiography and archival formation as well as to stereotypes about the Anatolian past promulgated by "lost homelands" rhetoric.

Yet, asking the refugees to speak if not Greek, always *as Greeks*, ultimately reflected a shocking and glaring blindness in the center's research: the failure to take into account the fact that people whose lives had been irrevocably shattered and destroyed by the divisive politics of nationalism and the violence of campaigns of ethnic supremacy (whether Greek or Turkish), people whose present existence in their "Greek homeland" had been painfully marked by racism and ghettoization, would identify naturally, proudly, and unproblematically through the discourse of the nation. By turning the refugees' oral testimony, often told in "strange" dialects of Greek or Turkish, into documents written in demotic Greek—which was implicitly posited as a unified and *unifying* mother tongue—and filing them in the country's symbolic center, the center's research could be said to have *hastened* the incorporation of this population into the nation's self-conception, and the history of Asia Minor Hellenism and the "Catastrophe" into national historical narratives. Similarly, in replicating modes by which the welfare state typically engages the poor (structured interviews with educated functionaries, written forms of documentation, character analysis), the center's research could be seen as complicit with the state's assimilation of this disadvantaged population into the ranks of the Greek working class.

In the final analysis, one of the things that is most striking about the center's oral archive is the fact that it contributed to institutionalizing the Anatolian past as a key *topos* of Greek cultural memory—and of its reform. Even though Merlier established the center to combat what she perceived as state-sanctioned amnesia about Greek Anatolia and used oral testimony to challenge orthodoxies of historical scholarship, over time the Asia Minor past and the refugee experience would become commonplace themes of popular and academic historical discourse as well as "obvious" subjects for oral history projects involving the use of new technologies of documentation (in recent years, for instance, video).[105] One day when speaking to a local historian in Volos, the author of a 1995 book about Greek Asia Minor based largely on oral testimony she had collected from her neighbors, I happened to ask her opinion of the center, only to find out that she had never even heard of it. Some months later, while flipping through a center publication, I happened to notice that one of the center's key informants in the city in the 1950s (when research had been conducted there) also was the key informant for her book! In retrospect, then, it is clear that the center's research established a precedent for central conceptual categories of "lost homelands" discourse: the former refugee quarters as ethnic enclaves (rather than politicized, working-class districts) and as privileged spaces of memory work; the refugee as "one-person unit of collective memory" (Wieviorka 1999: 141); and Greek Anatolian ethnicity as compatible with (if not an improvement on) Helladic Greekness. To be sure, in exposing the often dire living conditions of a marginalized population, the center's research provided a vision of Athens and the provinces that was a far cry from the images presented, for instance, in the booming postwar Greek film industry (the interiors of new apartments, modern furniture, the new airport, the city center, excursions to the beach). However, the center also contributed to establishing the trope of the "nobility" of the Anatolian poor, which in "lost homelands" rhetoric has often led to the disassociation of the historical experience of Asia Minor refugees from that of other impoverished and displaced populations of the past or present.

The ethnography of this archive also had much to tell us about how memory work shaped and was shaped by the culture of scholarship and identity politics of post–Civil War Greek society. The center's project, for one, testifies to a major paradigm shift in historical and cultural production, from the "genius" of a high bourgeois circle of liberal intelligentsia, each known by name, to the "work" of a mostly anonymous, educated middle-class "staff"; the center, thus, could be said to have presaged the transformation of historical re-collection from a marked (and signed) practice to a generalized social phenomenon. Second, the itineraries traced by the letters Merlier sent from France and Switzerland to the researchers in Athens as well as by the field reports that researchers sent her about their collecting journeys from the center of Athens to working-class neighborhoods where the refugees lived, defined routes, *topoi*, and contact zones, which mapped newly emerging cultural topographies while also confirming and transforming social hierarchies and class distinctions of the postwar period. The surprise in "discovering" the exotic East from Athens and *in Athens* reflected the development of a new nation-centered vision of a cosmopolitan Hellenism, which following the "Catastrophe" replaced the multifarious, de-centered relationships of the historic ethnic Greek communities of the Eastern Mediterranean. Remembering Anatolia, however, also had the effect of causing the willful *forgetting* of other stories. In treating their informants as "forever-refugees" (an identity some of their descendants are often more than happy to claim), center researchers working in the 1950s and 1960s repressed, both because of the center's goals and the prevailing political situation, the wartime experiences of their informants as well as their own; memory work thus transformed social spaces of recent and ongoing political and class conflict into idealized spheres of rural reciprocity and cultural difference. In retrospect, the silencing of the Civil War and its legacy entailed in the execution of this memory project is stunning.

The difficulties encountered in the process of eliciting much desired "refugee memory" also exposed how archiving itself contributes to defining the material—and materiality—of memory. While Merlier wanted to reform dry historical writing with the "warm and live speech of a person" who could "resurrect" Anatolia, she hardly embraced an all-out assault on historicism. Even though she pressed her researchers to infuse their writing with the aural and visual dimensions of new technologies of documentation, she ultimately wanted oral sources to assume the status and legitimacy of their written "counterparts": handwritten, sometimes typed, recently microfilmed, classified, quantified, categorized, labeled, concrete, and, above all, permanent. As a result, research ended up focusing on the "the *documentary* and *documentable* aspects of the spoken past" (Shryock 1997: 30)—as well as on their *translatable* ones.

The resultant tension in the archive between testimony and document derived from a deep and unresolved ambivalence at the core of the center's research: that between viewing informants as epic narrators of an unprecedented mass dislocation and "ethnic cleansing" or seeing them as reconstituted Anatolians whose oral discourse could be reified as replacement documents for a lost archive of Greek Asia Minor. This ambivalence extended to the researchers themselves: were they "second-degree witnesses" (Felman and Laub 1992: 213)—catalysts and witnesses to the act of testifying—who occupied a distinct and important "topographical and cognitive position" in relation to this traumatic event, or were they "objective" onlookers, collecting and relaying preformed social data? While discussions in historical circles about the significance (or irrelevance) of the center's oral archive often get bogged down in debates about the relative credibility of the oral source, the true innovation of the center for modern Greek historical studies is often overlooked. Despite the lack of mutuality in authoring testimony, unresponsiveness to the effects of trauma, and privileging of an Orientalist-style knowledge project, the center's research nonetheless entailed by Greek standards an unprecedented legitimation of the victim as historical authority and of the researcher as self-reflexive participant in the production of historical knowledge. In this project, as a result, history itself was partially refigured as narrative of collective suffering and trauma rather than as paean to national expansion, capitalist accumulation, and civilizational progress.

If in this chapter assumptions about the nature of testimony inculcated through researchers' own experience as readers (and sometimes also writers) of literature affected how they heard refugees' "real" testimony and, consciously or unconsciously, guided them to make history read as story, in the novel I discuss in the following chapter, the author works in the opposite direction: to deconstruct the subjectivizing, narrativizing, and integrating voice of testimony by making fiction read like fragments of an unwritable, unspeakable history.

Chapter 4

Reading (Civil) War, the Historical Novel, and the Left

In 1994, Thanassis Valtinos, one of Greece's most prominent contemporary fiction writers, published *Orthokosta*, a novel about the Civil War he had been working on for over twenty years.[1] The book presents a series of testimonies varying in length from a few lines to twenty pages concerning events that occurred in his natal village between 1943 and 1944: in particular, the burning of the village by leftist guerillas, the imprisoning of people considered collaborators in a nearby monastery named Orthokosta, the execution of some of the prisoners, and the interrogation of others in Valtinos's own house, in the same room where he would sleep when the family returned to the village after the war.

Orthokosta proved to be a lighting rod for controversy. Valtinos was condemned in the leftist press for revisionism and accused of betraying his leftist politics. Others defended him and hailed the book as a brave admission of "red" violence by someone who identifies with the Left. For these readers, the novel also provided an illuminating account of the devastating experience of the Civil War in a local context: a subject just beginning to be broached in historiography of the period. Still others simply found the book tedious because of the litany of personal names invoked in the text and the difficulty of piecing together events from a series of fragmented, and ultimately irreconcilable, narrations. Indeed, the book does take the shape of an archive, turning inquiry into plot and informants into characters while making reading pleasure often feel more like historical labor. For his part, Valtinos told me that he considers *Orthokosta* his best book because it elicited the strongest reaction. As for the controversy, he told me he has enjoyed it.

I first met Valtinos in the summer of 1997. During the following two years, we got together several times to talk about his writing and my research. By then, of course, the stir over *Orthokosta* had subsided.[2] The story of his "transgression," however, formed a natural focal point for our conversations about history, literature, and politics. Like other authors who came of age prior to and during the dictatorship, Valtinos has written about what he calls the "heavy historical load" (1997: 334) of the middle decades of the twentieth century: World War II, the Civil War, migration, and the abrupt modernization of Greece during postwar reconstruction. A novel published in 2000 takes on yet another "chapter" of modern Greek history: the 1922 "Asia Minor Catastrophe" and the Balkan Wars, in which his own father fought for eleven years.[3] While he often claims that he is not interested in history as the story of the past but in the past as source for stories, Valtinos can be seen as yet another reformer of cultural memory.[4] Drawing on childhood memories and a personal archive composed of various materials, including letters, diaries, old newspaper clippings, and testimonies gathered from covillagers, Valtinos has succeeded (whether he wanted to or not) in troubling hegemonic representations of the modern Greek past. Taken as a whole, then, his oeuvre could be said to stage the entire drama of twentieth-century modern Greek history and language, but from the perspective of its bit players and speakers.

In terms of narrative form, Valtinos's writing occupies a special place in modern Greek letters because of its painstaking cultivation of the rhetorics of testimony, or *martyria*.[5] His corpus treats a wide range of culturally and linguistically specific genres of first-person expression from fragments of telephone conversations and letters to the tall tales of old men, soldiers' diaries, Orthodox miracle stories, and courtroom depositions. Over the course of his writing career, Valtinos has turned from monologic narratives centered on a single person's testimony to polyphonic ones presented as fictional archives comprising transcribed oral testimonies or reproduced written documents. For instance, his *Stoiheia yia ti Dekaetia tou 60* (Data from the Decade of the Sixties), which won the Greek state literature prize in 1990, takes the form of a textual miscellany made up of letters written by hopeful migrants to a government immigration bureau, newspaper articles, and letters sent to a Greek radio station's "Dear Abby," while *Orthokosta* appears to be a haphazard selection of documents from the working archive of an oral historian. Although Valtinos remains fascinated with the aesthetics and cultural resonances of the modern Greek language, the narrative strategies he has employed in his later work could be seen as signaling a new concern with the social construction of authoritative discourse: a metahermeneutic focus on the "outsides," not just the "insides," of texts or what Foucault has famously described as "discourse in its own volume, as a *monument*" (1972: 138–9).

The debate that followed *Orthokosta*'s publication was symptomatic of struggles over the representation of 1940s violence and radicalism in the first decade after the "end of communism." In the 1990s, international attention was fixed, of course, on the bold rewriting of history occurring in former communist states where upheavals in cultural memory were graphically symbolized by the tumbling of statues, the shuffling of "dead bodies" of famous citizens in and out of public graves (Verdery 1999), and the opening of archives of totalitarianism to the public for historical research and social healing. Located on the capitalist side of the Iron Curtain, Greek society experienced the events of 1989 in less dramatic but perhaps more unexpected ways than its communist neighbors. The Cold War had begun early in Greece (or, for some, begun there *period*) when in Athens in December 1944 the British joined Greek conservative forces in fighting against members of the left-wing Greek resistance movement, EAM/ELAS[6]: as British forces opened fire against their former allies the superceding of the struggle against fascism with that between communism and anticommunism suddenly became clear (Mazower 1993: 340–54). In the ensuing Civil War, government forces, heavily backed by the United States, defeated the Greek Communist Democratic Army in 1949.

While the history of the antifascist wartime Resistance (or, at least, a very partial and much romanticized account of it) would serve to legitimate democratic and communist regimes across Europe, in Greece this history was forcibly repressed and distorted in state discourse. Communist resistance fighters were condemned as traitors to the nation who had been successfully vanquished in the Civil War or, as it was called in official discourse, the "*symmoritopolemos*" or "*kommounistosymmoritopolemos*" (literally, "bandit war" or "communist bandit war").[7] Meanwhile, during the postwar period, as leftists were imprisoned, exiled, and denied the right to work for the state, notorious war criminals escaped prosecution and in many cases Nazi collaborators assumed positions of power. If World War II, as Shoshana Felman (2002) has argued, was followed by unprecedented attempts to draw "conscious closure to the trauma of war" through high-profile public trials (Nuremberg, Eichmann), by contrast, Greek society would see a blatant travesty of justice in which many more people were convicted for resisting the Germans than for collaborating with them.[8] While as Felman points out the public adjudication of World War II would result in the profound reconceptualization of war crime (e.g., the emergence of the legal concept of "crime against humanity") and of witnessing (e.g., a radical opening to the relevance of private trauma to collective historical narratives), in Greece decades of state censorship and restrictions on open discussion of the war meant that the suffering of this period was relegated to the private sphere and the burden of judging the past ended up being taken up outside the courts (and outside historiography).

Although the war years of the 1940s long proved impossible to assimilate into official historical discourse, within the ranks of the Left memories of this period were, if not always dealt with, firmly "held on" to during years of harassment and more recently of political and cultural ascendancy. Given restrictions on free speech during the postwar period, literature would serve as an important alternative archive of this history, with the first novels about the war being produced immediately after the conflict.[9] Only with the end of the dictatorship in 1974 and more importantly the official recognition of the Resistance by the Panhellenic Socialist Movement (PASOK) party, which came to power in a landslide election victory in 1981, would the ideological blockages to writing the history of this period finally start to loosen.[10] Indeed, the Resistance—whitewashed, "nationalized," and disconnected from the history of the Greek Communist Party—would become essential to legitimizing socialist rule.[11] The fall of the Berlin Wall later paved the way for the incorporation of the Civil War into mainstream historical narratives after a lag of almost half a century.[12] However, the 1989 Government of National Unity, which included parliament members of both the conservative New Democracy (ND) party and the Left coalition party Synaspismos, would be vehemently criticized by many leftists, among them resistance fighters, as a superficial spectacle of "reconciliation" (*symfiliosi*).[13] That government's supreme and stunning act of oblivion, perpetrated in the name of "getting over" the past, would be the August 1989 incineration of leftists' old security files (*fakeloi*) in a surreal ritual staged at a state-owned steel mill.

To the extent that *Orthokosta* disturbed sacrosanct memories of the "National Resistance" in the midst of the Left's identity crisis, the reactions to the book were predictable. Yet, the anger with which Valtinos was "purged" was extreme, and detractors even included leftist intellectuals who usually distance themselves from "hard core" ideologues of the communist past and defend "postmodernism" and other perceived threats to historical truth. Ostensibly, the reason that *Orthokosta* disturbed leftist readers was that it depicted the violence of communist partisans (and implied that ensuing revenge killings committed by rightists were a *reaction* to it) while also suggesting that much of the fighting in the war was not motivated by ideology but by long-standing personal quarrels, chance events, and impulsive actions. As I will consider, however, other novels, including Valtinos's own, have made these points and been embraced by the Left. What seems to have made the book so hard for the novel's implied leftist reader to accept was that he or she was called on to assume the narrative perspective not of a disillusioned communist but of the wounded "enemy."

This difficult, even repugnant, exercise—which most readers tended to forgo, *Orthokosta* being a book that was much talked about and little read—revealed some of the assumptions about the politics of witnessing that have been cultivated in Greek readers through diverse literary and historical projects of recuperating the "voice of the people." Such uses of testimony, as we have seen, first developed around the representation of the "Asia Minor Catastrophe" in the interwar period. By the 1990s, though, the Resistance and Civil War had become privileged subjects for the production of eyewitness memoirs and the application of oral history methodologies.[14] In emphasizing rather than camouflaging the linguistic mediation involved in entextualizing and interpreting testimony, *Orthokosta* could be said to pose some simple but vexing questions of such projects of testimony production: What if persuasive testimony can be fabricated through literary means? What if people on the "other side" are interviewed in the same spirit as those with whom the researcher sympathizes (i.e., with a focus on "common people" not impassioned leaders, decorated fighters, or dogmatists), and this testimony is found to be convincing? How, in other words, does the novel jolt into view the unexamined positivism and redemptive drive informing currently authoritative discourses on this period?

For our purposes, the *Orthokosta* controversy in addition to illuminating contemporary debates over the representation of a particularly contentious subject of modern Greek history exposes yet another margin where historical authority is being negotiated: that between "history" and "literature" as disciplinary practices, powerful institutions of social memory, and adjudicating discourses. In Valtinos, we also have another case of a nonhistorian intruding on the grounds of history to challenge its subject matter and methodologies and being met with the outraged cry: "This is not history"—or rather "This is not *true*." The uproar over the book aimed at putting "fact" and "fiction" back in their places: in other words, in the two distinct epistemological fields indicated by the title of the 1995 conference "Historical Reality and Modern Greek Fiction" at which *Orthokosta* was discussed (and censured) by several of the presenters.[15] Valtinos himself has defended the novel by distinguishing the truth of facts from the persuasiveness of discourse and, by extension, historiography from literature. The novel, however, I argue, opened up ways to think critically about witnessing, historical discourse, and the archive that troubled the reduction of literature (and language) to a supplement of "historical reality" and, more radically, challenged the role of history itself as ultimate authority on the collective traumas of the past.

Fiction's Archive

In *Myth and Archive*, literary critic Roberto Echevarría has considered the persistent recurrence of the symbol of the archive in Latin American fiction. From the unfinished manuscript of Melquíades in Gabriel García Márquez's *One Hundred Years of Solitude* to Borges, the librarian, Latin American fiction has been as haunted by the archive as it has been obsessed with the subjects of myth and history. From its beginnings in the picaresque, he points out, themes of punishment, the law, and state power have figured centrally in the Latin American novel; the archive of fiction, thus, represents a "turning inside out of the Archive in its political manifestation, a turn that unveils the inner workings of the accumulation of power" (1998: 24).

For Echevarría, the novel does not merely depict the relationship between knowledge and power but also potentially intervenes in it. Lacking a set genre or "fixed form of its own," the novel, he argues, "often assumes that of a given kind of document endowed with truth-bearing power by a society at specific points in time" (legal discourse, journalism, ethnography, historiography, etc.). As the consummate "simulacrum of legitimacy," the novel has the potential to expose the fact that the truthfulness of authoritative texts is not immanent to them but bestowed from without by the dominant ideological forces of the day. Further, given that their "conception is itself a story about an escape from authority," novels often have plots that center on themes of power, punishment, and flight from the law.[16] Rather than comparing the novel solely to other literary works or to a "real world" it may purport to describe, Echevarría concludes that the novel might more productively be understood as "part of the discursive totality of a given epoch, occupying a place opposite its ideologically authoritative core" (8).

These insights might be extended to postwar Greek literature, which has similarly been consumed with themes of history, punishment, and political authority. Take, for instance, poet Aris Alexandrou's only novel, the 1974 *To Kivotio* (Mission Box), which is widely considered one of the masterpieces of Greek Civil War fiction. Composed of eighteen letters written by an imprisoned communist partisan, the novel could be read as a parable on the bureaucratic communist archive. These letters form an extended written deposition, initially addressed to a "comrade interrogator" but by the end to no one at all. In them, the narrator recounts the circumstances under which he, along with a squad of forty "volunteers," undertook a top-secret mission, which he was told was so important that it would determine outcome of the war. This mission was to transport a box from city N to city K. When the narrator, the only survivor of what turns out to have been a suicidal mission, arrives in K, he is thrown in jail as soon as the officials realize that he has brought them an *empty* box. The emptiness of the box, in which the narrator contemplates burying himself, parodies the formality of party bureaucracy, showing it to be a form without content: the archive's "secret" was generated simply by enclosing and barring access. As potential crypt, the empty box also unveils the archive's relation to death. Albeit in highly symbolic terms, the novel-*as-archive* could be said to document the impasse of Greek communists at the end of the Civil War. While the imprisonment of the narrator in a communist jail appears to mirror in inversion Alexandrou's own experience of political imprisonment and exile as a communist in various island prison camps, this reversal might in fact speak to his *double* exile as a dissenting communist who had renounced his membership in the party early in war. Ultimately, Alexandrou's novel condemns dogmatism, power, and ideology of any kind, pointing to the "void behind the institution of every law" (Gourgouris 2000: 72). As epitomized by this example, modern Greek historical experience has cultivated a deep distrust of the sovereignty governing the archive, whether fascist, liberal, or communist, while the novel has proved an effective medium to expose the dark underbelly of archival documentation and its relation to bureaucracy, surveillance, interrogation, exclusion, exile, and death.

Mission Box has been interpreted as an allegory for the crisis of realism, the box's emptiness signifying the absence of the sign's reference as well as the dead end of the literature of "militant commitment" (*stratevmeni logotechnia*) (Tsirimokou 1997: 247; Gourgouris 2000: 73). While in many national literatures World War II and particularly the Holocaust brought on the decline of realist forms of representation, by contrast, as literary critic Frangiski Abatzopoulou has pointed out, early postwar Greek fiction was marked by a "remarkable revival of realism" (1998: 86–94). Given that public discourse was long usurped by ideological dogmatism or silence, Greek literary authors were for some time the "only available historians" (Apostolidou 1997: 117), and many viewed their novels as temporary storehouses for forbidden histories and testimonies that could not yet be solicited. Conditioned by a heavy dose of social realist fiction, many Greek readers, as Abatzopoulou notes, became accustomed to treating literature *as history:* a point that will be important when we turn to the reception of *Orthokosta*. As an example, she notes that since serious scholarship on the deportation and genocide of Greek Jews did not begin to be produced until the 1990s, readers often approached Greek literary texts on the Holocaust as *historical* sources (1997: 281).

Contributing to the reality-effect of Greek war literature, many authors have written as eyewitnesses to and participants in the events they describe, continuing the tradition of testimonial fiction about the "Asia Minor Catastrophe" produced in the interwar years by refugee writers (Argyriou 1997: 63–4). This use of literature by authors to testify occurs, according to Felman, when authors feel that in the "court of history" there will not be enough evidence or that the evidence will fail or "cannot become consequential" (2002: 96). Thus, as literary critic Yiannis Papatheodorou has pointed out, Stratis Tsirkas takes on the role of historian in his trilogy *Akyvernites Politeies* (Drifting Cities) (1960–65), as he records a history whose documentation was "pending": namely, that of the April 1944 uprising in the Middle East of Greek armed forces who were agitating for a strong EAM presence in a postwar government of national unity. As he points out, this particularly "annoying" incident was condemned both by the Greek government-in-exile in Cairo and by EAM leadership and thus had been doubly expunged from the social memory of the period. Tsirkas himself would even be expelled from the Greek Communist Party for refusing to recant one of the trilogy's novels that the party felt presented a "distorted" view of these events (2002: 273–7).

Born in 1932 in a village located in the rugged Arcadian mountains of the central eastern Peloponnese, Valtinos, who now lives in Athens (fig. 4.1), was born too late to be part of the heroic, but doomed, generation of young people who fought in the Resistance and became embroiled in the Civil War but also too soon to escape its dislocations and disturbing memories. In contrast to many Greek authors of literary testimony and historical fiction, Valtinos has *not* written as a participant in the historical events to which his texts refer or as a "committed" writer (he has never belonged officially to a leftist political party), but rather as a consummate scribe of other peoples' experiences. The word scribe, though, is perhaps too removed and aloof to describe Valtinos's relation to his subjects. It might be more accurate to say that he was a "child witness" who was compelled by his partial memories and half glimpses of things to *ask* when he grew up.

The memory of the child witness should not be considered simply a secondary, derivative, and incomplete version of that of adult witnesses, as is so often the case in memory work projects in which attention is centered on the "last surviving" eyewitnesses to particular events.[17] Rather, as Marianne Hirsch (1999) has argued in her discussion of the "postmemory" of Holocaust survivors' children, the personal memories of child witnesses are often crowded out by the nightmares of their parents, leading them to engage in forms of tragic identification, projection, and mourning. For Hirsch, this form of "heteropathic identification," in which the subject identifies with

Figure 4.1   Domestic inscriptions. Thanassis Valtinos making Turkish coffee. Photograph by Christina Vazou.

the other's pain (it could have been me) but also disassociates (but it was not me), might be seen less as an "identity position" than as a powerful mode of identification and projection that is available for artistic and political, not just narrowly personal, acts of remembrance.

In situating his narrators as committed, engaged listeners to other people's stories, Valtinos embeds a metahistorical dimension in his fiction, which reflects a self-consciousness about historical re-collection as social, linguistic, and political praxis. In a 1979 short story entitled *Ethismos sti Nikotini* (Nicotine Addiction), the narrator, a thinly veiled version of the author, provides shocking glimpses of a war taking place at the edges of everyday life as he describes his first smoking experiences. The narrator explains how in 1943 when he was eleven years old, he and his friends had gone up into the mountains for a smoke. As his friends tease him for his tearful reaction to his first cigarette, the boys suddenly spot Nazi gunmen who were carrying out a reprisal action against resistance forces, and flee. The narrative breaks off at this point and joins the narrator five years later in the provincial city of Tripolis during the Civil War. While playing hooky from a school poetry reading to go for his second smoke, he and a friend happen to see an army truck full of corpses of left-wing partisans pass through the square. He notes:

> The first opinions had already been heard. In the nighttime attack, the marines had wiped out the small group of "bandits" (*symmoriton*). Another version had it that they had been taken prisoner. Then one of them tried to beat it and they executed them all.
>   The next day we were going to write History [examinations]. I closed myself in my room and tried to study. (35–6)

The quotation marks around "bandits" (*symmorites*) establish the narrator's skeptical distance from this key term of statist discourse. Similarly, the juxtaposition of the story (*istoria*) of this incident with the narrator's schoolwork casts ironic light on the textbook history (*Istoria*) approved and promulgated by the state. Although the phrase "*tha grafame Istoria*" corresponds to the English "sit for history exams," the literal translation of the phrase ("we would write History") is also implied, highlighting the disjunction between history as lived experience (*vioma*) and as authorized account of the past.

Like other reformers of cultural memory, Valtinos has mined these contradictions between personal and public histories, using them as jumping-off points for the informal historical inquiries on which much of his fiction is based. Of the testimonies in *Orthokosta*, for instance, Valtinos told me: "These were stories I had heard as a child. They were parts of a childhood mythology: the memories that bordered those of the neighbors you play with or your first loves. Most of the stories merged with my personal life." Since Valtinos's native Arcadia was the province with the greatest percentage of "first wave" migrants to the United States at the turn of the twentieth century, stories of migration have also provided Valtinos with a stock of personal memories that intrude on and trouble statist narratives of Greek history. Beginning from these hints and fragments of remembered experience, Valtinos often has gone on to seek out "informants" to tell him stories about a particular event or period. As he progressed in the writing of *Orthokosta*, he told me he spent time checking the accuracy of his memories, which for him had as much to do with listening to *how* stories of these events were told as with untangling *what* had happened. To do so, he engaged in what he calls, "a sort of documentation" (*ena eidos katagrafis*) by initiating conversations with his covillagers and sometimes interviewing them with a tape recorder. For his later fiction, Valtinos has consulted newspapers and other written texts and even used "found documents." His 1989 novel *Data from the Decade of the Sixties*, for example, was inspired in part by letters that originally had been sent to a state emigration agency by Greeks aspiring to work in Australia. Writer friends Stratis Tsirkas and Kay Cicellis had "salvaged" them from the trash for him. Since Valtinos was interested in these letters for his fiction and not because they were historical documents, he, in turn, has thrown them out a second time.

Literary critics tend to assign Valtinos's writing a place within genealogies of Greek literature (especially the long-standing tradition of testimonial fiction I referred to in the previous chapter) and relate his novels and short stories to Euro-American literary and cultural trends (German *Dokumentarliteratur*, Theatre of Fact, the Pop Art movement) and the work of specific foreign authors (e.g., John Dos Passos, Georges Perec). By including a discussion of one of Valtinos's novels in this book, by contrast, I follow Echevarría in asking what might be gained by situating the novel within the "discursive totality of a given epoch" and pressing it up against nonfictional forms of writing and historical archives. Testimonial fiction, like oral history, theoretically creates a crisis for archival practice based on positivist approaches to history: the production of new documents based on oral sources exposes supposed lacunae in the available documentary record while by extension demonstrating the social and linguistic construction of "real" (preexisting) docu-ments. I say *theoretically*, though, because in practice as we saw in the previous case study, the expansion of the documentary base can be guided by a strong neoempiri-cist agenda consistent with the dream of archival completion (cf. Trouillot 1995: 49). Valtinos's early use of testimonial fiction, which can be connected to international developments in oral history and "ethnobiography"[18] in the 1960s and 1970s, does reflect this realist ethic of "giving voice" but perhaps not in as clear-cut a manner as first appears to be the case.

Although Valtinos does not employ the archive as metaphor or allegory in the way of Márquez or Alexandrou, he could be said to have perfected the literary simulation of "authentic" and authenticating discourses described by Echevarría and thus to engage the archive concept from that direction. Consider, for instance, his 1964 novella *Synaxari Andrea Kordopati* (The Book of the Days of Andreas Kordopatis), based (as indicated in a prefatory note) on the "real life" of a Greek illegal migrant worker in the United States in the early part of the twentieth century. Literary crit-ics often compare this novel to Stratis Doukas's 1929 *Istoria enos Aichmalotou* (A Prisoner of War's Story), which similarly presents the laconic first-person testi-mony of an oral narrator to a narrator-scribe concerning his picaresque experiences as a fugitive. Both novels select a "common person" and a solitary man to stand as collective subject of modern Greek history. Both also highlight their informants' use of regional dialects and foreign languages (Turkish in Doukas's text and English in Valtinos's) in order to incorporate into the mainland Greek literary imagination sto-ries of Greek worlds outside the boundaries of the Greek state (the historic Greek communities of Asia Minor and the new ones formed through transatlantic migra-tion, respectively). Neither text radically challenges the literary author's right to record the testimony of a subaltern nor undoes the fictive pact by allowing the nar-rator to enter equally into the production of literary discourse and claim partial (or full) authorship over the text.[19]

However, when these works of fiction are compared not to each other but to historical discourses on these events, some important differences emerge. In *Kordopatis*, Valtinos does not document a crisis unfolding around him nor does he write as a witness-turned-scribe. Rather he recovers a story that had been forgotten and was not an open subject of literary and historical re-collection or social critique. As we have seen, literature about the refugee crisis began to be produced immediately following the "Catastrophe"; this experience was incorporated slowly, but smoothly, into Greek public narratives of history, with literature playing a critical role in its assimilation. The availability of this literary narrative, after all, had allowed the Center for Asia Minor Studies to institutionalize the category of factual "Exodus" testimony. Valtinos's novella, by contrast, created a space for an outlaw('s) history and a historical subject—the (return) migrant—at a time when the state was actively negotiating the "export" of a significant portion of its citizens as migrant laborers in foreign countries. As I will discuss in greater detail in the following chapter, migration as transnational phenomenon and "shame" for the nation was long unrecordable (and unrecorded) in national historical narratives. For Valtinos, however, as he explained to me, writing *Kordopatis* was less about documenting an understudied and politically sensitive history than of coping with his own anguish at being "left behind" in the wake of the postwar exodus of Greek migrants to places such as Germany and Australia. Rather than merely recording the forgotten story of U.S. migration, *Kordopatis* could be said to demonstrate how postwar migration repeated and reen-acted the unhealed collective trauma of "first wave" migration.

In his fiction of the late 1970s and 1980s, Valtinos moved away from the realistic portrayal of first-person testimony to the construction of intricate "documentary fictions" (cf. Foley 1986): in other words, plotless, narratorless collocations of fictionally reproduced (or forged) documents (i.e., letters, newspaper excerpts, court transcripts, transcribed testimony). This turn could be said to coincide with a trans-formation of Valtinos's narrators from scribes to "archivists." Rather than depict (or create) coherent subjects around the unity of voice and biography, these documentary fictions draw attention to the way that silences are produced in the volume of dis-course. They begin to explore the possibility of the *impossibility* of testifying and the unavailability of the integrated life-story narrative of the individual speaker. Attuned to the selectivity and artifice involved in framing documents, Valtinos's textualized archives might be seen as postmodern counterparts to the published archives and source books of historicism that I discussed in the case study on local historiography.

Valtinos's first documentary fiction, his 1978 *Tria Ellinika Monoprakta* (Three Greek One-Acts), for instance, is composed of three "files" of documents, each of which represents different social, political, and linguistic positions in the post–Civil War period. The first drama, "Praktika mias Dikis" (The Minutes of a Trial), is the transcript of a 1957 trial of army officers, written in a stuffy and pretentious *katharevousa*, the formal archaizing register of Greek. Laden with the stilted formu-laic phrases typical of what is known as the *xylini glossa* ("wooden language") of official-authoritative discourse, this one-act represents the bankrupt language of the post–Civil War state. The second one-act, "Grammata sti Fylaki" (Letters in Jail), consists of letters written to a political prisoner, primarily by his family who lives in Nikaia, a former refugee quarter, working-class neighborhood, and well-known communist stronghold. The letters are written in an "oral" demotic hastily and awkwardly transcribed in writing and combined with elements of hypercorrected *katharevousa*. A note in tiny print explains that these letters, which were sent to the prisoner from the end of the Civil War into the dictatorship, had been found in 1972 on the floor of a jail bathroom: a blatant sign of their exclusion from history. The third scene, "Nai, Alla Kenwood" (Yes, But Kenwood), consists of an instruction manual for a food processor. This text is written in a new idiom of the postwar period, an insipid mixture of "friendly," but impersonal, advertising language ("your new household companion"), pseudoscientific jargon ("at the same time a characteristic 'click' will be heard"; "planet-like movement"), and English words transliterated into Greek ("mixer or blender"[μίξερ ἡ μπλέντερ]; "chips" [τσιπς]).

In examining these heterogeneous documents, the reader is turned away from seeking meaning in the texts themselves to contemplating their juxtaposition from the perspective of an archivist or historian. The trial transcript in *Three Greek One-Acts*, for instance, depicts the bickering of high-ranking army officers about their conduct in the Civil War. As the trial proceeds, incriminating information about the army starts to leak out, but since the officers are speaking among themselves in the absence of representatives of the communist Democratic Army, a compromise is eventually reached. The president of the court is pleased. "Given that we all love the army," he explains, it is best not to discuss the details of the "bandit war" of 1948 and concludes, "forgetting of the past and peace." Similarly, the pamphlet for the food processor, as symbol of the aggressive modernization and Americanization of postwar Greek society, "pulverizes" historical memory by stripping language and the senses of their cultural body. By contrast, the letters found in the jail appear to be potential sources for a counterhistory capable of disrupting the smooth façade of postwar reconstruction by bringing to light the suffering, harassment, and violence that had been taking place for decades at the edges of everyday Greek life. However, the letters, which report the petty everyday problems of the prisoner's family members as they try to put the past behind them, defy that expectation. We hear about the remarriage of the prisoner's wife and the adoption of his children by the new husband. The prisoner's grandmother even coolly reports that the children told her to send kisses to their "uncle." Placed between the trial transcript and the instruction manual, these letters, in which the absence of the prisoner's voice is so glaring, exemplify the tremendous *forgetting* going on in the decades following the Civil War. At the same time, this novel signals Valtinos's disavowal of a literary project centered on "rescuing" marginalized voices (or, at least, one solely centered on such an aim) in favor of an exploration of the partial inscribing and alienated appearance of subaltern experience within the folds of hegemonic discourse.

Although *Orthokosta* was considered by some critics an aberration that negated Valtinos's oeuvre, from a literary perspective it clearly represents a logical continuation of his artistic vision. The novel returns to and reworks an earlier *topos* of his writing—oral testimony about the Civil War—through the prism of documentary fiction. Thus, the reader is not presented with the transcribed testimony of a single speaker but with excerpts from various interviews that were conducted by an oral historian. While those who denounced *Orthokosta* challenged the novel's depiction of the events of the Civil War, what they missed was the crucial fact that the novel does not so much represent the facts of the past as *discourse* about the facts of the past. As Echevarría has pointed out, discourse that claims to be novelistic is marked by its "mimetic quality, not of a given reality, but of a given discourse that has already 'mirrored' reality" (1998: 8). From this perspective, *Orthokosta* brings attention to the new legitimacy of oral history and anthropological fieldwork in historical scholarship on the Civil War.[20] This recent research, which forms a break with a preceding paradigm of archive-based diplomatic and political history, has been overwhelmingly centered on elucidating the experience of the Left. Although in the 1990s, the Civil War became a boom subject of Greek academic historiography, there has been relatively little research on right-wing organizations, practices, and discourses or on the violence that the Left waged before and contemporaneous with what it suffered (Liakos 2001: 84–5). What is so provocative about *Orthokosta*, then, is the fact that through its use of testimony the novel extends the narrative strategy of "giving voice" to the powerless, what Tzina Politi has described as a "deeply 'leftist' narrative position" (1996: 233), to speakers who are not considered valid historical subjects at this moment in time. In addition to exposing the transference of historians to their subjects (as symbols of radicalism, bravery, martyrdom), this gesture illuminates how much the truth value of testimony depends on factors outside the text.

By rescuing marginalized or discarded experience from collective dustbins or revealing the rhetorical structuring of archival silences, fiction can critique the historical record and make a bid to (re)define cultural memory. Furthermore, in returning persistently to the figure of the archive and mimicking authoritative discourses, the novel can expose the arbitrariness of power and the word of law. At the same time, as the stir over *Orthokosta* made plain, literature is also a part of history, and "fiction's archive" can refer to the archive of criticism that testifies to literature's dramas, scandals, heroes, and traitors as well as to books that have been "events" in their day. In Russia, for instance, Boym speaks of literature as a matter of such great political and national importance that in cityscapes "monuments to the poets rival the monuments to the tsars and party leaders" (1994: 170). In Greece, literature and literary criticism also represent a "national institution" of unusual prominence (Lambropoulos 1988). Deaths and funerals of major poets during times of national crisis have been occasions of mass public mourning: both the funerals of the poet Kostis Palamas in 1943 during the Nazi Occupation and of the Nobel-prize winning poet George Seferis in 1971 during the *junta* were attended by thousands of Greeks, who mourned in their deaths the nation's demise (Van Dyck 1998: 27). In the history of Greek communism, as we have seen, writing has also been viewed as a profound act of resistance. Thus, during the postwar period, the poet Yiannis Ritsos became something of a cult figure among communists both inside and outside Greece (Lambropoulos 1988: 172–7).

While Valtinos was never a figure of such national or international prominence, he nonetheless occupies—or, at least, used to occupy—a place in the pantheon of Greek leftist writers. During the military dictatorship, he had been part of the

"Group of 18" writers who produced *Dekaochto Keimena* (Eighteen Texts), a legendary volume of protest writing published in 1970.[21] His 1963 novella *I Kathodos ton Ennia* (Descent of the Nine) about a defeated band of soldiers of the communist Democratic Army is considered a classic of literature on the Civil War and was even made into a film during the heyday of leftist historical filmmaking in the 1980s.[22] Given this literary trajectory, then, one of the most outstanding dimensions of the *Orthokosta* controversy was that Valtinos was accused not only of historical revisionism but also of rewriting a literary history that he himself had had a hand in producing. As he described it to me, people began to treat him (and many continue to treat him) as an *exomotis*: as someone who has abjured his religion, a renegade. I realized the extent of his censure in leftist intellectual circles (and its contagiousness) when I was told by historian and literary critic friends that my choice to write about "Valtinos" was a mistake and that I had been misled by the author himself.

Literature on Trial and the Court of the Novel

"Mr. Valtinos participated in the *Eighteen Texts* during the years of the *junta*. That was definitely an act of resistance. After twenty years *you* produced *Orthokosta*, a book in which people say they saw other things. In other words we see a—," blurted out a man in the audience at one of Valtinos's book readings I attended in 1998, the abrupt switch from "Mr. Valtinos" to "you" making his charge palpably more personal.[23]

"A shift," interjected another audience member.

"And a big one in fact, an inexplicable one, and I don't know how people have explained it," the first speaker concluded.

Accustomed to these kinds of accusations since the publication of *Orthokosta*, Valtinos responded calmly:

"I think *Orthokosta* surprised people because it is difficult for us to accept that something that we believe, something that we worship—that something might not go right. The fact that the *Elasites* [members of ELAS, the military wing of the EAM resistance movement] killed no one can deny. Yes, but everyone killed. So what was the excuse they used? He speaks about the Security Battalionists. Therefore he vindicates them."

Valtinos's own use of pronouns in this comment ("difficult for *us* to accept" and "he vindicates *them*") underlines, as must be clear by now, that the controversy over *Orthokosta* took place within leftist circles, not between "Right" and "Left." If Valtinos had begun writing "light" or commercial literature, one suspects he would have been accused by his readers of "selling out" like so many who had once been involved in the struggle against the dictatorship; he may even have been praised for "growing up" and growing out of the need to write polemical fictions. The inexplicable (and, for many, inexcusable) thing that Valtinos had done was return to and revise his earlier interpretations of the period and use, or rather abuse, literature's power to pass judgment on the past but this time to pardon the enemy: specifically, former members of the notorious Security Battalions (*Tagmata Asfaleias*), the armed Greek forces that were set up by the Nazis to quell the Resistance.

In one of the angriest responses to the novel, the historian and publisher of the well-known leftist journal *O Politis*, Angelos Elefantis said that he read the book in a state of fury: "You feel the pressure being forced on you to forget what you your-self learned, what you understood, through your own means, about the people, the period and the drama of the Civil War in the Peloponnese" (1994: 63). For Elefantis, Valtinos has substituted amnesia for memory and forgotten the duty of (leftist) literature to serve history. These expectations are spelled out in the same reader's hysterical, apocalyptic vision of a future world in which all "other" historical docu-ments have been destroyed with the exception of *Orthokosta*. He begins his review with the following proposition: "Let's suppose that, after two or three hundred years, all the records (*stoiheia*) of human memory have been destroyed . . . the monuments, statues, photographs, films, inscriptions, books, libraries, archives . . ." If future generations only had *Orthokosta* to go on, how, Elefantis asks, could they make sense of the apparently senseless bloodshed of the barely human "beasts" (*zoulapia*) Valtinos describes? How, in other words, he also seems to be asking, can there be history without meaning, violence without purpose?[24]

In discussions of Valtinos's political about-face, *Orthokosta* was frequently contrasted with his novella *The Descent of the Nine*, published thirty years before. Another enraged reviewer of *Orthokosta* noted, "I have read the book *Descent of the Nine* five times up to now and I have given it as a gift to thirty friends, not to mention that I threw it into the grave of an eighty-year-old woman . . . who also read it many times and sang it like an epic-lyric Maniat funeral lament" (Stavropoulos 1995). In his opinion, *Descent* was nullified and dishonored by *Orthokosta*, which he likened to American journalist Nicholas Gage's 1983 *Eleni*, a best-selling English-language memoir that describes in histrionic tones the prose-cution and murder of the author's mother by a communist tribunal in the final days of the Civil War.[25]

By contrast, *The Descent of the Nine*, which was also set at the end of the war, had shed sympathetic, though not uncritical light, on communist soldiers who would be vilified and turned into de facto noncitizens during the postwar period. Through the first-person narration of one of the guerrillas, this novella describes the movements of a pitiful band of nine soldiers of the Democratic Army in the parched mountains of the Peloponnese as they try to reach the sea and find a way out of their fate and out of history. When the group finally reaches the coast, forces of the National Army and armed villagers open fire on them. Their struggle turned out to be in vain; as one char-acter remarks, "So much blood. And then to have nowhere to go" (61). At one point, the eighteen-year-old narrator, the only one of the nine soldiers to survive, muses on his lost youth: "It was the hour when the fairies awake, they were the noontime sounds of lost summers" (65). Aside from having stripped them of life's everyday pleasures and of life itself, their struggle has not been without its ethical price. During the course of the grueling and undirected march, one of the guerillas murders a civil-ian in order to steal his food, only to find that the man had had nothing, just "wet bread, half a tomato with the marks of his teeth in it and some cheese crumbs" (16). The murder he commits is savage and brutal, but the characters themselves are vanquished and pathetic. The book ends with the survivor's capture and the open question of his—and the Left's—fate in the years to come.

This portrayal of the communists as vulnerable and tragically defeated but with a good deal of blood on their hands refuses the moral reductionism of either communist or statist discourses during the Cold War period. As a *literary* strategy, however, this even-handedness is a commonplace of memorable Greek literature on the war as well as of war literature in general. Taking for granted an overarching condemnation of the right-wing establishment, much post–Civil War literature written by leftists expounds a self-critique, dwelling on "guilt for atrocities perpetrated in the name of a no-longer sustainable ideology" and mourning "ideals not betrayed but self-defeated" (Kantzia 2003: 119). Like *Descent*, Alexandrou's *Mission Box*—that "impersonal anti-epic of the Greek left"—also presents an astringent counterpoint to the strident and lofty rhetoric of the communist leadership. The novel's soldier-narrator is hardly a paragon of leftist virtue: he is cynical, self-centered, amoral, dishonest, and friendless (Tsirimokou 1997: 246). Just as memoirs of former *andartes* published in the 1980s exposed conflicts within EAM/ELAS and generated criticism of the communist party's actions during the war (Mazower 1995: 289), novels of the same period, such as Chronis Missios's 1985 *Kala, Esi Skotothikes Noris* (Well, You Were Killed Early) and Alki Zeï's 1987 *Arravoniastikia tou Achillea* (Achilles's Fiancée), which document the harsh personal toll of war through bitter stories of jail and exile, similarly deflated a lingering romance of the Left's noble struggle.

In a 1964 introduction to his first novel, *The Path to the Spider's Nest* (originally published in 1947), Italo Calvino explains that he had wanted to "launch an attack both against the detractors of the Resistance and against the high-priests of a hagiographic Resistance that was all sweetness and light" (15). In retrospect, he judges his aim—and his solution (writing about socially marginal people lacking class consciousness)—somewhat trite: "This was a new concept for me at the time, and I regarded it as a monumental discovery. I did not realize then that it had been and would continue to be the easiest material for fiction" (17). To a certain extent, then, Valtinos's detractors were correct. *Orthokosta* signals its author's refusal to reproduce a predictable genre of self-critical literature from within the safe (at this moment in time) province of leftist experience, if not its ultimate intent: the humanistic condemnation of warfare. For an author with Valtinos's past to write a novel focused on rightists and collaborationists *did* represent an unexpected move into an uncharted literary territory. Readers' frustration that *Orthokosta* departs from his earlier fiction—or, as one analyst laments, that Valtinos's critique of the Left did not come from the perspective of a disillusioned, but politically "engaged," author who, like Tsirkas (writing in the 1960s), continued to maintain "faith in the socialist vision as the only 'true' one" (Haralambidou 1997: 270)—ends up seeming like nothing more than an expression of sadness about the changing of the times and the fact that certain books cannot be written twice.

Orthokosta begins from the premise that in 1994—after the fall of the Berlin Wall as well as after over a decade of almost uninterrupted socialist rule—the Resistance and Civil War must be approached in a different way than they were in the years prior to and immediately following the fall of the dictatorship. Valtinos actually finished writing *Orthokosta* in the early 1980s. Although he is notorious for keeping manuscripts in his drawer for five or ten years until, as he describes it, his "wines have aged" (1994b), he denies that he deliberately waited to publish the book until after

1989. Nonetheless, he admits that he could not have written the book twenty or thirty years ago. In an interview, he explained:

> I was not sure that I had gotten beyond the reaction that comes in the heat of the moment. In emotional turmoil, you do not write literature, you write autobiography, you explode and get things out of your system, but you do not make art. The thirty-year period for me was more than enough to weigh things, for them to become clear, for there to stop being any, even sentimental, sympathy for one or the other side. (1994c: 28)

In the intervening decades, Valtinos suggests, the story that *needs* to be told about the Civil War has changed. In part, he makes this point by setting the action of *Orthokosta* not at the end of the Civil War as in *The Descent of the Nine*, but toward the end of the Nazi Occupation in 1943–44, which in conventional historical periodizations predates the beginning of the Civil War.[26] EAM then was at the peak of its strength and controlled large areas of the country, the so-called Free Greece, which in some areas constituted a state within the state. As Mark Mazower notes, although the new "people's democracy" undeniably introduced many radical social reforms and encouraged mass participation in politics for the first time in Greek history, the "new, wartime morality had its dark side too" and could be the cover for coercive and retributive practices (286). In *Orthokosta*, Valtinos has chosen to focus on a murky transitional period following mopping-up operations carried out by Nazi occupation forces and their Greek collaborators in preparation for German withdrawal. At this time, ELAS forces took revenge on the collaborationists and others considered to have sympathized with them.

That Valtinos himself has become sensitive to the mutability of the "past" not only as a political and historiographical problem but also as a literary one is evident in the different way in which the testimonies in *The Descent of the Nine* and *Orthokosta* are framed. While the narrator in *Descent* presents an inner monologue that unfolds contemporaneously with the events he describes, *Orthokosta* is composed of multiple responses, ranging from long statements to single words, given to questions posed by an "oral historian" figure whose precise objectives are never explained. These textual extracts possess neither clear beginnings nor ends while the disordering of chronology within and among the testimonies draws attention to only one firm date: that of re-collection itself.

Parenthetical comments throughout the text fix the moment at which the testimonies were taken: as the early 1980s when the PASOK government officially recognized the Resistance and awarded state pensions to those who had participated in the struggle against fascism. At this time, memories of the war years were brought back powerfully into people's thoughts, and the overturning of decades of stigma and censorship led to the outpouring of memoirs by former *andartes*. The "informants" in *Orthokosta*, thus, are not depicted as speaking either at any time or all the time but as having been prompted by historical circumstances to speak at *this* particular moment. Discussing the murder of a cousin who had attempted to form an independent resistance group, one narrator, for example, notes: "Until recently I did not know the circumstance under which he was killed. This year someone published a book. One of those self-published books (*idiois analomasin*). Stamos Triandafyllis. He presents himself as a captain" (175). Memories of harassment by communist soldiers are stirred by indignation at some of the people who stepped forward to file for resistance pensions. One testimony begins with this comment, cited provocatively on the back cover of the novel: "Vasilimi was killed by one of his brothers. One of his brothers and Mavroyiannis. Mihalis Mavroyiannis who now gets a pension for the resistance" (171). Another chapter contains the following exchange between the oral historian-narrator and the son of an old woman who was murdered by the partisans:

—The so-called recognition (*anagnorisi*). That I can't digest
—Forget the recognition. Can you tell me about the old woman? (104).

In refusing the easy reversal of "good" and "evil" that followed the recognition of the Resistance and on which PASOK so successfully capitalized, *Orthokosta* does not aim to tarnish the (recently redeemed) honor of the communists as the novel's detractors charge, but to refute a historicist philosophy of history focused on victory rather than suffering. The novel, in other words, does not highlight communist aggression in order to establish a new pantheon of heroes (i.e., the Security Battalionists). There are *no* heroes in *Orthokosta*, a book that sets out to abolish the idea of victory as a way of thinking about the outcome of war.

In rejecting, by extension, the fundamental assumption that the Civil War was fought by two clearly delineated "sides," Valtinos has been accused by Elefantis and others of having forgotten the "stakes" (*diakivevmata*) of the time and the different "visions, ambitions, interests, views, parties, camps, ideologies." In a photocopy of Elefantis's review, which Valtinos gave me along with a packet of other critiques of *Orthokosta*, I noticed he had double-underlined the phrase: "two different stakes clashed." In an interview in a national newspaper, Valtinos indirectly responded to this charge:

Interviewer: Do you think that the danger of writing off the battles of the "defeated" side of the Left—or also, something even more painful, of their not being impressed at all on the consciousness of the younger generations—is nonexistent? And if it is not, shouldn't these reactions be considered logical?

Valtinos: Understandable maybe. Logical, in no case. I believe that there wasn't a losing side. With quotation marks or without. Nor a winning side, of course. That which really existed was a defeated people as a whole. . . . As far as the desire for forgetting. I am categorically against it. Peoples should not forget. With the necessary clarification that there is a difference between memory and obsessive ideas (*emmones idees*, idées fixes). The trivialization of memory, in other words. (1994b)

Removing the quotation marks around "defeated" has two profound implications. For one, this gesture dispels the aura that continues to surround the Greek communist past, exposing the alibi that wartime defeat and postwar martyrdom gives to the production of heroic narratives of war to be "impressed" on the younger generations. Second, and most important, the removal of the quotation marks implies a significant expansion of the category of people who count as defeated in this war.

For some readers, in depicting the Civil War as suffering-for-all, *Orthokosta* has gone too far in dismantling the polarities of the Cold War and relinquishing the duty of literature to judge the past. Rather than an engagement with history, Valtinos's writing, in this view, represents quite the opposite: a retreat into allegory. One literary critic friend told me:

> My problem with Valtinos is that I think all his writing is an exit from history. He does not search for the causes, he just concludes in the ancient sentiment of tragedy and in stereotypes: that the leaders were bad and the rest of us innocent. I don't agree with what the Left said about *Orthokosta*, but I don't think that what Valtinos does is history. To tell me that there were some people in charge and the others were victims is to tell me nothing.

Despite its disparaging tone, if Valtinos had heard my friend's comment, he might not have entirely objected to it, with the exception of his assumption that Valtinos *believed* himself to be writing history (because history, it is implied, always has the last word in addressing the "truth" of the past). If the "victors" (or some significant portion of them) turn out also to be victims, the Civil War at last might be seen as a collective trauma that Greek society still has not addressed. In denying profound motive and meaning to violence, *Orthokosta* challenges political agendas that justify the loss of human life in their name. Elefantis, in appending a "true" document to his review (an extract from the memoirs of an ELAS captain describing a 1944 battle against the Security Battalions) demonstrates that he does not deny the existence of "red" violence but *legitimates* it as radical and revolutionary (cf. Raftopoulos 1994b).

Orthokosta's anonymous chorus of testimony, with its strong intertextual associations to the testimonies of Asia Minor refugees, by contrast, guides the reader to *mourn* the war rather than view it as an ideological touchstone or repressed horror to be either transcended through glorification of the Resistance and the communist struggle during the Civil War or circumvented through the rhetoric of "reconciliation." The testimonial format of the novel, thus, could be said to create a court in which the wounded, in a much broader definition than commonly has been accepted, are called forth to tell their stories at a public trial that never happened. This court-of-fiction, though, does not bring the criminal to the stand and pass down a verdict but asks victims to narrativize their pain and transform themselves from "mute bearers of a traumatizing destiny . . . [to] speaking subjects of a history" (Felman 2002: 126).

Notwithstanding the novelty of Valtinos's gesture in the context of Civil War memory politics, I believe that his book *can* be critiqued for its portrayal of a "suffering people"—not for failing to convict the guilty but for refusing to *historicize* the violence it describes and instead, as my friend suggested, turning history into "ancient tragedy." The setting of the novel in a communist prison camp exemplifies the author's tendency to distill "timeless" truths of human behavior from historical particularities. The choice of this setting is clearly meant to be ironic on several levels. For one, given that the Greek literary bibliography on leftist imprisonment and exile is lengthy (cf. Argyriou 2000 on Makronisos), *Orthokosta* blatantly disrupts an established literary *topos* by describing the imprisonment of *rightists*. Second, even though the communists might have wanted to tout their break with religion, the location of a prison camp in a holy place undermines their claims to be introducing a new system of a values along with a new political order. There are other signs in the novel, however, that the Orthokosta monastery is the most *natural* place for "ene-mies" to be rounded up and tortured. A "document" in italicized print following the novel's corpus of testimonies explains that the monastery of Orthokosta was built during the time of the Iconoclast debate, an earlier moment of ideologically moti-vated conflict. This "document," which appears to be a page from a descriptive his-tory or encyclopedia, refers back to and discredits another "document" preceding the testimonies: an extract from an eighteenth-century text, written by a bishop Isakkios and extolling the beauties of the monastery and its surroundings. In the closing doc-ument, though, Isakkios is accused of having been a liar who was imprisoned in the monastery for his "erroneous beliefs" (*kakodoxia*) and simony (cf. Politi 1996: 231; Calotychos 2000: 160–1). In short, the past repeats itself: those of "false" belief are persecuted by the "orthodox," and history is always both whitewashed and contested.

This metaphorization of violence, punishment, and ideology and their consignation to a sphere of recurring human behavior is further underscored by the novel's allu-sions to ancient Greek tragedy and the Bible (the novel's epigraph, "break them to pieces like a potter's vessel," is from *Psalms*). Like the labeling of Asia Minor refugee testimonies "Exodus," this use of allegory, in effect, treats the Civil War as a mere *repetition* of a human history of suffering and strife, which, it is implied, can be tran-scended and even redeemed.[27] In the novel, the narrativizing of traumatic experience represents a means to *rehumanize* the victims of this conflict by restoring them to language—and specifically to the *Greek* language in all its cultural and historical depth. (Valtinos even makes the rhetoric of ideology—*dilosi, Koukoue, metanooundes, organosi, vammenos, andartiko*—take on poetic color.) In doing so, however, the novel seems to provide an antidote to, rather than deeply penetrate the logic of, historically specific forms of violence. The novel does not lead the reader to dwell on the fact that World War II saw the emergence and dissemination of new bureaucratic modes of managing prisoners, exercising violence, and effecting serial death. In cel-ebrating language, *Orthokosta* also does not broach the subject of the annihilation, flattening, and distortion of language during this period, nor ironically the historic-ity of testimony itself as a response to the trauma of the war. Thus, even though the experiences described in the novel touch on a new political culture of violence, a new way of waging war, a new politics of living and dying, and a new language of history, its intertextual threads lead the reader away from the historical particularity of these transformations.

Returning to the controversy, one suspects that if *Orthokosta* had included "both sides" of the story or expressed the ambivalence of the Left through the voice of an embittered former partisan, the book might have been more acceptable to some of its critics. Juxtaposing "two sides," however, not only would be to acknowl-edge that the war should continue to be understood in terms of the ideological polarities that defined the Cold War but also confirm a logic of identification by which testimony, ideology, and the (individual) witness are understood as innately correlated. In a vicious circle, ideological essentialism (by definition) precludes the need to read ("He speaks about the Security Battalionists. Therefore he vindicates them"), thus also precluding an appreciation of the book's *critique* of ideological essentialism.

Voicing, Ideology, Responsibility

In his book-length study of Dostoevsky's poetics, Bakhtin observed that most critics of Dostoevsky's novels tended to focus on the ideological dimensions of his work and overlook its linguistic form: "The topical acuteness of those problems has overshadowed the deeper and more permanent structural elements in his mode of artistic visualization" (1984: 3–4). Similarly, the controversy over *Orthokosta* centered on the book's content, not its poetics. Or, to be more precise, even though the form of the novel was commented on frequently (and often found as irksome as its subject matter), the relationship between them was not addressed, or at least not systematically.

That the book was difficult to read simply made it bad and boring and a kind of propaganda, but reading as *experience* was not reflected upon. For leftist readers, how did it feel to be forced to listen to the intimate, confiding voice of the enemy resounding in their heads? What was it like to hear voice upon voice, and voice *inside* voice, without knowing who to trust or hold responsible? In the debate on *Orthokosta*, these questions were not posed as theoretical ones bearing on the nature of historical discourse and the ethical dimensions of witnessing. Instead, the multiplicity of voices in the text was understood primarily as the *repetition* of a single voice that should not have been allowed to speak in the first place: a barrage of banal "complaints" from the collaborators.[28] In an alternative reading, however, the novel's polyphony might be understood as a commentary on historical discourse itself and the rhetorical construction of authority through an unavoidable process of referring to others' speech (all the "he-said-she-saids"). Viewing testimony as emerging at the nexus of a chain of citations rather than as the closed account of an individual speaker centers attention less on testimony as narrative than on testifying as "project of address" (Felman and Laub 1992: 38), illuminating issues of responsibility, responsiveness, listening, and trust involved in historical re-collection.

The central question at stake in *Orthokosta* and around which the debate truly revolved, then, is whether the testimonies presented are monologic or dialogic: in other words, if the book's apparent polyphony is superficial or structural. For those who took offense at the book, *Orthokosta* is without doubt pure monologue, the blatantly one-sided and single-voiced account of events from the standpoint of the Right. Indeed, the most consistent charge leveled against the novel was that even though *Orthokosta* presents multiple testimonies broken into many chapters, these narratives were at root "all the same." As one critic complained:

> The characters in *Orthokosta* are multiple copies of one prototype. They are the same; only their names and their sexes change. They are "good" from divine inspiration (*epifoitisi*), they are "human" from their "birth." Their opponents are "bad" and "inhuman" for the same reasons. (Karali 1994)

Another critic argues that the monologism of the text reproduces the intolerance that characterized the war itself:

> The ideological construct put forth by Valtinos's *Orthokosta* is the *bigotry of the Civil War*, one-sidedly presented. With a single-minded narration, behind a language as heavy as a catapult blow, regardless of the deposition of multiple narrators. (Dallas 1997: 95)

The multiplicity of voices, then, is a façade. Behind them, it is implied, is *one* voice: that of the reactionary author himself who, like a puppet master, pulls the strings of the "speaker-marionettes" (Stavropoulos 1995). As a result, the "paratactic juxtaposition of narrative voices" in *Orthokosta* has been viewed by some critics as more of an "apposition" (*sym-parathesi*) than an "opposition (*anti-parathesi*) of voices and ways of seeing the world"(Haralambidou 1997: 269). For these readers, *Orthokosta*, by definition, provides only "half" the picture of the war and, thus, "butchers" a full interpretation: "In *Orthokosta*, the civil war is anguish only for one side. In that way, however, the authority of the book is automatically mutilated (*akrotiriazetai*)" (Kangelari 1994).

In not presenting "both sides," however, *Orthokosta* refuses the logic by which the *anti-parathesi* of "viewpoints," like the juxtaposition of historical "periods," composes a complete and continuous history of the nation. Or to be more precise, through this gesture the novel rejects such a total(izing) history as the product of a spurious philosophy of history. In not including all voices, then, the novel demands that the reader unpack the essentialized voice of the Right. Indeed, a close reading of *Orthokosta* reveals that this "single-minded narration" is in fact teeming with different voices. For one, each speaker possesses a unique narrative identity: some informants respond laconically to the questions of the oral historian while others speak at length. Some use political terminology and refer to particular politicians and major historical events; others discuss domestic life and agricultural work in local dialect, drawing on the language of folk songs and the Bible. The speakers also occupy a wider spectrum of political and ideological positions than critics typically appreciate, including uniformed Battalionists, anticommunists, rightists, noncombatants, and people who refused to be conscripted into EAM. Each stretch of testimony is also internally dialogic. Moments of conflict that proved to be turning points in characters' political decision making are marked by a proliferation of reported speech while narrators inevitably construct their accounts of events by referring extensively to hearsay and rumor.

Quoting the maximally unresolved discourse of others serves several purposes for speakers in the novel (and for "Valtinos" as speaker *of* the novel). Reflecting cultural conceptions of credibility and authenticity related to historical, journalistic, and judicial discourses, testimony is most authoritative when presented verbatim as direct rather than indirect discourse. There is a tremendous difference between the impact and persuasiveness of the statement "I heard Petros say: 'I burned your house'" and "Petros told me he burned my house." In reporting the speech of others as well as of a past self, speakers in the novel also strategically disassociate themselves from and make ambiguous their commitment to the veracity of what is being said: speaking with others' words can be a way of both saying something and not saying it, a way of borrowing authority from others or placing blame elsewhere. Historical testimony, *Orthokosta* suggests, is particularly rife with this kind of secondhand knowledge. Aphrodite, for instance, notes: "Tasia told me the year before last: Haroulis burned your house" (126). The truth of the past is sometimes revealed only after having passed through an extended chain of reported speech. Eleni Mavrou explains that she found out about the circumstances of her cousin Markos Ioannitzis's death many years later from a guest at a dinner party: "He tells me I know what my aunt told me. Markos Ioannitzis left our house and asked her for a towel and a knife. . . . I was a small child but I know where they buried him" (334). Through the medium of reported speech, we also sometimes hear the Left's direct confession of violence: "He told us I am Alimonos. And he turns to me, he tells me: I killed your compatriot Ioannitzis. Over there he tells me. And he showed me a mountain slope. A beautiful slope" (19). Similarly, when speakers damn the actions of the communist guerillas, they often prefer to do so using the words of others. Grigoriou, for instance, remembers the reaction of the deceased Penelope Kaloutsi to her capture by the partisans:

> When they got her she said to him, hey you, man, is it me you came to get, me you came to get, you know if you scrape your teeth, it's my bread that'll come out. (186)

The attribution of this charge ("you know if you scrape your teeth, it's my bread that'll come out") to a person who is dead endows it with both an authoritative finality and a profound dubiousness. As the speakers take the truth to their graves, we must rely on what other listeners, as witnesses to speech, report: in other words, we must depend on the inevitable links of *trust* underlying historical knowledge as a discourse on the dead, a matter that the historical discipline would prefer to cloak in the mystique of the archival sciences. To the extent that *Orthokosta* is replete with voices of the dead, the novel, furthermore, reminds us that discursive address is always, as Derrida has argued, "spectral": making an utterance inevitably entails a "conjuring" of that which is not there at the time of "incantation" (1994: 41). In drawing attention to a continual deferral of responsibility, quoted discourse reveals the emptiness of the signifier and the status of writing as an adjunct "in-the-place-of" (Derrida 1976). A theory of citationality, thus, fundamentally de-centers the fact/ fiction divide as the central problematic in a discussion of historical fiction, directing us to consider how discourses reproduce other discourses rather than "reality."

Ironically, reading testimony as a chain of citations undermines Valtinos's own assertions that in writing fiction, he is not also testifying "as a villager," quoting the hearsay and rumor of others to speak about the war without having to take responsibility for saying "I." In an article on anthropological approaches to literature, Thomas Lyons (2001) has drawn attention to the "narrative ambiguity," or the "ambiguity of 'who is the speaker'," implied in a Bakhtinian theory of voicing. Mitigating authorial intention, a theory of voicing approaches literature not as the imaginative product of a particular intellect but as a socially embedded utterance that registers and amplifies contradictions and struggles in consciousnesses; from this perspective, the sacrosanct border between "art" and "life" is a product of literary criticism not a principle of discourse. Giving the example of Salman Rushdie's *The Satanic Verses* and Rushdie's defense of his text as fiction not history, Lyons suggests that drawing distinctions between the "narrator in the fiction" and the "author in the world" cannot "quarantine" the author from discourse framed as fictional. Thus, Rushdie's outraged Muslim readers were not entirely incorrect in their reasons for condemning the book since "even discourse that is 'fictional' and 'hallucinated' can be political and make historical claims" (196). That the "real" author cannot stand outside his fictional text, of course, is an important point since it puts an ethical limit on representations of the past in literature or other cultural productions, which, while not denying the constructedness of the historical fact and the multiplicity of interpretations, does not let anything go. The implication of "Valtinos" and his views on the war in the text of *Orthokosta*, however, does not return us to the crude realism of some of his critics or turn him into an all-knowing puppeteer ventriloquizing his subjects' voices. If anything, the constant embedding of citation within citation and the dispersion of narration into multiple contradictory voices *downplay* the significance of the author and his or her masterful intentions, drawing attention to the status of literature as a social text haunted by the discourses and consciousnesses of others.

Even though all the speakers in *Orthokosta* were located on the Right (by choice or default) at some point during the war years, it would be a mistake to assume as many readers do, that the voice of the Left is absent—or *could be* absent—from the text. It perhaps bears repeating that the Bakthinian concept of dialogism is not based on a notion of interactional "dialogue" between two or more people. For Bakhtin, drama is not an inherently dialogic genre simply because it assigns clearly demarcated roles to different speaker-actors; on the other hand, the individual utterance can be highly dialogic. As Bakhtin writes of Dostoevsky's depiction of consciousness in the novel:

> In Dostoevsky, consciousness never gravitates toward itself but is always found in intense relationship with another consciousness. Every experience, every thought of a character is internally dialogic, adorned with polemic, filled with struggle, or is on the contrary open to inspiration from outside itself—but it is not in any case concentrated simply on its own object; it is accompanied by a continual sideways glance at another person. (1984: 32)

This understanding of consciousness as developing "alongside" other consciousnesses through these constant "sideways glances" counters a conception of consciousness as consistent and internally finalized: the very premise of ideological orthodoxies. In speaking this novel, "Valtinos" as "leftist writer" exposes what is programmatically repressed and refused in ideologically correct discourse: namely, the degree to which his (and others') consciousness is pierced by the voices of traumatized others: in Valtinos's case, those of his right-wing covillagers whom he may have tried for many years *not to hear*.

If *Orthokosta* had included speakers from "the other side" (in this instance, communists), the novel would have succumbed to a logic of dialogue that downplays the internal struggle and contestation within political consciousness as well as ignored those borderlines at which the voice of the Other breaks through. In *Orthokosta*, one way that the voice of the Left enters the text is as provocation: the speakers often reconstruct their discourse as remembered responses to the harassing voices of guerillas, thus casting their own actions and statements as reactions to others' aggression. Georgia, for instance, recalls: "He came, he threatened me, We are going to cut your hair. Why cut my hair, better to give me a bullet. And then Toyias tells me: No, you are a hostage, we are holding you for your brothers. We are going to cut the hair of the others" (17). Remembering the miserable rations at the camp, the same speaker reports the sarcastic voice of partisan: "Why don't you take your bread, the General asked me. Do you think you will upset us if you don't eat? I didn't answer him" (17).

Sometimes, though, the voice of the Left that intrudes on speaker's testimony is not villainous but brave, persuasive, and ethical. While speakers typically cite the discourse of others in order to support their assertions or dramatize their accounts, in doing so they take the risk that the quoted speech, especially if it retains the form of direct discourse, can undermine their narrating voice. Since, as Vološinov has argued, the direction in which the dynamism between reporting and reported speech moves varies, reported speech can be "more forceful and more active than the authorial context framing it" (1929: 120–1). At the end of one testimony, for instance, a speaker mentions how after having lived many years in the United States as an immigrant, he returned to Greece and found himself face to face with a former *andartis* whom he had brutally beaten in revenge for his brother's murder. An old man by then, the *andartis* holds out his hand for the speaker to help him climb into the bus but the speaker pretends not to see him. As soon as the *andartis* boards, though, he recognizes his former torturer and greets him warmly: "Hi there, Nikolaos, my man, he greeted me. Hi Anestis, I said. And I thought, why since we are going to die, why do we do those things. It was the revenge" (286). In this case, the words of the former *andartis*, and particularly his use of the particle "*re*" (man, hey, you) with its connotations of friendly intimacy, insinuate themselves into the speaker's rigid, unforgiving discourse to expose his blind, unhealed anger while at the same time marking a flickering moment of recognition and listening.

Although the testimonies in *Orthokosta* are all told to the "oral historian," the speakers' fellow villager, on a deeper dialogical plane they can be seen as responses to the accusing *logos* of the Left and the charge of Nazi collaboration or nonparticipation in EAM. In light of the 1980s recognition of the Resistance and the triumphant restitution of the Left's role in Greek history, the questions—Why didn't you fight the Nazis? Why did you betray your country?—resound, implicitly or explicitly, throughout the testimonies. One character, for example, reports this interchange with an *andartis*: "Are you going to go and become a partisan or not? I told him I can't go. I am not going to go" (296). In other testimony, Angelinaras remembers the comments of his uncle, an *andartis*, when he found out that his nephew had joined the Security Battalions: "He started as soon as he saw me. To curse me, naturally. What business do you have with those bums and so on and so forth."

One becomes a traitor, of course, when someone calls you one. Iraklis Politis describes his November 1943 capture by the partisans thus:

> In Meligou they tied me up. My feet—my knees, my ankles. And my hands. *Kapetan* Pavlos Bouzianis came, he gives me one with a rifle butt. I fall down, half my teeth fell out. I said to him why do you hit me? He says to me traitor cuckold. What did I betray? I asked him. I drove out the Italians, I fought them. You're a traitor. Tell us the officers who were with you. I say I don't know any officer, I don't remember. (308–9)

In the final analysis, this condemnation—"you are a traitor"—can be seen as the single statement to which all the testimonies in *Orthokosta* are addressed. The salience of such scenes of interrogation in witnesses' testimonies also makes clear what was underestimated in the testimony taking discussed in the previous chapter: namely, the degree to which the ritual of historical inquiry reinvokes and repeats previous, often harrowing, moments of interrogation in which speakers were subjected to an authoritative discourse demanding an answer, the names, the truth.

Contrary to what was implied by *Orthokosta*'s reviewers, the speakers who had been in the Security Battalions hardly present themselves as proud of this fact. Some characters avoid admitting that they were involved: To the question "You were in the Battalions then?" one speaker responds, "That's when the Battalions were formed" (106). Others do not hide their lack of political commitments. When Christina Mavrou, who earlier had participated in the theatrical productions of the communists, finds herself stopped by a Security Battalionist and taken in for interrogation by the Nazis, she admits that she would not hesitate to change sides again (and again): "He asked me you played theater for the *andartes*. I say I played. What could I do. And if you told me to play I would play" (93). This lack of conviction also extends to those who were more centrally involved in the events of the period. Consider, for instance, the testimonies of Kostas Dranias, a reserve army officer and veteran of the war in Albania who, unlike most of the rest of the speakers, held an official post in the Security Battalions. While other characters' testimonies tend to be narrowly focused on events that happened to their families, Dranias surveys the broader political landscape. Without any particular prompting from the "oral historian," he begins apologizing for his participation in the battalions. In his first testimony, he notes:

> How I found myself there is another story. In any case I found myself in deep water. The Battalions were not formed only in Tripolis. They were set up in all the cities of the Peloponnese. It was a situation of need. There were no Greeks who liked the Germans. Who wanted to collaborate with them. That was when the Battalions were formed in the Peloponnese. In the spring of '44. When it was clear that the Germans were losing the war. When it was also clear how much danger everyone would be in who was at the mercy of ELAS, after the collapse of the Germans. (23–4)

In this passage, Dranias, like many other characters in *Orthokosta*, describes joining the battalions as a last resort rather than a positive choice ("It was a situation of need. There were no Greeks who liked the Germans"). He explains that an earlier effort to form an independent, anticommunist resistance group had been thwarted: members of ELAS prevented them from collecting aid from the British as well as from capturing arms abandoned by retreating Italians. Following a failed attempt to flee to the Middle East where the Greek government-in-exile was based, Dranias explains that he returned to his village and, after refusing to join ELAS, signed up with the battalions: "The danger from ELAS and EAM was imminent. They would have knocked us all off" (37). Admittedly, it is precisely matter-of-fact comments of this kind in their guise as alibis (i.e., we could not do otherwise but to join the battalions) that get under the skin of many leftist readers. Yet, Dranias's statements probably should not be taken at face value as an assertion of "what really happened" (as far as "Valtinos" knows and believes), but be viewed as a particular *account* of what happened. As I will suggest below, triangulation with other testimonies, in fact, shows Dranias, whose testimony sounds so convincing and forthright, to have covered up some of the activities of the Security Battalions and his own involvement in them. As a result, we must read with some skepticism his claims to aloofness as well as its broader implications (i.e., Greeks "by nature" are not capable of fascist behavior).

Speakers who had been in the battalions mostly describe their actions in exactly the same terms that leftists typically use to describe them: opportunistic, cowardly, and knowingly complicit. Consider Dranias's brother Yiannis, who also claims to have ended up in the battalions less out of choice than desperation. Yiannis tells the "oral historian" that he had been interned at the Orthokosta camp in 1944 not because he *was* a collaborator but because he was *not* a communist. When Germans moved into the area during their clean-up operations, the guerillas headed the prisoners into the mountains on a forced march; they abandoned them when they realized the Nazis were approaching. While the rest of the prisoners surrendered themselves to the Germans, Yiannis beat a different path, along with a few others, and eventually returned to his village, hoping that the communists would look with favor on the fact that he had not surrendered to the Nazis. Indeed this was the case, and the next day against his will he was forcibly conscripted as "head of press and propaganda" and sent on assignment. At the first opportunity, he fled and joined the battalions ("there wasn't another solution," 148). Later, though, after he finds out that the Greek government-in-exile disowned the Security Battalions and that their leader, Papadongonas, had greeted Hitler, he claims to have been shocked. Similarly, he describes his horror the first time he saw the Germans make a Greek platoon execute Greek prisoners:

> They took the prisoners, they stood them against the wall. The girl with her patent leather shoes, with her white socks, like she was going to communion. We froze. The Germans had made a Greek platoon accompany the condemned, as an execution squad. . . . This made a tremendous impression on us. The Germans to kill, to do that job. But not we Greeks. (77)

Despite his disgust and dismay at the situation, Yiannis does not attempt to leave the battalions. Shortly after describing these disturbing incidents, he notes:

> I was and I wasn't in uniform. I had one, used to wear it when I went out. In fact, the Germans knew me in the neighborhood. They saluted me, and I saluted back. I had a woman I used to visit and there were the restrictions on going places. I had to know the password somehow. Sign countersign. (77)

A little further on, he also casually mentions going to the Nazi doctor for treatment of a knee injury. Ultimately, it is not clear whether this speaker stayed in the battalions out of fear of the retaliations of the communists ("there wasn't another solution") or because he regretted losing privileges garnered by working for the occupier.

Over the course of the book, such damning things are revealed about the battalions and the people who fought in them that it is difficult to understand how *Orthokosta* could be read as a one-sided portrayal of leftist violence. Some of the speakers quote the harassing comments of right-wing thugs or even reanimate their own thuggish voices. The speakers sometimes describe in gory detail the retaliation that they took on the *andartes* for the persecutions and killings at the Orthokosta camp. One speaker, for instance, describes how he took revenge on a man who was present at his brother's execution: he pummeled him viciously, cut off his ear and hair (together with the scalp), tied him up, stripped him, and left him in a basement. When Dranias tells the "oral historian" about a report that he once had to write about the battalions, he does not shy away from painting a grim picture of their activities:

> I sat and did the report. What was the general picture, of disarray and depravity. Those villainies. A situation that you could not control. Because there were other factors involved. A queer set of people, rounded up. Some in pain, others on the run, others, for instance, like the Maniats [from the region of Mani, known for its feuds] who have it in their blood. (204)

At another point, Dranias describes the battalionists' unwarranted brutality toward civilians. After Kastri had been burned by the guerillas, the Security Battalions moved in to loot whatever they could find among the ashes:

> We went to Kastri, we passed through Kastri. Kastri of course had been burned. The Battalion hordes seized whatever they found. We went to Agios Petros the same thing. We went down to Ayianni from there to Mesogeio Astros. And all of them were going into the houses, to loot (*pliatsikologoun*). Like they were on foreign territory. In a foreign country. A situation I had not imagined. (230–1)

By the end, one begins to wonder why people on the *Right* did not come forth to condemn *Orthokosta*.

Since the novel's dialogism is not trapped within its pages, one must ask at this point to *whom* the book is addressed, to what discourse *it* is a rejoinder. Obviously the book can be (mis)read by anyone and, theoretically, despite what I have just said, it could be embraced by former battalionists: Valtinos, in fact, mentioned to me how strange he felt one evening when a man approached him at a tavern to tell him that he was relieved of the burden and guilt of his family's right-wing past after reading the novel. Nonetheless, the reader *implied* in the text is clearly a leftist and, given the intricacy of the novel's allusions, one knowledgeable about the "stakes" of the time and not, as Elefantis suggests, "any reader" in a postdiluvium future. Given that for these readers exonerating the battalionists is not a serious possibility, the novel could be said to challenge them to listen not only to the voice of the Right but also to that of the Left as refracted through the discourse of the "enemy." From this perspective, the reading experience (if it is attempted) is potentially intense, even visceral.

Furthermore, since *Orthokosta*, as I have already pointed out, refuses to narrate history as "noble struggle," the novel does not so much dispute the "facts" of the Civil War (who killed whom, who killed more, who killed why) as the very philosophy of history undergirding leftist mythologies of the period. Search as one might, one will not find in this novel a portrait of the "brave battalionist" as *antilogos* to the figure of the valiant communist guerrilla. The confused, the wounded, the cowardly, the fearful, the vengeful, the callous, yes. But not the brave. Although literary critic Kostas Voulgaris, in a remarkably unliterary, literalist reading of the novel, cites confessions of violence on the part of *Orthokosta*'s speakers as proof of their guilt and points to omissions of historical figures of the local resistance movement as evidence of Valtinos's willful distortion of history (2004: 129–33), one might understand this choice of emphasis differently: as a challenge to the leftist reader to hear a story of this period not filtered through a historicist discourse on heroism and progress.

The novel's use of testimony also brings into crisis numerous assumptions about witnesses and witnessing that have been inculcated through practices of historical re-collection such as those I have discussed in this book. For one, the naturalization of the leftist subject (guerrilla, political prisoner, unionist, etc.) as (oral) witness. Given the emphasis of liberal and radical projects on recuperating the voice of the "folk" or the subaltern, interviewing *non*leftists appears as jarring as collecting testimony from a Turk about the "Asia Minor Catastrophe."[29] Second, in not presenting individual speakers but ideological voices that crosscut portions of testimony, the novel casts doubt on the notion that the individual can "take the stand" as witness to a collective history or represent a particular ideological viewpoint. Instead, the splintering of testimonies into discursive fragments and the novel's refusal to identify the original source of authoritative discourse or its final attribution implicitly critique documentary practices (naming, transcription, photographing, videotaping) that treat the biological individual as *embodied* proof of a given atrocity as well as coherent subject of discourse. *Orthokosta*, thus, could be said to fundamentally question the ability of memory workers to "give voice" to historical witnesses or enable them to possess (and sign) their testimony in its guise as icon of the self.[30] The novel, furthermore, shows the "person" behind testimony—whether the informants of the Center for Asia Minor Studies with their biographies, "Exodus" stories, and photographs, or "Andreas Kordopatis" in Valtinos's eponymous novel— to be the *product* of projects of historical and literary witnessing not their presupposition. Finally, although Valtinos has been accused of remaining within the mindset of the Civil War (and the Cold War) by presenting only "one side" of conflict, *Orthokosta*, in fact, upends the logic on which such ideological polarities are founded by depicting on multiple planes (right-wing neighbors vis-à-vis left-wing neighbors; "Valtinos" the leftist author vis-à-vis the testimonies of his right-wing neighbors; left-wing readers vis-à-vis *Orthokosta*) the struggle with—and also the possibility of listening to—the voice of another.

Even though, as literary critic Vangelis Calotychos has argued, Valtinos was condemned by historians for not reading the past properly, in his opinion the reverse charge should be leveled at historians for their problematically realist and literalist demands of literature. In Calotychos's words, the *Orthokosta* case cautioned against the "pitfalls of allowing historians to read—purport to read, or not read at all—literature" (2000: 153). In regard to the argument I have been making in this book, these "misreadings" by historians, but also literary critics, represent valuable evidence in their own right, revealing the expectations of some Greek readers about the relationship of literature (and language, more generally) to historical experience. On the other hand, the failure to read the novel might be seen as a significant *loss* for historians given the perspicuity with which *Orthokosta* problematizes historical reading itself.

Reader as Historian, Historian as Reader

That historians might read fictions in the archives discovering in legal depositions and other documents the persuasive plotlines of a particular age has become something of a given following the work of historians such as Carlo Ginzburg and Natalie Davis. In his recent documentary fictions, and especially in *Orthokosta*, Valtinos presents us with a different proposition: that the reader of literature, who normally expects a pleasurable experience when she picks up a novel, be forced to undergo the "ordeal" of primary historical research (checking sources, sifting through irreconcilable testimonies, untangling personal and place names). Reading *Orthokosta* thus can be seen as a simulation of the drudgery of historical reading, but one that undoes the smooth certainty of the finished historiographical narrative by emphasizing the performative, nonreferential excess of language pervading the "sources."

The reader and author of literature usually abide by an unspoken contract. According to literary critic Doris Sommer (1999), reader response theory only reinforced an already strong conviction in readers' power over the texts they read. Barthes's (1975) celebration of the "pleasure of the text" did not scandalize, she explains, because readers had already assumed the privilege of "self-empowering interpretation." Sommer's comments come as part of an analysis of a testimonial novel routinely assigned in American college classes. She notes that "public approval" for this text on ideological grounds was often accompanied by a "private boredom." The narrator of the testimony is not at all charming and manages to turn her eventful life into an uninteresting story lacking hidden meanings for the reader to discover. Sommer muses that Jesusa's straightforward account of her life leaves a reader who has been trained to deconstruct modernist literary puzzles with little "work" to do: "Where are we privileged readers, the darlings of flirtatiously difficult texts, of an entire industry in literary criticism that assumes our responsibility—and right—to activate a text and to coauthor it?" (149). Turned into the object of aggression by the testifying subject, the reader ultimately cannot but feel "hurt."

The situation to which Sommer refers (the refusal of a subaltern subject to respond to the empathy of a middle-class reader) is quite different from the one we are examining. Nonetheless, breaking the unspoken rules of literary etiquette to address boredom and textual resistance might help us think about the experience of reading *Orthokosta*, a novel that has been considered especially hostile to its readers. One particularly annoyed critic contrasts Valtinos's successful use of testimony in his earlier books with his employment of this genre in *Orthokosta*. In her opinion, *The Book of the Days of Andreas Kordopatis* was a "pleasurable read" (*anagnosi apolafstiki*): "the reader was drawn effortlessly [*aviasta*, literally "unforced"] into the story and followed its development with the interest that someone follows an engaging interlocutor, a live presence." On the other hand, in *Orthokosta*, she complains, the language is "stifling and monotonous, the multiplicity of narrators makes it difficult to understand, lessens the originality of what is narrated and the progress—if one can speak of progress—gets bogged down or goes forward at a ridiculously slow pace . . . " (Triandafyllou 1995: 163). She adds that the lengths of the paragraphs "panic" the reader and that by the end she was "annihilated" by the reading experience and anxious to simply finish. She notes that she even had to lie down while reading and found herself skipping pages without regret. In a similar vein, another reviewer complains that the book was "deadly boring" and admits he did not even finish reading it (though he did still write a review) (Stavropoulos 1995).

In conversations with people who defended the book, I heard many private confessions of a similar kind. Even sympathetic articles about the novel tended to avoid going too deeply into the details of the testimonies. Drawing on Tzina Politi's (1996) analysis, Calotychos, for example, explicitly takes the novel's unreadability as pointing the reader away from the testimonies to the book's "paratexts," such as the prefatory and concluding "documents" to which I have already alluded. One could even argue that these paratexts *cancel out* the intervening testimonies, making reading unnecessary. The final document, with its precise references to the topography of the area in which the Orthokosta monastery is located, condemns Bishop Isakkios, the author of the first document, for the inaccuracy of his writings and his "poetic" evasiveness. Since the bishop Isakkios, according to this account, had been imprisoned in the monastery for selling false pardons, he could, according to Calotychos, represent an alter ego that "Valtinos" has provided for himself, predicting full well the storm of accusations that would follow the publication of the novel: namely, that he too had taken poetic liberties with history and was peddling false pardons to the Right. The testimonies in this case are of dubious authenticity. But, then again, why do we believe that final document's account and not Isakkios's? The encyclopedic text is just as much a literary creation, a "simulacrum of legitimacy." This productive reading of the novel along its surface and calculated (if somewhat guilty) decision not to plunge into the text's hermeneutic depths suggest that the novel can be read as a commentary on discursive authority and historical interpretation rather than yet another salvo in the struggle over the accurate representation of the Civil War. In conversations with Valtinos, however, I often got the impression that he had deliberately planted these complex allusions in the novel, as if he were engaged in some sort of playful cat-and-mouse game with his critics, challenging them to use all their literary and cultural resources to figure them out.[31] While the framing of *Orthokosta* is very clever, I think that it still might be useful to return to the corpus of testimonies, which represent a more socially embedded text, less amenable to either authorial or critical control, and examine the sentiment of boredom that overcomes the reader when forced to read, evaluate, and say something about them.

Orthokosta might deny its audience a predictable kind of reading enjoyment but, unlike Sommer's example of the straightforward plodding testimonial, presents the reader with *too much* work to do and work of an unaccustomed, nonliterary kind. One critic described the reading of the novel as a struggle that requires "persistence and diligence" (*epimoni kai epimeleia*) and tests the patience of the reader to its utmost. He found that to read the book he had to make an index of names and keep track of the page numbers on which particular characters appeared (Focas 1995: 133). I admit that I followed a similar strategy when I read *Orthokosta*. I took notes on index cards, which I then shuffled to follow the testimonies of particular characters. One afternoon Valtinos even helped me put together a table of speakers and trace the prisoners' marches on a map of the Peloponnese we had stretched out on a café table. He vacillated between encouraging this way of reading the book and gently poking fun at it: one day as he glanced at my battered copy of *Orthokosta*, he told me that he gave me permission to attach as many sticky notes to the pages of the book as I liked. In the course of reading the novel in this scholastic way, I suddenly realized that I was engaged in that famous process of "cross-checking" information that defines (some) historians' idea of their labor. In challenging the reader to compose a *historical* account from its collocation of transcribed testimonies, *Orthokosta*, in turn, makes her confront in practice, not just in theory, the extreme reductiveness of treating testimony as a receptacle for a series of "facts."

Aside from the fragmentary nature of the testimonies, the other principal reason that *Orthokosta* has been considered a difficult, even trying, reading experience is the abundance of names used in the text: a seemingly endless stream of personal names, some repeated over and over, but most heard only once. Some critics have charged that Valtinos uses all these names in order to deliberately disorient the reader and warp her view of the past. One critic notes: "The hail of names, incidents, the continual recording of the same events by the characters of the drama leads to the intentional confusion of the reader" (Karali 1994). Another writes: "The events that are presented as personal experiences of the heroes create a stifling atmosphere of details, a sea of facts and information that are of no use, that confuse" (Triandafyllou 1995). Yet another critic charges that the use of names in *Orthokosta* is so overwhelming that reading the novel is like reading a "telephone book or the Yellow Pages, with lots of names without addresses" (Stavropoulos 1995).

Rather than a mechanism of "confusion," inventory, I will argue, represents one of the main tropes that Valtinos uses in *Orthokosta* to create an effect of orality through writing. Critics often describe Valtinos as a writer of oral literature: a description that he considers the "biggest lie." Although he is usually classified within its ranks, Valtinos is critical of literary demoticism, which through its various phases triumphed the oral vernacular over the purist register, *katharevousa*, once the official language of state. Even though Valtinos laments the gradual loss of local idioms, he claims not to hold a romanticized vision of the "language of the folk." As he remarked to me one day:

> I never went looking to find the *demotic language, the true language of the people!* Drums of squash (*kolokythia toubana*)! I believe that language is unified. Every time and in every period it changes.

Pointing to my copy of *Orthokosta* lying on the table in front of us, he added: "There is *katharevousa* in here. It is an equally live language. It just depends how it is used." He then went on to make the unlikely proposition that Cavafy's writing is "steeped in folk song" (*empotismenos apo to dimotiko tragoudi*). This comment seems odd at first since Constantine Cavafy, the famous Greek poet of Alexandria, was hardly interested in the "folk" and wrote in an idiolect that included archaizing elements. For Valtinos, however, Cavafy's poems respect the economy and structure of folk songs, if not its lexicon. He stressed: "Demoticism is not about writing *demotic words*. The demotic language has an internal functionality."

The often misunderstood "art" involved in literature such as Valtinos's lies in its transposition of the "internal functionality" of oral discourse to writing, which is not so simple a matter as "writing down what they say." Like many of Valtinos's other works of fiction, *Orthokosta* lays bare the poetics of transcription in ways that can be particularly illuminating, but at the same time troubling, for practitioners of oral history. Reflecting the deep-seated suspicion of writing in "Western" culture, many oral historians view transcription as an unavoidable disenchantment of the authenticity of oral language: at best a technique for minimizing losses, not a productive and creative process in its own right.[32] Perhaps even more problematic, and equally unacknowledged, is the fact that the literal transcription of oral testimony can be deeply *untrue* to the emotional force of witnessing. For Valtinos, then, transcription is a rigorous exercise in finding a written language that might do justice to what oral discourse does not say in words:

> Oral discourse is an imperfect [*atelis*, also "incomplete"] discourse. Anyone who has experience writing knows that. Often—though not always—its imperfections (*ateleies*) can prove productive. The silences, the gaps, the discontinuities—syntactic and others—whatever is related to the anguish of memory and expressed in the hue and tone of the voice, the elements, in other words, with which the imagination's projections on the historical fact are embodied, are exactly those elements that cannot be passed onto paper. In these sorts of cases, the aim remains always to inscribe those amorphous projections in writing, in a fictive discourse—in other words in an effective one. At this point begins the work of the writer. (1997: 339)

Valtinos's testimonial and documentary fictions bring attention to the editing involved in transcription, even supposedly *literal* transcription. The persuasiveness of his writing demonstrates how "minor" and "absolutely necessary" changes (removing repetitions, pauses, digressions, fixing syntax, etc.) required to make historical testimony "readable" often have the result of devaluing the performative dimension of speech (and of silence).

One of the ways that Valtinos makes his writing more "true" to oral discourse than literal transcription and transposes certain of these nondenotative aspects of testimony is through his use of tropes. In a 1991 article entitled "Polytropy," Paul Friedrich outlines a theory of tropes for anthropological poetics, elaborating and reinvigorating terms of classical rhetoric with Peircean semeiotics. Friedrich defines a trope as "anything a poet, politician, pundit or Everyman uses or employs—whether intentionally or unintentionally to create poetic texture and effect, poetic meanings, and integration" (26). He argues that critics' preoccupation with the most famous of tropes, metaphor, has led other tropes to be ignored. Valtinos himself uses metaphors sparingly in his writing; as a result, poetic effects in his texts are mostly achieved by means of more commonplace tropes. Inventory, the most striking trope used in *Orthokosta*, is, Friedrich notes, one of the most common forms of contiguity trope and to be found in a great variety of texts, including Russian saints' lives, the Homeric "Catalogue of Ships," and Walt Whitman's poetry. In *Orthokosta*, in testimony after testimony, we encounter inventory in passages such as these:

> There was an execution order. The Germans were approaching. And the Kastriots started to leave. To head down, fearing the Germans. All the Kastriots. Lambros Chronis. Kourvetaris, Athanassios. Ismini Athanassiou. Ismini who gave me a bag of raisins. And Lambros as soon as he saw me started to cry. They had learned. They had

learned about it. They knew about the execution. Others came through then also. Christos Kokkinias, Thanassis Kosmas. They took them to the camp later. Because the camp was reestablished. Dinis Pantazis. Lots of guys. All the guys. (143)

    Kyriakos Galaxidis was there. There was a Talas from Tripolis. There was a Kringas, uncle-Lias Kringas, from Rizes. When you enter the village his house is the one on the right. There was a Yiorgos, a brave kid, him I see in Tripolis. He has a gas station now, I don't remember his last name. (163)

In choosing a passage to quote from a testimony, a historian or anthropologist would surely skip over plotless lists of this kind. On a poetic level, however, this naming of an endless stream of unknown people is precisely what enhances the text's authenticity as seemingly unedited oral discourse.

In drawing his reader's attention to inventory, *Orthokosta* also highlights performative dimensions of testimony that can be overlooked in the pursuit of information (i.e., who did what, when, and to whom). A historian faced with an analogous jumble of first names, last names, and nicknames might list them in an index, pair them with other names, and speculate what ties of kinship, locality, or politics bound them to each other.[33] The fact of *naming* as social practice and existential need, however, remains difficult to account for within conventional categories of historical knowledge: it is a "fact" that is very easily erased in the process of producing historical data. In discussing the plethora of names in the novel, Valtinos told me that he wanted to create an effect that was "like a river" (*potamikos*): "The names make it confusing, I know, but at some point you have to ignore the confusion and see what they are carrying, how it is like a huge river, that descends—people, names, places." In putting name beside name, the inventory locates all these individuals within a common fate ("Lots of guys. All the guys"). For Politi, this roll call of the anonymous wounded undermines the importance accorded to political leaders whose names have monopolized the pages of official history (1996: 234–5). At the same time, individual identities are held on to with nicknames or little details ("Ismini who gave me a bag of raisins"), as if the anonymity of death might be countered by the will of memory. Some critics of *Orthokosta* have likened the use of inventory in the novel to a Greek Orthodox memorial rite; as one reviewer notes: "Everything is named in order to exist (people, wells, streams), a long punctuated list of names (*onomatologio*)/*mnimo-logio* (tomb [*mnima*] and memory [*mnimi*]) that recalls the lists of names read at memorial services for the peace of the soul" (Kouvaras 1994: 74).

Given his propensity to draw out the diachrony of Greek social practice and historical experience, Valtinos might have had religious ritual in mind in constructing these inventories; however, the naming of names also can be seen in a historical light and linked to global transformations in the conception of the relation of personal to cultural memory. In her work on the politics of memory in the United States, Marita Sturken, for instance, has spoken of the radical innovation in memorial practices occasioned by the Vietnam War Memorial in Washington, D.C., which was erected in 1982. The arrangement of the names of American casualties on its black marble surface according to the chronological order of soldiers' deaths, not their rank or honors, signals a refusal to perpetuate the glory of war or recognize the primacy of some deaths over others. Read aloud at ceremonies, the names become a "chant," a roll call of the dead and, because listed in chronological order, a history of the conflict (1997: 58–63).

In insisting on the collective mourning of war, naming names in the 1990s might be understood in the context of a new "activism of mourning" in which the "public vigil emerges as a performative practice of political protest with intense sensuous suggestiveness" (Athanasiou forthcoming). Another public memorial project, but one initiated to mourn a disease's victims, the NAMES Project AIDS Memorial quilt, which has been stretched out on the Mall in Washington, D.C. several times since 1987, deliberately appropriates the space of the national war memorial to make public the devastating death toll of a stigmatized and hidden disease. The collective gathering of victims, but also the insistence on their individuality through personalized patchwork quilt squares, represents a demand for recognition of this illness as a national problem, another "war" in which the U.S. government was highly culpable. The individual panels made by lovers, friends, and family, furthermore, humanize discourse about this disease and convey its suffering to a wider public (Sturken 1997: 183–219). The Greek Civil War, by contrast, has never been publicly mourned in these kinds of ways: it remains a taboo subject on a local level and highly ideologized in national public discourse, the tremendous investment in remembering the "National Resistance," in effect, legitimating the forgetting of this conflict.[34] As a result, the naming practices in *Orthokosta* take on particular significance, given that they can be said to resonate with the politicized performances of public remembrance to which I have just alluded, in their insistence on the mourning of collective trauma, refusal of the heroic death in war, and attempt to bring out of the shadows forgotten, marginalized, and shameful casualties.

Aside from naming, another aspect of the text that exhausts the reader, but also forces her to address testimony as more than merely a mode of transmitting information about the past, is the "cross-checking" of multiple accounts of the same (or roughly the same) set of events. As I have already suggested, the novel encourages the reader to follow the discovery process of a historian confronted with the problem not so much of reconciling conflicting or contradictory accounts of a particular past event as of defining what series of human actions constitute a meaningful event in the first place. Several of the speakers in the novel, for instance, refer to the execution of an old woman, a shoemaker named Braïlaina, and the miraculous escape of Kalabakas, a prisoner at the Orthokosta monastery who apparently survived by hiding under Braïlaina's skirt. In an early chapter, the woman's son tells the "oral historian" to make sure to interview Kalabakas since he is the only eyewitness to the murder. Over the course of the novel, we hear about this incident many times and become convinced we know what happened. At the end of the novel, then, when the man who discovered Braïlaina's corpse presents his testimony, we expect him to confirm the accounts of the incident that we have heard up to this point. The "oral historian" prompts him:

— Kalabakas had left?
— He had left.
— He got away [*Glitose*].
— He got away, yes.

— How did Kalabakas escape?

— He must have bribed someone. To get off like that. He hid under the skirt of Braïlaina and what not. Those things don't happen. It's not possible. (323)

The reader's certainty about this incident is somewhat shaken after reading this dialogue. The archival form of the novel, however, allows this conflicting view, this tiny doubt, to be registered rather than brushed aside in the interest of composing a coherent account of the past. Through the course of the book, other key "events" also take shape—and unravel—in this way.

Given the multiplicity of speakers, we not only hear different versions of events but also have them *framed* for us quite differently in each testimony. Consider, for instance, the story of the murder of Tsigris, a former major of the regular army who had been recruited against his will into ELAS. In order to leave ELAS without being called a traitor, he allowed himself to be captured by the Security Battalions so that it would seem that he had been taken against his will. As a formality, he then was sent to the battalion offices in Tripolis for interrogation. While Tsigris was undergoing questioning, a man suddenly burst into the office and shot him dead. The murderer apparently killed Tsigris to avenge the death of his brother Kyriakos, a battalionist. The murder is ironic, though, because Tsigris is not "really" a communist.

We first hear about this incident from Kostas Dranias, who tells us that he had been in the battalion office at the time of the interrogation and saw Tsigris die right before his eyes. This shooting incident represents a central component of Dranias's narrative of the war; he begins and ends a twenty-page testimony describing Tsigris's murder, suggesting that for him it encapsulated in some profound way the violent irrationality of the times. By contrast, Dranias's brother Yiannis does not foreground this event but refers to it along with many others. Interestingly, he also claims that his brother Kostas had been the one interrogating Tsigris. As I noted above, this piece of information sheds some doubt on Kostas's claims to have been a bystander to this particular event as well as to the battalions' operations more generally. "Kostas did this work, interrogations," Yiannis notes (80). In other testimonies, the shooting of Tsigris is so peripheral to the informants' narratives that they only mention it because the oral historian figure asks them about the incident directly (perhaps in an attempt to sort out the conflicting accounts provided by the Dranias' brothers [209–11, 297]).

As the novel proceeds, rather than becoming more confident about what happened, the reader instead starts to question whether Tsigris's murder is even *the* event. We know from the first testimonies that Mihalis Galaxidis murdered Tsigris in revenge for the death of his brother Kyriakos. As we read on in the novel, however, the circumstances of Kyriakos's death start to draw our attention more than those surrounding Tsigris's. Kostas Dranias tells us that Kyriakos had gone into the countryside with other battalionists to do some investigations (*erevnes*): "Maybe it was his own mistake. With an Italian carbine. He went to do something and the weapon went off and killed him" (23). Iraklis Politis, a fellow battalionist, who was on the raid with Kyriakos, gives a similarly matter-of-fact account of the incident: "He [Kyriakos] was killed at Agiorgi. We made a drive (*exormisi*) and he was killed. We brought him dead to Tripolis" (297). Other speakers, however, have more incriminating accounts to tell of the circumstances surrounding Kyriakos's death, which make it seem like he had not been engaged in routine, or at least respectable, army business. Dranias's brother, Yiannis, for instance, explains that Kyriakos, along with a party of battalionists, had headed to that area to make trouble: "It was a routine sortie. For kicks. Because down there, of course, who was there to go after. And maybe to bring back some provisions." Kyriakos, he explains:

> had gone to beat people (*na deirei*), he didn't beat her, he pushed her with the carbine, an Italian carbine, the mother of Vangelis Farazis. A little old woman. It was her house, with a little stair going down. Quiet people, sheep. And Kyriakos, he pushed the old woman. Where did you hide the oil, where did you hide it. The poor old woman was going downstairs, probably to show him where. Can oil be hidden? He was going to get the oil, Kyriakos, all-wild. And as he pushed her with the butt of the gun, the carbine went off and killed him. (80)

The account of Kyriakos's death provided by a woman named Aphrodite similarly makes this "revenge killing" for an accidental and self-inflicted death seem increasingly gratuitous:

> As soon as they saw the old woman they asked, where is your old man? And Kyriakos gave her a slap on the face. He pushed her. Why are you hitting the old woman, our Nikolas asked him. Why is the old woman to blame. Shut up, he replies. And with the gun butt he breaks down the door. The barrel reversed on him and caught fire, and he died on the spot. In front of Nikolas. In front of him. The others ran over, the officer came, what is going on, this and that. Maybe someone killed him, no, he killed himself. He still had the trigger in his fingers. (151)

In her testimony, Aphrodite describes the murder of the old woman from the perspective of people living in the village and makes no reference to the subsequent murder of Tsigris. For her, the harassment of the old woman and the senseless death of the rapacious battalionist simply represented one more act of violence of this time, an occurrence that does not seem to form a part of a causal chain of events and for this reason was particularly susceptible to misinterpretation ("Maybe someone killed him").

Far from the tiresome or irrelevant repetition of the same event, each account of the incident(s) paradoxically deepens the reader's sense of expertise and knowledge about what happened at the same time that it shifts the boundaries of the event. As a reader of this novel, I believe one ultimately *is* rewarded with a kind of pleasure, deferred after a good deal of reading labor, in going through this frustrating and fascinating process. Reading the overlapping and contradictory testimonies not only makes one appreciate a multiplicity of interpretive viewpoints and the contingency of events (the obvious point) but also takes one to the brink at which the event and causality recede as the ultimate reference of testimony. This does not mean, however, as those who jump quickly on the defensive about these issues might argue, that war as "fact" is recklessly denied in the novel. The testimonies in *Orthokosta* actually do not diverge that much; although ambiguities remain and the details are conflicting, one still feels justified in bringing Kyriakos, the battalionist, to justice in one's mind. The point is that in doing so, one becomes conscious of the reductiveness of the historiographical gesture. As in the case of naming, a shift from viewing testimony as knowledge statement to thinking about *testifying* as discursive performance does not refuse reference: it simply transforms it (cf. Caruth 1996). In this view, testimony that fails to communicate meaning is not devoid of historical importance but, to the contrary, often effectively enacts and (re)presents the terrifying and unhealed experience of trauma itself. Reflecting on the futility of cross-checking facts in *Orthokosta*, one might even conclude that the *unwitnessability* of the war in standard referential forms of historical discourse is precisely the "missing" plot of the novel.[35] Given this reading of the novel, then, the fact that *Orthokosta* has been assigned a place alongside other projects of right-wing historical revisionism aimed at "setting the record straight" about leftist violence appears deeply ironic.[36]

The Anthropology of "History and Literature"

The case study I have presented in this chapter forms a linchpin in this book's narrative and argument. For one, the discussion of the poetics of transcription and archive in *Orthokosta* is intended to reflect back on the previous chapters in which the linguistic mediation of historical knowledge was obscured or downplayed as well as to prepare the ground for the close textual reading in the following chapter. Second, on a thematic level the repression of the subject of the Civil War from other genres of historical writing and projects of historical re-collection I have considered in this book makes clear the importance of examining the postwar novel, in which the war years of the 1940s have constituted *the* subject. Yet despite my perception that this case study was crucial to my project as a whole, several readers of this manuscript surprised me by having the opposite reaction. Some suggested I revamp the chapter drastically by situating the novel and its reception in a broader "sociological" context; others that I remove it entirely. If mostly not for the reasons they put forth, these critiques compelled me to rethink and rewrite this chapter in fundamental ways. In closing, then, I felt it might be useful to explicitly address questions such as: Why treat literature in an anthropological study? Why this novel in a discussion of the Greek politics of historical representation?

For some Greek readers, the problem began and ended with the choice of this particular novel. In circles of leftist intellectuals in the late 1990s, *Orthokosta* really *was* taboo: "If you write about Valtinos, you vindicate him." As I have already suggested, one of the reasons that *Orthokosta* was taken so seriously (as history) has to do with the legacy of the literature of "militant commitment" and its role in documenting forbidden histories and proposing social critique. The debate over *Orthokosta* brought into sharp relief the intertwining of the political with the literary in modern Greek society as well as the part that authors and particular literary texts have played in shaping historical narratives of the postwar period. Nonetheless, when I first started looking into the *Orthokosta* controversy, I had assumed that more readers in my acquaintance would join in protesting the literalist expectations of the book's denunciators. By contrast, I found (and in retrospect I realize that I should have predicted) that this chapter of modern Greek history is too integral to the fashioning of political identities and legitimacies to be open to much negotiation. The imperative of archival activism, which I have discussed in other contexts, and the sense of serving a community of politicized historical seekers with which it is associated, send down their deepest roots around the re-collection of this historical period. The noncoincidence of the communist archive with power during the Cold War has generated both a suspicion of the archive as manifestation of law and cloak of hegemony *and* an unrequited faith in the archive as safeguard of otherwise distorted, repressed, and unknown histories. *Orthokosta* troubled this fragile balance by critiquing not the state's memory (as in his previous fictions) but that of the Left itself. Although the *Orthokosta* controversy exploded in the midst of the Left's post-1989 identity crisis, the debris was quickly swept away. In the final analysis, the book has provided a convenient whipping post for "right-wing revisionism," thus endowing a greater sense of urgency to the production of left-oriented historiography and literary criticism related to the Resistance and Civil War.

For some anthropologist readers, less concerned with the particular cultural politics of Valtinos's literary transgression, my case study in this chapter placed undue emphasis on literature and language. The peripheral status of literature in anthropological research (in comparison to more "popular" forms of verbal expression, such as oral poetry, folk song, oratory, etc.) can be attributed to entrenched divisions of disciplinary labor and distinctions between high culture and a more "democratic" anthropological cultural concept. Another reason for the anthropological oversight of literature, as Lyons has suggested, lies in the fact that the literary author as professional cultural producer and critic too closely resembles the anthropologist; writers, as a result, more often "come to us" than are "discovered" by us in the field. Moreover, as he argues, literary texts appear to interpret themselves and to too closely share the theoretical preoccupations of anthropological writings (2001: 183). While composing this chapter, I did struggle with some of these issues. If I traced the inner workings of a novel Valtinos had written in order to "show" rather than "tell" his ideas, what work had I done, and what kind of *anthropological* work?

In my approach to the text, I also found it difficult not to fall into a way of reading and talking about literature I had learned as an undergraduate English major: namely, elucidating and, to a large extent, justifying authorial "intentions." Given the personalism pervading literary criticism in Greece (i.e., critics write about "their" authors) and the relative dearth of interest in nonliterary (and unsigned) textual practice, I also had to struggle not to let my reading of the novel be overdetermined by established themes and problematics used to discuss particular literary works and authors.[37] While the controversy over *Orthokosta* clearly called out for some kind of *antilogos* in "defense" of the novel, as I reworked my argument in this chapter, I realized that I needed to be able to take a step back from the incident enough not only to describe the novel's reception as an ethnographic conjuncture but also to analyze the novel itself with a more critical eye (for instance, as regards its tendency toward dehistoricization). Deemphasizing the place of "Valtinos" in the text (and not taking for granted the literary asylum by which authors stand outside their fictions) in turn led me to examine the novel as a *social text* in complex dialogue with literary and nonliterary historical discourses. Rather than a polyphonic orchestra Valtinos "conducts" (since the "multiplicity of voices" appears to be the next big, radical thing after "giving voice"), the novel, I suggested, constitutes a repository of cultural knowledges and performative utterances that exceeds, disturbs, and ultimately escapes the control of an authorial masterdiscourse.

Anthropologists increasingly acknowledge that their analyses are "incomplete" without treatments of literature, film, and other cultural products that crucially shape cultural understanding and imaginings but had previously been outside the purview of anthropological research. The question remains, though, how to define an anthropological approach to literature without simply making recourse to a familiar logic of addition whereby culture is constantly expanded to take into account formerly unstudied subjects (according to the always adaptive formula of "anthropology of *x*"). One useful proposal for thinking about the relationship of anthropology and literature is to view novels, like films (cf. Fischer 1998; Caton 1999), as ethnographies in a different register: as intricate portraits of a social reality often powerfully iconic of social experience and struggle precisely because they are not constrained by the terms of social science analysis and its demands that causality be spelled out (cf. Handler and Segal 1990; Daniel and Peck 1996; Lyons 2001).

Another common understanding of the relation of anthropology to literature is ethnographic, but in a literal sense: the anthropologist's contribution is to locate (and even anchor) literature in the social and historical contexts of its production and reception. In this view, an anthropological reading comes less to unsettle than to supplement the literary critical analysis of text; the author is treated as yet another speaking subject to be interviewed while the textual intricacies of the fiction is again left to the literary critics. Aside from further supporting the cultural construction of the writer as authority on his or her work, this need to listen to the writer, I believe, stems from a difficulty in claiming reading as an anthropological method and practice. In this hesitance, the dichotomies of field/archive and writing/orality rear their heads once again. Yet, when I met with Valtinos, aside from some interesting background information about his writing practice and insights into the politics of literature in Greek society, he did not actually have much to tell me and certainly nothing of comparable significance to what I found in his novels. In reworking this case study, then, I found myself not sketching more social or biographical context in place of a discussion of literary and stylistic matters but staying closer to the text (including the text of criticism).

While the *Orthokosta* controversy interested me in being a vivid contest over cultural memory as well as an entry point into examining institutions and communities authorized to speak—and by speaking—about this particular historical event, the novel itself, I believe, also made an important contribution to theorizing the practice and poetics of historical re-collection in a modern Greek context. In my reading, the novel did not so much reflect an already established mode of thinking or writing about the Civil War as enact a new way of mourning the war that brought personal experience into the public realm to redefine, not multiply, historical knowledge. It is characteristic, for instance, that the novel rejects the logic of "*antiparathesi*" (opposition) whereby multiple viewpoints of the war could be juxtaposed in the "secular empty" space of the archive. *Orthokosta*, further, could be said to depict the war as a "critical event," in Veena Das's terms: namely, as an event that connects the world-historical dimensions of historical processes with the "inner life" of individual historical actors grappling with changed definitions of social action and subjectivity. Despite its redemptive undertones, the novel fundamentally challenges conventional notions of history as "victory" (or "noble struggle")—the terms *par excellence* through which the war years continue to be discussed—in order to address history through the prism of the unheroic death, meaningless violence, the traumatized survivor, and the shattered, elliptical testimony.

Contrary to dominant understandings (and often writers' own explanations), so-called historical fiction concerns a project such as this not because it paints a "portrait" of a particular historical period, blurring impressionistically a given historical reality that could be more precisely described in historiographical writing.[38] Rather, literature such as Valtinos's is of interest because in addition to its capacity to act as "precocious" testimony, it makes startling *precise* observations about historical discourse. Through its simulation of historical testimony, *Orthokosta* exposed the rhetorical constitution of authoritative discourse on the war and, in particular, the fascination with testimony in contemporary historical studies. At the same time, in demonstrating the performative excess of language, the novel identified levels of experience that could not be translated into familiar forms of historical discourse. The poetics of voicing, transcription, and archiving to which the novel drew attention, thus, proved not to be "merely" linguistic or stylistic issues but to register existential and ethical concerns about responsibility, authorship, witnessing, and mourning as well as about the ability to persuade, listen to another, and to trust. To the extent that a novel such as this has taken on the cultural task of putting unadjudicated historical experience on trial and bringing injustice and suffering to light, it is clear that literature cannot help meeting up with historiography, and vice versa. If brought into a true dialogue outside of their disciplinary frameworks (or even their "interdisciplinary" ones), literary and historical discourses might be evaluated in terms of their relative abilities to *respond* to historical experience.

Chapter 5

America Translated in a Migrant's Memoirs

Sometime in 1951 in an Arcadian village, Yiorgos Yiannis Ilias Mandas, then seventy-five years old, wrote the story of his life in a tiny notebook. Once he finished, he wrote the story down a second time in similar, though not exactly the same, words.[1] In the back of one of the two notebooks, he also recopied a long poem entitled "The Misfortunes (*Pathimata*) of the Greeks," which he claims to have originally written in 1907 while he was a migrant laborer in Los Angeles.[2] These notebooks remained tucked in a drawer in Mandas's house until 1996 when his grandson gave the original handwritten manuscript to the village local historian to transcribe into grammatical, vernacular, computer-processed Greek. Thirty years after Mandas's death, approximately two dozen laser-printed copies of his edited memoirs were distributed among family members and covillagers, and thus his autobiography circulated outside his house for the very first time.

Mandas might be considered a quintessential survivor of the traumatic twentieth century—or, at least, as experienced by citizens of "old Greece" (*palaia Ellada*).[3] Born in 1876 to landless peasants in the village of Vourvoura, Mandas, according to his account, emigrated to the United States in 1898, just after the end of the Greco-Turkish war. The fall of the international price of currants, Greece's principal cash crop at the time, had caused a severe national economic crisis that laid the grounds for a "first wave" of Greek transatlantic migration, consisting overwhelmingly of unmarried men of draftable age like Mandas. In his first journey to the United States, Mandas moved all around the country at a dizzying pace, working any job he could find: selling fruit and vegetables with a pushcart in Washington, D.C., New York, Chicago, Los Angeles, and San Francisco; drilling at a cement factory in California; and building railroad lines in Virginia, Wyoming, Nevada, Texas, and Utah. In 1909, after eleven years in the States, Mandas returned to Greece to marry his sisters off and get married himself. During this time, he also fought in the 1913 Balkan War against Bulgaria.[4] Finding that he could not make ends meet, he left for the United States again in 1915; as he tells us: "during the five years that I was here I always kept the Fare for America" (Τον Ναύλοδιατην Αμερική τον εβαστούσα πάντοτε). His second trip (1915–22) to the United States was less frenetic. He worked a pushcart in Chicago for several years before settling in Spartanburg, South Carolina, where his brothers-in-law owned a fruit store and "candy kitchen" (cake shop).[5]

In 1922, Mandas returned to Greece for good and finally bought some land. Having money to lend allowed him to achieve some local power; for many years, he served as president of the village council and was actively involved in various local benevolent associations. In 1937, though, when dictator Metaxas passed a law reliev-ing agricultural debt, he lost what remained of his original capital, most of which he had lent out to covillagers. The war, however, would bring Mandas much greater tragedies than bankruptcy. His two oldest sons fought in Albania in the 1940 war against Italy. One of them came back severely handicapped, only to be killed a few years later in Athens by a stray bullet during the 1944 *Dekemvriana* (December Days). In 1949, in the final year of the Civil War, government forces executed his oldest son, Yiannis, a left-wing partisan. During that same year, his youngest son, Ilias, suffered a severe and ultimately fatal head injury while serving in the govern-ment's mountain commando squad (LOK). Shortly after the war, one of Mandas's daughters died of cancer and the other emigrated to Canada, leaving Mandas in the village with his wife and one remaining daughter until his death in 1966 at the age of ninety.

Although punctuated by events of national and international significance, Mandas's story had long remained outside the frame of Greek historical narratives. He might tell the prototypical Greek migrant story within the pages of his memoirs but perhaps for this very reason his life experience could not be incorporated into either Greek or American national historiographies. Between 1890 and 1924, it is estimated that almost a tenth of the Greek population participated in the so-called first wave of transatlantic emigration, the highest percentage coming from Mandas's province, Arcadia, in the populated interior of the Peloponnese.[6] As a migrant worker who repatriated and went bankrupt, Mandas tells a story that does not con-form to American narratives of immigrant struggle and success (especially those pro-duced by upwardly mobile Greek American sociologists).[7] In pointing to a humbling lack and absence in the nation, his story also does not flatter Greek self-representa-tions: unsurprisingly, no archive was established by the Greek state or private indi-viduals to collect narratives about the Greek experience of migrant labor.[8] Thus, even though it is estimated that about 40 percent of the half-million Greeks who migrated during this period repatriated, the experience of the returned *American* Greek has not seemed important to document.[9]

Since Mandas's sons died on opposite sides during the Civil War, his family catas-trophe could also be considered a prototypical Civil War story. However, as we have seen, writings on this conflict were long focused on key players not uncommitted sideline onlookers such as Mandas. Along with his three sons, Mandas initially had joined the EAM/ELAS resistance movement, but decided to quit when he realized that the Greek Communist Party (KKE) lay behind the organization. Like some of the speakers in *Orthokosta*, Mandas ends up describing the war as nothing more than an attempt to protect what he has—his home, his family, his daughter's dowry clothes, and his meager larder—as his family is raided and interrogated by forces across the political spectrum (Nazis, left-wing guerrillas and right-wing Security

Battalionists). As a result, his account of the war is disjointed on a narrative level and lacks a clear ideological message. Even though Mandas, who had been a Royalist during the National Schism, would end up supporting the Right, his experience of history consigned him to a sphere of ethical reckoning beyond the securities of political allegiance: it was his right-wing covillagers after all who had one of his sons executed during the Civil War. In Mandas's autobiography, then, in sharp contrast with the genre of local historiography, community is not a given, but precisely that which is at stake and open to transformation at moments of crisis.

Finally, the fact that Mandas *wrote* rather than told his story might have been reason enough for its exclusion from established structures of public historical recollection. Mandas was a talkative man who used to love to debate politics in the village taverns and cafés, tell his grandson about the heroes of the Greek War of Independence, and analyze dream narratives; he was also a talented singer of folk songs. While Mandas probably would have been the perfect oral informant for a project of folklore or anthropology research—an ideal source for the "warm and live speech" of a peasant, historians might find the written account of his life, in which he attempts and "fails" to cast his discourse in "correct" written Greek, valuable for the historical details and information that might be gleaned from it but unremarkable as a form of expression in and of itself. Furthermore, given that Mandas had already recorded his memories on paper, what work was left to be done by others?

In the 1990s things changed, however, and Mandas's story became poised to be of interest to a number of readers. For one, with the sudden transformation of Greece, like Italy, from a country that "exports" migrant laborers to one that "imports" them, the conditions have taken shape to tell the story of modern Greek migration from *within* Greek public historical culture.[10] As I learned from Mandas's grandson, this changed political and economic context played a crucial role in his decision to publish the notebooks. With the emergence of a new theoretical language on transnationalism and diaspora (Chow 1993; Gilroy 1993; Clifford 1997) as well as the further consolidation of the paradigm of economic history in modern Greek historical studies, Greek academic historians also have begun studying the Greek migration experience.[11] In addition, as we saw in the previous chapter, in the 1990s the Greek Civil War started to be understood in less rigidly ideological terms, with the violence and dislocation suffered by particular communities, rather than military engagements and political debates, drawing increasing scholarly interest. A feminist historiography of militarization and war (Cooke 1996; Grayzel 1999) attendant to the gendering of the "home front" could serve as yet another optic through which to read Mandas's geography of war and descriptions of violation. Turning to the writing of the text itself, contemporary studies on memory and trauma suggest ways to view Mandas's memoir as an *act* of witnessing: in other words, as both a response to the deaths he survived and an address to a reader "on the outside" who might commiserate with him. Finally, textual and semiotic anthropologies might provide tools to read the "errors" and dysfluencies of Mandas's autobiography as a performance of his linguistic and social alienation but also as a creative product of his transnational experience.

By taking as my subject such a clearly minor text and focusing on an intimate circle of readers, editors, and writers who have constituted and activated it, I intend this final case study to serve as a counterpoint to those presented in the preceding chapters. Compared to the other projects of historical re-collection I have discussed in this book, Mandas' memoirs are marked by their extreme marginality to powerful institutions of social memory, including explicitly alternative or radical ones, as well as to mainstream networks of textual circulation and preservation. A poor-quality publication in terms of both editing and aesthetics, the memoirs have been printed on the cheap and read by few. A consideration of the circumstances surrounding this text's production and reproduction thus allows me to consider—this time from the perspective of exclusion not inclusion—how representations of historical experience are shaped by the political economy of documentation and archiving. This text's tenuous hold on materiality also leads me to examine the heretical notion of history as the story of *dispossession from community*, which comes as a startling challenge to discourses of local historiography as well as to Greek and Greek American mythologies of migration by narrating capitalism from the standpoint of those it displaces rather than grounds. Nostalgia, settlement, compatriot, community, and kinship, I contend, are reconceptualized in Mandas's text in ways that illuminate their strategic presupposition in other forms of historical writing that demand that the past be territorialized (nationalized, localized) a priori.

This case study also provides a different angle on issues of witnessing than I have considered up to this point by putting equal emphasis on the position of the witness as that of the scribe. As a result, I tack between two levels of analysis. First, with particular emphasis on Mandas's "migrant's tale," I consider the social and political conditions but also the engrained habits of historical interpretation that have shaped how Mandas's memoirs (or certain parts of them) could become "legible" in the 1990s. Second, I conjecture how a story such as this came to be recorded outside of established structures of historical re-collection in the first place. In this way, I intend to denaturalize certain fundamental categories and conventions of historical discourse (biological individual as historical actor and witness, historical period, causal explanation, monolingualism).

"The Bad Old Days": Repatriating the Story of *Ameriki*

The publication of Mandas's memoirs can be situated against the backdrop of the recent upsurge in local historical production I discussed in this book's first case study. Indeed, the immediate catalyst for the publication of Mandas's autobiography was the centennial anniversary of one of Vourvoura's benevolent associations. Even though neither the village council nor a village association funded the publication of the memoirs, new computer technologies have made the creation of texts such as this both feasible and affordable for independent historical producers. As a tale of labor exploitation, restless movement, and breakdown of community, Mandas's memoirs, however, present a vision of the world fundamentally at odds with the narratives of progress, continuity, and communal belonging to be found in local historiography. Thus, the text's publication, albeit in this marginal way, is noteworthy and can be ascribed, I will argue, to the fact that the poverty and violence Mandas describes, especially in relation to his migration experience, seem distant to the contemporary Greek reader.

In the 1990s, the word immigrant (*metanastis*), once a fundamental term of Greek self-description, became associated with the existential condition of the foreigner, the Other. Despite the fact that Mandas's memoirs speak at length about the Civil War, it was primarily as a "migrant's tale" that his autobiography was suddenly "discovered" and removed from the proverbial darkness and dust of a personal archive. In what follows, I consider two different readings of Mandas's memoirs, one by his grandson and the other by the memoirs' editor, which correspond with the two central ways in which the historical experience of Greek transatlantic migration has been drawn on to interpret the new immigration to Greece in the 1990s.

In the first reading of the text, Greek migration represents a closed story: a humbling but completed process that served as a steppingstone to contemporary advancement and prosperity. From this perspective, in the 1990s the history of Greek migration could, at long last, be (re)patriated and gathered into the corpus of modern Greek history as a diasporic resource extending and enriching rather than interrupting local and national historical narratives. This reading was exemplified in the way the memoirs were edited by Mandas's covillager Evangelos Mantzouranis, a philologist and local historian. For Mantzouranis, Mandas's memoirs represented just one in a series of local historical and genealogical texts he has published since his retirement from high school teaching: most notably, a massive volume of village genealogies entitled *The Families of Vourvoura from 1800 Until Today*. Reading Mandas's text in turn through the prism of village genealogy, Mantzouranis has included information about the births, deaths, and professions of Mandas's descendants in the edited version of the memoirs and also scanned in new and old family photographs. These images form a jarring parallel narrative of continuity and reproduction running counter to Mandas's desperate account of cataclysmic loss.

While Mantzouranis in a brief prologue notes the significance of Mandas's memoirs for the information they provide about the history of Vourvoura, the main reason he says he considers the transcription and transmission of Mandas's memoirs a worthwhile endeavor is that the text describes the "difficult life of immigrants in America." Viewing history as *historia magistrae vitae*, Mantzouranis interprets the memoirs pedagogically, as teaching "our children" that the money immigrants made in the United States did not "come out by the sack" but with "sweat and blood." Even though observations about the "honest toil" of immigrant ancestors sound familiar enough to American ears, their invocation in the Greek context is not so common. It cannot be taken for granted, for example, that the American immigrant experience has always been seen as part of "*our* children's" heritage or of the history of the village. After the publication of Mandas's memoirs, Mantzouranis gave them to a local newspaper in Tripolis, the provincial capital of Arcadia, where Mantzouranis and many people from Vourvoura, including Mandas's grandson, now live. The newspaper published excerpts relating to Mandas's childhood in the village and his two journeys to the United States but not any about his experience of the Civil War. When I met with Mantzouranis and asked him why the parts about the war were not included, he told me in a rather offhand manner that "everyone knows that story."

In his edition of Mandas's memoirs, Mantzouranis has included everything that Mandas wrote, with the exception of one scandalous story. This incident involved a village woman, to whom Mandas refers sarcastically as a *Brooklisa* (the feminine of *Brooklis*, a term derived from the word "Brooklyn" that was commonly used to refer to compatriots who had lived in the United States). While her husband was working abroad, this woman had had affairs with local men that eventually resulted in the birth of a bastard child; after killing the baby, she gave the corpse to some village men, among them one of Mandas's sons, to bury. After she refused to pay the men for this service, Mandas's son complained, and the story became public gossip, eventually leading to his brief imprisonment. Mandas's grandson told me that he decided not to include this story in the published version of the memoirs out of respect for the woman's descendants. This "family secret," though, illuminates some of the social costs of migration by revealing, ever so briefly, the figure of the "woman who waits," the Penelope whose story is rarely, if ever, told in studies of migration. The omission of this little story composes an image of the local past that does not upset mythologies of fidelity and narratives of normative, reproductive sexuality enshrined in village genealogies. By extension, this "polite" oversight contributes, as do other elements of the text's interpretation and editing, to downplaying the harrowing (but also potentially liberating) effects of migration on personal relationships.

The first time I met Mandas's grandson, he told me about this missing story and offered to let me read photocopies of the original notebooks. He also did not hide from me his disappointment in what he considered Mantzouranis's as well as other covillagers' shallow readings of the memoirs. Although Mandas told me that he treasures his grandfather's notebooks as family "relics" (*keimilia*), he explicitly rejected a local historical or genealogical interpretation of them in favor of a Marxist one focused on the sufferings of a global working class. Mandas, thus, did not consider his grandfather's story to be about Vourvoura, the Mandas family, or even about the Greek experience of transatlantic migration. Instead, he drew parallels between his grandfather's story and that of migrants in contemporary Greece, especially the largest, most stigmatized group of migrants, those from neighboring Albania. He said he wished that a prologue had discussed these similarities:

> From my grandfather's book you understand that Greece then was like Africa is today. His pain is that of a person who lived through circumstances that other people are living through now. Reading his story, people might learn not to be such asses (*gaidouria*) toward the Albanians.

Even though the immediate catalyst for the publication of the memoirs was the centennial of the Vourvoura benevolent association, Mandas stressed that if the memoirs had been published ten years ago, they would not have had any meaning or, to use his word, "profit" (*ofelos*). He explained:

> If you read it as a little story (*istorioula*) that has to do with how bad things were back then and how good they are now, you will come to the wrong conclusion. The point is to relate it to today's circumstances, to your life, your character, the things you believe (*to pistevo sou*): so that it will change you, not just pass over you like a fairy tale (*paramythi*) told by your grandmother.

If Mantzouranis could not remove the story from its context (since it is precisely the uniqueness of context that local history elaborates), Mandas, by contrast, chafed at seeing the text from a single, fixed corner, proposing instead that his grandfather's story be remolded to encompass other experiences and address unaffiliated readers.

Mandas's allegorical reading of the memoirs could be said to center on the slogan—"We were once Albanians"—which in recent years has been employed by leftist journalists to combat the climate of xenophobia in Greek society.[12] Interestingly, in public discussions about migration, this analogy has also been proposed to make precisely the *opposite* argument. As Ioanna Laliotou (1998) notes in her study of historical "enactments" of the Greek experience of transatlantic migration, the fact that Greeks themselves were once migrants has been treated as an "inoculation" against racism that ironically legitimizes its emergence. In everyday discourse, Greeks commonly represent themselves as "good" migrants who, unlike foreign migrant workers in Greece in the 1990s, had visas and working papers, contributed positively to the societies in which they lived, and were peaceful, law-abiding citizens. Mandas's grandson told me he decided to circulate his grandfather's memoirs because of his conviction that negative media representations of contemporary migrants in Greece were based precisely on this amnesia about actual Greek migration history.

At his house one day as we were talking, Mandas suddenly reached for and opened one of his grandfather's original notebooks. He started reading a section concerning an incident that had happened while his grandfather was working at a cement plant in Napa Junction, California. A number of strikes had been organized at the plant by workers, who were divided into factions according to their nationality. Relations between the Greeks and Italians, who outnumbered the Greeks 80 to 25, were particularly tense. When the Italians tried to break the strike, Mandas writes that the Greeks, along with the "English," beat them up (*tous espasame sto xylo*) but in court the Greeks lied and said that the Italians had attacked them with razors. A second story that Mandas's grandson read aloud concerned the time bailiffs in Los Angeles stopped Mandas and his brother for not having a dog license. One thing leads to another and the brothers soon find themselves in a scuffle with the officers. As Mandas hits the officer with a stick, his brother calls out to him: "not to hit him on the head or else we are finished" (*min ton varo sto kefali yiati ehathikame*). Realizing where the fight might lead, the brothers flee the scene, only to be rounded up shortly afterwards, brought to trial, and eventually released after paying a large fine. Closing the notebooks, Mandas's grandson concluded: "You see how easily this man, this good family man (*kalos noikokyris*), almost became a murderer. It does not take much for that to happen: that was my point." In his view, his grandfather, a man who in later life proved to be honest (*timios*) and logical, did not do break the law in the United States because he was a criminal, but because he—like foreigners in Greece in the 1990s—had been *criminalized* by the experience of migrant labor.

While Mandas's interpretation of his grandfather's story as a timeless parable of the underclass derived from his leftist politics, he seemed to be using his grandfather's story in order to argue for an "end to ideology" in the late 1990s. A telephone company employee in Tripolis and local cameraman for a private national television channel, Yiorgos Ilias Mandas is the father of three sons. Named after his grandfather, he was born in 1955 to Mandas's youngest son, Ilias, who would die shortly after his son's birth from a head wound inflicted during the Civil War. Growing up without a father in the years following the Civil War, Mandas's grandson had a difficult childhood, and he too should be considered a victim of that conflict. Prior to the fall of the Berlin Wall, which coincided with the birth of his twins, Mandas told me that he was extremely active in communist politics. "I had given myself to it" (*Imoun dosmenos*). Since the collapse of European communism, however, he explained that he has become disenchanted with politics and the course that the Greek Communist Party has taken. In his view, his grandfather's memoirs, in addition to providing a valuable lesson about the global political economy, also had much to say about what it means to be a "family man" and make ethical decisions in a world blighted by violence and partisanship. When I asked Mandas how he felt given his own politics about the fact that his grandfather was located on the Right, he told me:

> His politics had more to do with his opinion of what was good, not what was in his immediate interest (*symferon*). And all of us are like that. Tradition is a major thing, to have that kind of a heritage (*parakatathikes*; literally, "stock," "supply"). I was left-wing—and I am. I situate myself on the Left, but now I have become disappointed. I am not involved in the party anymore even though I could have a position of power now. Those things bring a person down.

He added that he particularly admired the fact that his grandfather, even though right-wing, had condemned the Security Battalionists and left-wing guerrillas alike for looting and violence. Ultimately, Mandas's "mature" outlook on the politics of the Civil War probably should not only be ascribed to his growing older and having a family himself but also linked to broader shifts I discussed in the previous chapter in how memories of the war years were being recalled and negotiated in the 1990s.

Despite the ostensibly opposed political visions underlying Mantzouranis's historical-particularist and Mandas's humanist-universalist readings of Mandas's "migrant's tale," they converge in viewing the *Greek* relation to migration as a subject of the past. In the editor Mantzouranis's reading, Mandas's story of life and work in *Ameriki* forms part of the prehistory of Greek American, but now also Helladic Greek, economic and cultural advancement. Notwithstanding the fact that Mandas's story demonstrates how economic transformations and political conflicts tore his family and village apart leaving him alone with memories of the dead, Mantzouranis paradoxically plots Mandas's narrative as a story of *life*—as the *rejuvenation* of a particular village genealogy through repatriation. Reframed as a story of community, the memoirs, thus, can take their place within a growing bibliography of local historical works about the village. Mandas's grandson, on the other hand, has attempted a more emotionally and politically strenuous reading of the text, one that sees his grandfather's experience as more than a "little story" or "folk tale" unrelated to present decision making and consciousness. Like other reformers of cultural memory we have seen in this book, Mandas has looked to the evidence of personal archives, to a family "stock" of memories, in a bid to challenge dominant public representations: in this case, of contemporary migration's veneer of shocking newness and lack of precedent.

Both Mandas and Mantzouranis converge, though, in understanding the memoirs to describe *another* Greece, a country teetering on the edge of economic collapse and marred by intractable political conflict, a place remote from the relatively prosperous, democratic, and peaceful present ("Greece then was like Africa is today . . ."). These are the so-called bad old days (*o palios kakos kairos*), as Mandas's grandson sardonically referred to them. As a result, even seen through Mandas's internationalist prism, new immigrants to Greece appear to be passing through a stage that Greeks as modern European citizens have already completed. Regardless of the reformist intentions behind it, the slogan "Greeks were once Albanians" implies that poverty, not capitalism, is the "problem" (i.e., the source of deviant behavior) and locates "Greeks" and "Albanians" (or other migrant groups) at different points in social evolution (Konstandinidou 2000). This denial of coevalness, a term that Johannes Fabian (1983) has coined to critique the construction of the ethnographic present of the Other as "Western" modernity's past, obscures the degree to which Greek "natives" are participating along with "foreign" migrants in a complex social transformation unfolding in a *global* present, arguably only superficially more peaceful, prosperous, and democratic than the past.[13]

Writing in the 1950s from the devastated post–Civil War countryside as young men and women, including one of his daughters, were about to set off in a second mass migration, Mandas himself surely would have felt that the story of his days in the United States was not a closed story, but a chronic symptom of an ailing Greek economy. In contemporary readings of the memoirs, Mandas's "migrant's tale," as marked (exotic, unknown) historical narrative, was unproblematically dissociated from the unmarked discourse on the Civil War ("everyone knows that story"): this strategic elision enabled migration to enter public historical narratives as a unifying story of national progress. Turning to Mandas's own act of re-collection, however, these two historical themes—migration and war—cannot be so easily disentangled into distinct "chapters" of modern Greek history.

Migrant, Soldier: Expendable Bodies and the Continuities of Class

It is little wonder that contemporary readers are tempted to excerpt a "migrant's tale" from Mandas's memoirs. This story not only resonates with contemporary concerns about the new migration but also coheres as a narrative. While Mandas's account of migrant labor is breathless and compelling, his story of the war years is disjointed and lacks a central hero, except when he flees the village during the Nazi incursion (in which thirty-three of his covillagers were murdered) and briefly becomes a traveler again. Chronology, which had been impelling the story forward, also breaks down toward the end of the memoirs as Mandas backtracks and reflects on his sons' lives. Furthermore, a reader with leftist sympathies would find Mandas a much more appealing narrator in the first part of his story: as a migrant laborer, he was an archetypal subaltern figure who participated in strikes and was conscious of his exploitation by the American industrial machine. In the second part of the text, even though Mandas, as his grandson pointed out, ends up assuming an ethical stance beyond partisan politics, some of his views can be hard to reconcile with the early Mandas.[14]

Carolyn Steedman's analysis of the memoirs of John Pearman, a nineteenth-century British railway worker, soldier, and policeman, in her *The Radical Soldier's Tale* (1988), might provide a useful starting point for thinking about Mandas's writing practice as well as the way that his text was later interpreted and edited. Like Mandas's autobiography, Pearman's memoirs consists of two distinct sections: an account of his experience as a British soldier in India and philosophical ruminations written during his service as a policeman back home. In British society, as Steedman points out, a cultural script was available both to tell and to receive a soldier's tale. As a result, Pearman's memoirs could be published (in the 1960s, in a series of diaries about nineteenth-century cavalry life). In this publication, it seemed reasonable only to reproduce the part of the text relating to Pearman's soldiering; his reflections on being a policeman and his seemingly irrelevant political-philosophical musings were simply summarized. Steedman argues that separating the two parts of the memoirs is highly misleading since it was in the context of Pearman's disciplined daily writing as a policeman that he had come to compose his text. During the writing process, he reevaluated his military service through the prism of his radical political views while his experience as a footsoldier of the British Empire naturally contributed to his developing those views in the first place. As Steedman suggests, writing must be seen as an active form of social practice: "an account of thinking as much as it is of living" (70).

Mandas's ease in narrating the first part of his story suggests that he similarly was drawing on an available cultural script. Despite the fact that the tale of migrant labor was not elicited from returned migrants for the project of writing Greek national history, this travel-adventure story—which Valtinos has aptly termed a *synaxari*, playing on the double meaning of the word ("saint's life," or religious story of suffering, and "tall tale")—must have been circulating among migrants themselves. Mandas certainly would have *told* the story of his travels many times in the United States in the cafés he used to frequent and then at home in Vourvoura. Notably, his grandson referred to incidents he thought he had read in the text but which he must have remembered from one of his grandfather's oral storytelling sessions. It seems highly unlikely, however, that Mandas would have *written* his tale of migrant labor if his sons had not died.

While speaking with Mandas's grandson one day, I told him that I found the photographs included in the published version of the memoirs incongruent with Mandas's narrative: "They seem to tell another story, almost the opposite of what your grandfather is saying. That he is alone. That his family is destroyed." Putting down his coffee cup, Mandas replied:

> If I were to write something in addition to the prologue. Maybe an epilogue. I would say something about his family. My grandfather had a whole family, the *Mantaioi*, the family tree. I am the last link (*krikos*). I am the only one left. The name, the root (*riza*), just stopped.[15] I would say something about how a man reaches his height (*apogeio*). A family man (*noikokyris*) in a village where he had a big family, which comes to nothing. They all were killed in the war. And they did not die only on one side. That was what

really shook him. Like his sons. One, on one side. One, on the other. And none was armed. A scumbag. An animal (*Kanenas den itan enoplos. Kathiki. Tomari*).

While Mandas's memoirs present themselves to the contemporary reader as a valuable source on the history of the first period of Greek transatlantic migration to the United States, Mandas himself appears to have written in order to testify to the traumas of the war period and specifically the many deaths of friends and family he had witnessed. From this perspective, Mandas's writing constitutes an act of mourning and his text a collective obituary.

In having his sons' deaths come before his own, Mandas is forced to take on the role of mourner, thus overturning the expected generational and gendered division of mourning labor in rural Greek society of the time.[16] With the reversal of the death order, Mandas, writing in his mid-seventies, can no longer expect to be remembered and commemorated by his children in the elaborate Orthodox memorial rite. Or, at least, by his male children: his wife and daughters, the "traditional" guardians of the dead, are entirely peripheral to his world and his story. As he contemplates his own death, Mandas instead finds himself overwhelmed by memories of his dead sons. Indeed, at several points in the narrative, he internalizes their voices to such an extent that it seems like he is really writing his story to tell *theirs*, or the story that they might have told if they had lived. Toward the end of the text, after he has described their characters, Mandas writes: "This is why I cannot forget them for a second many times I think about putting an end to my life I worry only that I will put my soul in hell."

If suicide is a form of communication rather than a solitary act, autobiography might be the note that makes the act unnecessary. As Veena Das has suggested, drawing on Wittgenstein, "Pain . . . is not that inexpressible something that destroys communication or marks an exit from one's existence in language. Instead, it makes a claim asking for acknowledgment, which may be given or denied. In either case, it is not a referential statement that is simply pointing to an inner object" (1997: 70). In putting his life on paper, Mandas can be said to be engaged in this kind of testimonial "project of address." His text is not premised on the existence of a potential listener but rather attempts to *constitute* an empathetic reader who might recognize his pain.

Rather than thinking of Mandas's use of autobiography as a reflection on his life, then, it might be more useful to think of his writing as a way of coping with survival in the midst of so much death. In her work on trauma and history, Caruth has posed the startling question: "Is trauma the encounter with death, or the ongoing experience of having survived it?" Can a narrative such as Mandas's be anything other than what she describes as a "double telling": an "oscillation between a *crisis of death* and the correlative *crisis of life*: between the story of the unbearable nature of an event and the story of the unbearable nature of its survival" (1996: 7)? Caruth's insights into the trauma of survival as entailing—and demanding—an "awakening" to the "necessity and impossibility of responding to another's death" (100) might help us think about the way Mandas folds his sons' lives and deaths into his text. Caruth describes hearing the voice of the other in pain as a reenactment of the trauma of loss but also as a reception and transmission of that voice; this transmission, however, does not necessarily involve *understanding*. Through the extensive use of reported speech in his memoirs, Mandas could be said to pass on a multiplicity of voices to which "he" as narrator is not fully present and which are not framed and controlled by an authoritative reporting voice. Rather than a sign of his "weakness" in regimenting other discourses, however, this profusion of voices might lead us to consider the ethical, not just referential, function of citation. Viewing Mandas's text as a "double telling," furthermore, precludes splitting it into discrete units based on historical theme or period while also troubling the assumption that the individual is the "natural" unit of historical subjectivity.

Reading Mandas's memoirs in terms of the juxtaposition of his migrant's tale and his sons' soldier stories, in turn, underscores deep continuities in the lives of working-class men and their bodies. A conceptual link for this reading might be found in the notion of *xenitia*, the Greek word for the state of being in a foreign land. *Xenitia*, as anthropologist Nadia Seremetakis has suggested, is a "foundational taxonomy" whose imagery informs Greek dreaming, death rituals, kinship systems, marriage, geography, history, ethnicity, and politics: "*xenitia* . . . encompasses the condition of estrangement, the outside, the movement from the inside to the outside, as well as contact and exchange between foreign domains, objects, and agents" (1991: 85). As Guy Saunier (1990) notes in his introduction to an anthology of folk songs of *xenitia*, motifs of sickness, death, and physical degradation are common elements in the depiction of the alienation, displacement, and suffering associated with *xenitia*.[17]

Xenitia also can be considered a root metaphor for death, as suggested in this folk song recorded in 1909: "the poor boys are tormented in foreign lands/dirt (*lera*) eats their body and a *kimer* [money belt] their waist/foreign women wash his clothes, foreign women wash his dirtiness" (1990: B/1a). In this striking image, the dirtiness of the body in *xenitia* reflects the absence of nurture as well as the corrosiveness of money in a wage-based economy. Money unnaturally adheres to a body that has become identical with the bearing of profit (rather than progeny). To be in *xenitia*, then, is to suffer a social death before one's physical one. In a brief comment Mandas makes about a coworker in the Napa Junction cement factory, an echo of these songs can be heard. After a strike at the factory, he says that all the Greeks left to find work elsewhere, except for one man who was engaged to a local woman. Although seemingly a minor detail, Mandas does not neglect to mention it in both notebooks: "he had become engaged in a nearby city/his fiancée ditched him however he stayed there and his bones stayed there too." This little tale encapsulates some of the greatest fears of *xenitia* as expressed in folk songs: being beguiled by a foreign woman to forget one's kinship obligations and leaving one's bones behind, unmourned, in a foreign land.

Xenitia humiliates the body. Its labor is not redemptive or transformative nor does it form the natural first step toward owning a small business, as the immigrant success story would have it. It is brute, polluting, sometimes fatal. It can lead nowhere. Mandas recalls his experience of migrant labor in the United States by reading the archive of his body: it is there that he finds "documents" not preserved elsewhere. Pieces of rock from a workplace accident in Napa Junction are still lodged in his back decades after its occurrence, reminding him that he almost lost his life "for nothing." Taken as a whole, Mandas's narrative charts the progressive decline of his body. In Chicago, during his first trip to the United States, he developed a bad case of typhus: "and I am amazed how I lived without going to the Hospital and without any care (χορείς περιπίεση)." At the cement factory in Napa Junction, he worked the ten-and-a-half-hour night shift. The factory, he tells us with some amazement, never shut down: "the workers had to work without a break [whether] it rained [whether] it was Sunday we had to work especially we who worked with the machines we had to not stop working at all we stopped only on christmas the new year and *thefourthjuly* [τοφορτζουλαϊα] on the 4th of July." He mentions being pleased when he started working on the drills (*Drilia*), remembering even fifty years later that in summer there was a breeze (το Καλοκέρη είχε αϊρα) and that it was a bit cooler than in the back of the plant where the Italians worked.

While Mandas endured the hard labor of his first trip to the United States, on his second trip (when he was in his late thirties and early forties), he developed a series of debilitating health problems, aggravated by questionable medical interventions. For example, after being bedridden for several months during a flu epidemic in Chicago in 1918, he had a hunk of flesh cut out from his nose by a doctor, causing him a major hemorrhage; the next doctor he consulted extracted all his top teeth. Later, in Spartanburg, Mandas would become obese (hence his nickname of *Hondros*, or "Fatty") and develop chronic insomnia and knee problems. Eventually, Mandas had no choice but to return home. At forty-six years old, he no longer had the strength to work. By the time he got on board ship for Greece in 1922, he was, according to his description, "almost a corpse" (*schedon ptoma*). Since he got on board so weak and pale from working two years, indoors, from 9:00 A.M. until midnight daily, he got an "ocean sunburn" the first day he sat out on the ship's deck. He did not even sleep on the ship, he tells us, because he feared the sailors might rob him and throw him overboard: "many of the passengers were sick and they were coming to Greece they were coming in third class and they died and they threw them into the sea." Mandas's fear of being disposed of before reaching home suggests the degree to which returning migrants had internalized the state's and their compatriots' view of them as pathology to the nation.[18]

In re-viewing his experience of *xenitia*, Mandas might have found a premonition of his sons' "cheap" deaths as well as the unmourned death that awaited him. In the second part of his memoirs, the degradation and humiliation of his body is mirrored in the violent destruction of his sons' bodies in war. Mandas's two sons fought in the Greco-Italian war, the middle one returning from the conflict a cripple. After a severe bout of frostbite, "they had cut the soles from both his feet and only the ankles were left and a little bit of the soles." During the Civil War, his oldest son, Yiannis, was executed and his youngest son, Ilias, was seriously injured while fighting as a mountain commando: "he had a wound through the head the shell had gotten him under the right eye and came out from behind the ear."

For Mandas, physical degradation is always linked to the potential for moral degradation: something that becomes all the more true during the Civil War when "home" becomes as foreign a land as any he saw as a migrant. Mandas's struggle to define moral behavior and the meaning of the word "compatriot" (*patriotis*) while living and working among a heterogeneous group of Greek laborers in the United States could be said to have been echoed and amplified in the crucible of the Civil War. If we see Mandas's migrant story as coming *after* his and his son's experience of that war, we can understand his dogged concern to judge particular cases of betrayal and fairness in interactions with his coworkers, friends, and bosses.

Although he does not speak of his migrant experience in explicitly political terms, Mandas does at one point in the text consider his son's fate through the prism of class analysis. Notwithstanding his own conservative politics, Mandas is prompted to accept some of the ideas proposed by the communists. In describing how a colonel moved his nephew out of the front lines during the Civil War, replacing him with Ilias, he notes:

> why did they do it because that's the way that this rags-and-tatters (*xekoureliasmeno*) state has it will the children of the rich fight? the worker (*ergatis*), the peasant (*agrotis*) will spill their blood so that communism will not prevail and they lose their villas and start to work because now others work for them and you will say you are a Communist I am like the King not a Communist but as some of the proclamations the guerrillas write they don't lie they say Soldier you who fight look around do you have any child of a rich person with you and that was Correct there wasn't a rich man's kid in the division

This passage is quite remarkable in terms of its deployment of voices. In quoting a communist proclamation, Mandas absorbs the rhetoric of communism into his own discourse to such an extent that he finds himself answering back defensively ("I am like the King not a Communist"). In the prologue to his memoirs, Mandas invokes a Biblical language of suffering, locating himself in the "rank of the life's poor toilers" (*viopalaiston*, literally "those who wrestle with life") and elsewhere in the text refers to himself as a "farmer" (*yiorgos*) and even a *deterlis* (from the Turkish word for "poor sufferer"). In this passage, however, he finds himself using politicized words from the communist lexicon such as "peasant" and "worker." In this instance, to use Vološinov's words, the speech of others could be said to have "infiltrated" the reporting context with "authorial retort and commentary," leading us to view Mandas's text from *its* perspective: just as Mandas was an expendable human cog in industrial America, his children were cannon fodder in World War II and the Civil War.

Constructed as a family story, Mandas's autobiography makes problematic testimony-taking projects that treat the biological individual as a one-person unit of collective memory. Instead, his text offers a vision of a transhistorical and transgenerational mode of re-collecting historical experience, centered not on a place of origin but on a bodies on the run (from the law, the bullet, a "cheap" death). Genealogy here holds together a story not of the village but of transnational movement and repetitive class injury: the immigrant of one generation is the footsoldier of the next, not the "small businessman." If the traumatic aspects of Mandas's experience easily can be downplayed by contemporary readers seeking to redeem his story for a narrative of community and national development, it is little wonder, as I will now consider, that the socially liberating and unfilial aspects of the migration experience described in his memoirs have also been overlooked.

Nostalgia in a Story of *Nostos*

94% of the residents are farmers. . . . The 87 male emigrants are included in the number of farmers because whether they were small businessmen abroad, or even important ones, when they come back to Vourvoura they become farmers again.

—"Statistics of Vourvoura," in the 1939 *Vourvoura Yearbook*

A photograph of Mandas as a grimacing old man has been scanned onto the front cover of the edited memoirs. A few pages into the text, however, one finds a quite different picture of him: as an "American" in his thirties, wearing a neat suit with a lapel pin. His hair is slicked down with brilliantine and parted down the middle. A thin rakish moustache graces his full, strong lip (see fig. 5.1). In reading Mandas's memoirs, one cannot help thinking that on some level his writing represents an attempt to reinhabit *this* photograph and explain to himself how his life, which seemed briefly to have some momentum and purpose, went so horribly wrong. While ostensibly confirming the conventional American (and Greek American) view that return to the homeland is always a step backwards, perhaps a disastrous one, Mandas's memories of a brief moment of personal freedom in the United States might be read as a more complicated meditation on the incompatible moral and economic orders in which his life was pitched. Mandas's longing for his bachelor days in California, a nostalgia on

Figure 5.1 Memory portrait. Yiorgos Mandas with a photograph of his grandfather in the United States. Tripolis 2003. Photograph by the author.

which neither Mandas's grandson nor Mantzouranis remarked, also could be said to counter the nostalgia for origins and the obviousness of the *topos* of local belonging institutionalized in the verbose genre of local historiography.

Recalling his youthful travels as an old and ruined man was bound to make Mandas nostalgic and lead him to regret his life decisions. Unlike middle-class authors of local history, however, Mandas does not recall his village childhood with regret; the *village* is not even a significant category in his text. Even though Mandas was involved in village politics, he never writes about the village *per se* (its history, the distinctive character of the villagers, its social networks, etc.) nor does he describe it as a physical place or built environment. Mandas, in any case, would not have had that many memories of his youth there, and these memories probably were not as vivid and formative as those of his childhood travels.

Contrary to stereotypical understandings of the migration experience and of Greek economic history, transatlantic migrants such as Mandas were not "shocked" out of their secure pastoral worlds for the first time when they set foot on American soil. Having begun his working life at the age of six, Mandas grew up traveling all around the Peloponnese doing seasonal rural labor as well as working jobs on road and railroad construction, at a roof tile factory, and as a shepherd's boy and digger. As he notes: "I did not stay in the village at all because as I wrote in the beginning we didn't have fields." Mandas tells us that during the summers his father worked as a shepherd, for which he received 100 drachma and his shoes (*tsarouchia*); in the winter, his father was a seasonal worker on the currant plantations along the western coast of the Peloponnese ("this is what all my compatriots did"). In addition, Mandas' family worked the grape harvest in Aigio and the wheat harvest in Sparta where, like many poor families, they gathered blades of wheat (*astachia*) that had been left behind on the threshing floors for use in their own households. Testament to his tenuous hold on residence, Mandas was not called up to fight in the Greco-Turkish war of 1897 because his parents had not registered his birth (*eimoun adilotos*). In any case, at the time the war broke out, he was away doing seasonal work in Olympia and the following year he left for the United States: "in '98 I left for America on the 26th of August." Given this life of restless movement, Mandas writes with bitterness but understanding of his mother's decision to send him to work at a railroad construction site when he was just a young boy: "When I was (8) years old my Mother sent me to the Railroad line with the other workers for me also to work as a worker an eight year old child what doesn't hunger do though." Home, for Mandas, certainly was not a cozy place nor was family intimacy and continuity a given.

Nostalgia, however, can be a longing not for a literal home, but for a place where one felt at home—a "place-of-provenance" in a more existential sense (Casey 1987: 363). Writing in the wake of a decade of war, it is hardly surprising that Mandas would view his past life in the United States, as difficult as it had been, as a time of freedom and relative contentment. Telling a story of his migrant days provided him a narrative field in which to recuperate his lost masculinity, youth, and agency. Even menial work like peddling fruit and vegetables with a pushcart takes on a glamorous, even transgressive, dimension in Mandas's account. He brags, for instance, that despite the "diabolic cold" in Chicago in 1900 and 1901, he could work outside very lightly dressed. His female customers, he reports, used to marvel at his endurance (ηγινέκες με εθαυμάζαν).[19] Stories of migration might be likened to tales of military service shared by old men in Greek village cafés. As Evthymios Papataxiarchis has noted: "At the conclusion of their lives, men in general, and especially those who have traveled a lot and seen a lot, are 'full of *istories* [stories],' which usually focus on a single theme: the making of the male self as that process was jointly experienced by friends" (1991: 74). For Mandas, his time in the United States represented the only period in his life when he could devote himself fully to his male friendships. When he first arrived in the United States in 1898, he mentioned that he had no friends because he was the "new guy" (*eimouna freskos*). This situation, however, changed over time, especially during the period he lived in California as a bachelor. "California," Mandas remembers, "is Paradise" (*I Kalifornia einai o paradisos*). In Los Angeles in 1907, he notes: "slowly I got to know the good Greeks of Los angeles and without a doubt I was very Well-liked (*Sympathitikos*)." Even though he did not have much money, he recalls, "I was invited to parties all the time at the Greek clubs I had many and good friends they respected me very much." Together with two other friends, he even claims to have set up the first Greek community in Los Angeles and arranged for a Greek Orthodox priest to come to their parish.

Notably, Mandas never refers to himself as a *metanastis* (migrant, immigrant, emigrant) but instead calls himself a *Brooklis*, one of several terms used by Greeks with both jealousy and derision to describe their repatriated or visiting compatriots from the United States.[20] If *metanastis* is a humbling word, which could be used to launch a protest for workers' rights, *Brooklis* is a boastful term in Mandas's use of it. Unlike Greek names transliterated into English via odd pronunciations and humiliating truncations (i.e., "Pappas," from all compound names beginning with "Papa-"), the word *Brooklis* represents the transformation of an American word into a Greek one (as well as the transformation of Greek into something else). It captures the sense in which the flow of people, ideas, and money in migration, though governed by a deeply unequal global economy, was also a "contrapuntal" (Coronil 1996) relationship, the meanings and terms of which were not entirely out of the hands of the migrants and the societies from which they came. In insisting on a difference that national ideologies are quick to erase (once a Greek always a Greek), *Brooklis* might be analogous to Roger Rouse's "(im)migrant," the term he uses to unsettle the assumed opposition of *immigration* (as unidirectional movement) and *migration* (as continual circulation), thus highlighting the "transnational migrant circuit" as the main setting around which people "orchestrate" their lives (1991: 14).

In his praise for the opportunities his sojourn in the United States afforded him, Mandas, however, seems to accept common American and Greek American mythologies of personal advancement through movement from a preindustrial economy to a modern, technological one. In his analysis of Greek American literature, Yiorgos Anagnostu (1993–94) describes the plot of the immigration story as involving a passage from "immigrant" to "ethnic," a movement typically entailing the relinquishing of an "Old World code of honor," revolving around obligation to home and a culture of revenge, for a "New World humanism" centered on obligation to others and oneself and an ethic of forgiving. According to this schema, return cannot be anything but a mistake, an anachronism, a hard lesson.[21] While the story of migrant repatriation was long untellable within categories of Greek national historiography, this is not entirely the case from the perspective of American history and sociology. In his 1956 *They Remember America: The Story of the Repatriated Greek-Americans*, Theodore Saloutos, a second-generation Greek American historian describes a journey he took to Greece in the early 1950s to collect the stories of Greeks like Mandas who had repatriated in the 1920s. As Yiorgos Kalogeras (1998) has argued, Saloutos depicts the repatriates' failure and alienation in Greece in order to emphasize that there was a "high price" to be paid for repatriation as well as to ease his own return to the United States as an *American* social scientist, not to be mistaken for a potential repatriate himself. Yet, as Kalogeras suggests, Saloutos could only posit the United States as the "completion" of Greece in developmental terms by failing to take into account the complex political and socioeconomic contexts the migrants left and returned to and, most glaringly, the devastating effects of World War II and the Civil War.

On some level, this teleological narrative *does* appear to apply to Mandas's case. For one, even though as a landless peasant Mandas had already worked for wages in Greece, his jobs in the United States in retailing and heavy industry did introduce him to a more abstract concept of labor and a new logic of money. He tells us that in Greece from the age of fifteen he had worn a leather money belt. As a migrant worker, this money belt, as I have already noted, came to symbolize the conflation (and corruption) of the laboring body with money. At one point in his narrative, Mandas notes that the room where he was staying in Los Angeles had been broken into by thieves who stole his and his friends' guns and clothes. Their money was safe, though, because as he explains: "we always had our money with us we had those belts the so-called *Kymeria* [from Turkish, *kemer*, leather money belt] and we had it all in Sovereigns all gold." In the physical form of gold, the money that Mandas made did not appear to be just a sign of value but its physical manifestation. Another time, following a quarrel with bailiffs in Los Angeles, Mandas paid his and his brothers' bail with two checks (*tsekia*) for $2,150. The officer, surprised by the amount of the checks, looked at Mandas's hands to see if he was a "worker or a Thief" (*ergatikos i Lopoditis*). Judging from the way he reports this incident, Mandas seemed to find it reasonable that his life of labor had been inscribed directly on his body.

Yet, the reference to checks in this comment also indicates that Mandas had started to deal with money in more abstract, dematerialized ways that invalidated the triptych of body-labor-money symbolized by the money belt. This "bodiless body of money," as Derrida has written of the "spectropoetics" at work in Marx's analysis of the commodity, is "not the lifeless body or the cadaver, but a life without personal life or individual property" (1994: 41). The moment in which Mandas was truly introduced to this "ghost" seems to have stood out quite distinctly for him. He tells us that during the four years (1903–07) that he worked at the cement factory at Napa Junction, two major events occurred. The first was the workplace accident that nearly cost him his life. The second was the burning down of his bank during the 1906 earthquake and fire in San Francisco. He writes: "we figured that we would lose it [the money] however even though it burned down the bank gave it to us even with the interest." This magical return of his capital appears to have "spooked" Mandas so much that he considered this miracle—and not so much the earthquake and fire—a central event of this period of his life.

In keeping with an "Old World" narrative, Mandas also explains his return to Greece and sacrifice of a bohemian lifestyle as motivated by a sense of responsibility to his family. After telling us about the good days in Los Angeles, he notes that he always had a "major worry" on his mind: namely, marrying off his sisters and seeing his old parents before they died. He remarks: "really I remembered the terrible state of Greece but this was more important" (πράγματη εθιμομου[ν] τα χάλια της Ελλάδος αλλα αφτό είτο πιοβαρή). While his decision might be interpreted as a clear instance of "clinging" to "traditional" values, especially since he ascribes his return to *filotimo*, or honor, the choice, as Mandas remembers it, was neither easy nor automatic. All his friends, he remembers, were against it: "no one told me that I was doing good and everyone tried to stop me." When he returns to Greece after his first trip to the United States, he experiences his marriage and brief period of working as a rural guard (*agrofilakas*) as profoundly humiliating, even emasculating. He writes: "In 1910 I married in the fall I became a Rural Guard a laughable profession (επάγγελμα ξεφιλειστειχον) who became a Rural Guard Yiorgos Mandas the prize (*o eklektos*) of Los angeles." As suggested by this comment, dropping out of a more advanced capitalist economy into a rural one is intimately linked in Mandas's mind with a loss of personal freedom and chance for advancement. Retrospectively, he chides himself for not settling in the United States after he married and thus escaping his family's and his nation's grim fate. As he does frequently throughout the memoirs, he poses himself a rhetorical question to frame his discourse: "What should I have done when I came from America I should have married off one of my Sisters and gotten married myself taken my wife and gone back to America."

As evident in Mandas's discussion of his marriage strategies, his return to the village appears to have created an acute crisis for him about how to measure his personal value in relation to money. At first he tells us that he did not want a big dowry because he—the former "prize of Los angeles" and a *Brooklis*—did not want to give up his independence and be controlled by his wife and her family:

> I decided to get married after people made me a lot of offers since I was both a *Brooklis* and very handsome (*efpariseiastos*) they offered me Girls to marry from important families with big dowries I however avoided them because I had a little money I did not want to be under the hand of a Woman I also had the intention to marry a woman whose Sister I loved who had already married however nothing came of that I was Engaged in January the year 1910, as dowry her family did not have a landed estate she had two Brothers in America and they promised to give me 4,500 dr[achmas] which of course at that time was 900 dollars

Even this dowry never comes through, and a few lines later Mandas writes in a self-mocking tone: "The *brooklis* who had big ideas ended up just getting as dowry money for the expenses of the wedding." At the time, of course, he might have thought it was a better investment to marry a woman who had brothers established in the United States than to receive land or cash as dowry, and indeed on his second trip Mandas did work with his brothers-in-law in South Carolina. Nevertheless, these contradictory comments reflect a profound conflict between seeing himself as an autonomous capitalist subject, free from the social obligations that a dowry entails, or as someone whose worth is reflected by marrying into an "important family" and attracting an impressive dowry.

Although Mandas returned to Greece from his second trip to the United States so fat and laden down with belongings that he barely staggered into the village with two hired mules, it does not take long before he is stripped down to size both financially and physically. His plan to employ usury as a banking system would fail miserably. After his first trip to the United States, Mandas had chastised himself for thinking he could survive in the village without owning land. Nonetheless, he tells the reader, he had had a plan to maintain his capital and also generate profit (εντούτεις είχα κάποιο πρόγραμμα): he would lend his covillagers the capital remaining after his sisters' weddings, which he estimated at 10,000 drachmas, and live off the interest. At 15 percent, he reckoned, he would be making 1,500 drachmas a year, equivalent to the then enviable salary of schoolteachers: "I said our family got by with 300 dr[achma] a year with 1500 wouldn't I get along well." However, his scheme does not pan out; since his capital had dwindled to 4,000 drachmas after the weddings, he would have to return to the United States to raise more funds. After his second sojourn abroad, he makes sure to buy some land in the village and set himself up as a farmer; his investment scheme, though, would go awry once again. He lent the majority of his capital ($3,000 of $4,700) to a covillager and merchant in Piraeus at 11 percent interest; when this man went bankrupt shortly afterwards, Mandas along with many other Vourvouriots lost their savings. Mandas did not have any better luck with loans to "poor relatives." He tells us that he was not a money lender (*tokistis*); he was just doing them a "favor" (*efkolia*) in order to secure their votes in local elections. However, after dictator Metaxas's relief of agricultural debt in 1937, as Mandas remembers bitterly, his debtors never came of their own accord to pay him back. Despite Mandas's intentions to turn his money into generative capital, his covillagers succeeded in treating it as wealth to be redistributed.

The fact that Mandas returned to Vourvoura, became a potato farmer, and went bankrupt would seem conclusive evidence for a (Greek) American narrative that scripts return to the Old World as regression. Like the argument "Greeks were once Albanians," however, a view of national economies as developing independent of each other—the bedrock of liberal historiography—obscures the global economic field in which processes such as migration take place. The fall of currant prices that led to Mandas's initial migration was hastened by the institution of national tariffs, itself a sign of growing international protectionism; as a result, Mandas was thrust into the global reserve army, only to be tossed back to his country when no longer productive. Rather than a failure to become a small businessman, Mandas's return to Greece also might be seen as an *opting out* of the American proletariat. Back in Vourvoura, Mandas with his newly bought land had established himself as "economically independent" (*oikonomikos anexartitos*).[22] After a period that had lasted from the age of six to forty-six, he was no longer a migrant laborer. As his grandson suggested, when Mandas writes that he worked "abroad" (*sta xena*) as a currant picker in Messinia, a neighboring province, his use of the word *xena* reflected not only that this area *was* far away because of the difficulty of travel at that time but also that he was working for others, doing "foreign work" (*xeni douleia*). Although Mandas in his grief does not tell us much about the first years in Greece after his return from the United States, it seems that he was actually quite happy. In addition to his active participation in local political life, he mentions that he used to host lots of social gatherings at his home: "my house that all the time had parties and entertainment now the last years constantly has bitterness and sadness misery" (το σπήτιμου οπου μια φορα ειχε κάθε λήγο γλέντει κε διασκέδασει ετορα τα τελευτέα χρόνια έχη σεινέχια πίκρες και λίπες βασανα). When he repatriates, Mandas does not return to a "premodern" lifestyle; instead he attempts to support himself and his family by cobbling together various sources of income in a quintessentially modern adaptation to his circumstances. It is the war more than Greece's chronic "underdevelopment" that brings on Mandas's personal catastrophe.

That Mandas cannot resolve the contradictions in his life reflects nothing other than that he is caught in them. Exploitation and autonomy were bound together in his experience of migrant labor in the United States and he cannot quite make sense of it. The dysfluencies of his text and its generic eclecticism testify to the obstacles involved in constructing a historical narrative that spans territories, cultures, and languages. At the same time, as I will now consider, the experience of migration—and the writing practices and print culture related to it—appears to have provided the discursive context in which his story came to be recorded in the first place.

Account-ing for the Past:
The Material Contexts of Writing

How did Mandas come to *write* his story? He had attended school for just a few years and learned only the bare rudiments of writing. Unlike educated refugees contacted by researchers from the Center for Asia Minor Studies, Mandas probably was not encouraged by anyone to write down his story. No one brought him a notebook and promised to type up his manuscript and preserve it in an archive. Even though Mandas's work did not provide him a routine of disciplined writing, his writing, nonetheless, could be said to have emerged out of the material contexts of his life and specifically from textual practices associated with migrant labor and the agricultural economy. His autobiography, in turn, builds on a model of *accounting*: an ongoing balancing of his finances that he extends to the events of his life.

It would be a mistake to assume that Mandas lived a life at a far remove from writing and reading. Given the romance of the oral, ethnographies of Greece have not always provided us much of a picture of the place of writing in village life. Written texts, however, were hardly absent from that world, especially in the twentieth century, and a rigid social hierarchy based on mastery of official written language and linked to various institutions (church, school, state bureaucracy) shadowed it.[23] According to his grandson, Mandas was an avid reader of newspapers (*Kathimerini*, not the more populist paper of the day *Akropoli*). During his terms as president of the village council, Mandas also must have handled a certain amount of paperwork. Even agriculture had its written dimensions: the two tiny notebooks in which he has

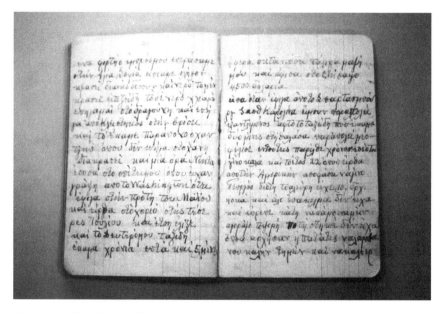

Figure 5.2   Visualizing orthographies. Mandas's notebook. Photograph by the author.

written his life story are lined account ledgers once commonly used in Greek villages to record agricultural income and expenses (see fig. 5.2).

The most important context for Mandas's writing, however, seems to have been migration itself. While in the United States, Mandas learned to put his basic literacy skills to use in dealing with banks, sending remittances, reading the local Greek press (he makes reference to some of the major Greek newspapers in the United States at the time), and writing an occasional letter home (such as the one in which his return was announced many months before his actual arrival on a very slow boat). Once back in Greece, he found himself on the other end of this transatlantic dialogue. In addition to his personal dealings with state bureaucracy and banks (he tells us, for instance, that in 1923: "I wrote to the bank in Chicago and they sent it [the money he had left on deposit] to me and I put it in the National Bank at $3\frac{1}{2}$% interest"), he handled money sent to the village by his compatriots in the United States as contributions for various local building projects, such as the construction of a new church, road, and clock tower.

Mandas's village, although quite tiny, also produced "yearbooks" (*epetirides*) in 1924, 1925–26, and 1939. These volumes, published by local benevolent associations, contain miscellaneous articles on subjects relating to the village, including historical, archaeological, and geographical information; folk songs; sayings; short stories; jokes; statistics; letters; obituaries; and photographs. Brief moralistic messages, many printed in red type and scattered throughout the 1924 yearbook, underscore the fact that these texts were addressed to Vourvoriot immigrants in the United States: "Bring us only dollars from America. Not the other customs though.

Keep away from any oppositional and un-Greek ceremony. We have to keep the customs of our village pure and unmixed." Or, echoing folk songs of *xenitia* to which I have alluded: "If you see that your life is beginning to go dark leave America quickly and come and die in the earth of your homeland. Don't leave your body in foreign soil. Foreign earth is a stepmother!!" (Η ξένη γης είναι μητρυιά!!). As nostalgic discourses on the village's past, these yearbooks represent a characteristic product of the transnational cultural space opened by migration; in contrast to classic village ethnography, they posit the "Vourvoriot" as an inherently cosmopolitan subject.[24] Although these texts, which proudly list the names and places of residence of villagers living abroad, promote a flexible view of the relationship between community and territory, they actively repress hybridity in order to assert the inalienability of origins. Diaspora, from their perspective, cannot be anything but an extension of and supplement to an otherwise self-sufficient and fully formed nation.

Although most contributors to these yearbooks were members of the village's educated elite living in Athens or Piraeus, Mandas himself wrote two brief stories for the 1925–26 edition, thus suggesting that he had some ambitions as a writer and that these textual productions might have played a central role in cultivating his interest in writing.[25] Given his heightened consciousness of the dissemination potential of print, one wonders if Mandas was not frustrated by having to resort to handwriting to produce his memoirs. To the extent that handwriting indexes class position and educational background, Mandas might have greatly preferred to hide his poor man's script—especially "quaint looking" to readers in the computer age—and escape into the uniformity of type that would have allowed him to "look the same" as bourgeois writers (cf. Kittler 1999: 199).

Migration provided the context for Mandas's writing in yet another way. If in the economy of travel, the return to the *oikos* is meant to provide some sort of "profit" (Van Den Abbeele 1992: xiii–xxx), a migrant's story of travel at base cannot but be an accounting of money made, spent, and lost along the way. Travel from place to place follows as a natural effect of these calculations rather than vice versa, as in a travelogue. Thus, in Mandas's text, narrative time moves forward by way of transactions, wages, purchases, and inventories: a constant balancing of his budget.[26] In his first year in the United States, Mandas lived in a squalid basement room in New York City and sold dates with a handcart. He writes of this time:

> what did we make from the Dates we had sales every day from 70 ¢ to 150 what were we left a profit each day of 30 to 40 Cents (*sentzia*) how many expenses did we have we paid 4 Cents a day for rent because we lived in a basement 10 steps down and we were close to the river and many times we had to put our shoes up on the bed because water would come into the basement black bread on the one hand cost 3 ¢ a loaf and white on the other 5 ¢ a loaf meat on the one hand lamb was 3 ¢ for the breast 5 for the back parts and 8 for the leg with the loins and thus our expenses were up to 20 ¢ a day

In this passage, Mandas's documentation of his expenses as well as his implicit contrast of prices "here" and "there" and "then" and "now" could be said to form a rudimentary mode of recalling the past and making cultural and historical comparisons.[27]

The failure to really get anywhere in life is measured in Mandas's text by this continuous discourse on his finances: rather than surplus, he charts a gradual loss both of human and fiscal capital. He ends up not far from where he started: "I was born in 1876 my father was poor my mother was an orphan by her father as dowry she got a one-room house (*domatio spiti*) and 3 to 4 *stremmata* [approx. 1 acre] of a dried-out field (*xerikon agron*)." In a note added to one of the notebooks after the death of his son Ilias, Mandas draws up his grand total:

> That's how the general catastrophe of Yiorgos Y. Ilias Mandas came about of the six girls and boys (*pedia*) he was left with 2 girls one in Canada and one here. The little fields that I have remain uncultivated the apple trees unsprayed unpruned they run wild we live with 5 dr[achmas] a day and those the state grants us

In her discussion of the "commonplace books" of literate eighteenth- and nineteenth-century upper-class Americans, Susan Miller has described the accounting of work, expenses, and property as an *aide-mémoire* that blurs the boundaries between memory and work, turning accounts of work into memory and making the notation of expenses a kind of work (1998: 177–83). "Time for writing, various forms of literary expertise, and a keen sense of significant identity," she suggests provided the context for the production, transmission, and safeguarding of these written accounts of miscellaneous daily events and acquisitions (1998: 30). Mandas's text as an accounting of a progressive stripping away of his family and belongings could be seen as a dark parody of these genres of bourgeois household management.

As any writer knows, a context for writing is also a physical space and stretch of time. Mandas's writing could only take place in that brief period between the end of a working life and death. Unlike bourgeois authors for whom writing is the means *par excellence* to extend the self into the public sphere, Mandas's act of writing was directly linked to his withdrawal from public life. In old age, Mandas had become confined to his house. He was too weak to work in his fields, and his doctors had told him to avoid drinking coffee and getting riled up. Recalling the simple pleasures of male socializing in rural Greece, he notes:

> and my time does not pass easily because I was used to working and I have had to make another concession I was something of a drinker and during feast-days I would spend the day in the taverns that's where the political games were going on because as I told you I was always into politics this was before the coffeehouses were established in the village when the coffeehouses came I also had stopped drinking even wine on account of Arteriosclerosis and I was by this time a man of the coffeehouses I played almost all the [card] games *prefa—piketo—skarbeli—koltsina—rami—kiamo* and any other game of the day

Since he could no longer go to the cafés, time, which used to be passed so pleasantly in these public spaces of male leisure, had become a burden for him: one temporarily filled by his writing project.

At the end of his text, after racing across expanses of the United States and walking across large stretches of the Peloponnese, Mandas's narrative slows down to the speed of writing. This is not necessarily surprising, of course, since stories of travel are usually told at moments of stasis. Mandas complains that he no longer has the strength to walk down to his olive groves. His outside world has become restricted to the garden surrounding his house:

> I do any odd job I tie up the branches of an apple tree that is loaded down so that it doesn't break I look to see if the apple trees have worms in their Trunks and are destroying them because worms go after apple trees a lot because they are sour-sweet (*glikoxines*)

One imagines Mandas getting up to check on his trees and then sitting down to write a few pages in his notebook. His garden is the site of re-collection on the edge of his life, the worms nibbling on his apples a portent of impending death. His notebook opens up an imaginative space, but also a material one, which is molded with manual labor of another kind. In his loneliness, Mandas did not necessarily seek out a quiet place to write and an audience to listen to his complaints; rather writing gave him a place to be and provided him with a listener—another sad and ruined person like himself—with whom he could review his life and seek acknowledgment for his pain.

The social and material contexts in which Mandas's memoirs were produced form a suggestive counterpart to the projects of historical re-collection we have considered up to this point. Given his social position, Mandas could be expected, from the standpoint of the guardians of literate tradition, to have a limited ability or desire to document his past. Yet, his case suggests that it is problematic to assume that the speaking (and writing) subject of discourse emerges only within the confines of disciplines and institutions culturally assigned to archive and judge the past, such as history, literature, and law. The de facto family archive created by depositing memoirs in a village drawer differs greatly from those I discussed in the chapter on local historiography; here, the family as institution of memory with its own base of material and psychological continuity proves to have the potential to register experiences at odds with established narratives of a nationalized past, a fact that lately has become of use to Greek academic historians as they seek evidence with which to write the history of migration. In this respect, it is notable that Mandas, despite his introduction to print culture, ended up writing his story *twice*, suggesting an "old-fashioned" set toward the book as unique object-artifact rather than reproducible text. However, given the differential hold that various social groups have over the "materiality that history needs both to explain and acknowledge" (Trouillot 1995: 45), there seems to have been little else to assure the preservation of Mandas's story besides the brute fact of the physical trace.

Becoming an Author:
Hero, Traveler, Father, Petitioner

At first, the fact that Mandas writes autobiography seems startling. Given the hierarchies that regulated access to written language, autobiographies of working-class people with little education were not common in Greek society at the time Mandas wrote, and his text could hardly be said to fall into the two principal categories of Greek autobiographical writing: war memoirs and reminiscences of the elite. In

Mandas's case, however, I would argue that he did not have a choice *but* to write his story as a personal one: autobiography was the only genre of historical discourse available to him given his tenuous hold on the codes of literate expression and, perhaps more importantly, the fact that his was a story of restless movement. Like the novel, autobiography is marked by its generic fluidity and openness to absorbing other discourses within its textual fabric. Thus, Mandas's autobiography appears to be composed of multiple other genres, such as Orthodox saints' lives, adventure comic strips, bourgeois obituaries, accounting ledgers, and complaint letters, which are themselves related to various performance contexts and media networks, such as coffeehouse banter, journalism, litigation, liturgy, and religious and diaspora print discourses. To parse out these genres, I draw loosely on Bakhtin's (1986) typology of the novel (travel novel, novel of ordeal, family-biographical novel, national *Bildungsroman*), ignoring its problematic evolutionary implications and using it in a more properly Bakhtinian way.

Before I speculate on the nature of these other genres, though, I want to consider briefly how "Mandas" himself as author has framed his text. Sensing that he has transgressed the rules of literary etiquette by casting his discourse in the first person, Mandas begins both notebooks with a note explaining why his writing autobiography should not be taken as an egotistical gesture:

Απομνημονεύματα Γεωργίου Μαντά
Ιωάννου του Ηλία ηγράφοντες τά
Απομνίμονευματάτους ην πλούσιη Στρα-
τηγεί Σοφεί εφεβρέτε εξερεβνιτέ καί
ακόμη καί αυτή ηγκάστερς η αρχή
λίσταρχη εγω όμος ανήκο στον κλάδον τον φτοχόν τονβιοπαλεστόν και τον
κάτεστρεμένον δεν ειμε εγώειστης
ημε ενας ανθροπος χορεις εγώησμο και
γράφο ολαμου τα βασανα και τας θλίψεις
δια να ηδούν και αλη θλιμένη και κατε
στράμενη οτη δεν εινε μόνιτους

Memoirs of Yiorgos Mandas
Son of Ioannis son of Ilias the authors of their
Memoirs are the rich the Generals the
Wise the inventors the explorers and
Even those ga[ng]*sters* and chief brigands
I however belong to the ranks of the
Poor the toilers and the
Wretched I am not an egotist
I am a man without egoism and
I write all my miseries and woes
So that others who are sad and wretched
Can see that they are not alone

Απομνημονεύματα
Γεωργίου Ιω. Ηλ. Μαντά

Ηγράφοντες τάαπομνιμονευ-
ματά τους εινε πλούσιη
Στρατήγί πρόθηπουγί
εφεβρεται εξερεύνηταί
Βασειλής δικτάκτορες
και ακομη και αφτη ειλή-
σταρχη και οκαθενας γρα-
φή πος εδρασε και τα μεγάλα
του κατορθόματα
εγώ δεν ανίκο σε αφτόν
τον κλάδον είμε ενας
πτοχός βείοπαλεστίς

Memoirs
Yiorgos Io. Il. Mandas

Authors of their memoirs
are the rich
the Generals the prime ministers
the inventors the explorers
the Kings the dictators
and even those brigands
and everyone writes
how they acted and their great
accomplishments
I do not belong to that
Rank I am a
Poor toiler

δεν ίμε εγοηστής θέλονα-	I am not an egotist I want to
γραψο πος ζή ενας πτοχος και	Write how a poor
κατέστραμένος ανθροπος	And wretched man lives
πόσα βάσανα καιληπες είχ(δ)α	How much misery and sadness I had/saw
στα (75) χρονια που εχο	in my (75) years

In Walter Benjamin's terms, Mandas could be said to be asserting an "authority which even the poorest wretch in dying possesses for those living around them" (1968: 94), an authority "borrowed" from the death of his sons, the death of his co-villagers, and his own impending death. In this prologue, Mandas also appears to be making the distinctly modern claim to possessing the right to witness history not as a "great man"(whether honest or dishonest) but as a sufferer and ruined man. The history he will witness is not that of military triumph or scientific progress, the "monumental history" of "struggle and action" that Nietzsche has described, but rather one of injustice, which since World War II, as Felman (2002) has argued, has come to give monumental dimensions to history. In other cases we have considered, this claim has been made by an educated mediator on the part of a subaltern subject. In making this assertion himself and insisting on full authorship over his text, Mandas finds himself faced with the nonobvious task of finding a language in which to testify.

In referring to his text as memoirs (*apomnimonevmata*) rather than as an autobiography (*aftoviografia*) or a diary (*imerologio*), Mandas invokes a tradition of memoir writing with which he would have been familiar: the autobiographies of heroes (the "Generals") of the Greek War of Independence as well as perhaps those of the more recent Balkan Wars, an event that had given further impetus to the development of Greek military memoir writing (cf. Abatzopoulou 1994: 28). In invoking the paradigm of the military memoir, Mandas signals a desire to inscribe his personal experience—and specifically his catastrophe—within the frame of a national historiography of battles and deeds. Yet, most of the story Mandas tells is plotted far from the reach of national-historical events and whenever his narrative does move into national-cultural time-space, it is almost always to describe a sense of disconnection from the major events of the day. He writes only one page about his participation in the Balkan War of 1913, and these few lines primarily concern an accident that occurred as he returned to his village after the war's conclusion:

> there came about some sort of Settlement (επηλθε καπιος Σύμβιβασμός) with Turkey and we were demobilized (απεστρατέφθημεν) from Nafplion as we were coming along with a cousin of mine as we neared the outskirts of the village he had a shotgun on his shoulder I was coming up from behind and it appears his hand was playing with the trigger and he almost killed me the bullets passed by and touched my hat

The formal Greek of the first sentence quickly segues into an informal vernacular. The events of national politics are distant from Mandas's war experience: "some sort of Settlement" was signed and they were "demobilized," but all Mandas knew was that he was coming home and that as in other moments in his life he almost died by accident.

By contrast, birth, childhood, school, marriage, work, death, parenting, and household accounting—the central subjects of bourgeois autobiography and journal writing—give structure to Mandas's story. Bakhtin has suggested that it is the concept of "generations" that defines the family-biographical story and expands it beyond the limits of a single life: "Generations introduce a completely new and extremely significant aspect into the depicted world; they introduce the contiguity of lives taking place at various times" (1986: 18). The family biography is typically addressed to children and meant to provide them with an exemplary text after which to model their lives. In defining a successful career, the biography establishes a unique family heritage; as material artifact, it also adds to the family archive, itself a sign of family continuity, prestige, and accumulation (Lejeune 1989: 169–70). Mandas would have had a model for the bourgeois biography in the biographical sketches and obituaries that appeared in the village yearbooks and other such publications. These narratives, which describe the lives of villagers who had notable or illustrious *stadiodromies*, or careers, could be said to promote not only specific ideas about the ideal career—but also the ideal *of* a career as well as of education, procreation, civil service, and public works. Mandas's text is structured in terms of generational time and ordered by an ethic of rational fiscal management. As a business enterprise, however, his life, as I have already suggested, is an utter failure: not only does he have little to pass on to his children, he has lost them as well.

Ultimately, Mandas spends too much time on the road to tell a story about home: his memoirs, thus, often invoke genres of adventure-travel narration. Movement through time and space might create the most basic chronotope and story line but a tale of travel can only take proper shape if the traveler returns to narrate it to friends and family. In Greek American and other ethnic American literatures, by contrast, a one-way journey from the homeland to the United States is often plotted as a *Bildungsroman*, in which, as Bakhtin describes, narrators "emerge" and "grow" along with the world as they come into consciousness. This kind of story unfolds in the chronotope of a "national historical time" in which the past has a "necessary place" in an "unbroken line of historical development" (1986: 19–54). Travel in the *Bildungsroman* denotes movement in the sense of education as well as transformation, often symbolized by the acquisition of a new name, language, and identity. As a story told in Greek about an "elsewhere," Mandas's account of repatriation, on the other hand, cannot but be a form of "travel story," in which no such existential change is experienced. According to Bakhtin, travel novels are dominated by "adventure" time: "moments, hours, days—snatched at random from the temporal process" (11). Mandas might have had a model for this kind of adventure time and its potential for the performance of rugged masculinity in the comic strips of his day, such as *Tsakidzis tou Aidiniou*, an Anatolian Greek Hercules figure whose exploits Mandas followed with keen interest, according to his grandson's account.

Against the backdrop of a highly sketchy cultural and physical landscape, then, "Mandas" appears in much of the memoirs as a picaresque hero who encounters one *peripeteia* (adventure, experience, mishap) after another, as he brushes up against the Law and alien Others.[28] The travel novel, Bakhtin explains, is also governed by a sense of the strangeness of foreign worlds and devoid of an "understanding of the wholeness of such sociocultural phenomena as nationalities, countries, cities, social groups and occupations" (11). Indeed, in his descriptions of the United States, Mandas does not attempt to characterize American life or provide a visual image of the American landscape, built or physical. He describes the country in terms of Greek climatic zones. For instance, he tells us that in winter he headed for *himadia* ("winter grazing lands") such as Texas, Florida, Utah, and Nevada, and that Fresno where grapes and figs grow is the "Mediterranean." The only time Mandas describes a human landscape in any detail is when he is on board ship in the Mediterranean, closer to home, but in a more "exotic" place than the United States. When the ship stops to get coal in Algeria, he is transfixed by the poor black "natives" and their strange, desperate poverty:

> for workers they had all Blacks (*Arapides*) all-naked the passengers threw them a little bread and they were fighting among themselves who would get it first imagine the hunger that those Africans also have I saw another interesting thing in Algeria there at the port where the ship was getting coal there was a diver who had gone down into the depths of the sea and he had a bamboo net and wherever coal had fallen from the boat he was collecting it and another guy was going around with a boat and pulling up the net with a string

As suggested by this passage, Mandas fits Others into crude categories of racial difference. It would be wrong to assume, however, that he brought these views along untouched from the "Old World." While working in Chicago just after the end of World War I, he notes, for instance, that his good customers on a particular street had started to sell their houses because Jews were moving into the neighborhood. He explains:

> there are three categories of Jews the Upper classes the middle and the bottom who think that they are in Jerusalem and have let their beards grow on that road the middle classes came and wherever Jews live the English and the Germans leave and wherever Italians live the Jews leave I had some Jewish women customers from the Aristocracy from the other two classes I didn't have [any customers] because I sold good stuff and they wouldn't pay for it

While Mandas's Greek world would have been divided up according to regional distinctions and antagonisms, in the United States he "learns" new ways to stereotype people according to ethnicity, religion, and race.

Perhaps the most important genre on which Mandas relies to plot his story, especially if we see it as a survivor's testimony, is what Bakhtin has described as the "novel of ordeal," which turns a text into a "court of law." Indeed, in the memoirs "Mandas" often plays the role of a much-suffering martyr in search of moral vindication. Time in Mandas's text is punctuated not by events accorded importance in historiography (Balkan Wars, "Asia Minor Catastrophe," Nazi Occupation) but by crises of justice and tests of humanity that often take the form of a dyadic encounter. Another genre of biographical expression that appears to have entered Mandas's text, then, is that of the Orthodox saint's life, centered on a martyr whose moral integrity and faith are tested through physical attacks to the body.[29] While Mandas does not speak much about religion (besides telling us that he considered himself very religious and always went to church), the descriptions of his and his sons' experience of violence, pain, and moral conflict draw heavily on the religious imagery of saint's lives (humiliation and torture of the body, the *topos* of the journey, the conflict with a hostile Other, the quest for justice, the ideal of ethical behavior, the sufferer as witness).[30]

Nonetheless, in taking up a pen to write his story, Mandas was engaging in a distinctly secular act. His "court of law" was located on earth, not in heaven, and the power that he bumps up against time and again is that of the state. The courtroom and the interrogation figure many times in his narrative, both in the United States and in Greece, and Mandas's part as narrator often seems to be that of perpetual defendant. At points, then, his text reads like the extended complaint (*parapono*) of an unhappy citizen-petitioner. Complaints, of course, are themselves an integral component of Greek male coffeehouse banter and a cornerstone of national discourse, with no better examples than the memoirs of the revolutionary war heroes themselves who institutionalized complaint along with the genre of national memoir. Mandas's complaints begin from the start: with his recollections of childhood. He notes, for instance, that students had to pay the teacher one drachma per month because the village did not have a public school: "even though the village had 90 houses at this time, the state however did not send a teacher." In Mandas's narrative, the Greek state goes from being negligent to being outright criminal and illegal. When his son Yiannis, the left-wing guerilla, is executed, he complains:

> he died with the great complaint that they spare the lives of criminals that the greek state is like that here you have to have someone pull the strings (*na eheis meson*) you have to be a crook (*apateonas*) to be in step with the times

As we have seen, Mandas blames the "rags-and-tatters state" (*xekourialsmeno kratos*) for his other son's death and throughout the text peppers his remarks with statements about the "mess of the Greek state" (*ta halia tou ellinikou kratous*) and the fact that his "bad luck and the Greek disgrace just doesn't stop" (εικακή τήχει και το ατειμο το ελληνικό δενσταματάν). Following Ilias's death, Mandas complains, "afterwards they tell you about the state and the Greeks with their long history wouldn't it be better to say thieves gluttons bribe-takers" (*den lene kleftes fagades kai rousfetologoi*). It might have been in the United States, however, that Mandas learned to *write* complaint letters and take on the more aggressive stance of the plaintiff. He tells us that in Los Angeles sometime between 1907 and 1909 when his first cousin died during the construction of a bridge, he lodged charges (αφτό με έκαμε να Καταγγίλο την ετερία) against the company and went to court to demand compensation, albeit to no avail.

In conjecturing about some of the genres whose performative contexts have permeated Mandas's text, I aim to draw attention to the complex discursive universe in which "Mandas" could appear as an author in this text. In part, I intend this brief discussion as a critique of assumptions often held by social scientists that their informants' "oral" utterances derive from discourses passed down "face-to-face" across the generations, untouched by print culture and other forms of sociotechno-logical mediation. The generic bricolage of Mandas's text also suggests the degree to which a distinct and coherent genre of testimony (which people like Merlier expected subaltern subjects to employ as a matter of fact) could only be the product of literary manipulation.

In comparison to the other more authoritative genres of historical writing I have considered in this book, Mandas's text is marked by a centrifugal tendency to decom-pose into its component parts. If historiography has ways to "defend" the reporting context from reported speech through conventional modes of citing evidence, Mandas's text, by contrast, is exceedingly open to other voices, voices that often take the liberty of imposing their own views and agendas. That Mandas's life does not "fit" into bourgeois autobiography—or, of course, local historiography—speaks to how these genres implicitly define the proper subjects of history (settlement, accu-mulation, development, etc.) as *stylistic* prerequisites. The fact of Mandas's writing, nonetheless, indicates the beginning of a historic rupture in the bourgeois hold on writing practices. At the same time, his authorship does not appear to be an end in itself, but a *means* to communicate his pain (*I write all my miseries and woes/So that others who are sad and wretched/Can see that they are not alone*).[31] The heterogeneity of Mandas's text can be ascribed in large part to his struggle to find a way to address a future reader and testify to history as injustice in a context in which available dis-cursive forms of historical representation had become inadequate.

Transliteration, Translation, Transition

Given his limited education, Mandas probably would not have been able to write as well as he does if he were not a charismatic figure and good talker. His storytelling gave him a practical kind of experience at describing scenes, crafting narratives, and isolat-ing incidents with a plot and moral. Writing, as opposed to speaking, however, pres-ents Mandas with a different set of possibilities as well as difficulties in presenting his story. His "failure" to smoothly record *Ameriki* in Greek, turn his fragmented and con-tradictory experience into a unified narrative, incorporate his multiple senses of self into a coherent "I," and tame the voices of hostile interrogators into an analytical indirect discourse, in turn, could be said to reflect back on the prolixity of other his-torical discourses and the ease with which passages between orality and writing, foreign languages and "standard" Greek, and reporting and reported speech were negotiated.

Mandas's attempt to write "proper" Greek (i.e., the formal archaizing register of *katharevousa*) but his actual code switching among the purist register, his local ver-nacular, and "Gringlish" (i.e., the "Greek-English" of Greek America)[32] point not only to the highly unequal social access to and mastery of official written language at the time he wrote but also to the inadequacy of monolingual historical discourse in gen-eral to express the transatlantic scope of his life experience. In editing Mandas's text, Mantzouranis has rounded the text's many jagged edges. Notably, even though Mandas's grandson complained about the way that the memoirs were edited, he did not say anything about the textual form that editing took, despite the fact that

Mantzouranis's interventions were often radical. In keeping with my focus on the continuum between witness and mediator, in what follows, I bring into tension the 1990s transcription and computer-processing of Mandas's handwritten text with my reconstruction of Mandas's performance of writing in the early 1950s.

Transcription, Johannes Fabian has remarked, is "never just a straightforward transposition from acoustic signals to graphic signs. It is an activity geared to, guided and constrained by the aim to make the transcript *readable* according to criteria which are always relative to culturally and historically specific situations (of both, the source and the 'target' text)" (1993: 86). In editing Mandas's memoirs, Mantzouranis has indeed made several changes to the text in the interest of making it "legible" to a contemporary Greek reader: namely, he has corrected grammatical errors, conflated the two versions of the memoirs into a single text complete on the level of information and details, and expunged the memoirs's "oral" dimensions as well as, importantly, signs of its *over*writing.[33] As Mantzouranis explains in the introduction: "I corrected the **spelling**, I added **commas and periods**. I also put in **parentheses** some explanations or supplementary information and lastly I included **headings and a table of contents as well as photographs**." In addition, as this comment reveals, he has put proper names and statements (which he deems significant) into bold face, according to the common practice of contemporary Greek newspaper journalism. Although Mantzouranis does not feel he needs to mention it, he also "demoticized" the text to a large degree, removing many of the signs of Mandas's struggle to write in the formal register of Greek: he dispensed, for instance, with diacritic marks and some accents in order to make Mandas's text conform to the *monotoniko* (single-accent system), which replaced the *polytoniko* (multiaccent system) in 1982.[34] Another change he does not mention is his elimination of Mandas's irregular capitalizations. While Mantzouranis has altered Mandas's text drastically and, as a result, strongly directed the reader's interpretation of it, it is interesting that he sees his editing as simply presenting the text in its original form (*aftousio*).

In turning to the original notebooks, it is tempting to simply ascribe Mandas's writing "problems" to that of an "oral" writer. Indeed, in producing *two* versions of his memoirs, neither of which is the "fair" copy of the other, Mandas demonstrates that he has not fully internalized the logic of writing as singular event or the ideal of the text as closed in its final draft. His most common "errors" (orthography, running words together, inconsistent accentuation, lack of punctuation, extensive use of direct discourse) also appear to involve an idiosyncratic infusion of auditory elements of speech into the visual order of writing.[35] In Mandas's text, articles and possessive particles, for example, are often run together with adjacent verbs or nouns: "they-calledme" (μελέγανε), "myfather" (οπατέραςμου), "mychild" (τοπεδίμου). These run-together spellings, though, might be seen as "contextualization cues," which is John Gumperz's (1982) term for indexical signs that keep speakers informed about how an interaction is proceeding while also attempting to guide how semantic content should be understood; in oral discourse, such signs include intonation, stress, accent, pitch, tempo, pauses, overlaps, and laughter. Although Gumperz does not directly address written discourse, such cues in writing might be the use of the space of the page, underlining, handwriting style, font, and paper quality. From this vantage point, the run-together spellings in Mandas's text might be said to convey a change of tempo, even emphasis, which the regularity of spacing cannot express.[36] When he writes of the Greeks he met upon arrival in New York in 1898 that "theydidn'thang-outwithme" (δέν μεκαμάνεπαρέα), this "misspelling" transmits to the reader a sense of his loneliness, which is further underscored by the extraneous accent on the word "not." Similarly, his exclamation "I said ohmyVirginMary (αχπαναγίαμου) how was I lost for nothing" depicts something of the shock of his near-death experience. Rather than a lack of skills and a failure to move out of orality, Mandas's run-together spellings also might be viewed in terms of *style* and seen in light, for instance, of the avant-garde movement in concrete poetry. In saying this, of course, I do not mean to imply that "Mandas" was consciously making an artistic statement in his writing, any more than that he was deliberately using "contextualization cues" to infuse his writing with extralingual effects, but that as in visual poetry Mandas's run-together spellings expose spacing to be a *convention* of written textuality and, especially, of print culture.[37]

Overemphasizing the creativity or subversiveness of these features of Mandas's text would be reckless if it came at the expense of considering how his memoirs testify to linguistic alienation, which Paul Friedrich has described as the process by which an "individual must adjust to the dominant language or suffer communicative death" (1989: 303). As can be seen in the original versions of the memoirs, Mandas clearly was *trying* to write formal Greek.[38] Indeed, only a bourgeois intellectual whose linguistic security was assured would attempt (at least, at that juncture in Greek history) to re-create orality in writing, transcribe dialect forms, or make visual poetry. For Mandas, writing his autobiography might have been primarily *about* recording it in official written discourse (and for this reason, he probably would have been pleased with Mantzouranis's revisions as well as with the technological upgrading of his text).

Many of the spelling errors in the memoirs can be attributed to hypercorrection, which as Bourdieu (1991) has argued, drawing on Labov's classic studies, reveals the symbolic violence of linguistic hegemony: namely, the asymmetry between the recognition of, and the ability to produce, the "correct." This hypercorrection in Mandas's text can be seen in his overuse of diphthongs (such as ει), which reflect so-called historical spellings in modern Greek (Triandafyllidis 1993: 70–1).[39] These nonphonetic spellings, which ideologically link the modern language to ancient Greek, have to be learned and, thus, represent just one more way that mastery and competence in the written form of the Greek language has been made more difficult for those outside the educated elite. Mandas's hypercorrection demonstrates an awareness that such diphthongs are an element of literate Greek but an inability to gauge when they should be used; refusing the instinct of his ear, he often appears to have gone by the rule "the more diphthongs the better."[40] Similarly, even though "Mandas" attempts to employ the multiaccent (*polytoniko*) system of formal Greek, he makes his exclusion from this discourse evident in not using *all* of the accents and sometimes placing them over the wrong letter.[41]

Mandas's memoirs are also rife with instances of code switching among various languages and registers (formal Greek, his regional vernacular, "Gringlish," and English) as well as between the Greek and Latin alphabets. While it is common to think of monologic discourse as the norm of human communication, work of linguistic anthropologists on bilingual and multilingual speech practices suggests that code switching is a norm that programmatically "pure," unmixed uses of languages make look like an aberration (cf. Heller 1988; Auer 1998). From this standpoint, historiography's "containment" of quoted discourse and translation of foreign languages or dialects into a national standard might be seen not as a "natural" process but as an ideological statement about the "proper" relationship among languages as well as a means of constructing "us" readers as an unmarked ethnic group and unified speech community. In a similar way, fiction in which a narrator's literate voice is separated off from reported speech given in dialect (for instance, in the short stories of Alexandros Papadiamantis) can be said to contribute to normalizing a linguistic hierarchy. Mandas's abrupt juxtaposition of voices and speech styles, by contrast, might be seen as more akin to modernist literature in which the depiction of heteroglossia, as in Joyce, conveys the conflict between different social and ideological standpoints. While linguistic anthropologists used to approach code switching as socioindexical (in other words, the social status and speech style of speakers were seen as "correlated"), recent scholarship has pointed to the need for a more interactional approach, sensitive to the ways in which language usage does not passively reflect social identities and relationships but actively constitutes them. As Joseph Errington has suggested in his study of the play of "shifting languages" in Indonesia, code switchings are "grounded in diffuse, transient, intersubjective stances which shape and are shaped in the biography of interaction" (1998: 173).

Code switching in Mandas's text could be said, for one, to underscore the irreducible multiplicity of the memoirs's potential addressees (another poor and destroyed person, Mandas's covillagers, his co-*Brooklides*, his grandchildren, the state, God, himself). Second, this switching testifies to the strain of writing in the formal register and following its rules about quoting, transliterating, and translating foreign discourses. Finally, Mandas's use of several registers reveals the semantic incompleteness of a single language and its inability to represent the breadth of his life experience while, at the same time, demonstrating the incommensurability and untranslatibility of languages. Mandas's code switching, thus, provides a sense of the plurality of Greek languages, which mechanisms of linguistic standardization have reduced and hierarchized.[42] His text, for instance, includes many words spelled in both demotic and *katharevousa* (i.e., Αραβόσειτον/Αραποσείτη, "corn"). In one version of his memoirs, he uses the formal Greek word for "poor" (*ptohos*) four times in the first three pages and then on the fourth page when quoting a saying, he uses the demotic *ftohos*: "such poverty that we didn't get our fill of corn flour" (φτόχια όπου δένεχορτέναμαι μπομπότα). Mandas also frequently employs words from his local dialect (verb forms such as ήμαστουν, instead of ήμασταν; nouns such as Κάτσουλα, instead of κουκούλα, "hood"); and Turkish words that had been purged from the purist register.

Unsurprisingly, Mandas's code switching (of language and alphabet) especially proliferates around the use of English. Although there are very few cross-outs in the text as a whole, words in English are riddled with little smudges, suggesting Mandas's confusion about the "proper" way to write an English word in Greek but also his difficulty in delimiting a single audience for his text. Consider, for instance, the graphic performance of linguistic ambivalence witnessed in his "Greek" transliteration of

"New York." Sometimes Mandas writes the word in Latin characters, sometimes in Greek, and sometimes in a mixture of the two, as in *New(a)Yorki* written in Latin characters but in which the "w" is overwritten with the "a" of the Greek "*Nea*" and an "i" is added at the end of the word in keeping with the Greek word for New York, *Nea Yorki*.[43] His different Greek spellings of the word indicate an uncertainty about how to convey an English word with Greek letters (and in Greek pronunciation): he especially struggles with the "Yo" in York (Νεαυόρκη, Νεαϋόρκη, Νεαηορκη, Νεα ηρκή). This miniature transliteration crisis exposes the seemingly necessary requirement that texts be written in *one* language and alphabet in order to be comprehensible as, in fact, an arbitrary constraint that eliminates certain aspects of transnational experience as "grammatically incorrect."

At many points in the memoirs, *both* Greek and English versions of the same place name are given. Thus, we read: Los Angeles and Λος αντζελες; Chicago, Chicago Ill., and Τσίκαγο; Spartan Bourg (Spartanburg) and Σπαρατανμπουργ; and Vartzinia (Virginia) and Βερτζίνια.[44] In the case of San Francisco, Mandas translates the meaning of the word *San* into the Greek for "saint": thus, sometimes he writes *Sanfrantzisko* (Σάνφραντζίσκο) but other times *Ayionfrantzisko* (Αγιονφραντζήσκο). In these spellings, the Greek pronunciation of these English words is also conveyed: *Βαϊομεν Στεϊτ* (i.e., "Wyoming State") sounds something like *Vyomen Stet* while "Fourth of July" (φορτζουλαϊ) sounds like *fortzoulay*. In the latter example, the "swallowing" of the "of" in "Fourth of July" indicates a simplification of the consonant cluster common in the English of native Greek speakers.[45]

These spellings suggest not only that transcription is a form of translation but also that the point at which a word stops being English and becomes Greek (or a new variety of Greek) is a much more contingent and complicated matter than a dictionary view of translation might have it. As Susan Gal (1987) has pointed out, redundancy is common in bilingual communities in which neither "native" or "host" language has a greater value in the eyes of speakers; in these cases, the repetition of the same words in both languages serves a basic pedagogical function, enabling newcomers to learn the second language quickly. Mandas's repetitions and transliterations could be said to open his text to people who know *Ameriki* like himself or those who have never been and are in need of a cultural translator. Mandas's use of foreign words effectively indexes this other world (of *Ameriki*, of the past), simultaneously authenticating his claims to being a cultural insider and qualified guide.

Mandas often transliterates (and sometimes glosses) English words for objects, technology, and customs specific to the United States or to the migration experience more generally. For instance, he explains that the "snowball" (σνομπολ) he sold on the streets of New York in 1900 was: "ice we scraped with a scraper like a grater and we threw on top a little syrup and with a piece of paper we put it in the hand of the child he gave us one cent 1 ¢ (*ena sentzi*) and when he sucked the syrup he would throw the ice in our face." In this passage, the words "one cent" (*ena sentzi*) are also followed by the numerical symbol ¢. Other times Mandas simply transliterates units of measure, such as παον (pound), without explaining them. He does the same for other words: ολανδομερκαινλαίν (Holland American Line, one of the major ship lines that brought the migrants to the United States), Ιούνιον (union), μεσίνεια (machines), εξιπρές (express), τσέκια (checks), μπόσεις (boss), and γκάστερς (gangsters). These words probably should be seen neither as Greek (Mandas's "mother tongue") nor as translit-erated English (the language of his cultural "assimilation") but as belonging to a new idiom that emerged in the transnational social world formed by migration. In Chakrabarty's terms, what this "translation" could be said to produce "out of seem-ing 'incommensurabilities' is neither an absence of relationship between dominant and dominating forms of knowledge nor equivalents that successfully mediate between differences, but precisely the partly opaque relationship we call 'difference' " (2000: 17).

There are also instances in the text when Mandas glosses a word that *does* seem translatable. For instance, he writes: "for me to go south (*saoth*) to the South (*Noto*)" (να παο στο σαοθ σε Νοτο) or "Fourth of July on July (4)" (φορτζουλάι στης (4) Ιουλίου). In this way, he indicates that what it means to say "South" or "Fourth of July" in English is something other than a literal translation can convey. In addition to English words, Mandas seems to have picked up new Greek words (actually Turkish-derived words used in Greek) from other migrants in the United States. In the beginning of his memoirs, he described the money belt he had worn in the village as a *selahi*. When he writes about his time in Los Angeles, however, Mandas refers to this belt as a *kymeri* (from a different Turkish word for money belt). Since this word probably was not used in Arcadia, he glosses it for an implied local reader: "belts the so-called *Kymeria*" (λουρίδες ταλεγόμενα Κυμέρια). As this small example suggests, migration in so many ways reconfigured Greekness by introducing Greeks not only to American culture but also to the diversity of Greek cultures and languages.[46]

Another kind of "error" that has been systematically corrected in the edited ver-sion of Mandas's memoirs involves punctuation. Mandas's original text lacks breaks (periods, commas, paragraph indentations, section divisions). Mantzouranis's intro-duction of punctuation marks and transitions does not just make the text "easier" to read but also could be said to bring along the *ideological* demands of historical dis-course for clear periodization, causal explanation, and the exposition of continuous unfolding time. On the broadest level, Mantzouranis has imposed (his) order on the text by splitting it up into eight sections that reflect distinct "chapters" of Greek and village historiography as well as of bourgeois biography: "Childhood Years and Life in the Village," "The First Trip to America," "Return to Greece," "Second Trip to America," "Definitive Return to Greece," "The War of 1940 and the Occupation," "The German Raid on Vourvoura," and "The Last Blows of Fate." Mandas himself actually had made a minor attempt to organize his text into sections. In one of the notebooks, for instance, blank lines separate some of the "episodes." In that same notebook, there is also a clear break between the prologue and the first chapter, which is entitled "Vourvoura." This, however, is the *only* chapter. As for many peo-ple, it seems, Mandas found it easier to narrate the beginning of his life than to locate its significant middle points or central themes.

In the absence of systematic punctuation, antithesis provides a modicum of syntactic order to Mandas's original text; however, this syntactic mechanism more often than not is unable to balance or connect the things that he describes as having happened to him, his family, and those around him. One of the most common grammatical constructions in the memoirs is the formal Greek "*o men . . . o de*," which means "the one . . . the other" or "on the one hand . . . on the other hand." In Mandas's text, this construction indicates a range of things, from the equilibrium of a work schedule (or at least the ideal of such an equilibrium) to irony and social critique. In the beginning of the memoirs, the *men/de* construction links labor and money to nature's calendar: "one year (*tin men mia chronia*) we sowed with *smigon* [corn, barley, wheat] and we made 100 to 120 *okades* [unit of measurement] and the other (*tin de alin chronia*) we sowed Corn and we made the same amount." He tells us of his father's seasonal labor in these terms:

> On the one hand my father on the one hand in the summer (*o men paterasmou to men kalokeri*) was a shepherd and got (100) drach[ma] for the half year they gave him bread and shoes on the other hand in the winter (*ton de kalokeri*) he went to Messinia or to Gargalianoi and worked the currants as a worker

In other cases, though, this construction links actions and events that seem incommensurable, even contradictory. During the Nazi raid on Vourvoura, Mandas finds himself at a monastery, where he learns from the abbot that the Nazis have murdered thirty-seven shepherds:

> on the one hand they killed the Shepherds because they gave milk to the Hospital of the *andartes* [located in the monastery] on the other hand the shepherds again thought that they would not bother them because they were not registered in the organization [*organosi*, i.e., EAM resistance force]

Antithesis links the assumption that noncombatants would not be targets and the assumption that everyone is "fair game," revealing the "sense" of this new kind of total warfare. In these grammatically awkward passages, Mandas's text demonstrates how traumatic experience *broke* available conceptual frames and expressive forms. In the description of this incident in the second notebook, there is no attempt whatsoever to connect these two facts; instead, they appear in a paratactic chain: "up above the monastery they killed all the shepherds in total (37) the *andartes* had the Monastery as a Hospital and they took milk from the shepherds."

Mandas's text is also structured syntactically by other forms of antithesis (such as *omos* [however] and the more formal *en toutis* [yet, however]), which run through the fabric of the entire memoir, exuding into the performance of his writing (and our reading) a sense of a life marked by sudden changes and reversals of fate. For instance, while living in Los Angeles between 1907 and 1909, he describes having a large group of friends and even founding a Greek community with some of them. This relative state of contentment, however, is shattered by the death of his first cousin in bridge construction:

> and so three Insignificant People (Ασείμαντη Άνθροπη) were the founders of the Today wealthy [Greek] Community of the city of Los angeles I had however the misfortune (ατήχιμα) to lose my first cousin he was working for a company that was building a pier in the sea they had built a Bridge and it went out quite deep into the sea that Bridge broke and the workers along with the stones went into the sea they all drowned

In this passage, antithesis verges on parataxis as events pile up without adequate linking terms and sometimes not even enough "and's": "the workers along with the stones went into the sea they all drowned." Mantzouranis has dealt with the abruptness of this passage by creating a new paragraph following "I had however." Yet, as Carolyn Steedman has pointed out in her discussion of the memoirs of soldier and policeman John Pearman, the contradictions of working-class experience are often iconically represented in paratactic chains of this sort, held together only by an "unsatisfying, unsynthesizing 'but'" (1988: 19). The brusqueness of this and other transitions in Mandas's text, thus, could be said to speak to the truly new and paradoxical way that entry into a more advanced capitalist system opened for him a space for self-development and personal growth at the same time that it entailed brutal abuse.

Mandas's inability to write "properly" exposes the social stratification of language use at the time he was writing as well as the great distance separating him from people whose life experiences not only fit more neatly into available generic forms but also had been trained to regiment their lives to the exigencies of writing. The awkward juxtapositions in Mandas's text, though, might say as much about the randomness with which he experienced certain events as about the requirements of historical discourse itself for causal explanation. In editing Mandas's memoirs for publication, Mandas's editor has erased many of the signs of Mandas's struggle to register personal and family memories in public language. At the same time, it would be wrong to see Mandas's account solely as a testament to linguistic subordination and not also as the creative textual expression of someone who had lived as a stranger abroad. The insufficiency of the nation as a category of collective ascription is played out as much in the story that Mandas tells as on the inscriptive surface of his text.

Hearing Other Voices

The most important indication of a writer's relationship to spoken language, but also more generally to the discourse of another, is the reporting of speech. For Vološinov, the reporting of speech represents an "*active relation* of one message to another;" thus, he suggests, the degree of assimilation and adaptation of quoted discourse to the syntactic form and compositional style of the authorial utterance can be read as a "document" of the reception of that speech (1973: 116–7). In his memoirs, Mandas almost exclusively employs an unpunctuated direct discourse that keeps the (oral) discourse of others maximally distinct and autonomous relative to his (written) narrative voice. As a result, the abrupt transitions between reporting and reported speech in Mandas's text might be read as a record of his confrontation with the raw limits of community and the arbitrary power of the law. In the instances when the quoted discourse is that of his sons or even his own remembered self, this relation between voices also points to the ethical, not just evidentiary, function of passing on the discourse of others.

While in conventional historiography the citing of direct discourse is understood in terms of reference and verification, the invocation of others' words can also be seen as a form of dramatization (cf. Rumsey 1990). Mandas's memoirs are shot through with voices of other people whom he usually quotes verbatim. He never uses commas or quotation marks, even though he usually does introduce other peoples' discourse with verbs of speaking. As a result, it was easy for Mantzouranis to slip in quotation marks, and sometimes even bold lettering, at the points when direct discourse enters the text. For instance, Mandas tells us that the first organizational meeting for the Greek community was a failure: "one night there was a Meeting and they started to say I give this much they shouted all together even though no one gave a penny." In invoking an "I" that the reader knows to be different from that of either the narrated or narrating "Mandas," the statement "I give this much" could be taken as indicating what Goffman has called a change of "footing." According to Goffman, during the course of an utterance ongoing shifts in footing, indicated by innumerable signs (body orientation, tone of voice, linguistic code, interjection, emphasis, volume, selection of speech recipient), imply changes in the alignment of the pragmatic roles played by narrator, characters, and audience in a given speech situation (1981: 128). In another example from Mandas's text, a shift from Greek to Italian accompanies the use of reported speech, further emphasizing the change of footing. On the boat back to Greece after his second journey, Mandas notes that the Italians bitterly complained about the incredibly slow pace at which the boat was moving (it took 62 days to cross the ocean) and vociferously spoke out against the Greek owner of the ship, a Mr. Stefanides: "the Italians started to curse Stefanides who was traveling with us they shouted Son-of-a-Bitch Stefanini (Σαναμπαμπήτσει Στεφανίνι)." In these cases, the embedded voices both authenticate and enliven Mandas's narration by invoking the "live" speech of another as well as by "setting up" entire performance contexts from the past: namely, the boisterous meeting in an immigrant café somewhere in Los Angeles at the beginning of the nineteenth century and the shipboard haranguing of bedraggled, repatriating first-wave European immigrants.

In bringing alien voices into his text in such a raw state, "Mandas" as author expresses a sense of tension and conflict with the foreignness of Others and the socioideological positions they represent. In receiving these voices in a maximally unresolved state, Mandas's text could be said to archive a diversity of performative utterances while also leaving itself open to appropriation by them. If these other voices had been presented through indirect discourse (with verb tenses and personal pronouns shifted to bring the narrating and narrated text into alignment), Mandas's narrating voice might have asserted a certain level of interpretive control over them. Alternatively, as in much historical and social science discourse, cited discourse is set off from the rest of the text and thoroughly analyzed, evaluated, and commented on, thus defusing (at least theoretically) the ability of the quoted discourse to propose alternative readings of itself or of the framing discourse. By contrast, Mandas's text, by dint of its construction, is highly susceptible to interpretive "hijacking" by its "sources" and "examples." For example, as we have already seen, the direct quotation from the proclamation of the communists (*Soldier you who fight look around do you have any child of a rich person with you*) and the infiltration of his text with words such as "worker" and "peasant" direct the reader to more politicized readings of his narrative than "Mandas" might well have intended.

Abrupt breaks in the text between the authorial frame and quoted discourse could be seen as iconic of Mandas's experience of life as confrontation. The predominance in Mandas's text of a rough direct discourse, which more often that not renders the voice of the other as a shout, accompanied by a blow to the body, might be related to philosopher Charles S. Peirce's phenomenological category of Secondness. For Peirce, Secondness, which he describes as "force without law or reason, *brute* force" (1.427), is the experience of "fact": namely, of resistance, contingency, the "here and now," struggle, and the "accidentally actual" (1.435). Since Secondness is marked by a sense of Otherness, it is often, according to Peirce, the primary way in which we perceive "reality" itself: "In the idea of reality, Secondness is predominate; for the real is that which insists upon forcing its way to recognition as something *other* than the mind's creation" (1.325).

Mandas frequently reports speech when he bumps up against the Law as embodied in the figures of police officers and clerks. Describing Secondness as the sense of the "actuality"of an event, Peirce clarifies: "A court may issue *injunctions* and *judgments* against me and I do not care a snap of my fingers for them. I may think them idle vapour. But when I feel the sheriff's hand on my shoulder, I shall begin to have a sense of actuality" (1.23–6). Mandas's awakening to the impersonal authority of the American state occurs one day when bailiffs in Los Angeles apprehend him and his brother for not having a dog license. The arrest leads to a brawl; as the agents beat up his brother, Mandas calls out: "I say to him you shouldn't Hit he is my Brother as I was near him he gives me a strong punch on the Forehead." In the description of this incident, Mandas, a usually sardonic narrator, conveys (or transports us back to) an earlier naïveté. The words of care and concern for his brother that slip out of his mouth are rudely answered with a punch. Why would the policeman care that Mandas was being forced to watch his brother—just another scofflaw—being beaten? Mandas's cry for empathy does not open a dialogue with the officer that might halt or, at least, soften and humanize this manifestation of the state's capacity for arbitrary violence. Instead, according to Mandas's account, his words go unanswered by the bailiffs while he responds in kind, picking up a stick to fight back.

In Mandas's text, the incessant invocation of alien and hostile voices draws attention to that thin line that separates someone who is *dikos mou* (my family, or literally, mine, my [person]) or *patriotis mou* (my compatriot) from someone who is a stranger or even an enemy. Mandas's experience in the United States is filtered through an ongoing attempt to define what it means to be a "friend" and a "compatriot" in a world of strangers. If "Americans" (whom he usually refers to as the "English"), other immigrants (especially the Italians), and the police are the foreigners (*xenoi*) and potential enemies, does this make all Greeks "friends"? Greek middlemen (*mesites*), or "padrone," who extracted fees for translating and arranging work, are an omnipresent feature of Mandas's account of his first journey. Mandas notes, for instance: "from Chicago I went to Wyoming again to the [railroad] Line 160 [cents] a day in every job that we went I would also pay (10) dollars commission and 1 dollar a month as many workers as the translator brought to the job he got (10) dollars supposedly for the fare even though the company gave a paper so you didn't pay a Fare." Even though, as we see in this passage, the middlemen were extortionists who played on the vulnerabilities of the migrants and especially their lack of English, Mandas has difficulty thinking of them as impersonal economic mediators and often speaks of these exchanges through the idioms of friendship. Thus, in 1902 when he could not find work in San Francisco, Mandas became so desperate that he went to find a "friend of mine among the Bosses" (εναφίλομου αποτους Μπόσειδες) and begged him to help him find work. After Mandas gives him forty dollars to arrange work for four people, this "friend" sends them to work on a team with a particularly brutal boss. Ultimately, community for Mandas is not rooted to particular territories, but represents a metaphysical opposition between betrayal and care, which was often provided by new friends and compatriots in the United States. After the accident at the cement factory in Napa Junction, for instance, he mentions going back to his room and having his friend put cupping glasses on him, an intimate gesture recalling a mother's care: "I went to my room and my friend did a blood-cupping for me" (επείγα στοδοματιὸν μου και φίλοσμου μου επιρε μιαβεντούζα ματωτή). When he suffered from the Spanesi flu in Chicago, he lived briefly with a *patriotis*: "I would have died if I hadn't gone to stay with a compatriot of mine who had a family."

Even though migration provided Mandas the possibility to create new communities of trust, care, and reciprocity based on friendship, he was often led to check his impulse to relate to others on the basis of a shared (Greek) humanity rather than common blood or homeland. Between 1903 and 1907, Mandas worked in the cement factory in Napa Junction, a job that paid him well enough and at which he was relatively happy. Once, however, he notes that in order to save a "stranger's skin," he almost lost his own: διαναγλιτόσο ξένο τομάρει παραλήγο ναχάσο τονδικόνμου. Some new Greeks, who had just come on the job, had been instructed by the boss to break a rock that had already been loosened with dynamite. Watching the new men struggle with this task, Mandas asks his coworker to help the new guys. When his coworker refuses, Mandas himself climbs up on the rock to give a hand, but with his weight the rock breaks loose and he comes tumbling down with it: "the rock fell and me with it and when I was going down with the rock I said ohmyVirginMary how was I lost for nothing (*dorean*)" (είπα αχπαναγίαμου πος εχάθηκα δορεάν). Unscathed, he gets up quickly from the ground and makes the sign of the cross.

Mandas's fall to the ground represents his sharp awakening to how cheaply a worker's life can be lost. In this instance, Mandas's spontaneous verbal outburst is accompanied by a shock to the body that simultaneously represents a piercing of his ontic shell. His use of the word *dorean*, which literally means "free," underscores how his death would negate, but also expose, his goal of turning his body into a tool for capital accumulation. The fall also shatters his innocence as he is awakened by his own voice, or rather by a new voice emerging out of this experience. His sense of duty to those other Greeks will not be repaid he realizes, and his death would have been the price for his kindness: his coworker knew better than to go help just because "some Greeks" had come along. As a parable about the disposable life of the working class, this story reveals Mandas's recognition of the emptiness of abstract discourses of patriotism. In retrospect, the generosity of his action comes to seem a foolish rather than profound gesture of care for an unknown Other, who now has become dehumanized, reduced to the status of a "foreign skin," or even an animal's "hide" (*tomari*).

Although Mandas typically quotes discourse at moments of conflict, at one important juncture his text receives the voice of another in a way that promises to expand the boundaries of community beyond kinship and locality. During the war, he finds himself alone in Athens going from hospital to hospital seeking help for a medical problem. Like migrant cafés and hotels in the United States, the different state hospitals he visits, such as Evangelismos and Ippokrateion, represent sites in which Mandas's path intersects with those of unknown—but, theoretically, fellow—Greeks. Here, too, though, the logic of filiation holds. At Ippokrateion hospital, an employee informs him that they have their "own sick people" (*dikous tous astheneis*). He protests by speaking back to an impersonal state—"and I too am Greek I told him"—but receives no response. He makes the circuits of the other hospitals, but does not have any better luck. In Evangelismos hospital, he complains to the other people in the waiting room and by chance a woman overhears his conversation and replies:

> a visitor from Piraeus asked me don't you have a person from your family (*dikos sou*) here no I told her she told me that I should give her a note to go to one of the hospitals that she in other words would lose a day's wages exclusively to help me out without us having any acquaintance what was she she was a refugee Girl (*prosfygopoula*)

On the one hand, Mandas automatically categorizes the woman in terms of her difference from him (the "visitor from Piraeus," a "refugee girl"). For Mandas, a Peloponnesian, the Asia Minor refugees represented an ethnically and culturally alien group of Greeks. Yet, in contrast to most of the incidents in which Mandas reports speech, here he depicts a brief dialogue he had with the woman. In using indirect discourse to report the woman's speech ("she told me that I should give her a note"), he also signals the extent of his internalization of her kind offer to help him gain entry to a hospital. By documenting his profound sense of thankfulness to this woman, Mandas leaves open the possibility of connecting to Greeks across the boundaries of *topos*, class, and—remarkably for Mandas—gender through acts of human concern and generosity. The possibility of such communion takes on particular significance in the post–Civil War period in which he is writing given that the reference of the word *patriotis* had become suspect, if not void.

Mandas's account of the war and Civil War, unsurprisingly, is pierced by many hostile and accusing voices that often, as in *Orthokosta,* evoke the interactional framework of political interrogation. The chaotic writing of this part of the narrative conveys a sense of the vortex of the war years as Mandas experienced them; namely, as an assault from all sides of the political spectrum. In the beginning of the war, for example, he and his youngest son were questioned by Nazis who captured them at a monastery that the *andartes* had been using as a hospital; according to Mandas, they were brought to the village of Agios Petros for interrogation:

> he started to ask us in Greek where were we from where were we who is in charge and he took the information a guy there was writing and we didn't look [at him] he says to

the kid you are in EPON [youth organization of the EAM/ELAS resistance movement] I was he said to him but now we have broken it up well then what the devil did you want at the Monastery that you went there

In this passage, the German officer's quoted speech consists of a remembered battery of questions that attempt to locate Mandas and his family both literally and politically: *Where were we from? Where were we? Who is in charge? You are in EPON?* In the beginning of the war, as suggested by this incident, Mandas's family was persecuted for being leftists. Later on in the memoirs, when the Greek government militia (*ethnofylaki*) comes to arrest his son Yiannis, the *andartis*, Mandas is accused on behalf of his children for possessing weapons; "one of those two-faced guys started to shout make them produce their arms." As they take away his son, a covillager, father of one of the men whose life his son had once saved, "says to the officer a beating and nothing else" (λεη στον αξιοματικό ξείλο και τείποτης άλο). Mandas, however, is also harassed by left-wing guerrillas who come to his house in 1948, enraged that he let his youngest son be conscripted into the government army. He describes his argument with the guerrillas:

> look guys at the time of the other Conscription you took 4 loads of stuff from me take (40) loads leave me my child to bury me who am at death's door Burn the house don't leave a nail no you sent your child to kill us to kill your child that's why we are taking him

When Mandas here invokes the voice of a past "I," along with the voices of the guerrillas, their "dialogue" can be said to be no more than a sum of monologic statements. As Mandas pleads them to take all his worldly belongings (*Burn the house don't leave a nail*), they, by contrast, make clear that they are only interested in taking back blood with blood (*no you sent your child to kill us to kill your child that's why we are taking him*).

Aside from the refugee woman in the hospital, the only voice that Mandas seems to hear as his own is that of his son Yiannis. The conflation of their voices suggests, as I have already argued, the degree to which Mandas seems to be writing his sons' soldier stories along with, as well as *through*, his migrant's tale. When Mandas is hospitalized in Athens, he remembers Yiannis' visit. Referring to his grown son with the sentimental *pedaki mou* (my little child), Mandas writes:

> my child Yiannis came and saw me and when I saw him I was moved and he consoled me I am in the best hospital in Athens and I shouldn't be scared and he stayed with me all the time right by my side (*sto kefali mou*) and asked the doctor how I am doing

In quoting his son's tender words (*I shouldn't be scared*)—so different from the rough cries he reports at other points in his narrative, Mandas internalizes his son's care, remembering it as he faces his old age alone. At another juncture, he recalls how Yiannis put the welfare of his covillagers above partisan loyalties, even though later on his covillagers betrayed him and sent him to his execution. Mandas explains that he went to the jail in which his severely beaten son was being held to complain about this unjust treatment; he wanted to remind his son's capturers that his son had protected local rightists during the left-wing revenge killings that followed Nazi withdrawal:

> my child always worked for the good of the village and he wasn't bloodthirsty and the proof is that when the Germans were doing clean-up operations the Germans killed besides the Shepherds Agiopetriots [people from the neighboring village of Agios Petros] and others that they caught up on [Mount] Parnon and when the Germans left the *Andartes* came to Agio Petro and at the suggestion of the organization [*organosi*, i.e., EAM] they executed 5 the best guys one of them slipped away from them and got off and the *organosi* of Agios Petros came outside of our village and called my child the Shepherd and Ch[ristos] Mandas and said to them that we in Agios Petros cleaned up the reactionaries (*antidrastikous*) you guys are going to do the same on the one hand the other two wanted to get going on the job however my child objected—no he said they want Comrades the reactionaries are not doing anything to us we aren't going to become murderers as a favor to the Agiopetriots

In taking on the voice of his dead son, "Mandas" draws on the authority of the dead in ways I discussed in the previous chapter. By putting the phrase "the reactionaries are not doing anything to us" in the mouth of an executed *andartis*, he perhaps could be accused of using his son's words to legitimate his postwar political position. And, yet, these rightists are his son's killers whom he is writing to condemn. Indeed, his memoirs document and expose precisely the kind of death that would be roughly silenced in the decades following the war. In the dichotomous logic of ideological essentialism, Mandas cannot "make sense" or write "clearly." At the end of the memoirs, when he speaks with his son's voice, reiterating his refusal to accept the legitimacy of political violence, Mandas's migrant's tale appears to finally merge with his sons' war stories. In the end, in Mandas's opinion, neither he nor his sons were rewarded for their attempts to transcend logics of identification that turn the Other—by definition—into a *xeno tomari*.

In writing his memoirs, Mandas could be said to be responding to all the angry voices in his head as well as to the baton of the policeman and the gun of the soldier. While reading his text, one sometimes gets the sense that the world is shouting at him, and he is shouting back. Rather than using the past to defend the boundaries of citizenship, community, nation, and class, as local(ist) and national(ist) historiography so often do, Mandas's text brings these "obvious" categories into crisis, revealing the centrifugal, rather than centripetal, forces of capitalist development and political ideology. His text gestures toward both the possibility and impossibility of communities of reciprocity and care *not* defined by kin, geographical *topos*, or "mother tongue." In Mandas's text, the invocation of the voices of Others and the embedding of interactional contexts of intense dyadic struggle draw attention to the performative and ethical dimensions of testimony. The vivid repetition of these past voices, especially those invoked in the context of political interrogation and state violence, can be seen as reenactments of particularly traumatic experiences in Mandas's life. The openness of Mandas's text to other voices, though, also enables his testimony to serve the cultural function of transmitting and passing on voices in pain. Ultimately, the most poignant of these is probably his own remembered one, surprising and awakening him to his "cheap" life and fragile body, as he was freefalling in Napa Junction: *Oh my Virgin Mary how was I lost for nothing.*

On Reading For and Against History

Growing up in the United States as a child of a Greek immigrant father, I must admit that the possibility of being "lost for nothing" was not a real consideration in the stories I heard told about migration. This is not to say that there were not ambivalences, but that these were exceptions that confirmed the logic of an inevitable forward movement. It says something about the times that I would meet this text on the other side of the Atlantic, where, as I have suggested, it was even more unlikely to be made public and read. The fact that this narrative engages, albeit critically, Greek American stories of success and struggle I had grown up with might have made it *more* difficult for me to situate it within *Greek* national historical culture: in other words, I had to resist my own ingrained "American" ways of thinking about immigration in order to appreciate the act (or acts) of re-collection constituted by Mandas's writing and its uptake in 1990s Greek society. This would mean attending to its relation to other key junctures of modern Greek history (the Civil War, postwar migration, contemporary migration) as well as to other projects of witnessing and historical re-collection (refugee testimony, Civil War testimony).

Furthermore, even though it was clear that the analysis of this text could open onto a multisited (temporally and culturally speaking) examination of the challenge migration poses to the archive of the nation (as well as to the notion of the nation as archive), what was much less obvious to me was its relation to the problematic of local historiography, which I discussed in the first case study of this book. I did not see at first that there was a connection between the strange ritual by which local historiographies had been lined up in glass cases in a provincial town and the cheap edition of Mandas's bibliography-less memoirs, a lone text whose presentation undermined in every way its possible importance. That this comparison seems obscure, even though histories of industrialization and migration are so profoundly intertwined, exposes the degree to which documentary genres and archival formations not only legitimate which parts of the past come to be recorded in historical discourse but also overdetermine the kinds of connections that can be drawn between different discursive accounts of social experience.

The territorializing of time and ethnicizing of territory in local(ist) and national(ist) historiography turn stories such as Mandas's into aberrations— "personal" experiences and "adventures"—when compared to the uneventfulness of "everyone being at home" and speaking their "own language." The accumulation, multiplication, and careful management of the documentary evidence of local belonging encouraged by the historicist fetish of the document makes Mandas's attempt to inscribe and concretize his life seem capricious and the tenuousness of his grip on materiality even more glaring. Pushing Mandas's text up against the tradition of local historiography, rather than viewing it within a field of "migration studies" (whether social–historical or transnational), puts in question keywords of local history (community, kin, nostalgia, home, compatriot, origin) while, at the same time, demonstrating another way to tell the same story, but from the outside.

In bringing into focus the dynamic between possession and dispossession, archival emplacement and dispersal, natives and "people on the run," this juxtaposition also exposes the well-hidden secret of liberal historiography's status as discourse not only on the nation but also on capitalism itself. If industrialization and the development of urban centers, on the one hand, and migration, on the other, were contemporaneous phenomena of late-nineteenth and twentieth-century Greek history, when placed side-by-side in a study of global capitalism, Greek migrant labor is clearly much more important than Greek capital. That in the 1990s, the shelves of provincial bookstores were bulging with accounts of local "industrial revolutions" but one could find little written along the lines of Mandas's text emphatically underlines the implication (and complicity) of (Greek) historiography in narratives of capitalist progress and expansion that measure "Greece" up to a "European" standard.

A second struggle I faced in constructing this case study had to do with the relationship between my analysis of historical re-collection in the 1990s (the reading and editing of Mandas's memoirs in the shadow of the new migration) and Mandas's own writing practice, which also constitutes a form of historical re-collection. Putting equal emphasis on the witness (and the witness as scribe) as on the mediator, I considered the politics of author(iz)ing the past from the vantage point of those typically represented (even in their "own words") in testimony-centered projects such as those I discussed in previous chapters. As my instincts drew me further into the semeiotic interstices of Mandas's text, though, I could not always explain to myself what exactly I was doing there.

If ethnographic and sociohistorical studies on Greece have not given us much of a sense of those disenfranchised by writing—the "victims" of textual hegemony—even less has been said about the producer of unpublishable texts and unsigned writing. As Susan Miller has suggested, studies of "commonplace writing" would do well to resist the temptation to read traces of dead or marginalized voices in order to find out what people "had on their minds"; instead these textual discoveries, she argues, should be understood as illuminating the "intersections of social vectors, forces that produce discursive actions that have simultaneously material, aesthetic, and ideological consequences" (1998: 2). In this vein, then, I attempted to address the way that conventions of written language (spelling, punctuation, syntax, citation, choice of register, translation, transliteration) rendered asymmetrical social access to written language into a mere class of linguistic "error." In crossing borders of territories, cultures, and languages in ways that could be stylistically creative, not just grammatically "flawed," Mandas's text also exposed the degree to which the "base" requirements of historical writing (as monolingual, referential, causal discourse) strongly predetermine the kinds of "facts" about the past that can be recorded.

My double temporal focus on Mandas's act of writing, ultimately, had two interconnected aims. For one, I sought to identify genres of documentation and archival formations outside established networks of historical practice in which a story such as this could be registered. I conjectured how practices of writing associated with migration, household accounting, and even petitioning as well as an institution of social memory such as the family, with its own ethic of historical re-collection and mourning, could provide the conceptual and material context for this story to be written down and preserved. Second, I juxtaposed the form of witnessing I located in Mandas's text to a "deep" historical common sense underlying many phenomenally conflicting schools of historical thought and involving such fundamental concepts as chronology, historical period, reference, causality, and subjectivity. Reading the text along its surface (by attending, for instance, to code switching, reported speech, footing shifts, and parataxis) allowed me to emphasize nondenotative aspects of Mandas's writing and examine how they conveyed the impact of events (particularly violent, unexpected, and inexplicable ones) without necessarily "saying something" about them. Finally, as a "double telling," in other words, as a survivor's story that embeds the story of loved ones' deaths, Mandas's memoirs challenged the assumption that the individual constitutes a "natural" unit of collective memory by suggesting instead that a transgenerational and transhistorical mode of witnessing might come closer to how subjects come to claim a history of their "own."

Epilogue

In a well-known article, historian Joan Scott challenged the assumption that individuals *have* experience; on the contrary, she insists: "Experience is a subject's history. Language is the site of history's enactment" (1992: 34). In her view, "experience" always needs to be historicized, not simply gathered. As we saw on numerous occasions in this book, however, the notion of experience as prediscursive bedrock authorized historical producers who could claim access to it while dispelling the shadow that their own politics cast on their archival constructions and historical texts. To unfix the evidence of "experience," then, one must get at its double aspect and trace how the experience of research and the experience of the researched subject become interlocked in the archive in a tightly wound empirical bundle. In this book, I have been primarily concerned with historicizing the experience of the historical producer. Following Scott, I have not asked how individuals and groups come to "undertake" historical projects, but rather how authors, archivists, and witnesses emerge as subjects in the course of historical praxis. In turn, I have attempted to show how political arguments, claims to belonging, assertions of cultural continuity, expressions of comradeship, and bids for collective redemption and reform of cultural memory were furthered from these positions.

The archival poetics I have proposed in this book provide a conceptual meeting ground for a notion of document as material artifact, possession, auratic object, and "building block" of an archival dwelling, on the one hand, and as nexus in a chain of citations, collocation of genres, and trace of various acts of textual appropriation, on the other. Placing emphasis on the materiality of the archive and its function as a mechanism for keeping memory "in place" allowed me to take account of the significance of the archive as monument (or antimonument) projecting a particular group's power, cohesion, and claim on place; the role of the archive as crossroads, social world, and second home; the authenticating power of the artifact as conduit to the event; and the sensual, even erotic, contact with the past enabled, ironically enough, by technological mediation. By locating the discursivity of the archive in the ongoing reiteration of the "originary" source, I engaged historical discourse not so much as "narrative" or as the work of particular authors, but as a network of cultural performatives crisscrossing purportedly meaningful borders between writing and orality, fact and fiction, history and literature, and text and context. Tracing links of citation and reported speech brought the interface of textual and social authority into focus, illuminating what a textual anthropology might gain from examining historical production and vice versa.

I discussed literature from the center of this study, not as a supplement to it, placing particular emphasis on the blurred genre of testimony. To the extent that literary testimony does not aim to present a referential monologue and factual "report" but to draw attention to *testifying* as address to a listening other, it poses fundamental questions about the politics and ethics of historical practice, revealing citation to be a mode not just of verifying information, but of receiving, transmitting, and responding to the pain of another. As we saw in the case of the Center for Asia Minor Studies, attempts made by social actors to elicit testimony on behalf of those normally excluded from historical accounts can founder before resistances to the narrativization and exteriorization of traumatic experience. At root, this failure could be said to stem from the profound challenge that testimony poses to historicist conceptions of history as knowledge of the past (rather than response to suffering). In this book, I considered some aspects of the historical emergence of testimony in the Greek context and also, importantly, how this new authority accorded to the witness has been strategically harnessed or refused. Even within projects of testimony taking, the relationship between scribe and witness can be articulated quite differently, ranging from the privileging of the mediator's intentionality to a greater mutuality in which the recorder plays the part of catalyst and redactor of testimony, and authorship is claimed by the witness. The scribe can also take on the role (and responsibility) of a "secondary witness" (Felman and Laub 1992: 213): in other words, a witness to witnessing who participates in and co-owns a given testimony, even partially experiencing the witness's trauma. The relationship between scribe and witness, though, can be one in which the scribe appropriates the witness's discourse in a self-authorizing and authenticating move, emphasizing her *distance* and distinction from the witness's temporal, cultural, and experiential otherness. Conventions of historical practice and methodology, particularly the historicist privileging of the "primary" written source, can even block at the outset the documentation of orally transmitted eyewitness or survivor testimony. The important ideological consequences of some of the projects of historical re-collection I examined in this book, then, could be said to lie in the degree to which they *limited* the potential for personal testimony about traumatic historical events to enter into public historical discourse.

I hope that this book will cast a new light on the commonly heard observation (and lament) that Greece is "poor" in archives. This "lag" in archival accumulation is implicitly (and sometimes explicitly) attributed to a failure of political will and a collective amnesia. As a result, questions about the history of "modern Greek history" are often left unposed, while existing archives are not fully appreciated as sites in which to peruse "Greece's" location in the global knowledge game. One day a colleague painted the following striking image for me as we were speaking about archiving in Greece: in the late 1990s, during the same period that he was cataloguing the archive of a leftist political party and spending his days "rescuing" documents out of big black garbage bags, he told me that he also happened to read Derrida's *Archive Fever*. This overlapping of seemingly incompatible archival practices and theories, of empiricist desires (the archive fever, the drive toward the "origin," the need for proof) and post-structuralist critique (*Archive Fever*), confounds as much as it intrigues. Viewing archival projects in relation to cultural politics and not some abstract model of academic paradigm shift, however, turns these apparently contradictory gestures into signs of the tense intersections of history, politics, and epistemology. Situating "modern Greek history" in history, furthermore, reveals not only belatedness, but also innovation (the precocious identification of the refugee as consummate witness of the traumatic twentieth century, for instance), against the habit of attributing originality to metropolitan theory and then tracing lines of diffusion and derivation.

The archives for twentieth-century Greek history thus cannot be evaluated without reckoning the relation of "Greece" to histories of colonialism, nationalism, and capitalism as well as to the political and ideological fault lines of the world wars and the Cold War. Only then might we explain the combined fetish and fear of the archive in modern Greek historical culture, evident in, to name a few startling examples, the passion for collecting signs of "industrial revolution" in a country known for its "underdevelopment"; a national archive "in the basement in boxes" for a century; peripatetic communist archives "in exile"; the dispersion of family archives in transnational circuits of labor migration; the multilingual personal archives of cosmopolitan Greeks of the historical diaspora; the penchant of leftist historians (and even leftists not trained as historians) to take on the "uniform of the archivist" because there is "not enough time," or they do not trust those trained in archival "science," to assemble the evidence needed to (re)write the history of the Left; and the mass conflagration of the state's files of political surveillance, as analogous archives were being opened to the public to establish the legitimacy of postcommunist states. In various concerted acts of gathering and localizing "Greek" histories, just a few of which I have considered here, the archive emerged Janus-faced and, yet, indispensable as sign of revelation, proof, (self-)knowledge, truth, rationality, progress, capital, legacy, patrimony, patriarchy, genealogy, nation, metropole, sovereignty, surveillance, law, monolingualism, bureaucracy, order, power, paper, garbage, dust, the dead.

Notes

I INTRODUCTION: TAKING TESTIMONY, MAKING ARCHIVES

1. K. Gavroglou, "Sweet Memories from Tzimbali." *To Vima*, August 29, 1999.
2. I am indebted for the use of the term *personal archive* to a panel organized by colleagues Laura Kunreuther and Carole McGranahan at the American Anthropological Association Meetings in San Francisco in November 2000, entitled "Personal Archives: Collections, Selves, Histories." On the historian's "personal archives," see LaCapra (1985b).
3. On the history and theory of collecting and collections, see, for instance, Benjamin (1955), Stewart (1993), Crane (2000), Chow (2001).
4. The interdisciplinary literature on memory is voluminous, including studies on the "art of memory" from antiquity to modernity (Yates 1966; Matsuda 1996); monuments, public commemoration, and "lieux de mémoire" (Nora 1989; Young 1993; Gillis 1994; Sider and Smith 1997); photography, film, and other kinds of "screen memories" (Kuhn 1995; Hirsch 1997; Sturken 1997; Davis 2000; Strassler 2003); public history and national heritage (Wright 1985; Hewison 1987; Samuel 1994); and trauma, testimony, and the "sciences of memory," such as psychoanalysis (Langer 1991; Felman and Laub 1992; Caruth 1995, 1996; Hacking 1995; Antze and Lambek 1996); as well as many theoretical analyses, review articles, and comparative cultural studies (Connerton 1989; Hutton 1993; Olick and Robbins 1998; Bal, Crewe, and Spitzer 1999; Ben-Amos and Weissberg 1999; Stoler and Strassler 2000).
5. For commentaries on the "memory boom" as a "postmodern" phenomenon, see Fischer (1986), Huyssen (1995). James Faubion has argued that anthropological interest in history and memory might be ascribed to astute "participant observation" of a world in which the past has become the "privileged ground of individual and collective identity, entitlements, of *la condition humaine*," but charges nonetheless that "anthropologists have been more likely to reflect this transformation than reflect upon it" (1993b: 44).
6. The term *cultural memory* derives from Maurice Halbwachs's (1992) concept of "collective memory" and his well-known assertion that although it is individuals who remember, they do so only as members of the various social groups to which they belong (family, nation, etc.); for Halbwachs, individual memory was far too elliptical and fragmented to amount to much without being integrated into collective memory narratives. Replacing Halbwachs's "collective memory" (with its the strong Durkheimian connotations) by "*cultural* memory" underlines the unavoidably confrontational, rather than consensual, means by which particular narratives of the past come to be seen as more persuasive and credible than others. Since as Marita Sturken notes in her work on the politics of memory and amnesia in the

contemporary United States, this struggle is really a struggle over which social groups have a hand in defining collective meanings, cultural memory can be seen as a process that "both defines a culture and is the means by which its divisions and conflicting agendas are revealed" (1997: 1). The composing and recomposing of public memory narratives (in popular culture, public ritual, monument making as well as in diverse media technologies, such as television and film), thus, can be said to play a crucial role in the formation of national culture and political identity more generally.

7. For critical work on historiography by scholars associated with the Subaltern Studies Collective, see Guha and Spivak (1988), Guha (1997a, b), Chakrabarty (1992, 2000), Prakash (1992), Chatterjee (1993), Amin (1995). For a historical anthropology, defined neither in terms of "borrowing" methods across the two disciplines nor as a form of "social history," but as a politicization of categories of cultural difference and social knowledge and hence their historicization, see Cohn (1980, 1987), Comaroff and Comaroff (1992), Dirks (1992, 1996, 2001), Trouillot (1995), Cooper and Stoler (1997), Stoler (2002a). For a recent set of essays on historical anthropology in this framework, see Axel (2002).

8. The limitations of White's literary readings of historiography may be more evident to scholars coming to his work from disciplines other than history. As Dominick LaCapra notes, even though White's mode of reading historical texts draws heavily on New Criticism, a theoretical approach that is now viewed as conventional, if not obsolete, by literary critics, in historical circles it can still seem radical and controversial (2000: 38).

9. Refusing familiar genres of historical writing, Trouillot does not plot a "chronology of silences," but telescopes between different stages and levels of historical production. He thus considers both the Haitian historical establishment's silencing of the role of African-born slaves in the Haitian revolution and the silencing of the Haitian revolution *as a whole* within a Western historiography he shows to be ideologically and politically unable to acknowledge the revolutionary agency and, ultimately, the humanity of the enslaved.

10. Despite the fact that this new critical work on archives is, in archivist Terry Cook's (2000) words, "sadly usually not written by archivists," he notes that practicing archivists are also beginning to treat the archive not as "product," but to consider archiving as "process." Instead of "static physical objects" to be described in terms of their "singularity" and original context, then, archival records are coming to be understood as "dynamic virtual concepts" to be analyzed in relation to their function and potential for multiple authorship during the course of use.

11. On anthropology, colonialism, and travel, see Pratt (1986), Geertz (1988), Trouillot (1991), Clifford (1997). On gender and racial hierarchies in the anthropological profession, see Behar and Gordon (1995); on the gendering of historical practice, see Smith (1998). For comparisons between ethnographic fieldwork and archival research, see Cohn (1987), Farge (1989: 65), Dirks (2002: 48). If anthropologists have been chided for their excessive self-reflexivity, the reverse could be said for historians, whose accounts of archival research often unabashedly celebrate the "bravery" involved in historical "time travel," while demonstrating remarkably little self-consciousness about the ethics and politics of such "explorations" (e.g., Farge 1989; Steedman 2001).

12. In *Tristes Tropiques*, Lévi-Strauss describes his anxiety about traveling across national borders with a chest full of ethnographic materials, what he calls his "sole wealth," which includes "linguistic and technological card-indexes, a travel diary, anthropological notes, maps, diagrams and photographic negatives—in short, thousands of items" (1992: 33). Although the postmodern ethnographer's archive might not resemble Lévi-Strauss's chest or Malinowski's *corpus inscriptionum*, the production of "ethnographic documents" (through taking notes, audiotaping, videotaping, photographing, etc.) remains a standard component of anthropological research. See Sanjek (1990) on anthropologists' ambiguous feelings about their fieldnotes.

13. In the evolutionary paradigm of late-nineteenth-century anthropology, writing was treated as the developmental watershed separating "primitive" and "civilized" societies. Explicitly antievolutionist and cultural relativist approaches in anthropology would continue to treat the absence of writing as the salient feature "earmarking" societies for anthropological study, but in that classic move of anthropological liberalism, the creativity of oral products of the folk imagination (songs, folk tales, oratory) would be celebrated, valorized, and sometimes even placed above those of written culture. As a result, a bias against native exegesis and suspicion of the expertise of local elites would be entrenched in the discipline from the outset.

14. Of the hermeneutics of culture, Geertz has written characteristically: "Doing ethnography is like trying to read (in the sense of 'construct a reading of') a manuscript—foreign, faded, full of ellipses, incoherencies, suspicious emendations, and tendentious commentaries, but written not in conventionalized graphs of sound but in transient examples of shaped behavior" (1973: 10).

15. In a recent textbook, Alessandro Duranti has defined linguistic anthropology as the "study of language as a cultural resource and speaking as a cultural practice" and identified "speakers" as its subjects (1997: 2–3). Keith Basso's (1974) call for an "ethnography of writing" that would treat writing as a fundamental mode of "communicative *activity*," situated "squarely in the context of ethnography of communication" (426), has not been taken up with especial fervor. One trajectory of linguistic anthropological research on written culture has emerged, though, out of the critique of the "autonomous model of literacy," which views properties inherent to alphabetic literacy as catalyzing fundamental changes in the structure of societies; the ethnographic approach, by contrast, contextualizes literacy in relation to local social practices and ideological systems (cf. Besnier 1995). Other avenues of research into written culture have been opened up by Bakhtinian readings of the political struggles of "voices" in texts (cf. Hanks 1986; Messick 1995; Lyons 2001). On the ethnography of reading, see contributions to Boyarin (1993).

16. Derrida's theorizing of the archive in his 1996 *Archive Fever* has not been central to recent anthropological approaches to the archive. Derrida's writings on the archive draw on and extend his long-standing concern with issues of citation, authorization, authenticity, origins, and the techniques and technologies of mediation and do not represent as some believe the opportune adoption of an academic buzzword or a direct intervention into historians' debates about archival research. Although Derrida, like Foucault, does not speak of literal, "historical" archives (*Archive Fever* is a meditation on psychoanalysis, memory, and religion), his semiotics, along with Bakhtin's and Peirce's, can in my view invigorate anthropological and historical investigations into the acts of quotation, transcription, translation, and textual reproduction at the core of the archive's discursivity.

17. For a recent volume of interdisciplinary writings on archives and archiving, including articles written by historians, anthropologists, and archivists, most of them focused on "archives of power," see Blouin and Rosenberg (forthcoming).

18. Michael Herzfeld argued in *Anthropology through the Looking-Glass* (1987a) that the "charming but theoretically secondary field" of anthropology of Greece might by dint of its peculiar relationship to European colonial projects and ideologies and its location on the "margins of Europe" open up new kinds of questions for the field as a whole.

19. The Internet does not so much *de*materialize, *dis*locate, and *de*nationalize archives, relegating them to a neutral and immaterial "nowhere," as redefine in radical ways the relationship of archives to materiality, territoriality, and sovereignty. The emergence of the digital archive has led to the development of new transnational archival collections and memory places, new virtual documents whose legitimacy is not staked on their physicality, new modes of surveillance and control over access to information (as well as radical resistance to them), new "surfing" social scientists (whose presence in the archive or field

is not a prerequisite for the production of authoritative research), and, of course, a proliferation of new categories of documents (e.g., e-mail records). These transformations, in turn, are refiguring relations between the real and the virtual, public and private, and national and transnational involved in the construction, use, and management of archives. While our current ability (and need) to think critically about the "paper archive" could be said to have been occasioned by this current "crisis" and reformulation of the archive concept, at the same time, critical studies of "traditional" archives can contribute importantly to theorizing the continuities and discontinuities in archiving practices entailed by the digitization of documents.

20. On the "domestic archive," see Kunreuther (2002).

21. The opening of the Stasi archives after the collapse of the East German communist state did not so much expose shocking, previously unknown, state secrets, as provide an unparalleled opportunity to examine a particular system of state surveillance and its role in constituting the East German state itself as subject and agent. Thus, in his 1997 personal memoir, *The File*, Timothy Garton Ash reconstructs the production of his Stasi file in order to reflect on the everyday culture of spying and betrayal under communist rule. In the Greek context, see the comments of historian Filippos Iliou on the archives of the infamous Makronisos internment camp; he describes the disappointment of not finding in the archives direct evidence of the torture of leftist inmates and instead a more elusive record of the workings of the camp's bureaucracy (2000: 166–7).

22. During the evacuation of Washington in 1814, the Constitution and Declaration of Independence were stuffed in a linen sack and stashed in a grist mill outside the city. Upon return to Washington, they were kept for a time at an orphan asylum (!) before being deposited at the Library of Congress and later "settled" in the National Archives in 1952 (O'Toole 1993: 250).

23. In contrast to annals or chronicles, which present the world as a "mere sequence without beginning or end or as sequences of beginnings that only terminate and never conclude," modern historiography, according to White, creates meaning through *closure* (1987: 24). As he notes: "The demand for closure in the historical story is a demand, I suggest, for moral meaning, a demand that sequences of real events be assessed as to their significance as elements of a moral drama" (21).

24. As Samuel Weber explains: "To retrace the mediatic articulation at work within the boundaries of the individual *work* is to call attention to the way in which what had hitherto been considered to be accessory and intermediary—the program, its transmission, reception, storage, recycling, retransmission, etc.—infiltrates the inner integrity of the work, revealing it to be inscribed in, and as, a *network*" (1996: 3).

25. Saussure's concept of linguistic "value" is modeled on that of economic value in a free-market global economy (cf. Bourdieu 1991): in Saussure's view, word-coins drawn from national "storehouses" of language can be easily exchanged for foreign linguistic currency. By contrast, as Marx once noted, objecting to the frequent use of money as metaphor for language, but implicitly assuming the "mother tongue" to be singular, unmixed, and authentic: "Language does not transform ideas, so that the peculiarity of ideas is dissolved and their social character runs alongside them as a separate entity, like prices alongside commodities. Ideas do not exist separately from language. Ideas which have first to be translated out of their mother tongue into a foreign language in order to circulate, in order to become exchangeable, offer a somewhat better analogy; but the analogy then lies not in language, but in the foreignness of language" (1973: 162–3).

26. In his study of the history of the footnote, Anthony Grafton has argued that Ranke overstated his role as originator of source criticism. He concedes, though, that the German historian was a master in bringing "the flavor and texture of documents into his own

text"; by turning his "book into a sort of archive," he allowed his "reader to share something of the impact of his own direct encounter with the sources" (1997: 57).

27. The relative authority accorded to written and oral sources is, of course, historically and culturally contingent. Derrida's (1976) concept of logocentrism refers to the privileging of the spoken word and its association with truth, presence, and authenticity in opposition to the written word as sign of the false, absent, and artificial. In his study of Yemen as a "calligraphic state," Messick (1993a) has described the development (*within* a context of literacy) of a recitational culture favoring the recited word over the written text. For interdisciplinary research on the history and culture of evidence, proof, and "fact," see Chandler, Davidson, and Hartounian (1994), Poovey (1998).

28. For attempts to apply Peirce's thought to cultural analysis and, in particular, to establish a "semeiotic anthropology," see Daniel (1984), Singer (1984), Deeley (1994). References to Peirce follow standard citation form (volume, paragraph number) from *Collected Papers* (1931–58).

29. In addition to their primary collections of documents and artifacts, archives often contain another tier of writings relating to the history of their manufacture and management, ranging from correspondence to programmatic statements about archival policy to those most neglected of writings—finding aides, catalogues, inventories, and publications about archival holdings. As prisms onto the imagining of the archive's future order and dreamed-of completeness, even amid a chaotic surfeit of materials or gaping lacunae, these texts expose the historically shifting criteria for categorizing holdings and publicizing the archive's collections. For the idea of finding aides as "the archivist's own manuscript," I draw on Nancy Bartlett, "Archivists as Mediators in the Production of Historical Knowledge," a presentation given on September 13, 2000 at the Sawyer Seminar, "Archives, Documentation and the Institutions of Social Memory," University of Michigan, Ann Arbor, Michigan.

30. The permanent building of the General State Archives long seemed to be under permanent *construction*. See M. Loverdou, "Archives without Beginning or End," *To Vima*, May 5, 1996. The supermodern structure, which was built on land donated by a private benefactor in 1972, finally opened in November 2003. Historical researchers also have many complaints about other Greek public archives and libraries. The underfunded Greek National Library is housed in a historic building much too small for its collections, while Greece ranks last among European Union countries (of the fifteen-member federation) in networks of public, municipal, and school libraries. See N. Bakounakis, "The Shallow Memory of Society," *To Vima*, May 11, 2003. The city of Athens also lacks a working municipal archive; documents relating to the modern history of the city (which have escaped destruction) "wallow" in the basement of the municipal building. See N. Yiakovaki, "Athens: A Capital . . . without a Municipal Archive," *To Vima*, April 7, 1996.

31. During the parliament session of October 6, 1914 at which the law mandating the establishment of the General State Archives was passed, a government minister lamented the Greek state's belated recognition of the importance of archives as well as its reckless treatment of documents as salable (or waste) paper: "It is well known that the Greek State, from the time of Capodistrias [the first Prime Minister of Greece] and thereafter, took no care at all for historical documents and the organization of archives. Many of great value were sold by the *oka* [unit of weight] by clerks and civil servants, while others are to be found in damp basements and have turned into pulp and yet other documents of great historic value have been found in groceries by various independent researchers. In all states there exist public institutions of this kind [i.e., archives]. I consider the discussion and voting of this bill imperative so that we can contribute, even if slowly, to the prevention of further destruction of all these historical documents."

32. See Articles of Association of the Athens-based Historical and Ethnological Society of Greece (Athens 1882) and the first volume of the *Bulletin of the Historical and Ethnological Society of Greece*, published in 1883.

33. For a century, the society's collections were on the move. In 1884, a first exhibition was held at the Polytechnic where the society's collections would remain "temporarily" for some decades despite repeated attempts to relocate them to various other sites, including the trophy room of the Royal Palace (today's Parliament Building). During World War II, the collections were packed up in wooden crates for safety and in the 1950s were briefly on display in rented rooms of the "Workshop of Destitute Women"(!). In 1960, the society's collections were installed in the former Parliament Building at the core of the new Historical Museum of Modern Greece (Lappas 1982).

34. See I.M. Varvitsiotis, "The Odyssey of the State Archives," *To Vima*, January 19, 2003. Varvitsiotis's distress at the *materialization* of documents as wrapping paper and garbage also echoes Vlahoyiannis: "In all the countries of the world the national archives gather, document and preserve all records that are necessary for the knowledge and documentation of the historical development of the nation. In Greece, however, the National Archives are stacked up in warehouses and basements, resulting in their often suffering destruction from rainstorms and fires and being in great danger of theft, which in fact recently occurred. I remind you that a few years ago it was discovered that in a grocery in the central market documents from the War of Independence were being used to wrap sardines!!!"

35. The founding of the Historical and Ethnological Society has been ascribed to just this kind of shame. One morning in 1882, the folklorist Nikolaos Politis complained to historian Dimitris Kambouroglou that German scholars with whom he had recently met were startled to hear that there was no historical society or museum in "our so historical country." Hence, the society's formation became an urgent priority (Lappas 1982).

36. Of course, they pose radically different arguments: leftists protest the technological enhancement and extension of surveillance, while the Orthodox demonize technology *tout court.*

37. Aside from national *katharsi* (cleansing, purging), the justification put forth for destroying the files was that they were "partial" (*meroliptikoi*) and "untrustworthy" (*anaxiopistoi*). Besides overriding historians' understandings of how even "faulty" sources can be used to write history, this incineration has significantly compromised the degree to which the history of the state's persecution of the Left can be reconstructed. Incensed historians would come together in attempting to stop the destruction of the files, which was undertaken with lightening speed during the middle of August summer vacation time. The fact that communists were participating in the short-lived coalition government then in power appears to have paralyzed critical discourse, while also nominally legitimating the destruction of the files. (Among the signatories of law N. 8504 for the "destruction of the personal files of the *ethnikon fronimaton* [national loyalties] of Greek citizens" was Nikos Konstandopoulos, currently president of the left coalition party *Synaspismos.*) Some historians interpreted this event as a stunning symbolic negation of the project of creating archives for modern Greek historical studies; as one historian wrote: "It is inconceivable . . . to be hunting after archives for thirty years, conducting missions, researching in damp basements, even finding ourselves amid dead rats and suddenly for contemporary archives to be destroyed" (Droulia 1991: 34). For the depositions of other outraged historians, see the rest of the contributions to the 1991 *Contemporary Archives, Files and Historical Research*, an appendix to volume 6 of the journal *Mnimon.*

38. In a review of trends in modern Greek historiography post-1974, Antonis Liakos notes that the "problem" of what Greece is *not* when compared to western European nations has formed the common theme of otherwise quite different schools of historical research

(i.e., history of the Greek Enlightenment, political history, economic history). These frameworks, he suggests, collude in viewing modern Greek history through the prism of a perpetual dilemma of stagnation vs. modernization, tradition vs. rationalization, and Western vs. anti-Western orientation (2001: 82). Gourgouris, for his part, explicitly ascribes the Greek academic discourse on "underdevelopment," and especially that on "clientelism," to the broader postcolonial predicament in which "Greece" has been inscribed: in viewing patronage as a precapitalist form and survival of Ottoman times, rather than as the product of modern capitalist relations, these theories, he argues, implicitly accept the rationale of the same colonialist ideologies of development on which a supposed European "superiority" is based (1996: 64–71).

39. Rather than a boon for the Greek nation, Philhellenism, according to Gourgouris, should be considered a "punishment," precisely because it consistently fails to be recognized as an "Orientalism of the most profound sense" that "engages in the like activity of *representing* the other culture, which in effect means *replacing* the other culture with those self-generated, projected images of otherness that Western culture needs to see itself in: mirrors of itself" (1996: 140). As Gourgouris also importantly notes, the enthusiastic Greek embrace of Enlightenment discourse resembles the Haitian case, in which, as famously described by C.L.R. James in *The Black Jacobins* (1963), the "wrong" subjects (i.e., slaves) took the universalist language of human rights literally (as really applicable to *all* humans). In Greece, the emancipatory project of the French Revolution seemed even more relevant given the metaphorical status of the "Hellenes" as Western subjects; after all, as Shelley once famously remarked, "We are all Greeks" (74).

40. Todorova (1997) has disputed the use of the term Orientalism to refer to all forms of Western domination. Instead, she proposes the term Balkanism to describe a power dynamic in the region that did not involve *direct* colonization by European powers. The commonplace representation of the Balkans as a "bridge" between East and West as well as the region's internal racial and religious heterogeneity make Balkanism, in Todorova's terms, an "imputed ambiguity" rather than, as in the case of Orientalism, an "imputed opposition." Moćnik argues that Balkanism should be seen as an even more "radical mechanism" than Orientalism: "Contrary to *Orientalism*, where the logic of domination is imposed by colonial rule, in Balkanism, it is the immanent logic of self-constitution itself that generates the incapacity to conceive of oneself in other terms than from the point of view of the dominating other" (2002: 95).

41. On the dilemmas of producing anthropological discourse *in* Greece (as well as in *Greek*), see Bakalaki (1997).

42. The postwar period was marked by a proliferation of social science research on Greece, much funded by American aid organizations and centered on the prospects for Greek "modernization" (Kovani 1986). In the 1960s and 1970s, during the first phase of anthropological research on Greece, the dominance of the "honor and shame" paradigm, with its focus on "farmers" and "shepherds" (who could possess honor even if they did not possess wealth) should be seen as an implicit (and sometimes explicit) disavowal of the politicized project of Marxist "peasant studies." Julian Pitt-Rivers, an anthropologist of Andalusia and one of the main figures in Mediterranean anthropology, remarked in 1995 that the first conference on Mediterranean anthropology, held in 1959, had deliberately been called "Rural Peoples of the Mediterranean" in order to avoid the "contention-ridden word 'peasant' " (26).

43. Arjun Appadurai (1986) has used the term "gatekeeping" to describe the distorting effect of viewing specific geographical areas through the lens of particular theoretical paradigms, and vice versa. One could argue that the shift in Greek ethnography toward themes of history and memory corresponds to a recategorization of "Greece" from the symbolic

topography of the "Mediterranean" (cf. Davis 1977; Herzfeld 1980, 1987b) associated with the *longue durée* to the "Balkans" where the politics of histories and their relationship to nationalisms have been as much a focus of contemporary geopolitics as of academic discourse, and, further, to "Europe" (or the "new Europe") where "local histories" are opposed to various "metahistories" (European integration, unification, and "end-of-history" narratives).

44. Exceptions to the ingrained ethnographic refusal of the written text can be found in James Faubion's (1993a) analysis of the novels of Margharita Karapanou and Michael Herzfeld's book-length study of a Cretan novelist-chronicler (1997). In both cases, though, literary writers are involved and the anthropological reading comes to supplement the textual analysis by elaborating a "social context," gleaned through interviews with the (speaking) author.

45. Following from critiques of anthropology's depiction of "people without history" suspended in a "timeless time" of "cyclical" memory (Wolf 1982; Fabian 1983), the "historicity" argument views all peoples as possessing some kind of historical sensibility, but asserts that conceptions of temporality, agency, and the event vary widely across cultures, with significant consequences for the social uses of historical knowledge (Rosaldo 1980; Sahlins 1981; Lederman 1985; Rappaport 1994). In some anthropological work on Greece, aspects of Greek historical consciousness, thus, have been ascribed to forms of cultural practice and belief (religion, kinship) typically defined as antithetical to modern, secular, "Western" history. Renée Hirschon (1989), for instance, has suggested that the resilience of Greek refugees' historical memory of their Anatolian homelands be attributed to the predominance of "oral culture" among the refugees as well as to the emphasis placed on memory and memorialization in the Greek Orthodox liturgy. According to David Sutton (1998), the intense hostility with which many Greeks reacted to the naming of one of the Yugoslav successor states "Macedonia" stems from indigenous kinship ideologies and specifically the significance given to passing down names and property within the family. In this case, "historicity" is marshaled to explain (to a "Western" audience) seemingly "irrational" historical and political claims by placing them outside the frame of purportedly normative historical discourse.

46. In her work on the "memory of the senses," Nadia Seremetakis (1994) has posited the existence of a Greek sensual register and aesthetic sensibility that differs fundamentally from a "Western," and especially an "American," one. In arguing for the recuperation of the realm of the "traditional" and the "rural" from their association with folklore, she attempts to delineate an autonomous archive of Greek cultural experience and historical memory. Also taking up the "tradition"/"modernity" opposition, but from the vantage point of modernity, James Faubion (1993a) has argued that the development of a cosmopolitan discourse on history among the Athenian elite testifies to the existence of "another modernity" in Greece despite the absence of Weberian technical rationalism.

47. In a 1991 ethnography of the Old Town of Cretan Rethimno, Michael Herzfeld describes residents' resistance to the designation of their neighborhood as a monument of the Venetian past by learned and powerful outsiders. As he demonstrates, the concomitant imposition of strict building codes rendered residents' lives literally, but also existentially, unlivable as intimate local meanings of buildings and public spaces were overwritten. Roxani Kaftantzoglou and F. Kamoutsi (2001) have studied the case of Anafiotika, a neighborhood originally settled in the nineteenth century by immigrant-squatters from the Cycladic island of Anafi, who constructed their island-style homes just below the Parthenon, the "West's" *Ur*-monument. She examines ongoing conflicts between local residents and the state archeological service over the meanings and proper custodianship of this place.

48. For anthropology as a "contribution to the social history of modern Greece," see Papataxiarchis and Paradellis (1993). For studies using oral history methodologies to address controversial subjects of modern Greek history such as the wartime Resistance, foreign occupation, the Civil War, and ethnic minorities, see Collard (1993), Hart (1996), Karakasidou (1997), Van Boeschoten (1997), Doumanis (1997). For the history and anthropology of memory, see Benveniste and Paradellis (1999).

49. Greek historians have begun to turn critical attention to the rhetorics of historical writing, but have focused on classic works of prominent Greek historians (Liakos 1994; Gazi 2000) or institutional discourses such as history textbooks (Koulouri 1988). The Greek historical journal *Historein* sponsored an important conference in Athens in 2001 entitled "Claiming History: Aspects of Contemporary Historical Culture," with historical culture being defined as the past's "second life beyond the bounds of the historical discipline." For interdisciplinary approaches to historical "narrativity," see Benveniste and Paradellis (1994).

50. A highly politicized "language question" (*glossiko zitima*) was a pronounced aspect of Greek national culture beginning in the late nineteenth century. In what has been considered a classic case of "diglossia" (Ferguson 1959), the purist register of *katharevousa*, as official language of state, bureaucracy, and schooling, was opposed to the vernacular *demotiki*, which was used in informal communication, but also in much literature. *Katharevousa*, which was created by intellectuals to serve the ideological needs of the new Greek state (i.e., to demonstrate historical continuity), purged "foreign" elements (i.e., Turkish, Italian, Slavic, Arvanitika (Albanian) words) from the modern Greek language as well as "returned" ancient Greek words and morphology. Although often depicted as the "authentic," "oral" language of the "people" in relation to the artificial, and patently exclusionary, purist register, *demotiki* also was a codified, *written* standard, espoused, promoted, and above all used by the progressive elite (cf. Skopetea 1988a: 111; Frangoudaki 2001: 57–8). Rather than fixed and autonomous linguistic essences, these registers are best understood in terms of a symbolic opposition with constantly shifting linguistic "content" and associated with historically contingent political ideologies. The 1976 institution of *demotiki* as language of state following the demise of the *junta*, whose language policies and own use of the purist register were widely reviled, promised the end of the "language question." Instead, a "language problem" emerged in the late 1980s and early 1990s, as conservatives spoke out about the "loss" of the Greek language in the wake of the liberal language reforms: namely, the language's "bastardization" from the influx of English loan words, disconnection from its ancient Greek "roots," and politicization (Christidis 1995). More recently, "Greeklish" (Greek written with Latin characters for use on the Internet) has come under attack by the linguistic establishment as a new form of (self-)colonization. This politicized relationship between "archaizing" and "vernacular" registers in Greek linguistic ideology has tended to obscure a complexly *polyglossic* situation in the Greek past and present, including in addition to non-Greek languages historically spoken by citizens of the Greek state (Turkish, Slavic, Arvanitika, etc.), regional dialects, new varieties of Greek (such as the "Gringlish" (Greek-English) of Greek-Americans), and hybrid orthographies that have developed as a response to the "new" media technologies of different eras (e.g., Karamanli, Turkish books printed in Greek characters; Internet "Greeklish").

51. In 1997 talk about the archives and private papers of Greek politicians reached a particularly feverish pitch with the publication of the "archive" of former Prime Minister Konstandinos Karamanlis (which actually comprises a much-edited volume of his writings and hardly an archive of "primary" documents, see A. Bayias, "Rigid Texts." *To Vima*, June 1, 1997); the personal memoirs of Prime Minister Andreas Papandreou's second wife, Dimitra

Liani-Papandreou, with its "Appendix of Documents," including some highly personal letters and notes; and the "lost archive" of famous communist guerrilla leader Aris Velouchiotis, one of the founders of ELAS, the armed wing of the EAM wartime resistance force.

52. Much research on contemporary Greek history has been conducted at the Greek Literary and Historical Archives (ELIA), the Gennadeios Library, and the Archive of the National Bank of Greece. Until the opening of the new permanent building of the General State Archives in 2003, the 1923 building in which the National Bank archives are housed was the only structure built in Greece specifically to house an archive.

53. In the Greek context, an analogous example might be the archive of the Alexandrian poet Constantine Cavafy, originally purchased by the philologist and literary editor Yiorgos Savidis in 1960 and later incorporated into the privately run Center of Neohellenic Studies in Athens (*Spoudastirio Neou Ellinismou*). Along with Cavafy's personal archive, the center also holds Savidis's library and that of historian and philologist Konstandinos Dimaras. In this way, the careers of these master interpreters and scholars of modern Greek literature and history are symbolically linked and intertwined with the work and life of the legendary poet. Since researchers are typically told that all the center's materials "soon" will be available on the Internet, access to "original," nondigitized materials "for the time being" is granted on a limited basis.

54. The 1991 law (N. 1946) for the organization and management of the General State Archives, which replaces the law of 1939 (N. 2027), significantly broadens the definition of "historical" to include activities not directly related to the state (e.g., banking and commercial activity, political parties and unions, culture and the arts, etc.) and nonwritten sources (e.g., audiovisual materials). Given the newness of the state's interest in cultural and economic history, the important "gap" filled by private archives such as the Greek Literary and Historical Archives (ELIA) and the Archive of the National Bank of Greece can be better appreciated. For the "belated" interest in Greek audiovisual archives, see K. Halvatzakis, " 'Electronic Guide' for the Salvation of Archives: Pan-European Effort for the Documentation of Audiovisual Memory." *To Vima*, April 29, 2000. See also the 1998 volume, *Martyries se Ihitikes kai Kinoumenes Apotyposeis os Pigi Istorias* (Testimonies in Auditory and Cinematic Records as Historical Source) (University of Athens, Department of History and Archaeology. Athens: Katarchi).

55. In the introduction to a finding aide for the EDA archive, historian Ioanna Papathanasiou describes the process of reconstructing an archive whose "original" sense had been shattered as a result of plundering and selective reordering by security forces as well as from haphazard storage following the regime change. In doing this work, she notes that a "historian did not just wear the uniform of an archivist; she began to study and discover the mysteries of archival science (*archeionomia*)" (2001: 15). The description of the EDA archive as "under persecution" (*ipo diogmo*) and "wounded" (*travmatismeno*) comes from a short preface to Papathanasiou's text written by Filippos Iliou and Ilias Nikolakopoulos.

56. In a brief article entitled "Closed Archives," Iliou (2003) cites A. Papapanagiotou, formerly in charge of the Greek Communist Party's Department of History, who describes parts of the Party archive relating to the wartime resistance movement as closed up with "forty locks" (*saranda kleidaries*) that opened only for " 'researchers' (interrogators)" looking to indict (*fakeloma*) other Party members and cadres.

57. During the Civil War and then following the communist defeat in 1949, the archives of the Greek Communist Party relating to the Resistance and the Civil War were gradually sent to Bucharest from where they were later transferred to the small Romanian town of Sibiou, the base of the translation department of the Communist Party-in-Exile. (KKE archives dealing with the period from 1918 to 1939 had been sent earlier, by boat, "up" to Moscow.) Following the 1968 party split, the parts of the archive that came into the hands of the Communist Party of the Interior were moved to Skopje for cataloguing and

microfilming; these materials, which make up the central collection of ASKI, were "repatriated" after the end of the military dictatorship (1967–74). On the history of the Greek Communist Party archives "in exile" and "refugeedom" (*prosfygia*), see Matthaiou and Polemi (1999), Iliou (2003).

58. In describing the "eclipse of the event" in French historiography, Ricoeur points to Braudel's critique of the notion that individuals are the ultimate agents of historical transformation and that "pointlike" changes of extreme suddenness and brevity are those that fundamentally transform people's lives (1984: 96–7).

2   COLLECTORS OF SOURCES: LOCAL HISTORIOGRAPHY AND THE POSSESSION OF THE PAST

1. Antonis Liakos (2001: 78–9) has described "new history" as the Greek turn toward social history and the social sciences. In relation to the historical discipline as a whole, new history's belated emergence and the style of its research, he argues, should be attributed to local political circumstances (especially the 1967–74 dictatorship) and the influence of specific scholars (such as Konstandinos Dimaras and Nikos Svoronos). As a result, even though many consider new history simply the Greek Annales, Liakos insists on key differences, such as the fact that while Annales initiated a break with Marxism, new history incorporated it. New history, he points out, has not proved particularly open to developments in 1980s and 1990s historiography (such as new historicism, the linguistic turn, and poststructuralism). Conflated under the capacious label of the "postmodern," research influenced by these theoretical approaches is often dismissed by those allied with new history as a betrayal of historical "truth" and leftist politics (see n. 2).

2. For instance, a heated interchange about "postmodern" historiography took place in various newspapers and periodicals (e.g., *To Vima, Avgi, O Politis*), following the conference "Historiography of Modern and Contemporary Greece (1832–2002)," organized by the Institute for Neohellenic Research–National Hellenic Research Foundation and held in Athens in fall 2002. The debate was sparked by Kremmydas's closing remarks, reprinted in *Avgi*, the newspaper of the left coalition party Synaspismos, in which he accused "young historians" of the "American" school of having confused historiography with history and, as a result, of having abandoned the archives: "I am reminded," he writes, "of something that a young historian told me a few years ago half-joking: 'Archives? What archives? Who looks at archives anymore?'—maybe he wasn't joking." See V. Kremmydas, "Six Days of Historiography: That's How We Ended . . . ," *Avgi*, November 17, 2002. For articles related to the debate, see http://www.historein.gr/index_gr.htm

3. For the social history and ethnography of local and amateur historical production in different historical and cultural contexts, see Levine (1986), Thiesse (1991), Mallon (1995), Manoukian (2001).

4. Academics, including historians, often write editorials in the Sunday editions of national newspapers, while amateurs frequently contribute articles to the popular history supplements of national newspapers (such as *7 Meres* in the newspaper *Kathimerini* and *Istorika* in *Eleftherotypia*). Occasionally, local histories are briefly reviewed in the book review sections of the national newspapers.

5. For the introduction of "scientific" national historiography in Greece in the second half of the nineteenth century, see Gazi (2000).

6. In folklore studies, the prominence of archaeological metaphors in phrases such as "monuments of the word" (*mnimeia tou logou*) or "living monuments" (*zonta mnimeia*), which

refer to folk songs, proverbs, fairy tales, and other linguistic customs, reflects the status of archaeology as paradigmatic discipline, demonstrating the "survival" of the past in the present and, by extension, the cultural continuity of the Greek people (Kyriakidou-Nestoros 1978: 66–7; Herzfeld 1986: 10–11).

7. The typical press run for academic historiography also happens to be 1,000 copies, except in the case of books earmarked for university classrooms (Liakos 2001).

8. Of course, the relationship between "local" and "national" historiography has also been in flux. Although local history now appears to be a quintessential form of national (if not national*ist*) history, Stathis Gourgouris points out that the publication of Konstandinos Paparrigopoulos's *History of the Greek Nation* (1860–74), the classic exposition of the masternarrative of Greek historical continuity, initially shocked local historians, who believed national history should be gradually composed from an aggregate of local histories. In practice, however, as Gourgouris notes, Paparrigopoulos's history ended up leading to a rise in the publication of local histories (1996: 253).

9. The 1990s introduction of desktop publishing technology has greatly affected the production of local historiography in Volos. *Ekdoseis Ores*, the vanity press at which most local writers were publishing their work during the time of my research, was established in 1991. Owner Yiorgos Tsitsinis did not hesitate to point out to me the commercial dimensions involved: he told me that he charged one-and-a-half-million drachma (approximately $5,000) to print 1,000 copies of a 300-page book. Also the editor of a local newspaper, Tsitsinis told me that he and his staff were journalists by trade who had gotten into this line of work accidentally, only to find themselves amazed by local demand. When I met with him in February 1998, the press had published 123 books, including history, fiction, textbooks, and conference reports.

10. For analyses of thematic and theoretical shifts in contemporary Greek academic historiography, see Kitroeff (1989); Liakos (2001). For the state-of-the-field in the late 1980s, see the 1988 three-volume issue of *Synchrona Themata* 35–36–37 ("Contemporary Currents in the Historiography of Modern Hellenism"). For an annotated bibliography of post-1974 historical production that includes developments in the 1990s, see the 1999 exhibition catalogue, *The Historical Book from the Regime Change until Today: Trajectories in Modern Greek History* (*Historein*/ National Book Center).

11. Since Thessaly was not liberated during the Greek Revolution of 1821 and, thus, did not play a prominent role in that historical "drama," local historians had focused anyway on the earlier period of the "Greek Enlightenment" and especially on several key local figures associated with it, such as Grigorios Konstandas, Anthimos Gazis, Daniel Filippides, and Rigas Velestinlis. A tome entitled *Figures of Magnesia* (Volos: Ekdoseis Nomarchias Magnisias, 1973), including biographical portraits of these and other "great men" of the region, was published during the dictatorship. Written exclusively by male historians, this volume is representative of the kind of chauvinistic historical discourse to which subsequent local historical production is counterposed.

12. See, for instance, the 1985 *The Modern Greek City: Ottoman Legacies and the Greek State*, two volumes of papers from a conference sponsored by the Etaireia Meletis Neou Ellenismou (EMNE). Academic research on the "neohellenic city" has been focused largely on "exceptional" cases, such as that of the port city of Ermoupolis on the island of Syros, a major hub for commerce, shipping, and industry in the mid-nineteenth century; the ethnically and religiously diverse city of Thessaloniki; and Athens, the megalopolis where the Greek state apparatus and the economic, cultural, and intellectual life of the nation have been disproportionately centered.

13. Despite the fact that the publication of memoirs has increased dramatically nationwide (see, for instance, M. Papayiannidou, "Autobiographies of Non-Famous People," *To Vima,* August 11, 1996), when I asked local writers in Volos to recommend memoirs or

autobiographies of local people, my query usually was met either with a grin (perhaps because writing autobiography was viewed as an act of vanity) or a confused look (since I had asked about a genre rather than a particular historical subject to which the text might refer). Although I ultimately located a few autobiographies written by local people, these were primarily war memoirs, not full life stories. Many autobiographies probably never end up getting published; municipalities and community groups, which have funded so many recent local historical publications, usually would not be interested in sponsoring the publication of an autobiography unless it concerned a famous person from the area. For more on the political economy of the memoir in Greece, see chapter 5.

14. Genealogies appear to be a relatively rare genre of Greek historical writing. My queries led me to three unpublished genealogies of local families. Two had been written by descendants of elite families, while the other was a deliberate parody of the genre by a left-wing typesetter from a Thessalian village.

15. One of the most rousing calls for Greeks to take up the writing of local history was made by Daniel Filippidis and Grigorios Konstandas, natives of a Pelion mountain village. In their *Modern Geography*, originally published in 1771, they exhort: "May others copy us and each person describe the land where they were born, not mathematically, not with geographical precision, in other words designating its width and breath . . . but narratively, each person writing the history (*istorondas*) of the places and villages of their native land (*topos*), its government, how many souls are in each village, what kind of people they are, with what morals, religion, trees, income, animals . . ." (1988: 172–3). Local writers in Volos often invoked this famous passage in conversations about local history or used it as an epigraph in their books.

16. This view of the city-as-character, of course, is modeled on the depiction of the state in national historiography. As Hayden White has pointed out, it was Hegel who first identified the modern state as the entity that provided not only the rationale for the production of historiography and the preservation of the records needed to write it but also with history's subject matter and leading "actor": a "legal subject that can serve as the agent, agency and subject of historical narrative" (1987: 13).

17. This is not to say, of course, that writers of local history have not made efforts in the other direction (i.e., to highlight the originality of their texts). Thus, Marxist historiography, for instance, presents itself as a radical break with and critique of "traditional" historiography.

18. See, for instance, Koliou (1994), Dimoglou (1995), Diomidi-Kormazou (1995).

19. See, for instance, Voyiatzis (1980, 1987), Koliou (1991), Triandou (1994), Mougoyiannis (1990, 1992).

20. See, for instance, Yiasirani-Kyritsi (1996).

21. See, for instance, Frezis (1994), Katsirelos (1994), Konstandaras-Statharas (1994), Kartsagouli (1995).

22. See, for instance, Koliou (1985, 1988, 1997), Haritos (1989).

23. On colonial era "ville nouvelles" in the Muslim world, see, for instance, Mitchell (1988), Rabinow (1989), Wright (1991), Messick (1993a: 246–7). In 1882–3, immediately following the annexation of Thessaly by Greece, Volos city officials approved a town plan that was an impoverished version of the early-nineteenth-century neoclassical town plan for Athens. In the same period, similar town plans were approved in other former "Turkish" cities of Thessaly, including Larisa, Karditsa, and Trikala (Hastaoglou 1995: 103).

24. In 1924, Asia Minor refugees were settled in an area north of the city: this refugee "settlement" (*synoikismos*) became the municipality of Nea Ionia (i.e., the "New" Ionia) in 1947, during the Civil War.

25. By the early 1960s, approximately 4,500 people had lost their jobs. Once-profitable textile and iron industries faced tremendous difficulties competing with foreign imports. A comparison of prewar and 1960 figures shows dramatic drops in employment: in

textiles (3,149 to 452), tobacco (2,340 to 903), and iron industries (1,789 to 533) (Dimoglou 1995: 136–7). In the 1970s, the city experienced another brief period of industrial development marked by the establishment of a national Industrial Zone in 1969, the remodeling of the port, and the opening of a cargo boat line between Volos and Syria (which was terminated during the Iran–Iraq war).

26. The 1999 desk calendar of the Volos municipal history center (DIKI) marks the date of the earthquake with the following comment: "Disastrous earthquakes. Old Volos is now history." The same "end point" is used in the history of the city published by DIKI, *Volos, One Century: From Incorporation into the Greek State (1881) until the Earthquakes (1955).*

27. Between 1981 and 1993, approximately 4,000 more jobs in manufacturing were lost (Maloutas 1995).

28. While Paparrigopoulos ended up proposing *five* Hellenisms (ancient, Macedonian, Christian, Medieval, and modern), his schema has been remembered in terms of these three periods (Liakos 1994: 184).

29. Indian historiography similarly has "explained" the chasm separating ancient and modern India through recourse to the concept of a middle ages. As in the Greek case, the attribution of that "night of medieval darkness" to Muslim rule had the further "advantage" of catering to European prejudices against Islam (Chatterjee 1993: 98). As Liakos has argued, the incorporation of the Ottoman era, that most "recalcitrant" period of Greek history, into the diachronic narrative of Hellenism was enabled by the emergence of the "Greek Enlightenment" as a historical thematic. By focusing on Greek scholars of the diaspora and their contribution to developing Greek national consciousness, the Ottoman period, he explains, was transformed from one characterized by Greek subjugation and passivity to one animated by Greek agency and accomplishment (1994: 195–6).

30. This antithesis was most pronounced in the rivalry between Volos and nearby Larisa, a prosperous city that derived its wealth primarily from agriculture. Voliotes typically juxtaposed their history of cultural refinement to the "provincial" ways of people from Larisa, who always seemed to be in the news for sex scandals, clergy corruption, or unruly farmer protests.

31. While many elite families did leave the city after the war, the mantra about the "disappearance" of the bourgeoisie mostly seems to operate as a deus ex machina to account for the changing relation of class to occupation.

32. I heard numerous explanations for this term, the simplest being that the Voliotes have the cold, snooty, and superior manner "typical" of Austrians. One local historian traced the origin of the term to the end of the nineteenth century when Thessalian peasants used to come to sell their goods in the city: seeing flags of foreign consulates, they thought they had left Greece and entered a foreign country (i.e., "Austria"). A cardiologist, himself a descendant of an established Voliote family, provided me with a more elaborate story. He believed that the real significance of the term lay in the relationship of Austrians to other Germanic peoples (i.e., more refined and epicurean, they were the "supervisors" who occupied high positions in the army). He suggested that Voliotes used to play a similar role in Thessaly, overseeing economic activity both on Mt. Pelion and the fertile Thessalian plain. Occasionally, I even heard Voliote urbanity distinguished from that of Athenians. Echoing a common neohellenic barb about western Europeans (i.e., "When they were hanging from the trees and living in caves, we built the Parthenon . . ."), a young civil engineer, who had worked on several of the municipality's restoration projects, reminded me: "When they were still tending sheep in Athens, here in Volos we had the industrial revolution. We had the consulates of European countries . . ."

33. A repositioning of Greek cultural particularity within a universalizing framework of "primitive" humanism also can be seen in postwar social science research on Greece. As

Michael Fotiadis (1995) has argued with reference to the first large-scale archaeological survey in Greece (1950s to 1970s), the shift from salvage excavations at isolated sites ("treasure hunting") to field surveys producing demographic and economic data created a new focus on "man-in-his-environment" in place of one on the "uniqueness" of Greek antiquity. Similarly, the postwar turn from folklore (with its emphasis on locating "survivals" of ancient Greek language and culture) to anthropology (with its "universal language" of kinship) led to the classification of the "Greek folk" within the "family of man." Testament to this "discovery" of the Greek as "aboriginal" European (Herzfeld 1987a), anthropologist John Campbell in the first ethnography of Greece, his 1964 study of the transhumant Sarakatsanoi, compares the huts of this shepherd group to those of the African Nuer, famously described by Evans-Pritchard, Campbell's teacher.

34. This interest in Pelion as a *natural*, not just a historical, landscape appears to have developed in the interwar period. At this time, the Hiking Club of Volos was established (1922) and Voliote commercial photographer Kostas Zimeris, a founding member of the club, extensively photographed the "picturesque" landscapes and peasants of Mt. Pelion and other rural areas near Volos.

35. On the allegorical use of the symbols of the 1821 Greek War of Independence in descriptions of the World War II Resistance and left-wing insurgence, see Petropoulos (1978: 175), Collard (1993: 378), Liakos (1994: 195). In representing communist guerrilla fighters (*andartes*) as successors to *kleftes*, the mountain rebels who fought against the Ottomans in 1821, leftist discourses emphasize the *nationalist* dimensions of the resistance movement, thus, countering accusations of disloyalty and treason made by opponents of communism. Tracing a diachronic history of Greek "freedom fighting," however, has had the effect of obscuring connections between European and Greek wartime radicalism, making resistance seem like a particularly *Greek* legacy.

36. Makris can be considered the Voliote Angeliki Hatzmihali, the Athenian aristocrat whose study of Greek traditional material culture (furniture, handicrafts, architecture, etc.) formed part of an elaborate strategy of self-fashioning that culminated in her construction of a neotraditional home in the center of Athens (Hatzimihali 1949; Faubion 1993a: 95). Like Hatzimihali's house, Makris's seems to have been built with a future folklore museum in mind and indeed posthumously was donated to the University of Thessaly as a museum.

37. Maloutas (1995) reports a decline in local employment in manufacturing from 34.6% in 1981 to 20.3% in 1993 and an increase in service sector jobs from 18.9% to 39.2%. The municipality itself became an important local employer during this period and the rise in service sector jobs was attributable, in part, to hiring by the municipality.

38. With funds from the European Community Initiative URBAN, the municipality of Volos took possession of nine industrial buildings or building complexes. Volos was one of seven Greek cities that participated in the 1995–96 program "Inventory and Appraisal of Historical Industrial Equipment," which documented information about Greek factories in operation between 1850 and 1950.

39. The *trenaki* ("little train") of Mt. Pelion, which runs along a tiny 60-cm-wide track, was built in 1895 and operated until 1971. A private association "Friends of the Train" was instrumental in its restoration and return to operation as a tourist attraction in 1996. The engineer responsible for the construction of the Thessalian railways was the Italian Evaristo de Chirico, father of the artist Giorgio de Chirico, who was born in Volos.

40. Greek municipal investment in historical production is not entirely new. As far back as 1879, the Athens Town Council funded the publication of a history of an Athenian archbishop written by Spyridon Lambros, a prominent history professor at the University of Athens (Gazi 2000: 96–7).

41. Established in 1971, the Society for Thessalian Studies previously had been at the center of the city's historical activity. The Society, to which many amateur history writers in the 1990s belonged, publishes a journal, *Archive of Thessalian Studies*. In 1991, the Local History Archive of Thessaly, originally founded by the Society, became a local branch of the General State Archives. In addition to holding archival material from state institutions, the archive also collects some of the same kinds of materials of interest to DIKI, such as the archives of local factories. During the time of my research, neither the Society for Thessalian Studies nor the local branch of the state archives was nearly as active as DIKI in generating public interest in the city's history.

42. For instance, after the 1993 DIKI conference, "Industry of Volos," Koliou (1994) and Diomidi (1995) wrote brief books about the history of local industry. Eleni Triandou (1994), the author of the most patently nostalgic book about the city, told me that she decided to write her book after participating in the 1994 DIKI event, "Volos . . . until the Earthquakes," which featured the panel "Ten Voliotes Discuss Their Memories of the Volos of Then."

43. The term *topiki aftodoiikisi* deliberately echoes that of *laiki aftodoiikisi*, the system of local self-government set up in so-called Free Greece, the parts of the country run by the communist-led Resistance during World War II. Other historical precedents drawn on by the Left to legitimize this institution include the "community" (*koinotita*) of the Ottoman period and the political philosophy of the revolutionary Rigas Velestinlis, who proposed a model of a decentered democratic state based on the Ottoman *millet* system in his 1797 constitution (cf. Tomara-Sideri 1999).

44. The conflation of local history and industry is striking in the case of Maroula Kliafa, a local historian from the Thessalian city of Trikala. One day while we were speaking at her house, she pointed through a lace curtain to the old building of the beverage factory owned by her husband (the new factory is located outside city limits). With their own money, she and her husband are turning the now-defunct factory into a cultural center to which she will donate her large personal archive of local newspapers and old photographs.

45. According to David Harvey, the study of urbanization should entail the examination of the capitalist process as it "unfolds through the production of physical and social landscapes and the production of distinctive ways of thinking and acting among people who live in towns and cities. The study of urbanization is not the study of a legal, political entity or of a physical artifact" (1989: 6–7).

46. Although my interlocutors in this chapter all share the negative self-identification, "I am not a historian," there are, needless to say, many distinct groups and subgroups among local history writers based on differences of age, politics, education, and research interests as well as affiliation with various cultural associations and historical societies.

47. In theory, if not in practice. Instead of banishing religion from the cemetery, the new civic cemeteries made the non-Orthodox "matter out of place." Thus, in Volos, as elsewhere in Greece, a separate Jewish cemetery borders the "municipal" one. One day at the Volos cemetery, Yiasirani showed me a nineteenth-century tombstone that had an inscription written in the Armenian alphabet. She claimed that cemetery officials had planned to remove it to make space for a new grave until she protested that it was a "historical monument." On Greek municipal cemeteries and their liminal position in public space, see Panourgia 1995: 185–6.

48. On the social construction of autochthony through the narration of originary history, see Papataxiarchis (1990) and Panourgia (1995: 54–8).

49. An exhibition of photographs taken by the local commercial photographer Kostas Zimeris entitled "Old Volos" was held in 1981. The following year the municipality installed a permanent slide exhibition (also entitled "Old Volos") of the photographs of Stefanos Stournaras, another of the city's commercial photographers.

50. In DIKI's *Volos: One Century* (1999), everyday records of commercial activity (old receipts, bills, correspondence) have been enlarged and reproduced, thus highlighting their period letterheads and antiquated handwriting and, by extension, their status not only as documents (to write the history of industry) but also as aesthetic objects.

51. Nitsa Koliou's *Typo-foto-graphic Panorama of Volos* (1991) is an example of a history of the local press and Maroula Kliafa's *Trikala, From Seifoullah to Tsitsanis: The Transformations of a Community as Recorded in the Press of the Day* (2 vols., 1996, 1998) of a history as told from the "pages" of local newspapers.

52. In testimonial genres, as I will discuss in the following two chapters, the same reverence has been accorded to the *spoken* voice. In his 1929 *A Prisoner of War's Story*, Stratis Doukas, for instance, describes the process of documenting testimony as a self-conscious effort to efface the intervention of writing. He explains that he made his cousin read aloud to him the transcription of his informant's testimony so he could reoralize his retranscription.

53. That photography is itself part of the "romantic" past can be discerned in the nostalgic comments of Voliote local historian Yiannis Mougoyiannis in a 1997 article entitled "The Charm of the Old Photograph" (*Makrinitsa* 15: 39): "The publication of some of these photographs is intended to acquaint younger generations with ways of life from the past, when every peasant of Pelion came down to Volos to be photographed, when people abroad sent their photographs to relatives back home so that they would remember them, when weddings still were held at home and photographs were taken in the courtyard. When people lived with a different view of life, more human and romantic."

3   WITNESSES TO WITNESSING: RECORDS OF RESEARCH AT AN ARCHIVE OF REFUGEE TESTIMONY

1. In 1844, politician Yiannis Kolletis introduced the term *Megali Idea* (Great Idea) into the political discourse of the newly established Greek state. Ever since the Ottoman conquest of Byzantine Constantinople in 1453, however, the dream of "return" had been a part of Greek popular culture: many folk stories and songs center on the theme of the eventual "redemption" and "salvation" of the lands of classical and Byzantine Hellenism (Layoun 2001: 24). In its implication that Greeks' destiny should have been to rule in the East as a "chosen people" and that their "martyrdom" in 1922 fulfilled some kind of divine prophecy, the term "Catastrophe" draws on and amplifies the religious undertones of Great Idea discourse (Gazi n.d.).

2. The terms "Asia Minor" (in Greek *Mikra Asia* or *Mikrasia*, "Little Asia") and "Anatolia" (from the Greek *anatoli*, or "east") refer to the Asian peninsula of contemporary Turkey. Prior to 1922, "Infidel Smyrna" (*Giaour Izmir*), as the Turks called it, had been the center of ethnic Greek commercial and cultural life in the Ottoman Empire. At the time of the "Catastrophe," European parts of the Ottoman Empire, such as Istanbul and Eastern Thrace, also had sizable populations of ethnic Greeks.

3. The 1923 Convention Concerning the Exchange of Greek and Turkish Populations stipulated "a compulsory exchange of Turkish nationals of the Greek Orthodox religion established in Turkish territory, and of Greek nationals of the Moslem religion established in Greek territory." Only the Greek Orthodox of Istanbul and the Muslims of Thrace were exempted from the exchange. In 1919, Greece and Bulgaria had ratified a similar Convention Respecting the Reciprocal Emigration of their Racial Minorities but emigration had been voluntary (Pentzopoulos 1962: 60–1).

4. The majority of refugees arrived in Greece in 1922 following the withdrawal of the Greek army. After the signing of the Convention in Lausanne, 200,000 Greek Orthodox residents of Turkey and approximately 350,000 Muslim residents of Greece were "exchanged." The League of Nations estimates that 20% of refugees died within one year of their arrival in Greece due to wretched health conditions. For a detailed discussion of the population exchange, see Pentzopoulos (1962). Many ethnic Greeks of the Ottoman Empire (Pontians, for instance) had fled their homes years before the "Catastrophe," victims of the persecution and violence of an increasingly aggressive Turkish nationalism.

5. See K. Koulouri, " 'Catastrophe,' 'Campaign' and 'War' in School," *To Vima*, Sunday, September 1, 2002. Although the events of 1922 were always included in Greek history textbooks, Koulouri notes that the 1983 textbook represented a turning point in the representation of the "Catastrophe" because of the amount of material presented and the fact that refugee testimonies were included along with information about political and military history.

6. Ironically, even though the exchange was proposed as a means of creating homogenous "national" populations, religion was considered the principal determinant of ethnic identity, thus demonstrating, as Layoun notes, the "confusion of ethnic, religious, linguistic and political citizenship that underlies the attempt to forcibly (construct) and exchange populations of 'the same' " (2001: 32). Turks, for their part, continue to mark the difference between citizens of the Greek state and ethnic Greeks living in other post-Ottoman lands (i.e., Asia Minor, Istanbul, Thrace, Cyprus, etc.) by calling the former Yunanlı, from the Turkish word for Greece, *Yunanistan*, and the latter *Rum*, a word deriving from "Roman" and alluding to these Greeks' historical descent from citizens of the former Roman-Byzantine Empire.

7. For instance, testimony is used as a narrative frame in works of fiction, such as Stratis Myrivilis's 1924 *Zoi en Tafo* (Life in the Tomb), Stratis Doukas's 1929 *Istoria Enos Aichmalotou* (A Prisoner of War's Story), Ilias Venezis's 1931 *To Noumero 31328* (The Number 31328), Dido Sotiriou's 1962 *Matomena Homata* (which literally means "bloodied earth" but has been translated into English as *Farewell Anatolia*), Elli Papadimitriou's 1975 *O Koinos Logos* (The Common Language) and more recently Evgenia Fakinou's 1983 *To Evdomo Rouho* (The Seventh Garment) and Yiorgos Mihalidis's 1991 *Ta Fonika* (The Murders). For discussions of the impact of the "Asia Minor Catastrophe" on modern Greek literature's thematic and stylistic repertoire, see, for instance, Doulis (1977), Haas (1992), Mackridge (1992).

8. Merlier had formed the Folk Song Society (*Syllogos Dimotikon Tragoudion*) in 1930 along with some of the most distinguished Greek politicians and liberal intellectuals of the time, including Penelope Delta, Chrysanthos Trapezoundos, Filippos Dragoumis, Panagiotis Kanellopoulos, and Eleftherios Venizelos. When Merlier decided to focus on the songs of Asia Minor refugees, she established the Asia Minor Folklore Archive (*Archeio Mikrasiatikis Laografias*) in 1933 and the Musical Folklore Archive (*Mousiko Laografiko Archeio*) in 1934. In 1949, at the end of the Greek Civil War and following her return to Greece from France in 1945 (where she and Octave had lived during the Occupation), she renamed the Asia Minor Folklore Archive the Center for Asia Minor Studies (CAMS). These name changes—from "Society" (*Syllogos*), which brings to mind a philanthropic club, to "Archive" (*Archeio*), which suggests a nineteenth-century historicist collecting project, and finally to "Center" (*Kentro*), which proclaims an area studies program—give a sense of Merlier's growing scholarly ambitions and sensitivity to scholarly trends.

9. Two volumes of Exodus (1980, 1982) have been published by the center and a final volume is in press. In the prologue to the first volume of Exodus narratives, Yiorgos Tenekidis notes that the term "Exodus" had originally been used in the 1926 League of Nations'

report on refugee settlement in Greece to refer to the "uprooting" (*xerizomos*) of the ethnic Greek populations of Asia Minor. The center, he explains, had chosen to employ this term in order to convey the tragic dimensions of the event, as well as to offset the phrase "exchange of populations," which made the ethnic homogeneity of Turkey appear a "fait accompli," thus obscuring Turkish expulsions of ethnic Greeks prior to and after the signing of the Treaty of Lausanne. With its overt Biblical connotations, the term "Exodus," however, also bestows *meaning* on the refugees' movements, implicitly scripting them into the role of a divine people fleeing the scourges of Turkish tyranny and casting "Greece" as their "promised land." Furthermore, the use of the word "Exodus" draws attention away from the fact that the population exchange was *two-way* and that ethnic Turks were displaced from their Greek homes.

10. Greek social and political life had already been polarized by the so-called National Schism (*Ethnikos Dihasmos*) of 1917 between Venizelists, who sided with the liberal politician Eleftherios Venizelos, and Royalists, who supported King Constantine.

11. See A. Liakos, "The Ideology of 'Lost Homelands.' " *To Vima*, September 13, 1998.

12. Although the Lausanne Convention had specified that refugees would be compensated for immovable property abandoned in Turkey, the Ankara Convention signed by Venizelos and Atatürk in 1930 withdrew these obligations. In the same year, the Refugee Settlement Commission (RSC), an autonomous organization that had overseen resettlement, also was disbanded. Even though the problems of the refugees were far from solved, the international community and the Greek state clearly signaled their desire to close this chapter of Greek history.

13. Octave Merlier served as director of the French Institute of Athens from 1938 until 1961 when he was summarily removed from this position for political reasons and appointed professor of Modern Greek at the University of Aix-en-Provence. Merlier, a specialist in Modern Greek literature, was an important figure in Greek cultural and political life in his own right. He is well known for having helped many bright, young Greek leftists, including the philosopher Cornelius Castoriadis, escape the Civil War by arranging scholarships for them in Paris in 1945.

14. Specifically, I have focused on the fieldwork reports (*Deltia Metavasis*) and informant reports (*Deltia Pliroforiton*) held in the Archive of Oral Tradition (*Archeio Proforikis Paradosis*) and the Work Letters of Melpo Merlier and Notes in Place of Minutes (*Grammata Ergasias Melpos Merlier kai Simeiomata anti Praktikon*) in Melpo Merlier's personal archive.

15. Prior to 1948, the Asia Minor Folklore Archive was held at the Society for the Propagation of Beneficial Books (*Syllogos Pros Diadosin Ofelimon Vivlion*). Between 1948 and 1962, the (renamed) Center for Asia Minor Studies was housed in the French Institute. In 1960, the French ambassador had demanded that the center's archives be given over to France as French property. Octave Merlier refused to comply, and between 1962 and 1982, when the center moved to its present location and came under the auspices of the Greek state, it occupied a rented space in Kolonaki, near the border of the student quarter of Exarcheia. In these movements through Athens, one can read major shifts in the institutional frameworks for the study—and funding—of modern Greek historical scholarship as much as the "fate" of this particular archive.

16. In a 1951 paper, Merlier notes that there were two researchers between 1930 and 1935, three between 1935 and 1938, and five in 1939. During the war, the center (then the Asia Minor Folklore Archive) was closed and reopened in 1945 with a three-person staff. Ten people were working at the center in 1948, nineteen in 1949, and thirty-two in 1951, the majority of whom were volunteers.

17. Melpo Merlier was director of the center from 1930 to 1976 and Fotis Apostolopoulos from 1976. Paschalis Kitromilidis served as acting director from 1980 until his election

as director of the Institute for Neohellenic Research in 2000, at which point the operation of the center passed to Vice Director Stavros Anestidis.

18. In the years immediately following the "Catastrophe," these associations focused on practical matters related to refugee settlement, such as advocating for housing reform; over time, however, these original groups as well as new ones (which still continue to be founded) turned to the preservation of the "culture" of specific "lost homelands" (through staging public events involving music, dance, theater, and food as well as sponsoring publications, exhibitions, and other cultural productions). These associations also have been actively engaged in the memorialization of the "Catastrophe" (through monument-building and the celebration of "days of memory") (cf. Kyriakidou-Nestoros 1993: 238; Varlas 2003).

19. For a characteristic example, see the best-selling autobiography of Yiorgos Katramopoulos, the 1994 *How Can I Forget You Beloved Smyrna*, which describes his comfortable life as son of a well-off Smyrna goldsmith and classmate of Aristotle Onassis. From his perspective, few Greeks knew Turkish in Smyrna because Greek was essentially the "national language" (26). Since in "lost homelands" discourse Greek Asia Minor is forever "frozen" in 1922, the strange impression is often created that if Asia Minor had not been lost, urban life itself might have retained the glamour and flair seen in old black-and-white photographs of Anatolian Greek clubs, cafés, and residences. Thus, in "The Social Life of Smyrna," an article in a popular history newspaper supplement entitled "Smyrna: The Pride of Ionia" (*Kathimerini* May 3, 1998), N. Viketou, general secretary of the Union of Smyrniots, can note of pre-"Catastrophe" Smyrna: "Generally the social life in Smyrna rolled along with simplicity and liveliness and in a carefree way, totally different from the anxious, rushed and pleasureless life of today's big cities."

20. In Turkish public culture, the fate of Muslim refugees from Greece also was a nonsubject until quite recently. No analogous discourse on lost *Greek* homelands developed following the refugee crisis, which is usually referred to in Turkish rather prosaically as the *mübadele* ("exchange"). In Turkey, refugees from Greece, like those from other neighboring Balkan countries who fled to Turkey at this time, are not even known as refugees, but simply as "migrants" (*muhacir*) with no indication given of their place of origin. This profound silencing can be attributed, at least in part, to the fact that the events of 1922 represented a triumphant victory for the Turks; stories of suffering and loss were incompatible with a national narrative proclaiming the glorious formation of the modern Turkish state. In the past fifteen years, though, against the backdrop of an internal war against the Kurdish minority, there has been a growing Turkish scholarly as well as popular interest in the "missing" minorities of the former Ottoman Empire. The population exchange has been the subject of several contemporary novels, such as F. Otyam's 1985 *Brother Pavli*, F. Çiçekoglu's 1992 *The Other Side of the Water*, A. Yorulmaz's 1997 *The Children of War*, K. Yalçın's 1998 *The Entrusted Wedding Trousseau*, E. Aladağ's 1997 *Sekene* and 1999 *Maria: The Pain of Migration*. For more on the population exchange from a Turkish perspective and on the cultural politics of Turkish representations of Self and Other through the "Greek," see Arı (1995), Iğsız (2000), Millas (2001).

21. In her ethnography of the social life of Asia Minor refugees, the anthropologist Renée Hirschon describes memory as refugees' and their children's "most valuable property" and argues that it has served as a "rescuing bridge" between a "meaningful past" and a difficult present. According to Hirschon, the centrality of memory for the Asia Minor refugees can be attributed to their predominantly "oral culture" and the salience of memory practices in Greek Orthodoxy (1998: 15–17). For a discussion of trauma that rejects this assumption of the transmissibility of memory, see Anna Vidali's (1996) study on the transgenerational blockage of memories of the Greek Civil War.

22. The center's use of testimony to record Greek-Turkish cooperation and cultural symbiosis takes on particular significance when juxtaposed to uses of refugee testimony as evidence to *incriminate* the Turks as incorrigible enemies. Immediately following the "Catastrophe," Greek police, for instance, had taken depositions from refugees about their violent expulsion from coastal regions of Asia Minor. As Mihalis Varlas (2003) has pointed out, this practice of documentation was modeled on that of the Greek Orthodox Patriarchate in Istanbul, which had recorded Turkish atrocities against Greek populations during World War I in publications such as the 1919 *Mavri Vivlos Diogmon kai Martyrion tou en Tourkia Ellinismou 1914–1918* (The Black Bible of the Persecutions and Torments of Hellenism in Turkey 1914–1918) and the 1919 *O Golgothas tou en Tourkia Ellinismou* (The Golgotha of Hellenism in Turkey).

23. Personal Interview. February 6, 1999, Athens.

24. Dominick LaCapra has described the transferential relation of historians to their subjects as involving the unavoidable projection of contemporary concerns onto supposedly "objective" accounts of the past (1985a: 123–4). Rebel points out that in addition to the transference and countertransference of the historian, analysts might attend to the way that the "construction of historical texts by historical subjects is itself grounded in *imagined* contexts that permeate the creation, interpretation, and implementation of their texts and may span and conflate several temporalities in creative interpolations of the 'present' and the 'historical'— and is therefore not just a directed, consciously selective and controlled project but also operates unconsciously, projectively, transferentially, transtemporally" (1991: 52–3). These multiple and overlapping layers of desire for the past can be detected in the comments of literary critic Mary Layoun about her experience of doing research in the center's Archive of Oral Tradition. Seeking to counter the mythologies of ethnic purity and incompatability on which the population exchange was based, Layoun drew heavily on the center's "Exodus" testimonies, themselves created on the basis of similar impulses. Unaware of the archive's context of production, Layoun, however, does not consider the acts of re-collection that lay between her research and the descriptions of the refugees. Thus, she can describe her discovery of the harmony in which Greeks and Turks lived as "one of the trenchant ironies of reading through the almost one thousand pages of testimonials" (2001: 42).

25. According to Paschalis Kitromilides (1987), British linguist Richard Dawkins's interest in linguistic survivals (such as dialects of medieval Greek spoken in Cappadocia) and cultural syncretism (such as Karamanli, Turkish language literature printed in the Greek alphabet) played an important role in shaping the center's research priorities. The fact that the center's research began with the remote Farasa of Cappadocia, whose dialect preserved forms of medieval Greek, also can be attributed in large part to Dawkins's influence on Merlier.

26. The refugees were not all Greek speakers (some were primary speakers of Turkish, Kurdish, or Armenian while others spoke dialects of Greek, such as Pontic), Greek Orthodox (some were converted Protestants, for instance), or even ethnic Greek (at least 50,000 Armenians were among the refugees who came to Greece). As Petropoulou (1997) gleans from reading between the lines of the refugee settlement reports, the "local" Greeks whom the refugees encountered also were more linguistically, religiously, and ethnically diverse than is often acknowledged.

27. The poet George Seferis dedicated his 1953 travelogue *Treis Meres sta Monastiria tis Kappadokias* (Three Days in the Monasteries of Cappadocia) to the Merliers. The novelist Ilias Venezis was to undertake the final editing of the "Exodus" narratives. The poet Angelos Sikelianos and his wife Eva Palmer were close friends. Merlier had even participated in their "revivals" of the Delphic Rites (1927–30), a seminal cultural event of the interwar period in Greece.

28. Many of the authors who comprised the core group of the "Generation of the Thirties" were themselves from Asia Minor or Istanbul, including the novelists Kosmas Politis, Stratis Doukas, Ilias Venezis, Fotis Kondoglou, Maria Iordanidou, Yiorgos Theotokas, and Dido Sotiriou as well as the Nobel Prize-winning poet George Seferis. While Greek literary history associates their writing with modernism and some of these authors did experiment with aspects of a high modernist style, much of their writing is actually closer to neorealism. More radical experimentation can be found in the works of surrealist poets (Emberikos, Engonopoulos, Rantos, Elytis, Sarantis) and in some writers of that period who were more marginal to the canon (Axioti, Pentzikis, Skaribas). For critical discussions of Greek modernism, see Vitti (1977), Tziovas (1989), Layoun (1990).

29. These historic folk song recordings are the prize collection of the Musical Folklore Archive. The novelty of the technologies of voice recording introduced to Greece by Merlier is attested by the archive's unique recordings of the speech (and even singing) of prominent Greek writers and politicians, such as Venizelos and Palamas. As Friedrich Kittler has pointed out, with the advent of voice-recording technology that could preserve the "live voice" for posterity, famous people were often called on to "immortalize" themselves (1999: 78).

30. Before participating in the center's project, writer Elli Papadimitriou, who in 1975 would publish a well-received literary collection of refugee testimonies, *O Koinos Logos* (The Common Language), had worked for the Refugee Settlement Commission. This experience might explain her politicized orientation toward recording the voice (and image) not of the folk, but specifically of the refugee. Testament to this early interest in documenting refugee experience is a text in her personal archive dated 1927 and entitled "Uncle-Ilias Speaks," which consists of a refugee's testimony and his photograph (Petropoulou 1999–2000: 298). While other people close to Merlier were pushing her toward an Orientalist-style project of ethnological knowledge-gathering, Papadimitriou would certainly have been among those who encouraged Merlier to focus on the pathos of the refugee as displaced person.

31. In *The Last Hellenism of Asia Minor*, Octave Merlier explains how in the case of Asia Minor refugees it was impossible to maintain the pretence that history and politics did not impinge on the life of the "folk." As an awakening to this fact, he points to his attempt one day to take a photograph of some refugees dressed in traditional costume; while he was changing film, they disappeared. He later learned from a shoemaker that the men had left because he was French and they were angry about France's role in the "Catastrophe": "We are not folklore images or photographs. We are Christian, Europeans, allies, who were betrayed by our allies, European, Christian like us—but surely without memory or heart" (1974: 17–18).

32. The Folklore Archive, established in 1918 by Nikolaos Politis, the "father" of Greek folklore, and the National Music Collection, founded in 1914, were the center's archival precursors. The questionnaires used by center researchers were adapted from questionnaires originally designed by folklorists Yiorgos Megas and Stilpon Kyriakidis.

33. Malkki (1995b) notes that the "refugee" did not become an object of social science research and a global legal problem until after World War II. Then the unprecedented numbers of people displaced by the war led to the development of refugee law and standardized procedures for settling refugees as well as to the institutionalization of the refugee camp. However, earlier in the century, albeit in a more piecemeal manner, populations that had been displaced during the dismantling of various empires (e.g., Ottoman, Hapsburg, Romanov) had started to become the subject of international attention and management. Attesting to the protean nature of the category "refugee" as well as the prevailing view that the "population exchange" entailed a "return" to a native land, the proposal for the 1923 Convention Concerning the Exchange of Greek and Turkish

Populations was introduced under the heading of "repatriation of prisoners," and the exchanged populations were referred to as "involuntary emigrants."

34. As early as 1958, Merlier had decided to write the history of the center (Work Letters. April 21, 1958).

35. Work Letters. September 22, 1956, p. 59.

36. Work Letters. March 16–17, p. 19.

37. Work Letters, p. 156.

38. With the founding of the Greek state, the distinction between Greeks living within the nation's borders, *Elladites* or *autochthones*, and those in the diaspora, *Ellines* or *eterochthones*, already had taken on significance (cf. Skopetea 1988a).

39. By 1958, the center's researchers had spent so much time studying Cappadocia that, in a seminar to which many Cappadocian refugees were invited, Merlier called on educated refugees to help them "finish" Cappadocia (i.e., by writing up historical and folklore materials themselves) so research on other provinces of Asia Minor could proceed: "We must not forget, said Mrs. Merlier, that we are not the Center for Cappadocian Studies, but the Center for Asia Minor Studies." Work Letters. December 22, 1958, p. 436.

40. Ilias Anagnostakis and Evangelia Balta (1990) argue that the Greek "discovery" of Cappadocia took place in three stages: (1) prior to 1860, the Orthodox church had attempted to "protect" Orthodox populations in the region from the proselytizing of Protestant and Jesuit missionaries; (2) between 1860 and 1890, Greek-speaking communities in Cappadocia were "discovered" and folk songs were collected avidly with the hope of finding survivals of ancient Greek; (3) after 1890, with the growing interest in Byzantine studies and the 1875 discovery of the manuscript of the medieval vernacular epic Digenis Akritas, Cappadocia not only found a place within a narrative of Hellenism but also came to be seen as Hellenism's *first* homeland. For more on "Greek" Cappadocia, see Ballian, Pantelaki, and Petropoulou (1994).

41. Work Letters. May 7, 1964, p. 1127.

42. Work Letters. June 14, 1962, pp. 768–70.

43. Work Letters. August 19, 1956, p. 8.

44. Historical and ethnological material was filed according to province, region, and settlement. The "region" (*perifereia*), a unit devised based on conversations with refugees, refers to a group of towns and villages centered on a small or large city (M. Merlier 1948: 15).

45. In an early essay on her folk song research, Merlier explained why she ascribed such importance to "re-placing" refugee singers in their native homelands: "For Eastern Thrace (Turkey), Northern Thrace (Bulgaria), and Asia Minor (Turkey), we have fictively maintained the map of Hellenism prior to 1922, the date of the Asia Minor disaster. It is only in relocating (*replaçant*) these populations of refugees in their country of origin, in their geographical and historical frame, that it is possible to know them and study their folklore" (1935a: 12).

46. At the end of the nineteenth and beginning of the twentieth century, as the Ottoman Empire's collapse appeared imminent, Balkan mapmaking flourished. German cartographer Heinrich Kiepert, whose ethnological maps of the Balkans, such as his famous 1876 ethnographic map of the "European Orient," were considered particularly sympathetic to Greek territorial claims in the region, was recruited personally by historian Konstandinos Paparrigopoulos to make maps for the Society for the Propagation of Greek Letters. Through its vigorous mapmaking campaign, this group aimed to demonstrate the Greekness of various regions not yet under Greek control, such as Macedonia and Epirus, and published maps (many produced especially for use in Greek school classrooms) highlighting Greek historical presence in the area (i.e., Macedonian Hellenism under Alexander the Great, medieval Hellenism in the age of the Macedonian Emperors, etc.) as well as Greek versions of Kiepert's ethnological maps (Tolias 1992).

47. In a letter to staff in Athens, Merlier describes her punctilious vision of the "order" of the archive thus: "I will tell you if you like how I would like the Archives, today and in the future. Envelopes for every village separately; naturally, in the case of chapters with few pages, two or more chapters will go in the same envelope, and every village, of course, will have as many envelopes as are needed for its material. The envelopes will stand *straight* and on their spine, as on their envelope—on their façade, we might say—will go the title or titles, and the number of pages will be in *red*. It will be the only number (we might say the 'personal number' of the chapter)—which will be given on the spine, but it will be the only one, because that will be the only thing that will interest the researcher . . . I return to the subject of the envelopes; I would prefer them to be plain, one after the other, straight—neither envelopes like your pretty one, or boxes. When the envelopes of one village end and there is still room on the shelf, one village will be separated from the other by two metal bookends such as I have here for my books" (Work Letters. May 17, 1967, pp. 2007–9).

48. Work Letters, p. 46.

49. In 2003, over 200 files with information about how research was conducted, including meticulous monthly and yearly reports recording how many pages of material were collected (according to theme, geographical region, and researcher), were "discovered" and brought up from the "dust" of the center's basement for cataloguing and rearchiving. This find suggests that the center's research is just starting to be viewed as of historical interest in its own right.

50. Researcher Sophia Dondolinou's father and two brothers were killed by the Nazis. Researcher Hara Lioudaki's sister Maria, who also had worked briefly at the center, was murdered by the Nazis as was Hara's fiancée, a famous early union leader. Researcher Kaiti Reppa-Kritsiki's brother was murdered during the Nazi Occupation and her sister was executed during the Civil War.

51. I, thus, primarily examine reports of center fieldwork conducted in the 1950s and 1960s. Although interviews were also done during the interwar period, they appear to have been less formal and fieldnotes about them were not kept systematically. Merlier herself had trouble remembering when researchers started keeping fieldnotes: "I found one of Loukopoulos' from 1935," she notes, "but it was only 4 or 5 lines." (Work Letters. April 29, 1967, p. 147). I focus on fieldwork done in Athens because research in the provinces was less thorough and did not engage individual informants in depth and over time.

52. Personal Interview. February 6, 1999, Athens.

53. In response to drastic changes in the ethnological composition of the Greek state following the Balkan Wars and the population exchanges with Turkey and Bulgaria, Merlier believed that Greek folklorists should have begun to address the multiplicity of Greek ethnicities. In 1948, she wrote: "I might add that in Greece we folklorists should have widened the borders of our science after 1912 as a natural and logical consequence of the events of recent Greek history . . . since then Greek folklore—and Greek scholarship generally—should have been moved by the migrations and movements of Greek populations" (26). Over time, rather than attempt to reform Greek folklore, though, Merlier turned away from the discipline and embraced ethnology and geographical history.

54. In the preface to her *Tripolis of Pontos*, Tatiana Gritsi-Milliex says she wrote the book to "pay back an old debt of her father" who disliked refugees and did not live long enough to realize how much Greece gained from them and their labor (1976: 14–15). Researcher Kaiti Reppa-Kritsiki told me that her first contact with refugees was through maids who worked at her house in central Athens when she was a child (Personal Interview. March 14, 2000, Athens).

55. Personal Interview. December 17, 1999, Athens.

56. Work Letters. March 1, 1957, p. 123.
57. Personal Interview. March 14, 2000, Athens.
58. Archive of Oral Tradition, Fieldwork Report: Pontos, Tripolis. March 15, 1949.
59. Archive of Oral Tradition, Fieldwork Report: Pontos, Kerasounda. Researcher: Tzoulia Souli-Tsouri. October 3, 1956.
60. Archive of Oral Tradition, Fieldwork Report: Cappadocia, Nigdi-Kayiavasi. April 12, 1957.
61. Archive of Oral Tradition, Fieldwork Report: Cappadocia, Kaisareia [Kayseri]. January 23, 1959.
62. Merlier planned to have well-known folklorist Angeliki Hatzimihali (cf. 1949), who had popularized the study of peasant material culture and decorated her own home in Athens in a neotraditional style, study the folk art of Cappadocia (1948:45). For more on Hatzimihali, see, Faubion (1993a: 95–8) and chapter 2.
63. Archive of Oral Tradition, Fieldwork Report: Cappadocia, Kaisareia [Kayseri]. January 8, 1955.
64. While Renée Hirschon's ethnography of a refugee community in Piraeus, based on participant-observation research conducted in the 1970s, has been hailed as the first urban ethnography of Greece, she describes the city neighborhood in which she did her research as if it were a transplanted rural community: "In contrast to the ubiquitous modernity of angular cement, marble, and glass structures which increasingly suffocate the city, low houses appeared with tiled roofs and walls painted in pastel shades of blue, deep ochres, greens and pink. Jasmine and honeysuckle twined around gates and walls, pots of geranium and sweet basil lined wooden balconies. Streets were clean and pavements marked with fresh lines of whitewash" (1998: 2).
65. Archive of Oral Tradition, Fieldwork Report: Pontos, Sampsounda. November 2, 1964.
66. A most egregious example was the so-called Book of Simela. Although researcher Tzoulia Souli-Tsouri had worked for many years collecting testimony from Simela, a particularly "good" informant from Cappadocia, Merlier presented this material to the well-known novelist Ilias Venezis to edit and publish under his name. Venezis, who had also agreed to edit the center's "Exodus" narratives, did not complete either project, though he did publish his own book with the title *Exodus*. Frustrated that their books were either delayed many years in publication or, most often, never published, several researchers chose to leave the center (Personal Communication. Christos Samouilidis [February 6, 1999] and Maria Asvesti [December 17, 1999]). Although for many researchers the center would serve as a stepping stone to graduate study abroad and successful careers, as in the case of Eleni Glikatzi-Ahrweiler, a renowned Byzantine scholar in France and President of the University of Europe, for others it turned out to be a bitter dead end. When Fotis Apostolopoulos became the director of the center in 1976 and started the publication of the *Bulletin of the Center for Asia Minor Studies*, the center's research finally began to reach a broader public (Petropoulou 1996: 419).
67. Work Letters. October 2, 1959, p. 58.
68. Work Letters. April 1–5, 1965, pp. 1354–5.
69. Archive of Oral Tradition, Fieldwork Report: Cappadocia, Askerai-Gelveri [Karvali]. April 12, 1953.
70. Archive of Oral Tradition, Fieldwork Report: Cappadocia, Kaisareia [Kayseri]. November 17, 1958.
71. Archive of Oral Tradition, Fieldwork Report: Pontos, Trapezounda [Trabzon]. October 5, 1956.
72. Archive of Oral Tradition, Fieldwork Report: Cappadocia, Farasa. August 12, 1939.
73. Archive of Oral Tradition, Fieldwork Report: Cappadocia, Nigdi-Kayiavasi. Researcher: Eleni Gazi. May 10, 1957.

74. Archive of Oral Tradition, Fieldwork Report: Pontos, Trapezounda [Trabzon]. Researcher: Hara Lioudaki; Informant: Vasiliki Papadopoulou. September 25, 1957.

75. As Varlas (2003) has pointed out, papers issued to refugees by various agencies (municipalities, settlement committees, refugee organizations), including travel papers, certificates of property abandoned in Turkey, refugee identity cards, and receipts of dues paid to refugee organizations, testified to the process of *becoming* a refugee while also representing "proof" of a lost identity (and often wealth). Thus, for some refugees, these documents became valuable tokens to be preserved in family archives years after they had expired and donated to refugee societies or local folklore collections.

76. Archive of Oral Tradition, Fieldwork Report: Pontos, Tripolis. June 13, 1950.

77. Archive of Oral Tradition, Fieldwork Report: Cappadocia, Nigdi-Kayiavasi. Researcher: Eleni Gazi. March 29, 1957.

78. Archive of Oral Tradition, Fieldwork Report: Pontos, Tripolis. Researcher: Tatiana Milliex; Informant: Dimakos Chrysopoulos. April 6, 1949.

79. Archive of Oral Tradition, Fieldwork Report: Cappadocia, Farasa. Informant: Anastasia Zaharopoulou. August 12, 1953.

80. Archive of Oral Tradition, Fieldwork Report: Cappadocia, Nigdi-Kayiavasi. Researcher: Eleni Gazi. April 24, 1957.

81. Archive of Oral Tradition, Fieldwork Report: Pontos, Tripoli. May 15, 1950.

82. Work Letters. July 11, 1960.

83. Work Letters. December 19, 1958, p. 403.

84. Archive of Oral Tradition, Informant Report: Pontos, Tripolis. Researcher: Eleni Karatza. May 13, 1957.

85. Evmorfili is lucky to have even survived. In 1916, the Greek Orthodox population of Tripolis was exiled to the interior of Turkey: 2,500 of 2,800 perished. Many Pontians who, like Evmorfili, subsequently crossed the Black Sea to Russia later become victims of Stalin's ethnic purges. Since 1982, but especially after 1989, a new wave of Pontic Greeks has come to Greece from the former Soviet republics of Kazakhstan, Uzbekistan, Armenia, and Georgia, many settling in "traditionally" Pontic neighborhoods, such as Kallithea in Athens. Ironically, if predictably, they have been targets of discrimination by "native" Greeks, who commonly refer to them derogatorily as *Rossopondi* (Russian-Pontians).

86. The Balkan Wars of 1912–13 would set the stage for the development of Greek war photojournalism. In turn, the Asia Minor Expedition, the subsequent defeat of the Greek army, the expulsion of the ethnic Greek populations from Asia Minor and most sensationally the burning of Smyrna and the arrival of the bedraggled refugees in Greece would be extensively covered in news photography and film (Xanthakis 1985: 140–52). The plight of the refugees and their living conditions in Greece would be the subject of a new genre of photographic social reportage pioneered by, among others, Nelly's. For more on the use of photography and film in documenting the "Asia Minor Catastrophe," see Varlas (2003).

87. Work Letters, p. 47.

88. By contrast, the Latin American testimonial (*testimonio*) has mobilized a more mutual coalition between intellectuals (as compilers and activators) and the poor (as narrators), thus more emphatically empowering the subaltern narrator as author(ity) (Beverley 1996a). See also chapter 4, n.19.

89. Most observers agree that given the great numbers of refugees and the political and economic instability of the Greek state, the relatively smooth settlement of the refugees under the aegis of the international Refugee Settlement Commission represented a significant achievement. Nonetheless, the mishandling of refugee compensations and the liquidation of Greek properties in Turkey led to decades of frustration and economic hardship for many

refugees. For the most part, rural refugees fared better than urban ones. In 1952, there were still 14,241 refugee families entitled to settlement living in shanties and even as late as 1978 3,000 urban families were awaiting settlement (Mavrogordatos 1983: 186–91).

90. Venezis's *The Number 31328* and Doukas's *A Prisoner of War's Story*, two of the most important literary works about the "Catastrophe" written during the interwar years, were republished in slightly revised versions after the war. As Abatzopoulou (1998: 82–4) has argued, changes made to the texts draw attention to the connections between genocides. In the 1958 edition of *A Prisoner of War's Story*, Doukas, for instance, dedicates the book to the "common ordeals of people everywhere" instead of, as in the first two editions, to the common ordeals of the Greek and Turkish people. In a similar spirit, in the second edition of *The Number 31328* published in 1945, Venezis has inserted epigraphs from Psalms. Indeed, the themes raised in these two books, which both depict the experiences of ethnic Greeks as prisoners in Turkey do resonate with literature on World War II and the Holocaust in focusing on the civilian population in wartime, the scapegoating of an ethnic "Other," the functioning of a system of persecution and total domination, the marginalization of victims and their dehumanization (the title of Venezis's book refers to the substitution of the narrator's name by a number), and the physical suffering and humiliation of the body of the persecuted.

91. Archive of Oral Tradition, Informant Report: Cappadocia, Kaisareia [Kayseri]. Researcher: Ermolaos Andreadis; Informant: Mihalis Avramidis.

92. In her 1975 *The Common Language*, Elli Papadimitriou, who had worked at the center and also been actively involved in communist politics, highlights, in Petropoulou's words, "precisely the unseen and forbidden dimension" of the refugee narratives collected by the center; her book casts the refugee testimonies within a leftist narrative that presumes the "natural" evolution of refugees into communists. Dido Sotiriou gave a similar leftist spin to her 1962 *Matomena Homata* (Farewell Anatolia), one of the best-selling Greek novels of the 1960s. This book features the testimony of a man who had been sent to Turkish labor camps during World War I, participated in the Greek military campaign in Asia Minor, and later come to Greece as a refugee. In the novel, international capital is identified as the real cause of the suffering of ordinary Greeks and Turks.

93. In her discussion of the famous moment in the Eichmann trial when prosecution witness K-Zetnik faints on the stand, Felman suggests that he was "re-traumatized" by the authoritarian discourse of a court that "ordered" him to speak in a certain way, thus "trigger[ing] a legal repetition of the trauma that [the legal institution] put on trial . . ." (2002: 146). Like law, historical inquiry (especially oral history) often overlaps with practices of political interrogation and bureaucratic documentation but tends to remain "blind" to such resemblances.

94. Archive of Oral Tradition, Informant Report: Cappadocia, Farasa. Researcher: Aglaia Loukopoulou. April 29, 1955.

95. Archive of Oral Tradition, Informant Report: Cappadocia, Farasa. Researcher: Aglaia Loukopoulou. January 24, 1954.

96. Archive of Oral Tradition, Informant Report: Cappadocia, Farasa. Researcher: Aglaia Loukopoulou. April 22, 1955.

97. Archive of Oral Tradition, Fieldwork Report: Cappadocia, Askerai-Gelveri [Karvali]. Informant: Alexandros Leondopoulos. February 12, 1958.

98. Archive of Oral Tradition, Fieldwork Report: Cappadocia, Nigdi-Kayiavasi. March 26, 1957.

99. Work Letters. July 18, 1963, p. 171.

100. In total, 474 manuscripts were collected, the majority of which were written after 1950 when the center made concerted efforts to encourage refugees to write. Many refugee-writers followed the guidelines of the center questionnaire and in some cases

produced multivolume studies; others wrote brief, entirely unstructured texts. For a discussion of one of these manuscripts, see, Petros Pasalidis (1992). "To Vivlion tis Zois mou" (The Book of My Life), comp. I. Petropoulou. *Bulletin of the Center for Asia Minor Studies* 9: 253–80.

101. Archive of Oral Tradition, Fieldwork Report: Cappadocia, Farasa. August 25, 1953.

102. Archive of Oral Tradition, Fieldwork Report: Cappadocia, Kaisareia [Kayseri]. November 21, 1958.

103. Archive of Oral Tradition, Fieldwork Report: Pontos, Trapezounda [Trabzon]. July 5, 1960.

104. In her work on the Partition between India and Pakistan, Veena Das (1995: 9) has argued that women who refused to be "recovered" by the Indian state following their abduction, preferring instead to stay with their abductors, protected their love from the state's order and in the process "escaped being inscribed in history"; as a result, though, these women represent "an enigma to the orders of the state and the family" and often remain "invisible" to researchers.

105. In the late 1980s and 1990s, the recording of filmic and video testimonies of refugees was sponsored by state television and private cultural organizations, such as the Historical Archive of Refugee Hellenism in Kalamaria (Thessaloniki) and the Institute for the Hellenic World in Athens (Varlas 2003).

4   Reading (Civil) War, the Historical Novel, and the Left

1. Valtinos's fiction has been widely anthologized in collections of postwar Greek literature as well as translated into several foreign languages, including German, Dutch, Swedish, Italian, French, and English. Valtinos is also well known in the world of cinema. He collaborated for many years on screenplays for the films of the prominent Greek director Theo Angelopoulos and was awarded the screenplay prize at the Cannes Film Festival in 1984 for Angelopoulos's *Voyage to Kythera*.

2. As this book was going to press, however, the controversy had sparked once again in the pages of the newspaper *Ta Nea*. A so-called dialogue on history was opened by Stathis Kalyvas and Nikos Marantzidis's controversial article entitled "New Trends in the Study of the Civil War" (March 20, 2004). Held up as an example of right-wing historical revisionism, the views of the authors have been condemned in a long series of articles, many of which refer directly or indirectly to Valtinos and *Orthokosta* (see, for instance, M. Piblis, "They Kill Your Mother. What 'Stakes' Are You Talking About?" *Ta Nea*, August 14–15, 2004). Testament to the extent to which Valtinos's novel has become *the* touchstone for Greek debates on history and literature was the publication, also in 2004, of *The Deal: A Game of Literature and History* (2004), a book-length harangue on *Orthokosta*. Written by literary critic and author Kostas Voulgaris who comes from a village near Valtinos's, *The Deal* attempts to dissect—and defuse—*Orthokosta*, which Voulgaris says he respects for its literary artisanship but castigates as part of this contemporary trend of right-wing revisionist historiography. Voulgaris openly professes that an *antidote* to Valtinos's novel is needed, an "anti-*Orthokosta*," in other words, a documentary fiction that could "play" in the same "ballpark" but with different players (141). Voulgaris, in fact, has already tried his hand at finding a "cure" to *Orthokosta* in his novella *Always in My Dream the Peloponnese* (2001), a strained imitation of Valtinos's spare style, even printed to *look* like a Valtinos novel (i.e., a small format book with

thick, good-quality paper, typical of the publisher *Agra* where Valtinos published his work in the 1990s), but narrated by a politically conscious EAM partisan.

3. Valtinos's novels include the 1963 *I Kathodos ton Ennia* (The Descent of the Nine), 1964 *Synaxari Andrea Kordopati, Vivlio Proto: Ameriki* (The Book of the Days of Andreas Kordopatis, Book I: America), 1978 *Tria Ellinika Monoprakta* (Three Greek One-Acts), 1985 *Ble Vathi Schedon Mavro* (Deep Blue Almost Black), 1989 *Stoiheia yia ti Dekaetia tou '60* (Data from the Decade of the Sixties), 1992 *Ftera Bekatsas* (Woodcock Feathers), 2000 *Synaxari Andrea Kordopati, Vivlio Deftero: Valkanikoi-'22* (The Book of the Days of Andreas Kordopatis, Book Two: Balkan Wars-'22), and 2001 *Imerologio: 1836–2011* (Journal: 1836–2011). Collections of his short stories *Tha Vreite ta Osta mou ipo Vrohin* (You Will Find My Bones Under Rain) and *Ethismos sti Nikotini* (Nicotine Addiction) were published in 1992 and 2003, respectively.

4. Responding to a question about why he writes about history so often, Valtinos has explained: "History, from the standpoint of literary interest, is an extremely stimulating sphere. An extremely dramatic sphere that, even in its rougher dimensions, comprises a patchwork of individual fates. If assessing the coordinates of this sphere consists in the knowledge of history, personally I am interested in the partial fates of which it is composed, which is the opposite of knowledge, it is the feeling of History" (1997: 333).

5. The modern Greek word for testimony and evidence, *martyria*, combines the ancient Greek juridical concept of "witnessing" with the Orthodox Christian *martyrio* (martyrdom, suffering, ordeal). The verb *martyro* has numerous meanings, including to bear witness in court, to be tortured and killed as a martyr, to tell on, to be an informer, to reveal, to give away. This etymology underscores the fact that the line between telling the truth and betrayal is thin indeed while exposing the degree to which oral historical inquiry borders on political and legal interrogation. For Valtinos as a key figure in modern Greek testimonial fiction, see, for instance, Tziovas (1987: 100), Abatzopoulou (1998: 106–7), Nikolopoulou (2002).

6. EAM is the acronym for *Ethniko Apeleftherotiko Metopo* (National Liberation Front) and ELAS, its military wing, for *Ethnikos Laikos Apeleftherotikos Stratos* (National People's Liberation Army). The Greek Communist Party (KKE) lay behind EAM/ELAS, which was the largest and most powerful of the wartime resistance organizations.

7. As Tasoula Vervenioti notes, the term "Civil War" was not used by the Left either until after the end of the dictatorship. Instead communists usually referred to the conflict as "the second guerrilla war" (*deftero andartiko*) against a second foreign occupation, this time by the United States (*Amerikanokratia*) (2002: 164).

8. Of the over 80,000 people prosecuted in Greece in 1945, the great majority were leftists. Remarkably, by the late 1940s, the ratio of those charged for collaboration to those charged for fighting in the Resistance was estimated at about one in ten (Mazower 1995: 275). During the *junta*, a law was passed that declared EAM/ELAS partisans enemies of the state and awarded pensions to former Security Battalionists. Several members of the *junta* leadership themselves had been in the Battalions (Mazower 1993: 376). For more on the grossly uneven prosecution of war crimes in the postwar period, see contributions to Mazower (2000).

9. An extreme example is Reno Apostolidis's *Pyramid 67* (1950), based on 5,000 pages of letters the author wrote over the course of his thirty-month service in the government army, during which time he participated in thirty-five battles of the Civil War. Apostolidis, who had been recruited against his will and claimed allegiance to neither side, swore he would never (and never did) shoot a bullet in the conflict, instead directing his energies into writing about it.

10. The "Law for the Recognition of the Resistance of the Greek People against Occupation Troops, 1941–1944" was passed in 1982. In 1989, another law would officially "reform"

the discourse on this period: in the first article of "Abrogation of the Repercussions of the Civil War 1944–1949," the term "brigand war" (*symmoritopolemos*) was replaced with "Civil War," and the word "brigands" (*symmorites*) with the "Democratic Army."

11. Mark Mazower (1995) has described how the legacy of EAM/ELAS was used strategically by PASOK's founder, the charismatic Andreas Papandreou, to form a popular center-left coalition around a platform of anticapitalism *and* anticommunism. The EAM/ELAS resistance movement was cast as part of an unfolding drama of "national liberation" linking the Greek Revolution against Ottoman rule in 1821 to the 1970s anti-*junta* protest movement. As Mazower argues, memorializing a "*national* EAM" had the effect of stripping the history of the resistance movement of its specific political (i.e., Marxist) agenda as well as repressing its "non-Greek" dimensions (the most egregious example being the differential treatment of Slavic-speaking political refugees after the socialists came to power). Despite this depoliticization of the Resistance, many on the Left, as Mazower notes, were exhausted from years of persecution and, thus, supported the "recognition" of the Resistance without closely interrogating the motives behind it. Historian Filippos Iliou similarly has spoken of the transformation of the Resistance into an "alibi for Greeks and for us ourselves [i.e., communists]" that refers to something "obvious" (i.e., that "Greeks fight foreign conquerors") while its politically subversive aspects are forgotten (2000: 162). Based on her oral history research, Riki Van Boeschoten has observed how this misleading portrayal of a unified, national Resistance has obscured histories of social conflict, and especially that of the Civil War itself, in the name of a "painless," but superficial, reconciliation (1997: 137, 230).

12. The first academic conference on the Greek Civil War has held in Copenhagen in 1984; not until 1995, however, did a conference on that war take place on Greek soil. The year 1999 was marked by a notable density of conferences and publications on the Civil War (Margaritis 2000; Liakos 2001: 83–4). In 2000, the popular encyclopedic *Istoria tou Ellinikou Ethnous* (History of the Greek Nation) (1970–78) was finally brought up to date: after having been stalled for decades in 1940 with the Greco-Italian war in Albania, that last moment of unified *national* resistance preceding Nazi, Italian, and Bulgarian Occupations, the series addressed the war years and the military dictatorship. Liakos has suggested that this updating could occur because the national-religious revival of the 1990s had enabled a "silent mutual acceptance" of former political differences (2001: 74–5).

13. The tensions that emerged at this time resulted in the fracturing of the radical Left. After the Greek Communist Party (KKE) withdrew from the original *Synaspismos* coalition, which had been founded in 1989 by leftist and progressive parties and groups, a new *Synaspismos* party was formed in 1992. Its current appellation is "Coalition of the Left of Movements and Ecology" (*Synaspismos tis Aristeras ton Kinimaton kai tis Oikologias*).

14. On the post-1981 flood of autobiographical accounts about the war years and postwar political imprisonment and exile, see, for instance, Papathanasiou (1996), Margaritis (2000). For a brief discussion of the place of oral history in contemporary Greek historiography as a whole, see, Liakos (2001: 84). In a survey conducted by the Oral History Group of the National Center for Social Research (EKKE) in 1999, the "decade of the 1940s" was the preferred area of research of those polled (Boutzouvi and Thanopoulou 2002: 13). For oral history methodologies in research on the Resistance and Civil War, see Collard (1993), Hart (1996), Van Boeschoten (1997, 2002), Vidali (1999), and Vervenioti (2002). For a discussion of an archive of audiovisual recordings of resistance testimony, see Varon (1994). Needless to say, the common use of the label "oral history" to describe all interview-based historical research on this period obscures the actual range of (often contradictory) theoretical approaches (empirical, interpretive, psychoanalytic)

currently being employed. For our purposes, however, this convergence of different analytical frameworks and academic disciplines manifests the degree to which "oral testimony" emerged as a privileged object of study in the 1990s.

15. Papers from the conference, many to which I will refer in this chapter, were published in 1997 in the volume *Istoriki Pragmatikotita kai Neoelliniki Pezografia* (1945–1995) (Historical Reality and Modern Greek Fiction [1945–1995]) put out by the Etaireia Spoudon Neoellinikou Politismou kai Genikis Paideias.

16. Explicitly linking authorship to punishment, Foucault (1977) argues that discourse was not originally considered a "thing" or a "product," but a transgressive *act*. The author function, he points out, emerged when authors became subjects of punishment. At the end of the eighteenth and beginning of the nineteenth century, as authors were placed in a new system of property and ownership that codified rights related to textual property (copyright, etc.), discourse's trangressive potential came to be seen as an "imperative peculiar to literature." For Foucault, the concepts of "author" and "work" are profoundly ideological: thus, he argues that in reducing fiction to the "genius" (and property) of the author and limiting its circulation, manipulation, decomposition, and recomposition, the *danger* of fiction was also reduced.

17. Questioning the point of presenting the reader of *Orthokosta* with multiple testimonies of the "same" event (an issue I discuss at length below), Voulgaris espouses the view that the witness who is "closest" to the event is naturally the best witness: in the name of "narrative economy," he suggests, Valtinos might have provided this person's testimony and dispensed with the "repetition" (2004: 55). Propounding the commonsense logic of "salvage" ethnography in the face of Valtinos's "assault" on the historical record, he asks in dismay, "What will the historian of the next generation do, who does not have my information? Will she/he turn to oral history, collecting the testimonies of the second generation?" (90). Ironically, Voulgaris's own performance of memory undermines this mocking dismissal of the testimony of the "second generation." Even though Voulgaris, born in 1958, is much younger than Valtinos, his essay on *Orthokosta* attests to a deep knowledge of the events of the war years as experienced in his village and the surrounding region and, perhaps most importantly, to their profound impact on him—despite the fact that he did not live through them.

18. In the 1960s and 1970s, along with the rising influence of Marxism in historiography as well advances in voice-recording technology, "ethnobiography" started to become a popular genre among journalists, academics, and activists in many parts of the world. The Latin American testimonial (*testimonio*), perhaps the most well known of such genres, developed when sympathetic intellectuals set about interviewing illiterate and semiliterate working-class people (Gugelberger 1996). As a result, the *testimonio*, which developed alongside armed national liberation movements in Latin America, has a pronounced political and juridical dimension as its narrator "testifies against abuses suffered by a class or community" (Sommer 1999: 117). Or, as John Beverley puts it: "The situation of narration in testimonio has to involve an urgency to communicate, a problem of repression, poverty, subalternity, imprisonment, struggle for survival . . ." (1996a: 26). Philippe Lejeune (1989) has written of the emergence of "ethnobiography" in France in the 1970s, as individual informants, the "ones who do not write," were called forth to speak to educated mediator-scribes on behalf of a social class or occupation or in regard to a particular historical experience.

19. In discussing the Latin American *testimonio*, John Beverley has argued that this genre not be seen as merely a kind of oral history. In oral history, the intentionality of the recorder of testimony remains dominant while in *testimonio*, by contrast, the intentionality of the narrator takes precedence over that of the educated "compiler" or "activator" (1996a: 26).

Beverley, thus, suggests that *testimonio* not be treated as a mere "reenactment of the anthropological function of the colonial or subaltern 'native informant' ": in *testimonio*, the relationship between the oral narrator and literate compiler is not characterized so much by "liberal guilt" or "charity" as by a politicized reciprocity, stemming from the union of radical intellectuals and the poor and working class in a struggle for social justice and change (31–3).

20. While critics often refer to Valtinos's writing as "ethnological" or "anthropological" (see, for instance, Raftopoulos 1994a), Vangelis Calotychos has more usefully compared *Orthokosta* to contemporary research on the Civil War based on ethnographic fieldwork and/or oral history, including that of M. Mazower, R. Van Boeschoten, J. Hart, Y. Margaritis, and S. Kalyvas. Calotychos notes that *Orthokosta* appeared just as such work was "beginning to pick up speed and achieve a critical mass" (2000: 152). For his part, Yiannis Dallas (1997) connects trends in "foreign historiography" (the Italian school of "microhistory") with recent "domestic" literary production (in which he includes *Orthokosta*). By contrast, Tzina Politi's (1996) argument that *Orthokosta* presents us with a "preliterary, prehistoriographic" discourse and an "older understanding of the role of narration" that replaces "official history" and "bourgeois reading habits" ignores the long history of constructing the "voice" of the "common people" in bourgeois literature, as well as the contemporary authoritativeness of testimony-based historical accounts.

21. Valtinos's short story, "The Plaster Cast" (O Gypsos), one of the more memorable contributions to that volume, plays on and mocks dictator Papadopoulos's favorite metaphor, "Greece as a patient in a cast" (the narrator of the story is wrapped in plaster as he speaks). Instead of speeding national recovery, as Papadopoulos intended, the cast is depicted as suffocating, stifling, and ultimately murdering Greek society. In her study of literary resistance to the military dictatorship and its tactics of censorship and "textual authoritarianism," Karen Van Dyck has highlighted Valtinos's attempt in this story at "erasing the figurative with the literal" as a means of parodying the regime's rhetoric and stripping it of its legitimacy (1998: 37–50). The story ends when *glossa* (language, the tongue) itself is cut off as plaster fills and gags the narrator-patient's mouth.

22. The film *Descent of the Nine*, directed by Christos Shiopachas, won the Golden Prize in the Moscow Film Festival in 1985.

23. This reading was held on the island of Skopelos on March 21, 1998.

24. Voulgaris's (2004) essay on *Orthokosta* (see n. 2) elaborates on Elefantis's line of argumentation, even to the point of including a fictional historian-of-the-future. It is 2014 and this (male) historian is attempting to write the history of the Civil War in Kynouria after the last eyewitnesses have died. With only a few badly written and cheaply produced Resistance memoirs to go on, the historian, in Voulgaris's vision, is unable to *not* treat *Orthokosta* as a "primary source" on the history of the region (32–42, see also n. 33). In depicting this future historian as employed in a (fictional) provincial university where he teaches the history of the "Age of Extremes" (i.e., an apologetic history of fascism and communism viewed as two equally fanatical and totalitarian ideologies, two evils, two sides of the same coin), Voulgaris implicitly links the critique of leftist metanarratives on this period with the emergence of a new breed of theory-minded, careerist, professional historians who have come of age within academia rather than spheres of political (and historical/archival) activism.

25. In his 2002, *They Took Athens from us . . . : Rereading some Points of the History of 1940–1950* (Athens: Vivliorama), Elefantis also makes this connection by reprinting his review of *Orthokosta* just following one for Gage's *Eleni*.

26. The standard periodization of the Civil War is 1946–49. At the October 1999 conference in Athens, "The Greek Civil War from Varkiza to Grammos," however, the "beginning" of

the Civil War was set in 1945 at the time of the Varkiza agreement that officially demobilized ELAS. Another common start date for the Civil War is December 1944 (*Dekemvriana*). Going even further back, the period to which *Orthokosta* refers is sometimes described as the Civil War's "First Round." Needless to say, these different chronologies pose arguments for (or against) seeing particular moments of internecine conflict as related.

27. Referring to Hannah Arendt's critique of the prosecution case at the Eichmann trial, Felman judges Arendt "jurisprudentially conservative" because she is unable to accept the new revolutionary conception of the *victim* that emerged at the trial to de-center the *criminal* (i.e., Eichman or the "banality of evil") on whom Arendt remained transfixed. On the other hand, she considers Arendt's commentary on the trial "historiographically revolutionary" because she refuses to accept the prosecution's depiction of Nazism as a "traumatic *repetition* of a monumental history of anti-Semitism." For Arendt, this interpretation problematically "screens the new" (2002: 122). In her discussion of Paul Celan's poetry, Felman also points out how Celan turned Christian metaphors of resurrection and transcendence on their head, making them testify to the historical specificity of the Holocaust and showing the "concrete historical reality of massacre and race annihilation" to be "unerasable and untranscendable" (Felman and Laub 1992: 30).

28. The description of the novel as a "literary reproduction of the complaints of the anonymous Security Battalionist" comes from "The Security Battalionists are Vindicated" (October 26, 2003), a special issue of "Sunday's 'Virus'" ("*O* "*Ios*" *tis Kyriakis*), a left-wing investigative news supplement to the high-circulation Sunday edition of the *Eleftherotypia* newspaper. In this reportage, *Orthokosta* is described as the "first step" in a program of revisionist historiography funded by right-wing think tanks and spearheaded by particular historians with ultimate aim of establishing the reputation of the Security Battalionists as "defenders of the peace."

29. Interestingly, in the 2000 sequel to *The Book of the Days of Andreas Kordopatis*, Valtinos turns his attention to the "Asia Minor Catastrophe," that other key moment in the production of Greek literary testimony. In this book, though, he highlights the violence of Greek military campaigns of territorial expansion during the Balkan Wars (focusing, for instance, on the rape of Turkish women by Greek soldiers) and not only their tragic conclusion in 1922 with the expulsion of innocent Greek victims by Turkish aggressors.

30. At the end of Stratis Doukas's *A Prisoner of War's Story*, the narrator-scribe remarks of his informant: "When he'd finished telling his story, I said to him, 'Sign your name.' And he wrote: *Nikolaos Kozakoglou*" (1999: 64). With this command ("Sign your name"), the narrator reinvests his informant with his Greek name (as a fugitive in Turkey the narrator had disguised himself as a Turk), as well as establishes that this name with its Turkish suffix (-oglou) is (now) Helladic Greek. Having the informant *sign* his name, however, also symbolically forces him to "claim" his testimony and recognize the fullness of his subjectivity through it. Finally, given the highly asymmetrical nature of this linguistic exchange, the signature might be seen as evidence that the informant willingly consented to signing over the "rights" to his story to Doukas.

31. In an interview, Valtinos observed that the discerning critic would find that the structure of *Orthokosta* had been inspired by music: "a graduate student also could note that 24 rhapsodies comprise the spine of the book. Exactly 24. And not a 'collection of narrations.' I have to make clear here that I was not interested in the number alone. There are other such things to be discovered. I am not going to be the one to list them though" (1994b).

32. As Raphael Samuel has noted in the tellingly entitled 1971 essay "Perils of Transcription" (reprinted in 1998 in *The Oral History Reader*): "The spoken word can very easily be

mutilated when it is taken down in writing and transferred to the printed page. Some distortion is bound to arise, whatever the intention of the writer, simply by cutting out pauses and repetitions—a concession which writers very generally feel bound to make in the interests of readability" (389).

33. In what he remarkably describes as a purely "textual" analysis (by which he means that he does not compare the story in the novel to his knowledge of "real" events), Voulgaris reads several testimonies in precisely this plot-centered way, parsing out chronologies, kinship relations, and political maneuverings (2004: 104–36). (Desperately trying to make sense of the Civil War with *Orthokosta* as a key "source" and hoping to put things "in some order" [46–7], Voulgaris's fictional historian-of-the-future even goes so far as to scan *Orthokosta* into a digital file so that he can cross-check names in the novel with a CD of the local census he secured from the municipality!) If, for Voulgaris, the "first reading" of the novel, the one at which most readers stop, produces a sense of "chaos," the second reading proves this chaos to be incredibly well organized and masterfully orchestrated and, thus, a dangerous fabrication, a trap (76, 138). Despite the fact that Voulgaris identifies himself as "not a historian, but a literary critic" (100), he does not show any particular sensitivity to the textual or poetic (something evident in his use of arbitrary passages from the novel as epigraphs); in blatantly privileging the historical reading over the literary, he treats the fictional as little more than a *mask* to be lifted from reality (as most notably in his identification of the "real people" behind *Orthokosta*'s pseudonyms).

34. By far the most common monuments relating to this period celebrate the battles and heroes of the "National Resistance" (*Ethniki Antistasi*) in familiar national-military terms (often including implicit or explicit reference to other moments of "Greek" resistance to a foreign enemy, e.g., the 1821 War of Independence against the Turks). These monuments were constructed following the "recognition" of the Resistance and replace an earlier genre of monument commemorating battles against the "communist bandits" (*kommounistosymmorites*), some of which still stand, especially in villages of northern Greece. State discourse on "reconciliation" had stipulated the (re)construction of memorials with names of those who died in the Civil War from both government and communist sides; however, there has been no notable collective and spontaneous mobilization to mourn the trauma of (the) war, and emphasis remains on excavating its "heroic" moments. The 1989 declaration of the Makronisos concentration camp a "national historical monument" by then culture minister Melina Mercouri importantly transformed a site of state-inflicted postwar violence on communists into a memory *topos*, but one associated not only with the Left but also with its most politicized part (cf. *Historical Landscape and Historical Memory* 2000). Testament to the symbolic capital associated with this site, politicians of the conservative New Democracy party ironically have also participated in recent "pilgrimages" to Makronisos.

35. As Felman notes, the *historical particularity* of traumatic events such as the Holocaust paradoxically lies in their "disappearance as an historical actuality and referential possibility." Since these events cannot be incorporated into existing conceptual frameworks for thinking about "History," they take on specificity precisely in the fact that they "cannot, historically, be witnessed" (Felman and Laub 1992: 104).

36. *Orthokosta*, as I have already noted, has often been spoken about in the same breath with journalist Nicholas Gage's *Eleni*. As Maria Skamaga (1999) has argued, this comparison is particularly unconvincing, as Gage's dogged pursuit to discover the single, undeniable "Truth" of his mother's death partakes of none of *Orthokosta*'s self-consciousness about the (re)construction and interpretation of the historical past. Valtinos's novel also has been frequently paired with political scientist Stathis Kalyvas' research on left-wing violence (e.g., Kalyvas 2000). Again this comparison seems unwarranted: Kalyvas's explicit aim in his

research is, as he puts it, "to set the record straight" and contribute to a "full exploration of the nature of violence during the Greek civil war" (2000: 143). He treats testimony as merely a source for otherwise unrecorded information. By contrast, as we have seen, *Orthokosta* explicitly refuses this kind of totalizing masternarrative of the war and uses testimony to speak to issues of narrative responsibility, the ethics of listening, and the pitfalls of ideological essentialism. It is, thus, curious that in recent left-wing interrogative reportage about contemporary representations of the Security Battalions (see n. 28), Kalyvas's work has been described as a "postmodern—and definitely selective—description of 'red terror' between 1943–4 in the Argolid" ("The Security Battalionists are Vindicated." *Eleftherotypia*, October 26, 2003). In regard to the contested history of the Civil War, it seems "postmodernism" can be used as a synonym for "revisionism," even if the contingency of historical events, the mediation of experience through language, and the multiplicity of subject positions and historical narratives are not at issue.

37. The work of Frangkiski Abatzopoulou on Greek Holocaust testimonies (1993, 1994: 25) represents an important exception to literary scholars' avoidance of texts that make claims to historical truth.

38. In response to charges that *Orthokosta* fabricates and falsifies the past, Valtinos has countered that "to talk of a painting—*Orthokosta*—with the negative of a photograph is hardly satisfying" (cited in Calotychos 2000). In other self-reflections on his writing, Valtinos has also resorted to metaphors from the visual arts not only to underscore the "impressionism" of historical fiction in relation to "scientific" accounts of the past but also to defend the work of literature as rightful product of its maker's art. In responding to the frequent charge that his writing simply reproduces things other people have said, Valtinos has pointed out that painters would never be accused that a "painting is its model" (1991: 14). The switch in media (from writing to painting) on which such an analogy depends is not, however, insignificant. In emphasizing the aura of the original artwork (not its technological reproducibility), Valtinos does not seem to take into account the citational principles of writing—to which his novels, ironically, make us more sensitive—and the fact that literary authenticity is so often produced through "conjuring," and borrowing the authority of, another's "live" voice.

5   America Translated in a Migrant's Memoirs

1. It is difficult to tell which notebook was written first. The copy I have labeled version A (6″ × 4″) has 84 written pages, followed by several blank pages and a 23-page poem. Version B, contained in a tinier notebook (5″ × 3½″), has 158 pages (though only every other page has been numbered). I think Version B was written second because it contains a much fuller account of Mandas's journey to the United States, but also because topic changes are more frequently indicated by page breaks. Version B, however, does not constitute the "clean" copy or revision of Version A (as "original" text); the events narrated and the language used to describe them are both similar and different enough in each version to suggest that Mandas did not write the second copy while looking at the first, but rather that he had a well-rehearsed account of the story in his head. Since Mandas's spelling errors are impossible to convey in translation and the original texts are not in circulation (and the edited text barely is), I quote extensively from Mandas's original Greek text. In cases in which I have transliterated phrases into English, Mandas's spelling errors are sometimes "concealed" by my transliterations.

2. In this poem, which has as its fictional addressee a lover back home, Mandas describes the hard lives of Greek immigrants in the United States from the textile plants of Lowell, Massachusetts to the railroad companies out west. He complains that the Greeks are a "small" people in comparison to other ethnic groups and that Americans do not care if they die or are exploited in their workplaces. He also laments that while living in the United States, Greeks lose their cultural identity and religion. The poem concludes with a rousing call for Greece to retake Hagia Sophia in Istanbul and realize the "Great Idea" of Greek territorial expansion. The fact that the poem is written in such a different style than the memoirs and uses phrases from popular songs of the time (such as "Columbus is to blame for discovering America") suggests that the poem draws heavily on other poems and songs that were circulating in Greek immigrant communities in the United States at the beginning of the century.

3. *Palaia Ellada* refers to the territories that comprise the original kingdom of Greece, including Mandas's native Peloponnese, as opposed to the so-called New Lands (*Nees Hores*), such as Macedonia, which were annexed post-1830. For *Palaioelladites*, migrant labor and soldiering in the Balkan Wars formed characteristic aspects of their historical experience of the first quarter of the twentieth century. Thus, we can understand why in the sequel to *The Book of Days of Andreas Kordopatis*, Valtinos "sends" Kordopatis, also an Arcadian, to the Balkan Wars after his return from working in the United States.

4. Mandas's age group had not in fact been called up (he was thirty-seven at the time), but when his parents registered his birth, they had declared him three years younger than his actual age. At the time of the Balkan Wars, many Greeks who were working in the United States returned to Greece to enlist. Mandas, by contrast, does not appear to have been so eager to fight; he simply happened to have already returned to Greece.

5. According to a study on the Greek community of Spartanburg, the first Greek "settler" arrived in 1900 from Arahova, a village near Vourvoura, and set up a "candy kitchen" (Boyd n.d.). "Candy kitchen" appears to be the Anglicization or "Gringlish" (i.e., "Greek-English") for *zaharoplasteio*, patisserie or cake shop. Arahova was the principal village from which Vourvoriot men took their brides.

6. According to an official Greek government study on migration, between 1890 and 1911 Arcadia was the province with the highest number of migrants in relation to its population: 15.10 percent (cited in Kitroeff 1999: 143). Migration had a tremendous impact on Mandas's own village of Vourvoura. A 1924 village yearbook, which has a section entitled "Vourvouriots in America," lists the names of a hundred villagers living in Washington, D.C. According to statistics compiled in the 1925–6 village yearbook, 173 of a total Vourvouriot population of 1,064 were in the United States, including one-quarter of the male population.

7. See, for instance, Saloutos's (1964) landmark study of the successful assimilation of the immigrant Greek population into U.S. society. For critiques of the overwriting of Greek working-class history in the United States and the labor organizing and radical politics of the community's past, see contributions to special issues of the *Journal of the Hellenic Diaspora* ("The Greeks in America" 14(1–2), 1987; "The Greek American Experience" 16(1–4), 1989; "Rethinking Greek America" 20(1), 1994) and Georgakas (1992). For a fascinating study of the 1914 Greek strike in the Colorado coal mines and the murder of strike leader, Louis Tikas, see Papanikolas (1982). Early sociological studies had assigned immigrant Greeks a low status in racial hierarchies: see Fairchild (1911), Burgess (1913); on the relation of race, class, and ethnicity in shaping immigrant discourses as well as on the progressive "whitening" of Greek Americans, see Anagnostu (2004).

8. While studies of immigrant communities began to be conducted in the United States quite early because immigration could be viewed as part of a story of "national accumulation," by contrast, emigration as "loss of national capital" was not for a long time a subject of mainstream European historiography (Laliotou 1998: 36).

9. If one factors in the large number of Ottoman Greeks (from Crete, the Aegean islands, Epirus, Macedonia, Thrace, and Asia Minor) who began emigrating to the United States around 1905, it is estimated that a total of as many as 900,000 people of Greek ethnicity emigrated to the United States during the "first wave" of transatlantic migration (Petmezas 1995: 428). Migration did form a subject of intense public discussion and cultural production in Greek society, with returned migrants symbolizing either physical and moral degradation or "reformed Greekness" (Laliotou 1998). For an overview of the salience of the theme of diaspora in Greek cinema, see Sotiropoulou (1995). Cultural texts produced *by* Greek migrants themselves about their experiences of migration and repatriation, however, have been mostly ignored in the historiography of Greek migration to the United States (Kalogeras 2001).

10. See, for instance, the extensively illustrated 1997 coffee-table book, tellingly entitled *Anywhere on Earth Greece: The Epic of Migration in Pictures*, ed. Fondas Ladis.

11. The most recent (academic) encyclopedia of modern Greek history, the *History of Greece in the Twentieth Century*, ed. Christos Hatziyosif (1999), is organized around socioeconomic and cultural historical topics, with migration constituting an important "chapter." For an important study that considers Greek transatlantic migration from the perspective of transnational movement and diasporic cultural formation rather than as an adjunct to national historiography, see Laliotou (1998). Postwar Greek migration to western Europe and Australia has also recently emerged as a subject of historical study; see, for instance, Ventoura (1999).

12. See, for instance, reportage in the newspaper *Eleftherotypia* by the left-wing journalist team *O Ios tis Kyriakis*: "The Unknown Pogrom against the Greeks" (June 14, 1998), "The Criminality of the Greeks in the U.S.A., 1929–30" (November 28, 1999) and "Australia: The Undesirable Greeks" (October 10, 2000).

13. For more on the use of the slogan "Greeks were once Albanians" in Greek public discourse as well as on the way 1990s Albanian migration to Greece has reenacted Greek histories of migration and poverty, activating Balkanist tropes of representation without, however, "coming to terms" with them, see Papailias (2003).

14. Describing his interrogation by the Nazis, Mandas, for instance, admits to being very impressed by the German officer who eventually released him. He notes: "after I said to myself may god bless him we left he was a Man of great Stature handsome and he wore a small medal on his chest and spoke greek like us hicks."

15. In statistics compiled for the 1925–26 Vourvoura yearbook, the Mandas family was listed as the largest in the village: of 1,064 "Vourvouriots" (including those in the United States), 159 were *Mantaioi*.

16. For the classic philological study on the Greek funeral lament, see Alexiou (1974); for anthropological and performative approaches to mourning practices, see Seremetakis (1991), Panourgia (1995).

17. Most songs of *xenitia* actually were produced during an earlier wave of Greek migration (between the fifteenth and eighteenth centuries, mostly to central Europe). Rather than reflecting a continuity of practice, the reproduction of these songs in twentieth-century print discourses such as folklore compendia might be seen as a re-creation of this "tradition." The 1924 Vourvoura village yearbook, for instance, contains two versions of the classic folk song of *xenitia*, "The Death of the Emigrant (*Xenitemenou*)."

18. While emigrant remittances provided a great boon to the Greek economy, the state was concerned about the drop in population caused by migration (and the concomitant loss of military conscripts) as well as by the poor physical and "moral" health of returned emigrants, many of whom were suffering from tuberculosis (Petmezas 1995: 428–9; Laliotou 1998: 124).

19. As Laliotou notes, cultural discourses represent first-wave migrants as nostalgic for the bachelor life of the early years of immigration and especially the "flirtatiousness of . . . everyday life interaction with women of different nationalities" (1998: 132).

20. Other common terms included: "That's-all-right-*ides*" (*Δετσοράκηδες*) from the Greek American habit of inserting the English phrase "that's all right" into their Greek; "Jimmy-*des*" (*Τζίμηδες*) from "Jimmy," the Anglicization of Dimitris; and *Kounimenoi*, "shaken," from the immigrant's boastful shaking of their bodies as they walked (Triandafyllidis 1963: 275).

21. To the extent that Mandas presents his life as an example (or counterexample), his text might be compared to the explicitly pedagogical 1945 *Engkolpion Metanastou* (Manual of an Immigrant) by Emmanuel Polenis. This author, who had lived in the United States between 1907 and 1921, advises future migrants not to make the mistake of letting nostalgia tempt them to return to Greece: with great regret, he recalls the day a prophetic bank cashier told him that it was a bad idea to withdraw his money and leave the United States, because Greece is poor and "good only for her History" (74).

22. As Susan Buck-Morss has suggested in reference to Greek migration to Germany in the 1970s, the dominance of family-based capitalism in Greece might have made Greek products noncompetitive in global markets, but family control over the means of production prevented the divorce of a large labor force from the land, thus maintaining ownership as an alternative productive means. Temporary proletarianization through periods of migration, thus, often strengthened family capitalism or created the basis for its establishment (1987: 226).

23. In their ethnographies, Campbell (1964) and Couroucli (1985: 136) note the oppression of common people by the formal discourses and paperwork of state bureaucracy, but do not make the relation of writing to social power an explicit subject of inquiry. In his discussion of the Greek "language fetish," Herzfeld (1992) has underscored the conjunction of language, bureaucracy, law, and nation-state in the "rhetorics of normativeness." For a subtle analysis of the workings of Greek linguistic hegemony from the perspective of speakers of a "minority" language, see Tsitsipis (1998).

24. In the 1939 Vourvoura yearbook, the authors of a statistical study on the village remark that to come to a correct conclusion about the population of Vourvoura, one must stop trying to do the statistics of "Vourvoura" and instead do those of "Vourvouriots."

25. One of Mandas's stories pokes fun at the fact that there were so many people in Vourvoura named Yiorgos (or, more informally, Yiorgis) Mandas. He writes: "To find a Yiorgis Mandas in Vourvoura you have to know his nickname (*paratsoukli*). A good friend of mine, whom I met when we were traveling from New York to Piraeus, promised me that he would come to see Vourvoura, such a famous place. And indeed he came two years later" Mandas's friend had trouble finding him, though, because he was looking for "Fatty" and by then Mandas had become quite thin.

26. In the same spirit, see the brief autobiographical note written in the 1930s by a Greek migrant laborer in the United States named Gus Markos (Anagnostu 1999). A contemporary of Mandas's, who eventually settled in Columbus, Ohio, Markos's account of his work and travel in the United States is composed almost entirely as a story of wages. It begins: "On March 18, 1902 I arrived in Chicago, America. On April 1st of the same year I got a job as a bootblack in Milwaukee, Wisconsin for $100 a year. I worked in the shoeshine parlor for fifteen months, made a total of $130. In July, I left Milwaukee and went back to Chicago. I worked in a hotel for two months for $15 a month and in a factory for a month for $5 a week."

27. The "tactful" suppression of the subject of money in the travelogues of the select few who are considered travelers (as opposed to migrants, exiles, refugees) is merely one of the

many ways such movement conceals its privilege. Contemporary tourist guidebooks, bristling with costs and estimates, however, unabashedly proclaim the significance of money as a standard of cultural comparison. As Buck-Morss notes in an article about tourism in Greece in the late 1970s and early 1980s: "In the cafés talk of money is incessant. The most frequently asked question to foreigners is *posso kostizi*? ('how much?') How much was your plane fare? your camera? your watch? The question is the means by which the villagers attempt to position themselves within a world system of abstract exchange" (1987: 224).

28. An analogue to Mandas's text might be *To Imerologion tou Viou Mou* (The Diary of My Life), the autobiography of a Cypriot migrant worker named Savvas Tserkezis (1874–1963) whose travels overlapped with Mandas's. Tserkezis was in Los Angeles between 1908 and 1912 and fought in the Balkan Wars before returning to the United States where he lived from 1915 until 1923. Tserkezis, who also wrote an adventure novel, casts his story entirely in a travel–adventure mode and only writes about his travels not his life at home.

29. Mandas's story resonates with narratives of the lives and deaths of "neomartyrs" (saints who were canonized after the fall of Constantinople in 1453). Unlike earlier saints, the neomartyrs were poor, socially marginalized people [cf. Nikodimos (tou Agioreitou) 1794]. Laurie Hart (1992) notes that in the Greek rural village where she did her fieldwork in the 1980s, the most common kinds of printed matter that entered the home were little pamphlets about the lives of saints or histories of monasteries. In addition, she notes that the stories of saints were very present in the public discourse of the village. She suggests that saints' lives be seen as a successor to the "late antique romance, concerned with the theme of 'capricious fate' " (203). For the relationship between saints' lives and early Greek biographical novels, see Farinou-Malamatari (1997).

30. In a discussion of the significance of martyrdom in Orthodox Christianity, Hart (1992) notes that the early Christian concept of the martyr placed stress on witnessing: the *martyras* was viewed as someone who could testify through observation or revelation to the truth of God's power or Christ's sacrifice. Over time, however, the concept of *physical suffering* became predominant, and martyrs were considered people who could testify because they had endured a particular *martyrion* (physical torture, torment, ordeal) and nonetheless had maintained their faith (1992: 193–223). It is important to note the difference between a religious and a historical or legal *martyras*: while the *synaxari* (saint's life) was a biography written in the third-person about a martyr who had died, the historical/legal witness, also called *martyras* in Greek, testifies in the first-person as a *survivor*.

31. Even though Latin American testimonial (*testimonio*) has been incorporated into U.S. multicultural literary canons, Beverley (1996a, b) argues that its narrators never claimed to have come into their "true" identity when they became writers (as is the case in some working-class and ethnic literature). For narrators of *testimonio*, literacy represents just one of several tactics to effect social change, not an end in itself.

32. In a 1953 article, written on the basis of a trip to the United States in 1939, Manolis Triandafyllidis (1963), the renowned demoticist linguist, describes the "Greek of the Greeks in America" not as a separate idiom, but as "native Greek" that has gradually "weakened" and been spiritually "emptied" because of having lost contact with the "live, renewing source" of the Greek "mother tongue" as well as as a result of coming under the pressure of American life and language. His analysis focuses primarily on changes to the lexicon: "misused" Greek words; Greek words used to express new meanings; and neologisms based on English words but adapted to Greek morphology, which were used to represent new meanings or replace "original" Greek words. "Gringlish," like "Spanglish" (Spanish-English), however, might be seen less as a "degeneration" from a putatively

"pure" mother tongue than simply as a new variety of Greek that developed in the context of migration and cross-cultural interaction.

33. The conflation of the two versions of Mandas's memoirs in the edited text not only undoes the rough poetry of Mandas's prose and disrupts the integrity of each account as a distinct act of writing, but also in many cases results in even more grammatically unclear sentences.

34. In the *monotoniko* (single-accent system), there are no breathing marks, monosyllabic words are written without accents, and words of more than one syllable are written with only one accent (an acute) over the stressed vowel (Mackridge 1985: 367–8). Due to technical limitations, I am afraid that I, too, have rendered citations from Mandas's original text in *monotoniko*.

35. The most common spelling errors for writers of Greek involve the many different spellings of /i/, which can be represented by various letters or combinations of letters. Mandas's text includes all sorts of incorrect spellings of this sound: for example, *απομνιμονεύματα*, instead of *απομνημονεύματα*; *συμέα*, instead of *σημαία*; *πλούσιη*, instead of *πλούσιοι*. He also does not use the letter omega at all, representing all "o" sounds with omicron: (*ανικο*, instead of *ανήκω*). As a result, Mandas often accidentally produces homonyms of the words he wants to write *αφτή* instead of *αυτοί* (feminine nominative singular, instead of masculine nominative plural) or *τον ανταρτόν* instead of *των ανταρτών* (accusative singular, instead of plural genitive).

36. The use of capital letters and underlining in Mandas's text also seems to indicate extra stress. When reflecting on the communist argument that only poor men end up fighting in the front lines, Mandas notes: "and that was Correct" (*και αυτό είτον Σοστό*). Of his departure for he United States he writes: ". . . in [18]98 on 26 of August I left."

37. As reified by particular technological media (such as the printing press and the typewriter), the space has been central to the postulation of the sign's arbitrariness and abstract exchangeability. It is not insignificant, for instance, that Saussure, even though he lionized orality, treated the "word" as his model for the linguistic sign. As opposed to the "flow" of handwriting, typewriting, as Kittler has argued, turns writing into a process of selection from discrete elements of the keyboard: what matters are the *differences* between letters as marked by spaces. See also Ong (1982) on the historical role of print and moveable type in transforming writing into a visual object.

38. Evidence of Mandas's use of *katharevousa* can be found throughout the text: including (1) word choice (*εντούτις* [sic] [however], his favorite conjunction; the use of the preposition *δια* [for] instead of the colloquial *για*); (2) the use of archaizing verb forms (*εγενίθην* [sic], instead of *γεννήθηκα*); (3) spelling (*πανδρέψο* instead of the demotic *παντρέψω*); and (4) grammatical forms (the use of the terminal *-ν* in accusative nouns, the use of formal accusative plural noun endings [*τας εορτάς*]).

39. In the tradition of Greek historical orthography, a specific closed set of digraphs (two-letter sequences) are referred to as diphthongs.

40. Mandas systematically overuses the diphthong "*ει*" (as in *ειϰογένια*, instead of *οιϰογένεια*, or *είταν*, instead of *ήταν*), but does not use other diphthongs when he should. He also commonly hypercorrects verb endings by employing those of "more difficult" middle and passive verbs: i.e., *πλιρόναμαι*, instead of *πληρώναμε*, or *εφιγαμαι*, instead of *εφύγαμε*. As this last example indicates, Mandas uses the augment for aorist verbs, which is an element of formal, not demotic Greek; in local idioms of Arcadia, however, the use of the augment was common.

41. Mandas does not use the circumflex (*perispomeni*) at all. He only uses smooth breathing marks (*psili*), even when a rough breathing mark (*daseia*) is in order. Mandas also assumes that the breathing mark always goes on the first letter of words and, as a result, often incorrectly accents those that begin with diphthongs.

42. On the social history and politics of the modern Greek standard, see Frangoudaki (2001). On Greek multilingualism and "minority" languages, see Tsitsipis (1998), Embeirikos (2001). For Greek sociolinguistics more generally, see the 1992 special issue of the *Journal of Modern Greek Studies* on "Language, Power, and Freedom in Modern Greece" (10: 1) and the 1997 special issue of the *International Journal of the Sociology of Language* on "Aspects of Sociolinguistics in Greece" (126).

43. Mandas has similar problems transliterating the word "junction" in "Napa Junction." He starts and ends the word in Latin letters, but for the "ct" alternately use the Greek letters "ξ" and "χ": *Ναραζιοξιον, Ναραζιονχιον.*

44. Gus Markos's brief autobiographical text (see n. 26) also includes many American place names written in both English and Greek, such as "*Τσικάγο της Αμερικής*, Chicago, Ills. U.S.A." and "*Μηλοβόκη Βισκάνσον*, Milwaukee Wisconsin" (Anagnostu 1999).

45. Triandafyllidis (1963: 281) refers to this phenomenon as the "lightening of the consonant cluster" (i.e., "pictures" becomes "pitses"). Another example is "swee-heart" (*σουϊχάρτ*) for "sweetheart" as in the Greek American *rembetiko* song "Why my sweetheart/Do you wound me so hard?" (*Αχ, γιατί γλυκό μου σουϊχάρτ/Αχ, να με πληγώνεις τόσο χάρντ*). See the 1995 CD *Cafe Aman Amerika: Greek American Songs Revised and Revisited* (Music World Productions).

46. Triandafyllidis notes the remarkable profusion of dialects and idioms of Greek used by immigrants in the United States, many of whose speech had not been significantly affected by schooling in the national standard. He himself also learns some new Greek words during his trip to the United States (1963: 271–2).

References

Abatzopoulou, Frangiski (1993). *Το Ολοκαύτωμα στις Μαρτυρίες των Ελλήνων Εβραίων* (The Holocaust in Testimonies of Greek Jews). Thessaloniki: Paratiritis.

——— (1994). Ιστορία και Μυθοπλασία: Οι Αυτοβιογραφικές Αφηγήσεις Πολέμων (History and Fiction: Autobiographical War Narratives). In *Narrativity, History and Anthropology*, ed. Rika Benveniste and Theodoros Paradellis. Mytilini: University of the Aegean, Department of Social Anthropology.

——— (1997). Λογοτεχνικά Πρόσωπα και Εθνοτικές Διαφορές στη Μεταπολεμική Πεζογραφία (Literary Characters and Ethnic Differences in Postwar Prose). In *Historical Reality and Modern Greek Fiction (1945–1995)*. Etaireia Spoudon Neoellinikou Politismou kai Genikis Paideias. Athens: Moraitis School.

——— (1998). *Ο Άλλος εν Διωγμώ. Η Εικόνα του Εβραίου στη Λογοτεχνία: Ζητήματα Ιστορίας και Μυθοπλασίας* (The Persecution of the Other: The Image of the Jew in Literature: Issues of History and Fiction). Athens: Themelio.

Agamben, Giorgio (1999). *Remnants of Auschwitz: The Witness and the Archive*, trans. Daniel Heller-Roazen. New York: Zone Books.

Alexandrou, Aris (1996). *Mission Box*, trans. Robert Crist. Athens: Kedros. Originally published as *Το Κιβώτιο* (Athens: Kedros, 1974).

Alexiou, Margaret (1974). *The Ritual Lament in Greek Tradition*. Cambridge: Cambridge University Press.

Amin, Shahid (1995). *Event, Metaphor, Memory: Chauri Chaura, 1922–1992*. Berkeley: University of California Press.

Anagnostakis, Ilias and Evangelia Balta (1990). *Η Καππαδοκία των "Ζώντων Μνημείων": Η Ανακάλυψη "της Πρώτης Πατρίδος της Ελληνικής Φυλής" (19 αι.)* (The Cappadocia of "Living Monuments": The Discovery of the "First Homeland" of the Greek Race [19th c.]). Athens: Poreia.

Anagnostu, Yiorgos (1993–94). Anthropology and Literature: Crossing Boundaries in a Greek American Novel. In *Fantasy or Ethnography? Irony and Collusion in Subaltern Representation*, ed. Sabra J. Webber and Margaret R. Lynd. Papers in Comparative Studies 8, Ohio State University.

——— (1999). Writing the Past: A Memoir of a Migrant Laborer (1902–1906). *Greek America* 5 (4–5): 50–3.

——— (2004). Forget the Past, Remember the Ancestors! Modernity, "Whiteness," American Hellenism, and the Politics of Memory in Early Greek America. *Journal of Modern Greek Studies* 22(1): 25–71.

Anderson, Benedict (1983). *Imagined Communities: Reflections on the Origin and Spread of Nationalism*. London: Verso.

Antze, Paul and Michael Lambek, eds. (1996). *Tense Past: Cultural Essays in Trauma and Memory*. New York: Routledge.

Apostolakou, Lito (1997). "All for One and One for All": Anarchists, Socialists and Demoticists in the Labour Centre of Volos (1908–1911). In *Greek Society in the Making, 1863–1913: Realities, Symbols and Visions*, ed. Philip Carabott. Aldershot, Hampshire: Variorum.

Apostolidou, Venetia (1997). Λαϊκή Μνήμη και Δομή της Αίσθησης στην Πεζογραφία για τον Εμφύλιο. Από την "Καγκελόπορτα" στην "Καταπάτηση." (Popular Memory and the Structure of Feeling in Civil War Prose: From *Kangeloporta* to *Katapatisi*). In *Historical Reality and Modern Greek Fiction (1945–1995)*. Etaireia Spoudon Neoellinikou Politismou kai Genikis Paideias. Athens: Moraitis School.

Appadurai, Arjun (1986). Theory in Anthropology: Center and Periphery. *Comparative Studies in Society and History* 28: 356–61.

Arendt, Hannah (1963). *Eichmann in Jerusalem: A Report on the Banality of Evil*. New York: Penguin.

——— ([1955]1968). Introduction. Walter Benjamin: 1892–1940. In *Illuminations: Essays and Reflections*, ed. Hannah Arendt, trans. Harry Zohn. New York: Schocken.

Argyriou, Alexandros (1997). Αποδόσεις της Ιστορικής Εμπειρίας (Renderings of Historical Experience). In *Historical Reality and Modern Greek Fiction (1945–1995)*. Etaireia Spoudon Neoellinikou Politismou kai Genikis Paideias. Athens: Moraitis School.

——— (2000). Η Πεζογραφία περί Μακρόνησο και Μερικά Παρεπόμενα (The Prose on Makronisos and Some Sequels). In *Historical Landscape and Historical Memory: The Case of Makronisos*. Minutes of the Academic Meeting, 6–7 March 1998. Athens: Filistor.

Arı, Kemal (1995). *Büyük Mübadele: Türkiye'de Zorunlu Göç (1923–1925)* (The Great Exchange: Forced Migration in Turkey, 1923–1925). Istanbul: Tarih Vakfi Yurt.

Asad, Talal, ed. (1973). *Anthropology and the Colonial Encounter*. London: Ithaca Press.

——— (1986). The Concept of Translation in British Social Anthropology. In *Writing Culture: The Poetics and Politics of Ethnography*, ed. James Clifford and George E. Marcus. Berkeley: University of California Press.

——— (2002). Ethnographic Representation, Statistics, and Modern Power. Ethnography and Statistical Representation. In *From the Margins: Historical Anthropology and Its Futures*, ed. Brian Keith Axel. Durham, N.C.: Duke University Press.

Asdrachas, Spyros (1993). Σχόλια (Notes). Athens: Alexandreia.

Athanasiou, Athena (n.d.). The Politics of Mourning: Charting the Future of Feminist Dissent, Countering the Empire's "States of Exception." *Historein* (forthcoming).

Auer, J.C. Peter, ed. (1998). *Code-switching in Conversation: Language, Interaction and Identity*. London: Routledge.

Austin, J.L. (1962). *How to Do Things with Words*. Cambridge: Harvard University Press.

Axel, Brian Keith (2002). Introduction: Historical Anthropology and Its Vicissitudes. In *From the Margins: Historical Anthropology and Its Futures*, ed. Brian Keith Axel. Durham, N.C.: Duke University Press.

Bakalaki, Alexandra (1997). Students, Natives, Colleagues: Encounters in Academia and in the Field. *Cultural Anthropology* 12(4): 502–26.

Bakhtin, M.M. (1981). *The Dialogic Imagination: Four Essays*, ed. Michael Holquist, trans. Caryl Emerson and Michael Holquist. Austin: University of Texas Press.

——— (1984). *Problems of Dostoevsky's Poetics*, ed. and trans. Caryl Emerson, intro. Wayne C. Booth. Minneapolis: University of Minnesota Press.

——— (1986). *Speech Genres and Other Late Essays*, trans. Vern W. McGee. Austin: University of Texas Press.

Bal, Mieke, Jonathan Crewe, and Leo Spitzer, eds. (1999). *Acts of Memory: Cultural Recall in the Present*. Hanover, New Hampshire: University Press of New England.

Ballian, Anna, Nota Pantelaki, and Ioanna Petropoulou (1994). *Cappadocia: Travels in the Christian East*, trans. J. Giannakopoulou. Athens: Adam Editions.

Barthes, Roland (1975). *The Pleasure of the Text*, trans. Richard Miller. New York: Hill and Wang.

——— (1977). *Image–Music–Text*, ed. and trans. Stephen Heath. New York: Hill and Wang.

——— (1981). *Camera Lucida: Reflections on Photography*, trans. Richard Howard. New York: Hill and Wang.

Basso, Keith (1974). The Ethnography of Writing. In *Explorations in the Ethnography of Speaking*, ed. Richard Bauman and Joel Sherzer. Cambridge: Cambridge University Press.

Bauman, Richard and Charles Briggs (1990). Poetics and Performance as Critical Perspectives on Language and Social Life. *Annual Review of Anthropology* 19: 59–88.

Behar, Ruth and Deborah A. Gordon, eds. (1995). *Women Writing Culture*. Berkeley: University of California Press.

Ben-Amos, Dan and Liliane Weissberg, eds. (1999). *Cultural Memory and the Construction of Identity*. Detroit: Wayne State University Press.

Benjamin, Walter (1968). *Illuminations: Essays and Reflections*, ed. and intro. Hannah Arendt, trans. Harry Zohn. New York: Schocken.

Benveniste, Rika and Theodoros Paradellis, eds. (1994). *Αφηγηματικότητα, Ιστορία και Ανθρωπολογία* (Narrativity, History and Anthropology). Mytilini: University of the Aegean, Department of Social Anthropology.

———, eds. (1999). *Διαδρομές και Τόποι της Μνήμης: Ιστορικές και Ανθρωπολογικές Προσεγγίσεις* (Itineraries and Sites of Memory: Historical and Anthropological Approaches). Athens: Alexandreia.

Besnier, Niko (1995). *Literacy, Emotion, and Authority: Reading and Writing on a Polynesian Atoll*. Cambridge: Cambridge University Press.

Beverley, John (1996a). The Margin at the Center. In *The Real Thing: Testimonial Discourse in Latin America*, ed. Georg M. Gugelberger. Durham, N.C.: Duke University Press.

——— (1996b). The Real Thing. In *The Real Thing: Testimonial Discourse in Latin America*, ed. Georg M. Gugelberger. Durham, N.C.: Duke University Press.

Bhabha, Homi, ed. (1990). *Nation and Narration*. London: Routledge.

——— (1994). *The Location of Culture*. London: Routledge.

Bjelic, Dušan I. and Obrad Savić, eds. (2002). *Balkan as Metaphor: Between Globalization and Fragmentation*. Cambridge: MIT Press.

Blouin, Francis X. and William Rosenberg, eds. (n.d.). *Archives, Documentation, and the Institutions of Social Memory*. Ann Arbor: University of Michigan Press (forthcoming).

Bolter, Jay David and Richard Grusin (1999). *Remediation: Understanding New Media*. Cambridge: MIT Press.

Bourdieu, Pierre (1991). *Language and Symbolic Power*, ed. and intro. John B. Thompson, trans. Gino Raymond and Matthew Adamson. Cambridge: Harvard University Press.

Boutzouvi, Aleka and Maria Thanopoulou (2002). Προφορική Ιστορία στην Ελλάδα. Οι Εμπειρίες μιας Δύσκολης Πορείας (Oral History in Greece. Experiences of a Difficult Journey). *The Greek Review of Social Research* (Special Issue: Perspectives on Oral History in Greece, ed. Maria Thanopoulou and Aleka Boutzouvi) 107: 3–21.

Boyarin, Jonathan, ed. (1993). *The Ethnography of Reading*. Berkeley and Los Angeles: University of California Press.

Boyd, Rosamonde Ramsay (n.d.). *The Social Adjustment of the Greeks in Spartanburg, South Carolina*. Spartanburg, S.C.: Williams Printing Co.

Boym, Svetlana. (1994). *Common Places: Mythologies of Everyday Life in Russia.* Cambridge: Harvard University Press.

——— (1998). On Diasporic Intimacy: Ilya Kabakov's Installations and Immigrant Homes. *Critical Inquiry* 24(2): 498–524.

Briggs, Charles and Richard Bauman (1992). Genre, Intertextuality, and Social Power. *Journal of Linguistic Anthropology* 2(2): 131–72.

Buck-Morss, Susan (1987). Semiotic Boundaries and the Politics of Meaning: Modernity on Tour—A Village in Transition. In *New Ways of Knowing: The Sciences, Society and Reconstructive Knowledge*, ed. Marcus G. Raskin and Herbert J. Bernstein. Totowa, N.J.: Rowman & Littlefield.

Burgess, Thomas (1913). *Greeks in America: An Account of Their Coming, Progress, Customs, Living, and Aspirations.* Boston: Sherman, French.

Calotychos, Vangelis (1992). Westernizing the Exotic: Incorporation and a Green Line Around a Non-Space. *Journal of the Hellenic Diaspora* 18(2): 35–67.

——— (2000). Writing Wrongs, (Re)Righting (Hi)story?: "Orthotita" and "Orthographia" in Thanassis Valtinos's *Orthokosta*. *Gramma* 8: 151–65.

Calvino, Italo ([1947]2000). *The Path to the Spiders' Nest*, trans. Archibald Colquhoun, rev. Martin McLaughlin. New York: Ecco Press.

Campbell, John (1964). *Honour, Family, and Patronage: A Study of Institutions and Moral Values in a Greek Mountain Community.* Oxford: Oxford University Press.

Caruth, Cathy, ed. (1995). *Trauma: Explorations in Memory.* Baltimore: Johns Hopkins University Press.

——— (1996). *Unclaimed Experience: Trauma, Narrative, and History.* Baltimore: Johns Hopkins University Press.

Casey, Edward S. (1987). The World of Nostalgia. *Man and World* 20: 361–84.

Caton, Steven (1999). *Lawrence of Arabia: A Film's Anthropology.* Berkeley: University of California Press.

Center for Asia Minor Studies (1980). *Η Έξοδος: Μαρτυρίες από τις Επαρχίες των Δυτικών Παραλίων της Μικρασίας* (Exodus: Testimonies from the Provinces of the Western Coast of Asia Minor), vol. 1, ed. Fotis Apostolopoulos, prol. Yiorgos Tenekidis. Athens: Center for Asia Minor Studies.

——— (1982). *Η Έξοδος: Μαρτυρίες από τις Επαρχίες της Κεντρικής και Νότιας Μικρασίας* (Exodus: Testimonies from the Provinces of Central and Southern Asia Minor), vol. 2, ed. Yiannis Mourelos, intro. Paschalis Kitromilides. Athens: Center for Asia Minor Studies.

——— (n.d.). *Η Έξοδος: Μαρτυρίες από τις Επαρχίες της Βόρειας και Βορειανατολικής Μικρασίας* (Exodus: Testimonies from the Provinces of Northern and Northeastern Asia Minor), vol. 3. Athens: Center for Asia Minor Studies (forthcoming).

Chakrabarty, Dipesh (1992). Postcoloniality and the Artifice of History: Who Speaks for "Indian" Pasts? *Representations* 37: 1–26.

——— (2000). *Provincializing Europe: Postcolonial Thought and Historical Difference.* Princeton: Princeton University Press.

Chandler, James, Arnold I. Davidson, and Harry Hartounian, eds. (1994). *Questions of Evidence: Proof, Practice, and Persuasion across the Disciplines.* Chicago: University of Chicago Press.

Chatterjee, Partha (1993). *The Nation and its Fragments. Colonial and Post-Colonial Histories.* Princeton: Princeton University Press.

Chow, Rey (1993). *Writing Diaspora: Tactics of Intervention in Contemporary Cultural Studies.* Bloomington: Indiana University Press.

——— (2001). Fateful Attachments: On Collecting, Fidelity, and Lao She. *Critical Inquiry* 28(1): 286–304.

Christidis, A.F. (1995). Γλωσσικές Μυθολογίες: Η Περίπτωση της Ελληνικής (Linguistic Mythologies: The Case of Greek). *Synchrona Themata* 54: 21–6.

Clifford, James (1990). Notes on (Field)notes. In *Fieldnotes: The Makings of Anthropology*, ed. Roger Sanjek. Ithaca: Cornell University Press.

———— (1994). Diasporas. *Cultural Anthropology* 9(3): 302–38.

———— (1997). *Routes: Travel and Translation in the Late Twentieth Century*. Cambridge: Harvard University Press.

Clifford, James and George E. Marcus, eds. (1986). *Writing Culture: The Poetics and Politics of Ethnography*. Berkeley: University of California Press.

Cohn, Bernard S. (1980). History and Anthropology: The State of Play. *Comparative Studies in Society and History* 22(2): 198–221.

———— (1987). *An Anthropologist among the Historians and Other Essays*. New Delhi: Oxford University Press.

Collard, Anna (1993). Διερευνώντας την "Κοινωνική Μνήμη" στον Ελλαδικό Χώρο (Investigating "Social Memory" in a Greek Context). In *Anthropology and the Past: Contributions to the Social History of Modern Greece*, eds. Evthymios Papataxiarchis and Theodoros Paradellis. Athens: Alexandreia.

Comaroff, Jean and John Comaroff (1992). *Ethnography and the Historical Imagination*. Boulder, Colo.: Westview Press.

Combe, Sonia (1994). *Archives Interdites: Les Peurs Françaises Face à l'Histoire Contemporaine*. Paris: Albin Michel.

Connerton, Paul (1989). *How Societies Remember*. Cambridge: Cambridge University Press.

Cook, Terry (2000). Archival Science and Postmodernism: New Formulations for Old Concepts. *Archival Science* 1(1): 3–24.

Cooke, Miriam (1996). *Women and the War Story*. Berkeley: University of California Press.

Cooper, Frederick and Ann Stoler, eds. (1997). *Tensions of Empire: Colonial Cultures in a Bourgeois World*. Berkeley: University of California Press.

Coronil, Fernando (1996). Beyond Occidentalism: Toward Nonimperial Geohistorical Categories. *Cultural Anthropology* 11(1): 51–87.

———— (1997). *The Magical State: Nature, Money, and Modernity in Venezuela*. Chicago: Chicago University Press.

Couroucli, Maria (1985). *Les Oliviers du Lignage: Une Grèce de Tradition Vénitienne*. Paris: Maisonneuve et Larose.

Crane, Susan (2000). *Collecting & Historical Consciousness in Early Nineteenth-Century Germany*. Ithaca: Cornell University Press.

Cunliffe-Owen, Betty (1927). *Silhouettes of Republican Greece (Romances and Refugees)*. London: Hutchinson.

Dallas, Yiannis (1997). Η Μεταπολεμική Πεζογραφία και η Μικροϊστορία: Η Λανθάνουσα Συνάντηση μιας Τεχνικής και μιας Μεθόδου (Μέσα από τις Ατομικές Φωνές ως Μαρτυρίες του Υποστρώματος) (Postwar Prose and Microhistory: The Latent Encounter of a Technique and a Method [Through Individual Voices as Testimonies of the Underclass]). In *Historical Reality and Modern Greek Fiction (1945–1995)*. Etaireia Spoudon Neoellinikou Politismou kai Genikis Paideias. Athens: Moraitis School.

Daniel, E. Valentine (1984). *Fluid Signs: Being a Person the Tamil Way*. Berkeley: University of California Press.

———— (1996). *Charred Lullabies: Chapters in an Anthropography of Violence*. Princeton: Princeton University Press.

———— (1997). Suffering Nation and Alienation. In *Social Suffering*, ed. Arthur Kleinman, Veena Das, and Margaret Lock. Berkeley: University of California Press.

Daniel, E. Valentine and Jeffrey M. Peck, eds. (1996). *Culture/contexture: Explorations in Anthropology and Literary Studies.* Berkeley: University of California Press.

Das, Veena (1995). *Critical Events: An Anthropological Perspective on Contemporary India.* Delhi: Oxford University Press.

———— (1997). Language and Body: Transactions in the Construction of Pain. In *Social Suffering*, ed. Arthur Kleinman, Veena Das, and Margaret Lock. Berkeley: University of California Press.

Davis, John (1977). *People of the Mediterranean: An Essay in Comparative Social Anthropology.* London: Routledge & Kegan Paul.

Davis, Natalie (1987). *Fiction in the Archives: Pardon Tales and Their Tellers in Sixteenth-Century France.* Stanford: Stanford University Press.

———— (2000). *Slaves on Screen: Film and Historical Vision.* Cambridge: Harvard University Press.

de Certeau, Michel (1988). *The Writing of History*, trans. Tom Conley. New York: Columbia University Press.

de Pina-Cabral, João (1989). The Mediterranean as a Category of Regional Comparison: A Critical View. *Current Anthropology* 30(3): 399–406.

Deeley, John (1994). *The Human Use of Signs, or Elements of Anthroposemiosis.* Lanham, Maryland: Rowman & Littlefield.

Delta, Penelope (1959–60). *Αρχείον Μακεδονικού Αγώνος* (Archive of the Macedonian Struggle), ed. Vasileios Laourdas and Louizas Sundika-Laourdas, 3 vols. Thessaloniki: Society for Macedonian Studies, Institute for Balkan Studies.

Derrida, Jacques (1976). *Of Grammatology*, trans. Gayatri Chakravorty Spivak. Baltimore: Johns Hopkins University Press.

———— (1978). *Writing and Difference*, trans. and intro. Alan Bass. Chicago: University of Chicago Press.

———— (1988). Signature, Event, Context. In *Limited Inc*, trans. Samuel Weber and Jeffrey Mehlman. Evanston, Ill.: Northwestern University Press.

———— (1994). *Specters of Marx: The State of the Debt, the Work of Memory, and the New International*, trans. Peggy Kamuf. New York: Routledge.

———— (1996). *Archive Fever: A Freudian Impression*, trans. Eric Prenowitz. Chicago: University of Chicago Press.

Dimoglou, Aigli (1995). Συγκρότηση και Εξέλιξη της Βιομηχανίας του Βόλου (Constitution and Development of the Industry of Volos). In *Volos: The Search for Social Identity*, ed. Thomas Maloutas. Thessaloniki: Paratiritis.

————, ed. (1999). *Βόλος, Ένας Αιώνας: Από την Ένταξη στο Ελληνικό Κράτος (1881) έως τους Σεισμούς* (Volos, One Century: From Incorporation into the Greek State (1881) until the Earthquakes). Volos: Dimotiko Kentro Istorias & Tekmiriosis.

Diomidi-Kormazou, Eleni (1995). *Μιχαλάκης Καζάζης: Ο Πρωτοπόρος στην Ανάπτυξη της Βιομηχανίας στο Βόλο και στη Θεσσαλία* (Mihalakis Kazazis: Pioneer in the Development of Industry in Volos and Thessaly). Volos: Ekdoseis Ores.

Dirks, Nicholas, ed. (1992). *Colonialism and Culture.* Ann Arbor: University of Michigan Press.

———— (1993). Colonial Histories and Native Informants: Biography of an Archive. In *Orientalism and the Postcolonial Predicament: Perspectives on South Asia*, ed. Carol Breckenridge and Peter van der Veer. Philadelphia: University of Pennsylvania Press.

———— (1996). Is Vice Versa? Historical Anthropologies and Anthropological Histories. In *The Historic Turn in the Social Sciences*, ed. Terence MacDonald. Ann Arbor: University of Michigan Press.

———— (2001). *Castes of Mind: Colonialism and the Making of Modern India.* Princeton: Princeton University Press.

——— (2002). Annals of the Archive: Ethnographic Notes on the Sources of History. In *From the Margins: Historical Anthropology and Its Futures*, ed. Brian Keith Axel. Durham, N.C.: Duke University Press.

Doukas, Stratis ([1929]1999). *A Prisoner of War's Story*, trans. Petro Alexiou, intro. Dimitris Tziovas. Birmingham: Centre for Byzantine, Ottoman and Modern Greek Studies. Originally published as Ιστορία ενός Αιχμαλώτου (Athens: Ekdoseis Ganiaris, 1929).

Doulis, Thomas (1977). *Disaster and Fiction. Modern Greek Fiction and the Impact of the Asia Minor Disaster of 1922*. Berkeley: University of California Press.

Doumanis, Nick (1997). *Myth and Memory in the Mediterranean: Remembering Fascism's Empire*. London: Macmillan.

Droulia, Loukia. (1991). Η Συνειδητοποίηση του Έργου του Ιστορικού (The Realization of the Work of the Historian). In *Contemporary Archives, Files and Historical Research. Mnimon* 6 (supplement). Athens: Etaireia Meletis Neou Ellinismou.

Duranti, Alessandro (1997). *Linguistic Anthropology*. Cambridge: Cambridge University Press.

Echevarría, Roberto González (1998). *Myth and Archive: A Theory of Latin American Narrative*, 2nd edn. Durham, N.C.: Duke University Press.

Elefantis, Angelos (1994). "Ορθοκωστά" του Θανάση Βαλτινού (Thanassis Valtinos's *Orthokosta*). *O Politis* 126 (June–July): 61–6.

Embeirikos, Leonidas *et al.*, ed. (2001). Γλωσσική Ετερότητα στην Ελλάδα (Linguistic Difference in Greece). Center for the Study of Minority Groups. Athens: Alexandreia.

Emborikos Syllogos Volou ([1901]1997). Οδηγός Νομού Μαγνησίας (Guide to the Prefecture of Volos). Volos.

Emerson, Caryl (1997). *The First Hundred Years of Mikhail Bakhtin*. Princeton: Princeton University Press.

Errington, J. Joseph (1998). *Shifting Languages: Interaction and Identity in Javanese Indonesia*. Cambridge: Cambridge University Press.

Etaireia Meletis Neou Ellinismou (1985). Νεοελληνική Πόλη: Οθωμανικές Κληρονομιές και Ελληνικό Κράτος (The Modern Greek City: Ottoman Legacies and the Greek State). Athens: Etaireia Meletis Neou Ellinismou.

——— (1991). Σύγχρονα Αρχεία, Φάκελοι και Ιστορική Έρευνα (Contemporary Archives, Files and Historical Research). *Mnimon* 6 (supplement). Athens: Etaireia Meletis Neou Ellinismou.

Etaireia Spoudon Neoellinikou Politismou kai Genikis Paideias (1997). Ιστορική Πραγματικότητα και Νεοελληνική Πεζογραφία *(1945–1995)* (Historical Reality and Modern Greek Fiction [1945–1995]). Athens: Moraitis School.

Fabian, Johannes (1983). *Time and the Other: How Anthropology Makes its Object*. New York: Columbia University Press.

——— (1986). *Language and Colonial Power*. Berkeley: University of California Press.

——— (1993). Keep Listening: Ethnography and Reading. In *The Ethnography of Reading*, ed. Jonathan Boyarin. Berkeley: University of California Press.

Fairchild, Henry Pratt (1911). *Greek Immigration to the U.S.* New Haven: Yale University Press.

Farge, Arlette (1989). *Le Goût de l'Archive*. Paris: Editions de Seuil.

Farinou-Malamatari, Georgia (1997). Μυθιστορηματική Βιογραφία, 1830–1880 (Novelistic Biography, 1830–1880). In *From Leandros to Louki Lara: Studies on Prose of the Period 1830–1880*, ed. Nasos Vayenas. Iraklio: Panepistimiakes Ekdoseis Kritis.

Faubion, James (1993a). *Modern Greek Lessons: A Primer in Historical Constructivism*. Princeton: Princeton University Press.

——— (1993b). History in Anthropology. *Annual Review of Anthropology* 22: 35–54.

Felman, Shoshana (2002). *The Juridical Unconscious: Trials and Traumas in the Twentieth Century*. Cambridge: Harvard University Press.

Felman, Shoshana and Dori Laub (1992). *Testimony: Crises of Witnessing in Literature and Theory*. New York: Routledge.

Ferguson, Charles F. (1959). Diglossia. *Word* 15: 325–40.

Filippidis, Daniel and Grigorios Konstandas (1988). Γεωγραφία Νεωτερική (Modern Geography). Vienna, 1791. Reprint, with an introduction by Aikaterini Koumarianou, Athens: Ermis.

Fischer, Michael J. (1986). Ethnicity and the Post-Modern Arts of Memory. In *Writing Culture: The Poetics and Politics of Ethnography*, ed. James Clifford and George E. Marcus. Berkeley: University of California Press.

——— (1998). Ο Κινηματογράφος ως Εθνογραφία και ως Πολιτισμική Κριτική (Cinema as Ethnography and as Cultural Critique). In *Anthropological Theory and Ethnography: Contemporary Trends,* ed. Dimitra Gefou-Madianou. Athens: Ellinika Grammata.

Focas, Nikos (1995). Review of *Orthokosta*, by Thanassis Valtinos. *Planodion* 22: 129–33.

Foley, Barbara (1986). *Telling the Truth: The Theory and Practice of Documentary Fiction*. Ithaca: Cornell University Press.

Fotiadis, Michael (1995). Modernity and the Past-Still-Present: Politics of Time in the Birth of Regional Archaeological Projects in Greece. *American Journal of Archaeology* 99: 59–78.

Foucault, Michel (1972). *The Archaeology of Knowledge*. New York: Pantheon.

——— (1977). *Language, Counter-Memory, Practice*, ed. Donald F. Bouchard, trans. Donald Bouchard and Sherry Simon. Ithaca: Cornell University Press.

Frangoudaki, Anna (2001). Η Γλώσσα και το Έθνος 1880–1980: Εκατό Χρόνια Αγώνες για την Αυθεντική Ελληνική Γλώσσα (Language and the Nation 1880–1980: One Hundred Years of Struggles for the Authentic Greek Language). Athens: Alexandreia.

Frezis, Rafael (1994). Η Ισραηλιτική Κοινότητα Βόλου (The Israelite Community of Volos). Volos: Ekdoseis Ores.

Friedrich, Paul (1989). Language, Ideology, and Political Economy. *American Anthropologist* 91: 295–312.

——— (1991). Polytropy. In *Beyond Metaphor: The Theory of Tropes in Anthropology*, ed. James W. Fernandez. Stanford: Stanford University Press.

Gage, Nicholas (1983). *Eleni*. New York: Random House.

Gal, Susan (1987). Codeswitching and Consciousness in the European Periphery. *American Ethnologist* 14(4): 637–53.

Gatsos, Nikolas (1998). Βολιώτικαι Αναμνήσεις (Voliote Reminiscences), ed. Eleni Kontaxi. Athens: Dimotiko Kentro Istorikon Erevnon, Tekmiriosis, Archeion kai Ekthematon Volou.

Gazi, Effi (2000). *"Scientific" National History: The Greek Case in Comparative Perspective (1850–1920)*. Frankfurt am Main: Peter Lang.

——— (n.d.). "Farewell Asia Minor": Writing and Telling the History of the Anatolia War (1919–1922). Unpublished paper.

Geary, Patrick (1994). *Phantoms of Remembrance: Memory and Oblivion at the End of the First Millennium*. Princeton: Princeton University Press.

Geertz, Clifford (1973). *The Interpretation of Cultures*. New York: Basic Books.

Georgiadis, Nikolas (1894[1995]). Θεσσαλία (*Thessalia*), 2nd edn. Reprint, Larisa: Ella.

——— (1997). *Νικόλαος Γεωργιάδης: Δήμαρχος Παγασών (Βόλου) 1899–1907* (Nikolaos Georgiadis: Mayor of Pagason [Volos] 1899–1907), ed. Yiannis Koutis. Volos: Dimotiko Kentro Istorikon Erevnon, Tekmiriosis, Archeion kai Ekthematon.

Georgakas, Dan (1992). *Greek America at Work*. New York: Labor Research Center.

Gillis, John R., ed. (1994). *Commemorations: The Politics of National Identity*. Princeton: Princeton University Press.

Gilroy, Paul (1993). *The Black Atlantic: Modernity and Double Consciousness*. Cambridge: Harvard University Press.

Ginzburg, Carlo (1980). *The Cheese and the Worms: The Cosmos of a Sixteenth-Century Miller*, trans. John and Anne Tedeschi. Baltimore: Johns Hopkins University Press.

Goffman, Erving (1981). *Forms of Talk*. Philadelphia: University of Pennsylvania Press.

Gourgouris, Stathis (1996). *Dream Nation: Enlightenment, Colonization and the Institution of Modern Greece*. Stanford: Stanford University Press.

———— (2000). The Ark's Void—Communism and Poetry, circa 2nd Millenium. In *Step-Mothertongue. From Nationalism to Multiculturalism: Literatures of Cyprus, Greece and Turkey*, ed. Mehmet Yashin. London: Middlesex University Press.

Grafton, Anthony (1997). *The Footnote: A Curious History*. Cambridge: Harvard University Press.

Grayzel, Susan R. (1999). *Women's Identities at War: Gender, Motherhood, and Politics in Britain and France During the First World War*. Chapel Hill, N.C.: University of North Carolina Press.

Gritsi-Milliex (1976). *Η Τρίπολη του Πόντου* (Tripolis of Pontos). Athens: Kedros.

Gugelberger, Georg M., ed. (1996). *The Real Thing: Testimonial Discourse in Latin America*. Durham, N.C.: Duke University Press.

Guha, Ranajit (1994). The Prose of Counter-Insurgency. In *Culture/Power/History*, ed. Nicholas B. Dirks, Geoff Eley, and Sherry Ortner. Princeton: Princeton University Press.

———— (1997a). *Dominance without Hegemony: History and Power in Colonial India*. Cambridge: Harvard University Press.

————, ed. (1997b). *A Subaltern Studies Reader, 1986–1995*. Minneapolis: University of Minnesota Press.

Guha, Ranajit and Gayatri C. Spivak, eds. (1988). *Selected Subaltern Studies*. New York: Oxford University Press.

Gumperz, John (1982). *Discourse Strategies*. Cambridge: Cambridge University Press.

Haas, Diana (1992). The Poetic Response to the Asia Minor Disaster. *Bulletin of the Center for Asia Minor Studies* 9: 199–222.

Hacking Ian (1990). *The Taming of Chance*. Cambridge: Cambridge University Press.

———— (1995). *Rewriting the Soul: Multiple Personality and the Sciences of Memory*. Princeton: Princeton University Press.

Halbwachs, Maurice ([1952]1992). *On Collective Memory*, ed. and trans. Lewis Coser. Chicago: University of Chicago Press.

Handler, Richard and Daniel Segal (1990). *Jane Austen and the Fiction of Culture: An Essay on the Narration of Social Realities*. Tucson: University of Arizona Press.

Hanks, William (1986). Authenticity and Ambivalence in the Text: A Colonial Maya Case. *American Ethnologist* 13(4): 721–44.

Haralambidou, Nadia (1997). Ο Λόγος της Ιστορίας και ο Λόγος της Λογοτεχνίας: Δομές Αναπαράστασης της Ιστορίας στην "Ορθοκωστά" του Θανάση Βαλτινού και στην Πεζογραφία του Εμφυλίου (The Language of History and the Language of Literature: Structures of Historical Representation in Thanassis Valtinos's *Orthokosta* and in the Fiction of the Civil War). In *Historical Reality and Modern Greek Fiction (1945–1995)*. Etaireia Spoudon Neoellinikou Politismou kai Genikis Paideias. Athens: Moraitis School.

Haritos, Haralambos (1989). *Το Παρθεναγωγείο του Βόλου* (The Girls' School of Volos), 2 vols. Athens: Geniki Grammateia Neas Genias.

Hart, Janet (1996). *New Voices in the Nation: Women and the Greek Resistance, 1941–1964*. Ithaca: Cornell University Press.

Hart, Laurie (1992). *Time, Religion, and Social Experience in Rural Greece*. Lanham, Maryland: Rowman and Littlefield.

Harvey, David (1989). *The Urban Experience*. Baltimore: Johns Hopkins University Press.

Hassam, Andrew (1990). "As I Write": Narrative Occasions and the Quest for Self-Presence in the Travel Diary. *Ariel* 21(4): 33–47.

Hastaoglou, Vilma (1995). Ο Βόλος από τον 19 αιώνα στον 20 αιώνα: Η Ανάλυση της Βιομηχανικής Πόλης (Volos from the 19th century to the 20th century: Analysis of the Industrial City). In *Volos: Search for Social Identity*, ed. Thomas Maloutas. Thessaloniki: Paratiritis.

Hatzimihali, Angeliki (1949). *Maison Grecque*. Athens.

Hatziyosif, Christos, ed. (1999). Η Ιστορία της Ελλάδας του 20 Αιώνα: Οι Απαρχές 1900–1922 (The History of Greece in the Twentieth Century: The Beginnings 1900–1922), vol. 1, part 1. Athens: Vivliorama.

Heller, Monica, ed. (1988). *Codeswitching: Anthropological and Sociological Perspectives*. New York: Mouton de Gruyter.

Herzfeld, Michael (1980). Honour and Shame: Problems in the Comparative Analysis of Moral Systems. *Man* 15: 339–51.

——— (1986). *Ours Once More: Folklore, Ideology and the Making of Modern Greece*. New York: Pella.

——— (1987a). *Anthropology through the Looking-Glass: Critical Ethnography in the Margins of Europe*. Cambridge: Cambridge University Press.

——— (1987b). "As in Your Own House": Hospitality, Ethnography, and the Stereotype of Mediterranean Society. In *Honor and Shame and the Unity of the Mediterranean*, ed. David D. Gilmore. Washington, D.C.: American Ethnological Association.

——— (1991). *A Place in History: Social and Monumental Time in a Cretan Town*. Princeton: Princeton University Press.

——— (1992). *The Social Production of Indifference: Exploring the Symbolic Roots of Western Bureaucracy*. Chicago: University of Chicago Press.

——— (1997). *Portrait of a Greek Imagination: An Ethnographic Biography of Andreas Nenedakis*. Chicago: University of Chicago Press.

Hewison, Robert (1987). *The Heritage Industry*. London: Methuen.

Hirsch, Marianne (1997). *Family Frames: Photography, Narrative and Postmemory*. Cambridge: Harvard University Press.

——— (1999). Projected Memory: Holocaust Photographs in Personal and Public Fantasy. In *Acts of Memory: Cultural Recall in the Present*, ed. Mieke Bal, Jonathan Crewe, and Leo Spitzer. Hanover, New Hampshire: University Press of New England.

Hirschon, Renée ([1989]1998). *Heirs of the Greek Catastrophe: The Social Life of Asia Minor Refugees in Piraeus*. New York: Berghan.

Historein/National Book Center (1999). Το Ιστορικό Βιβλίο από τη Μεταπολίτευση ως Σήμερα: Διαδρομές στη Νεότερη Ελληνική Ιστορία (The Historical Book from the Regime Change until Today: Trajectories in Modern Greek History). Athens: Historein/National Book Center.

Humphreys, S.C. (1997). Introduction: Let's Hear It for the Magpies. In *Cultures of Scholarship*, ed. S.C. Humphreys. Ann Arbor: University of Michigan Press.

Hutton, Patrick (1993). *History as an Art of Memory*. Hanover, N.H.: University Press of New England.

Huyssen, Andreas (1995). *Twilight Memories: Marking Time in a Culture of Amnesia*. New York: Routledge.

Iğsız, Zehra Aslı (2000). Memleket, Yurt ve Coğrafi Kardeşlik: Arşivci Kültür Politikaları (Homeland, Fatherland, and Geographic Fraternity: Archival Cultural Politics). In *Social Memory of Turkey*, ed. Esra Özyürek. İstanbul: İletişim.

Iliou, Filippos (1999). Ἀνοιχτὰ Ἀρχεῖα (Open Archives). *ArcheioTaxio* 1: 4–6.

——— (2000). Οι Βιωμένες Ιστορίες και η Ιστοριογραφική Προσέγγιση (Lived Histories and the Historiographical Approach). In *Historical Landscape and Historical Memory: The Case of Makronisos*. Minutes of the Academic Meeting, March 6–7, 1998. Athens: Filistor.

——— (2003). Κλειστά Αρχεία: Η Μαρτυρία του Αλέκου Παπαπαναγιώτου (Closed Archives: The Testimony of Alekos Papapanayiotou). *ArcheioTaxio* 5: 183–90.

Jackson, Michael, ed. (1996). *Things As They Are: New Directions in Phenomenological Anthropology*. Bloomington: Indiana University Press.

James, C.L.R. (1963). *The Black Jacobins: Toussaint L'Ouverture and the San Domingo Revolution*, 2nd edn. New York: Vintage Books.

Joyce, Patrick (1999). The Politics of the Liberal Archive. *History of the Human Sciences* 12(2): 35–49.

Kaftantzoglou, Roxani (with the participation of F. Kamoutsi) (2001). Στη Σκιά του Ιερού Βράχου: Τόπος και Μνήμη στα Αναφιώτικα (In the Shadow of the Holy Rock: Place and Memory in Anafiotika). Athens: National Center for Social Research (EKKE)/Ellinika Grammata.

Kalogeras, Yiorgos (1998). The "Other Space" of Greek America. *American Literary History* 10(4): 702–24.

——— (2001). Introduction to Ιστορίες της Πατρίδος Μου (Stories of My Homeland), by Konstandinos Kazantzis. Athens: Typothito.

Kalyvas, Stathis N. (2000). Red Terror: Leftist Violence during the Occupation. In *After the War was Over: Reconstructing the Family, Nation, and State in Greece, 1943–1960*, ed. Mark Mazower. Princeton: Princeton University Press.

Kangelari, Dios (1994). Για την "Ορθοκωστά" του Θ. Βαλτινού (On Th. Valtinos's *Orthokosta*). Book Review. *Anti* 559, September 16.

Kantzia, Emmanuela (2003). Literature as Historiography: The Boxful of Guilt. In *Modern Greek Literature: Critical Essays*, ed. Gregory Nagy and Anna Stavrakopoulou. New York: Routledge.

Karakasidou, Anastasia (1997). *Fields of Wheat, Hills of Blood: Passages to Nationhood in Greek Macedonia 1870–1990*. Chicago: University of Chicago Press.

Karali, Aimilia (1994). Ξαναγράφοντας ἢ Παραγράφοντας την Ιστορία (Rewriting or Writing off History). Review of *Orthokosta*, by Thanassis Valtinos. *Prin*, September 18.

Kartsagouli, Eleni (1995). *Εκεί που τα Ρόδα δεν Είχαν Αγκάθια* (There Where the Roses Had No Thorns). Volos: Ekdoseis Ores.

Katramopoulos, Yiorgos (1994). *Πώς να σε Ξεχάσω Σμύρνη Αγαπημένη* (How Can I Forget You Beloved Smyrna). Athens: Okeanida.

Katsirelos, Panayiotis (1994). *Ο Προσφυγικός "Συνοικισμός": Το Χρονικό της Ίδρυσης στο Βόλο της Σημερινής Ν. Ιωνίας* (The Refugee "Settlement": The Chronicle of the Foundation in Volos of Today's Nea Ionias). Volos: Dimos Neas Ionias.

Kentrikos Syndesmos Vourvouron (1924). *Επετηρίς των Βουρβούρων* (Yearbook of Vourvoura). Athens: Stavros Christos.

——— (1925–26). *Επετηρίς των Βουρβούρων* (Yearbook of Vourvoura). Athens: Ekdotiki Etaireia Athina.

Kitroeff, Alexander (1989). Continuity and Change in Contemporary Greek Historiography. *European History Quarterly* 19: 269–98.

Kitroeff, Alexander (1999). Transatlantic Emigration. In *The History of Greece in the Twentieth Century: The Beginnings 1900–1922*, vol. 1, part 1, ed. Christos Hatziyosif. Athens: Vivliorama.

Kitromilides, Paschalis (1987). The Intellectual Foundations of Asia Minor Studies: The R.W. Dawkins-Melpo Merlier Correspondence. *Bulletin of the Center for Asia Minor Studies* 6: 9–30.

Kittler, Friedrich A. (1990). *Discourse Networks 1800/1900*, trans. Michael Metter with Chris Cullens. Stanford: Stanford University Press.

———— (1999). *Gramophone, Film, Typewriter*, trans. and intro. Geoffrey Winthrop-Young and Michael Wutz. Stanford: Stanford University Press.

Kliafa, Maroula (1983). *Θεσσαλία 1881–1981* (Thessaly 1881–1981). Athens: Kedros.

———— (1996–98). *Τρίκαλα από τον Σεϊφουλλάχ ως τον Τσιτσάνη: Οι Μεταμορφώσεις μιας Κοινωνίας όπως Αποτυπώθηκαν στον Τύπο της Εποχής*. (Trikala, From Seifoullah to Tsitsanis: The Transformations of a Community as Recorded in the Press of the Day), 2 vols. Athens: Kedros.

Koliou, Nitsa (1985). *Άγνωστες Πτυχές Κατοχής και Αντίστασης 1941–44: Ιστορική Έρευνα για το Νομό Μαγνησίας* (Unknown Aspects of the Occupation and Resistance 1941–44: Historical Research for the Province of Magnesia). Volos.

———— (1988). *Οι Ρίζες του Εργατικού Κινήματος και ο "Εργάτης" του Βόλου* (The Roots of the Workers' Movement and the *Worker* of Volos). Athens: Odysseas.

———— (1991). *Τυπο-φωτο-γραφικό Πανόραμα του Βόλου* (Typo-foto-graphic Panorama of Volos), 2 vols. Volos.

———— (1994). *Η Βιομηχανία του Βόλου* (The Industry of Volos). Volos: Dimotiko Kentro Istorias & Tekmiriosis, Ekdoseis Volos.

———— (1997). *Ενθύμιον Εκπαιδεύσεως Θηλέων* (Souvenir of Girls' Education). Volos: Thessalikes Ekdoseis.

Konstandaras-Statharas, Dimitris (1994). *Το Χρονικό της Νέας Ιωνίας 1924–1994: Εβδομήντα Χρόνια Ζωής* (The Chronicle of Nea Ionia 1924–1994: Seventy Years of Life). Nea Ionia, Magnesia: Ekdoseis Ores.

Konstandinidou, Christina (2000). *Κοινωνικές Αναπαραστάσεις του Εγκλήματος: Η Εγκληματικότητα των Αλβανών Μεταναστών στον Αθηναϊκό Τύπο* (Social Representations of Crime: The Criminality of Albanian Migrants in the Athenian Press). Athens: Sakkoula.

Kordatos, Yiannis (1960). *Ιστορία της Επαρχίας Βόλου και της Αγιάς* (The History of the Province of Volos and Agia). Athens: Ekdoseis 20 Aionas.

Koulouri, Christina (1988). *Ιστορία και Γεωγραφία στα Ελληνικά Σχολεία 1834–1914: Γνωστικό Αντικείμενο και Ιδεολογικές Προεκτάσεις* (History and Geography in Greek Schools 1834–1914: School Subject and Ideological Ramifications). Athens: Geniki Grammateia Neas Genias (Istoriko Archeio Ellinikis Neolaias).

Kouvaras, Yiannis (1994). *Εμφυλίου Ονοματικόν* (Civil War Roll Call). Review of *Orthokosta*, by Thanassis Valtinos. *Entevktirio* 97: 73–5.

Kovani, Eleni (1986). *Οι Εμπειρικές Έρευνες στην Αγροτική Ελλάδα* (Empirical Studies in Rural Greece). Athens: National Center for Social Research (EKKE).

Kuhn, Annette (1995). *Family Secrets: Acts of Memory and Imagination*. London: Verso.

Kunreuther, Laura (2002). *Domestic Archives: Cultural Memory and Home in Kathmandu*. Ph.D. Dissertation. Ann Arbor: University of Michigan.

Kyriakidou-Nestoros, Alki (1978). *Η Θεωρία της Ελληνικής Λαογραφίας: Κριτική Ανάλυση* (Theory of Greek Folklore: A Critical Analysis). Athens: Moraitis School.

———— (1993). *Τρεις Γενιές Προσφύγων της Μικράς Ασίας: Η Σημασία της Προσωπικής τους Μαρτυρίας* (Three Generations of Asia Minor Refugees: The Importance of their Personal Testimony). In *Folklore Studies II*. Athens: Poreia.

LaCapra, Dominick (1985a). *History & Criticism*. Ithaca: Cornell University Press.

——— (1985b). On Grubbing in My Personal Archives: An Historiographical Exposé of Sorts (or How I Learned to Stop Worrying and Love Transference). *Boundary* 2(13): 43–67.

——— (1998). *History and Memory after Auschwitz*. Ithaca: Cornell University Press.

——— (2000). *History and Reading: Tocqueville, Foucault, French Studies*. Toronto: University of Toronto Press.

Ladis, Fondas, ed. (1997). *Όπου Γη Ελλάδα: Το Έπος της Μετανάστευσης σε Εικόνες* (Anywhere on Earth Greece: The Epic of Migration in Pictures). Athens: Mnimes.

Laliotou, Ioanna (1998). *Migrating Greece: Historical Enactments of Migration in the Culture of the Nation*. Ph.D. Dissertation. Florence: European University Institute.

Lambropoulos, Vassilis (1988). *Literature as a National Institution: Studies in the Politics of Modern Greek Criticism*. Princeton: Princeton University Press.

Langer, Lawrence (1991). *Holocaust Testimonies: The Ruins of Memory*. New Haven, Conn.: Yale University Press.

Lappas, Takis (1982). *Τα 100 Χρόνια της Ιστορικής-Εθνολογικής Εταιρείας και του Μουσείου της, 1882–1982* (A Century of the Historical-Ethnological Society and its Museum, 1882–1982). Athens: Historical and Ethnological Society of Greece.

Layoun, Mary, ed. (1990). *Modernism in Greece? Essays on the Critical and Literary Margins of a Movement*. New York: Pella.

——— (2001). *Wedded to the Land? Gender, Boundaries, and Nationalism in Crisis*. Durham, N.C.: Duke University Press.

Lederman, Rena (1985). Changing Times in Mendi: Notes toward Writing Highland New Guinea History. *Ethnohistory* 33(1): 1–30.

Lejeune, Philippe (1989). *On Autobiography*, ed. Paul John Eakin, trans. Katherine Leary. Minneapolis: University of Minnesota Press.

Leonardos, Ioannis (1992). *Νεώτατη της Θεσσαλίας Χωρογραφία* (Modern Survey of Thessaly). Pest (Hungary), 1836. Reprint, Larissa: Thettalos.

Leontis, Artemis (1995). *Topographies of Hellenism: Mapping a Homeland*. Ithaca: Cornell University Press.

Levine, Philippa (1986). *The Amateur and the Professional: Antiquaries, Historians and Archeologists in Victorian Britain, 1838–1886*. Cambridge: Cambridge University Press.

Lévi-Strauss, Claude ([1955]1992). *Tristes Tropiques*, trans. John and Doreen Weightman. New York: Penguin.

——— (1966). History and Dialectic. In *The Savage Mind*. Chicago: University of Chicago Press.

Liakos, Andonis (1994). *Προς Επισκευήν Ολομέλειας και Ενότητος: Η Δόμηση του Εθνικού Χρόνου* (Toward the Repair of Membership and Unity: The Structuring of National Time). In *Academic Meeting in Memory of K. Th. Dimaras*. Athens: Institute for Neohellenic Research–National Hellenic Research Foundation.

——— (2001). *Η Νεοελληνική Ιστοριογραφία το Τελευταίο Τέταρτο του Εικοστού Αιώνα* (Modern Greek Historiography in the Last Quarter of the Twentieth Century). *Synchrona Themata* 76–7: 72–91.

Lyons, Thomas (2001). Ambiguous Narratives. *Cultural Anthropology* 16(2): 183–201.

McDonald, Terrence J. (1996). *The Historic Turn in the Human Sciences*. Ann Arbor: University of Michigan Press.

Mackridge, Peter (1985). *The Modern Greek Language*. Oxford: Clarendon Paperbacks.

——— (1992). Kosmas Politis and the Literature of Exile. *Bulletin of the Center for Asia Minor Studies* 9: 223–39.

Magnis, Nikolaos ([1860]1985). *Περιήγησις ή Τοπογραφία της Θεσσαλίας και της Θετταλικής Μαγνησίας* (Tour or Topography of Thessaly and Thessalian Magnesia). Athens: Noti Karavia.

Makris, Kitsos ([1939]1996). *Ο Ζωγράφος Θεόφιλος στο Πήλιο* (The Painter Theofilos on Pelion), 3rd edn. Volos: Dimotiko Kentro Istorias & Tekmiriosis Volou, Ekdoseis Volos.

Malinowski, Bronislaw ([1922]1984). *Argonauts of the Western Pacific: An Account of Native Enterprise and Adventure in the Archipelagoes of Melanesian New Guinea.* Prospect Heights, Ill.: Waveland Press.

Malkki, Liisa H. (1995a). *Purity and Exile: Violence, Memory, and National Cosmology Among Hutu Refugees in Tanzania.* Chicago: University of Chicago Press.

———— (1995b). Refugees and Exile: From "Refugee Studies" to the National Order of Things. *Annual Review of Anthropology* 24: 495–523.

Mallon, Florencia (1995). Whose Bones are They, Anyway, and Who Gets to Decide? Local Intellectuals, Hegemony, and Counter Hegemony in National Politics. Chap. 9. In *Peasant and Nation: The Making of Postcolonial Mexico and Peru.* Berkeley: University of California Press.

Maloutas, Thomas, ed. (1995). *Βόλος: Αναζήτηση της Κοινωνικής Ταυτότητας* (Volos: The Search for Social Identity). Thessaloniki: Paratiritis.

Mandas, Yiorgos (1996). *Απομνημονεύματα από το 1876 έως το 1966* (Memoirs from 1876 to 1966), ed. Evangelos Mantzouranis. Tripolis (Arcadia).

Manoukian, Setrag (2001). *City of Knowledge: History and Culture in Contemporary Shiraz.* Ph.D. Dissertation. Ann Arbor: University of Michigan.

Marcus, George E. and Dick Cushman (1982). Ethnographies as Texts. *Annual Review of Anthropology* 11: 25–69.

Margaritis, Yiorgos (2000). Ο Ελληνικός Εμφύλιος Πόλεμος και η Ιστορία του: Το "Επετειακό" 1999 (The Greek Civil War and its History: The "Anniversary Year" of 1999). *Archeio Taxio* 2: 137–43.

Marx, Karl (1973). *Grundrisse: Foundation of the Critique of Political Economy (Rough Draft)*, trans. Martin Nicolaus. Middlesex: Penguin Books.

Matsuda, Matt (1996). *The Memory of the Modern.* New York: Oxford University Press.

Matthaiou, Anna and Popi Polemi (1999). Από την Ιστορία του Αρχείου του ΚΚΕ (From the History of the Archive of the Communist Party of Greece). *Archeio Taxio* 1: 62–5.

Matthaiou, Sophia (1988). Αρχειακή Πολιτική και Ιστορική Έρευνα (Archival Policy and Historical Research). *Synchrona Themata* 35–7: 137–9.

Mavrogordatos, George (1983). *Stillborn Republic: Social Coalitions and Party Strategies in Greece, 1922–1936.* Berkeley: University of California Press.

Mazower, Mark (1993). *Inside Hitler's Greece: The Experience of Occupation, 1941–44.* New Haven, Conn.: Yale University Press.

———— (1995). The Cold War and the Appropriation of Memory: Greece after Liberation. *East European Politics and Societies* 9(2): 272–94.

————, ed. (2000). *After the War was Over: Reconstructing the Family, Nation, and State in Greece, 1943–1960.* Princeton: Princeton University Press.

Merlier, Melpo (1935a). *Essai d'un Tableau du Folklore Musical Grec: Le Syllogue pour l'Enregistrement des Chansons Populaires.* Athens: Société pour la Propagation des Livres Utiles.

———— (1935b). *Η Μουσική Λαογραφία στην Ελλάδα* (Musical Folklore in Greece). Athens: Sideris.

—— (1948). *Το Αρχείο της Μικρασιατικής Λαογραφίας: Πως Ιδρύθηκε—Πως Εργάστηκε* (The Archive of Asia Minor Folklore: How It was Founded—How It Worked). Athens: Collection de l'Institut Français d'Athènes.

—— (1951). Présentation du Centre d'Etudes d'Asie Mineure: Recherches d'Ethnographie. Communication faite au 22e Congrès des Orientalistes à Istanbul. *Byzantion, Revue Internationale des Etudes Byzantines* 21: 189–200.

Merlier, Octave (1974). *Ο Τελευταίος Ελληνισμός της Μικράς Ασίας: Έκθεση του Έργου του Κέντρου Μικρασιατικών Σπουδών 1930–1973* (The Last Hellenism of Asia Minor: Exhibition of the Work of the Center for Asia Minor Studies). Athens: Center for Asia Minor Studies.

Messick, Brinkley (1993a). *The Calligraphic State: Textual Domination and History in a Muslim Society.* Berkeley: University of California Press.

—— (1993b). Written Culture. Unpublished Paper Presented at the Comparative Study of Social Transformations (CSST) Conference on "Culture." University of Michigan. Oct. 1–3, Ann Arbor, Michigan.

—— (1995). Textual Properties: Writing and Wealth in a Shari'a Case. *Anthropological Quarterly* 68: 157–70.

Millas, Herkül (2001). *Εικόνες Ελλήνων και Τούρκων: Σχολικά Βιβλία, Ιστοριογραφία, Λογοτεχνικά και Εθνικά Στερεότυπα* (Images of Greeks and Turks: Textbooks, Historiography, Literature and National Stereotypes). Athens: Alexandreia.

Miller, Susan (1998). *Assuming the Positions: Cultural Pedagogy and the Politics of Commonplace Writing.* Pittsburgh: University of Pittsburgh Press.

Milligan, Jennifer (n.d.). The Problem of Publicité in the Archives of Second Empire France. In *Archives, Documentation, and the Institutions of Social Memory*, ed. Francis X. Blouin and William Rosenberg. Ann Arbor: University of Michigan Press (forthcoming).

Mitchell, Timothy (1988). *Colonizing Egypt.* New York: Cambridge University Press.

Moćnik, Rastko (2002). The Balkans as an Element in Ideological Mechanisms. In *Balkan as Metaphor: Between Globalization and Fragmentation*, ed. Dušan I. Bjelic and Obrad Savić. Cambridge: MIT Press.

Mougoyiannis, Yiannis (1990). *Ο Βολιώτικος Πολιτισμός του Μεσοπολέμου* (Voliote Culture in the Interwar Period). Athens: Pyli.

—— (1992). *Πτυχές του Βολιώτικου Πολιτισμού, 1940–90* (Aspects of Voliote Culture, 1940–90). Volos: Ekdoseis Ores.

Nietzsche, Friedrich ([1874]1983). On the Uses and Disadvantages of History for Life. In *Untimely Meditations*, trans. R.J. Hollingdale. Cambridge: Cambridge University Press.

Nikodimos (tou Agioreitou) ([1794]1993). *Νέον Μαρτυρολόγιον* (New Martyrologion). 4th edn. Athens: Astir.

Nikolopoulou, Maria (2002). Η Μαρτυρία στο Έργο του Θανάση Βαλτινού (Testimony in the Work of Thanassis Valtinos). *Porfyras* 103: 95–103.

Nora, Pierre (1989). Between Memory and History: Les Lieux de Memoire. *Representations* 26: 7–25.

Olick, Jeffrey K. and Joyce Robbins (1998). Social Memory Studies: From "Collective Memory" to the Historical Sociology of Mnemonic Practices. *Annual Review of Sociology* 24: 105–40.

Ong, Walter (1982). *Orality and Literacy: Technologizing the Word.* London and New York: Methuen.

O'Toole, James M. (1993). The Symbolic Significance of Archives. *American Archivist* 56: 234–55.

Panourgia, Neni (1995). *Fragments of Death, Fables of Identity: An Athenian Anthropography*. Madison: University of Wisconsin Press.

Papadimitriou, Elli (1975). *Ο Κοινός Λόγος* (The Common Language), 3 vols. Athens: Kedros.

Papailias, Penelope (2003). "Money of *Kurbet* is Money of Blood": The Making of a "Hero" of Migration at the Greek-Albanian Border. *Journal of Ethnic and Migration Studies* 29(6): 1059–78.

Papanikolas, Zeese (1982). *Buried Unsung: Louis Tikas and the Ludlow Massacre*. Salt Lake City: University of Utah Press.

Paparrigopoulos, Konstandinos (1860–74). *Ιστορία του Ελληνικού Έθνους από των Αρχαιοτάτων Χρόνων Μέχρι των Νεοτέρων* (History of the Greek Nation from the Most Ancient Times until the Modern Ones), 5 vols. Athens.

Papataxiarchis, Evthymios (1990). Διά την Σύστασιν και Ωφέλειαν της Κοινότητος του Χωριού: Σχέσεις και Σύμβολα σε μια Αιγαιακή Κοινωνία (For the Establishment and Benefit of the Community of the Village: Relations and Symbols of Nativity in an Aegean Society. In *Community, Society and Ideology: Konstandinos Karavidas and the Problematic of the Social Sciences*, ed. Maria Kominou and Evthymios Papataxiarchis. Athens: Papazisi.

——— (1991). Friends of the Heart: Male Commensal Solidarity, Gender, and Kinship in Aegean Greece. In *Contested Identities: Gender and Kinship in Modern Greece*, ed. Peter Loizos and Evthymios Papataxiarchis. Princeton: Princeton University Press.

Papataxiarchis, Evthymios and Theodoros Paradellis, eds. (1993). *Ανθρωπολογία και Παρελθόν: Συμβολές στην Κοινωνική Ιστορία της Νεότερης Ελλάδας* (Anthropology and the Past: Contributions to the Social History of Modern Greece). Athens: Alexandreia.

Papathanasiou, Ioanna (1996). Βίωμα, Ιστορία και Πολιτική: Η Υπόσταση της Προσωπικής Μαρτυρίας. Σκέψεις με Αφορμή Δύο Βιβλία του Τάκη Μπενά. (Experience, History and Politics: The Substance of the Personal Testimony. Reflections Occasioned by Two Books of Takis Benas). *Ta Istorika* 13(24–5): 253–66.

——— (2001). *Ενιαία Δημοκρατική Αριστερά: Αρχείο 1951–1967* (United Democratic Left: Archive 1951–67). Athens: Themelio/National Center for Social Research (EKKE).

Papatheodorou, Yiannis (2002). Ο Σκληρός Απρίλης του '44: Μυθοπλασία, Ιστορία και Μνήμη στις "Ακυβέρνητες Πολιτείες" του Στρατή Τσίρκα (The Bitter April of '44: Fiction, History and Memory in Stratis Tsirkas's *Drifting Cities*). *Mnimon* 24: 269–96.

Peirce, Charles Sanders (1931–58). *Collected Papers of Charles Sanders Peirce*, ed. Charles Hartshorne and Paul Weiss. Cambridge: Harvard University Press.

Pentzopoulos, Dimitris (1962). *The Balkan Exchange of Minorities and its Impact upon Greece*. Paris: Moulton and Co.

Petmezas, Socrates D. (1995). Diverse Responses to Agricultural Income Crisis in a South-Eastern European Economy: Transatlantic Emigration from Greece (1894–1924). In *Fra Spazio e Tempo: Studi in Onore di Luigi de Rosa*, 3 vols, ed. Iliara Zilli. Naples: Edizioni Scientifiche Italiane.

Petropoulos, John A. (1978). The Modern Greek State and the Greek Past. In *The "Past" in Medieval and Modern Greek Culture*, ed. Spyros Vryonis. Malibu: Undena Publications.

Petropoulou, Ioanna (1995). Κέντρο Μικρασιατικών Σπουδών: Μια Επέτειος (Center for Asia Minor Studies: An Anniversary). *Ta Istorika* 12(23): 461–5.

——— (1996). L'Image de L'Orient. *Bulletin of the Center for Asia Minor Studies* 9: 415–20.

——— (1997). Κτερίσματα Προσφύγων (Refugee Artifacts). In *The Uprooting and the Other Homeland: Refugee Cities in Greece*. Etaireia Spoudon Neoellinikou Politismou kai Genikis Paideias. Athens: Moraitis School.

——— (1998). Η Ιδεολογική Πορεία της Μέλπως Μερλιέ: Το Κέντρο Μικρασιατικών Σπουδών και η Συγκρότηση του Αρχείου Προφορικής Παράδοσης (The Ideological Trajectory of Melpo Merlier: The Center for Asia Minor Studies and the Formation of the Archive of Oral Tradition). In *Testimonies in Auditory and Cinematic Records as Historical Source*. University of Athens, Department of History and Archaeology. Athens: Katarchi.

——— (1999–2000). Αρχείο Έλλης Παπαδημητρίου (Archive of Elli Papadimitriou). *Bulletin of the Center for Asia Minor Studies* 13: 269–338.

Pitt-Rivers, Julian (1995). Introduction: Friendship, Honor and *Agon Jus Sanguinis* and *Jus Soli*. In *Brothers and Others: Essays in Honour of John Peristiany*, ed. Stathis Damianakos et al. Athens: National Center for Social Research (EKKE).

Polenis, Emanuel (1945). *Εγκόλπιον Μετανάστου* (The Immigrant's Handbook). Athens.

Politi, Tzina (1996). Το Βουβό Πρόσωπο της Ιστορίας: "Ορθοκωστά" (The Silent Face of History: *Orthokosta*). In *Conversing with Texts*. Athens: Agra.

Politis, Alexis (1984). *Η Ανακάλυψη των Ελληνικών Δημοτικών Τραγουδιών* (The Discovery of Greek Folk Songs). Athens: Themelio.

Poovey, Mary (1998). *A History of the Modern Fact: Problems of Knowledge in the Sciences of Wealth and Society*. Chicago: University of Chicago Press.

Prakash, Gyan (1992). Writing Post-Orientalist Histories of the Third World: Indian Historiography is Good to Think. In *Colonialism and Culture*, ed. Nicholas Dirks. Ann Arbor: University of Michigan Press.

Pratt, Mary Louise (1986). Fieldwork in Common Places. In *Writing Culture: The Poetics and Politics of Ethnography*, ed. James Clifford and George E. Marcus. Berkeley: University of California Press.

Rabinow, Paul (1989). *French Modern: Norms and Forms of the Social Environment*. Cambridge: MIT Press.

Rafael, Vincente L. (1993). *Contracting Colonialism: Translation and Christian Conversion in Tagalog Society under Early Spanish Rule*. Durham, N.C.: Duke University Press.

Raftopoulos, Dimitris (1994a). Thanassis Valtinos, *Orthokosta*. Book Review. *Grammata kai Technes* 71: 32–4.

——— (1994b). "Ορθοκωστά" δεν είναι Σαπουνόπερα: Το Μυθιστόρημα του Βαλτινού και η Κριτική Ελεφάντη (*Orthokosta* is Not a Soap Opera. Valtinos's Novel and Elefantis's Review). *Anti* 559, September 16.

Rappaport, Joanne (1994). *Cumbe Reborn: An Andean Ethnography of History*. Chicago: University of Chicago Press.

Rebel, Hermann (1991). Reimagining the *Oikos*: Austrian Cameralism in Its Social Formation. In *Golden Ages, Dark Ages: Imagining the Past in Anthropology and History*, ed. Jay O'Brien and William Roseberry. Berkeley: University of California Press.

Richards, Thomas (1993). *Imperial Archive: Knowledge and Fantasy of Empire*. London: Verso.

Ricoeur, Paul (1984). *Time and Narrative*, trans. Kathleen McLaughlin and David Pellauer, vol. 1. Chicago: University of Chicago Press.

——— (2000). *La Memoire, L'Histoire, L'Oubli*. Paris: Editions du Seuil.

Rosaldo, Renato (1980). *Ilongot Headhunting, 1883–1974: A Study in Society and History*. Stanford: Stanford University Press.

Rouse, Roger (1991). Mexican Migration and the Social Space of Postmodernism. *Diaspora* 1(1): 8–23.

Rumsey, Alan (1990). Wording, Meaning, and Linguistic Ideology. *American Anthropology* 92: 346–61.

Sahlins, Marshall (1981). *Historical Metaphors and Mythical Realities: Structure in the Early History of the Sandwich Islands Kingdom*. Ann Arbor: University of Michigan Press.

Said, Edward (1989). Representing the Colonized: Anthropology's Interlocutors. *Critical Inquiry* 15: 205–25.

Saloutos, Theodore (1956). *They Remember America: The Story of the Repatriated Greek-Americans.* Berkeley: University of California Press.

———— (1964). *The Greeks in the United States.* Cambridge: Harvard University Press.

Samuel, Raphael (1994). *Theatres of Memory: Past and Present in Contemporary Culture.* London: Verso.

———— ([1971]1998). Perils of Transcription. In *The Oral History Reader,* ed. Robert Perks and Alistair Thomson. London: Routledge.

Sanjek, Roger, ed. (1990). *Fieldnotes: The Makings of Anthropology.* Ithaca: Cornell University Press.

Saunier, Guy (1990). *Το Δημοτικό Τραγούδι της Ξενιτιάς* (The Demotic Folk Song of Xenitia). Athens: Ermis.

Scott, Joan (1992). "Experience." In *Feminists Theorize the Political,* ed. Judith Butler and Joan Scott. New York: Routledge.

Seferis, George (1953). *Τρεις Μέρες στα Μοναστήρια της Καππαδοκίας* (Three Days in the Monasteries of Cappadocia). Athens: Collection de l'Institut Français d'Athènes.

Seremetakis, C. Nadia (1991). *The Last Word: Women, Death, and Divination in Inner Mani.* Chicago: University of Chicago Press.

————, ed. (1994). *The Senses Still: Perception and Memory as Material Culture in Modernity.* Boulder, Co.: Westview.

Shryock, Andrew (1997). *Nationalism and the Genealogical Imagination: Oral History and Textual Authority in Tribal Jordan.* Berkeley: University of California Press.

Sider, Gerald and Gavin Smith, eds. (1997). *Between History and Histories: The Making of Silences and Commemorations.* Toronto: Toronto University Press.

Singer, Milton (1984). *Man's Glassy Essence: Explorations in Semiotic Anthropology.* Bloomington: Indiana University Press.

Skamaga, Maria (1999). Re-writing History in the 80s and 90s. The Greek Civil War Revisited in Two Post-1981 Novels. Presentation at the Conference "Domestic and International Aspects of the Greek Civil War." April 18–20. London: King's College.

Skopetea, Elli (1988a). *Το "Πρότυπο Βασίλειο" και η Μεγάλη Ιδέα: Όψεις του Εθνικού Προβλήματος στην Ελλάδα, 1830–1880* (The "Model Kingdom" and the Great Idea: Perspectives on the National Problem in Greece, 1830–80). Athens: Polytypo.

Skopetea, Elli (1988b). Ο Κωνσταντίνος Παπαρρηγόπουλος του Κ.Θ. Δημαρά και Μερικές Σκέψεις περί Εθνικής Ιστοριογραφίας (K.Th. Dimaras's Konstandinos Paparrigopoulos and Some Thoughts on National Historiography). *Synchrona Themata* 35–7: 286–94.

———— (1992). The Balkans and Modern European History. In *Teaching Modern European History.* Szeged, Hungary: Attila Jozsef University, Department of Modern & Contemporary History.

Smith, Bonnie G. (1998). *The Gender of History: Men, Women, and Historical Practice.* Cambridge: Harvard University Press.

Sommer, Doris (1999). *Proceed with Caution, When Engaged by Minority Writing in the Americas.* Cambridge: Harvard University Press.

Sontag, Susan (2003). *Regarding the Pain of Others.* New York: Farrar, Straus and Giroux.

Sotiriou, Dido (1991). *Farewell Anatolia,* trans. Fred A. Reed. Athens: Kedros. Originally published as *Ματωμένα Χώματα* (Athens: Kedros, 1962).

Sotiropoulou, Chrysanthi (1995). *Η Διασπορά στον Ελληνικό Κινηματογράφο: Επιδράσεις και Επιρροές στη Θεματολογική Εξέλιξη των Ταινιών της Περιόδου 1945–1986* (Diaspora in

Greek Cinema: Effects and Influences on the Thematic Development of Films of the Period 1945–86). Athens: Themelio.

Stavropoulos, Kostas (1995). Οι Αφύλακτες Διαβάσεις της Ιστορίας (The Unguarded Passes of History). Book Review. *Avgi*, January 29.

Steedman, Carolyn (1988). *The Radical Soldier's Tale: John Pearman, 1819–1908*. London: Routledge.

——— (2001). *Dust*. Manchester: Manchester University Press.

Stewart, Susan (1993). *On Longing: Narratives of the Miniature, the Gigantic, the Souvenir, the Collection*. Durham, N.C.: Duke University Press.

Stoler, Ann (1992). "In Cold Blood": Hierarchies of Credibility and the Politics of Colonial Narratives. *Representations* 37: 151–89.

——— (2002a). *Carnal Knowledge and Imperial Power: Race and the Intimate in Colonial Rule*. Berkeley: University of California Press.

——— (2002b). Colonial Archives and the Arts of Governance: On the Content in the Form. In *Refiguring the Archive*, ed. Carolyn Hamilton et al. Capetown: David Philip.

——— (2002c). Developing Historical Negatives: Race and the (Modernist) Visions of a Colonial State. In *From the Margins: Historical Anthropology and Its Futures,* ed. Brian Keith Axel. Durham, N.C.: Duke University Press.

——— (n.d.). *Along the Archival Grain: Colonial Cultures and Their Affective States*. Princeton: Princeton University Press (forthcoming).

Stoler, Ann and Karen Strassler (2000). Castings for the Colonial: Memory Work in "New Order" Java. *Comparative Studies in Society and History* 42(1): 4–48.

Strassler, Karen (2003). *Refracted Visions: Popular Photography and the Indonesian Culture of Documentation in Postcolonial Java*. Ph.D. Dissertation. Ann Arbor: University of Michigan.

Sturken, Marita (1997). *Tangled Memories: The Vietnam War, the Aids Epidemic, and the Politics of Remembering*. Berkeley: University of California Press.

Sutton, David E. (1998). *Memories Cast in Stone: The Relevance of the Past in Everyday Life*. Oxford: Berg.

Svoronos, Nikos (1982). Η Επιστήμη της Ιστορίας και το Επάγγελμα του Ιστορικού (The Discipline of History and the Profession of the Historian). In *Selected Writings in Modern Greek History and Historiography*. Athens: Themelio.

Syllogos ton Apantahou Vourvouraion (1939). Επετηρίς των Βουρβούρων (Yearbook of Vourvoura). Athens.

Taylor, Lucien, ed. (1994). *Visualizing Theory: Selected Essays from V.A.R., 1990–1994*. New York: Routledge.

Tenekidis, Yiorgos (1980). Prologue. In *Exodus: Testimonies from the Provinces of the Western Coast of Asia Minor*, vol. 1, ed. Fotis D. Apostolopoulos. Athens: Center for Asia Minor Studies.

Thiesse, Anne-Marie (1991). *Ecrire la France: Le Mouvement Littéraire Régionaliste de Langue Française entre la Belle Epoque et la Libération*. Paris: Presses Universitaires de France.

Todorov, Tzvetan (1981). *Introduction to Poetics*, trans. Richard Howard. Minneapolis: University of Minnesota Press.

Todorova, Maria (1997). *Imagining the Balkans*. New York: Oxford University Press.

Tolias, Yiorgos (1992). 1830–1930, People and Territory. In *1830–1930. The Cartography of Hellenism: One Hundred Years. Exhibition Catalogue*. Athens: Society for Hellenic Cartography/Hellenic Literary and Historical Archive (ELIA).

Tomara-Sideri, Matoula (1999). Η Ελληνική Τοπική Αυτοδιοίκηση (Greek Local Self-Government). Athens: Papazisi.

Topping, Peter (1952). The Public Archives of Greece. *The American Archivist* 15(3): 249–57.

Triandafyllidis, Manolis ([1941]1993). Νεοελληνική Γραμματική (της Δημοτικής) (Modern Greek Grammar [of the Demotic]). Thessaloniki: Aristotle University of Thessaloniki.

———— (1963). Τα Ελληνικά των Ελλήνων της Αμερικής (The Greek of the Greeks in America). In *Apanta*, 2 vols. Thessaloniki: Aristotle University of Thessaloniki.

Triandafyllou, Maro (1995). Μερικές Σκέψεις για την "Ορθοκωστά" του Θ. Βαλτινού (Some Thoughts on Th. Valtinos's *Orthokosta*). Book Review. *Planodion* 22: 160–4.

Triandou, Eleni (1994). *Ο Βόλος Μέσα από την Ομίχλη του Χρόνου* (Volos Through the Mist of Time). Volos: Grafi.

Trigonis, Athos ([1934]1987). *Χρονικά του Βόλου* (Chronicle of Volos). Athens: Omospondia Syllogon Apodimon Magnisioton Attikis.

Trouillot, Michel-Rolph (1991). Anthropology and the Savage Slot: The Poetics and Politics of Otherness. In *Recapturing Anthropology: Working in the Present*, ed. Richard G. Fox. Santa Fe, N.M.: School of American Research Press.

———— (1995). *Silencing the Past: Power and the Production of History*. Boston: Beacon Press.

Tserkezis, Savvas (1988). *Το Ημερολόγιον του Βίου Μου* (The Diary of My Life), ed. Foivos Stavridis. Lefkosia: Ekdoseis Laikis Trapezas.

Tsirimokou, Lizi (1997). Το Τελευταίο Τσιγάρο: Σχετικά με "Το Κιβώτιο" του Άρη Αλεξάνδρου (The Last Cigarette: Regarding Aris Alexandrou's *Kivotio*). In *Historical Reality and Modern Greek Fiction (1945–1995)*. Etaireia Spoudon Neoellinikou Politismou kai Genikis Paideias. Athens: Moraitis School.

Tsitsipis, Lukas D. (1998). *A Linguistic Anthropology of Praxis and Language Shift: Arvanitika (Albanian) and Greek in Contact*. Oxford: Clarendon Press.

Tsopotos, Dimitris (1933). Ο Βόλος. Ίδρυσις και Εμπορική Κίνησις Αυτού Κατά τα Πρώτα Δέκα Έτη (Volos. Its Founding and Commercial Activity During the First Ten Years). Pamphlet. Athens: Vartsos.

———— (1991). *Ιστορία του Βόλου* (History of Volos). Volos: Kallitechnikos Organismos Dimou Volou.

Tziovas, Dimitris (1986). *The Nationism of the Demoticists and Its Impact on Their Literary Theory (1888–1930)*. Amsterdam: Hakkert.

———— (1987). *Μετά την Αισθητική* (After Aesthetics). Athens: Gnosi.

Tziovas, Dimitris (1989). Οι Μεταμορφώσεις του Εθνισμού και το Ιδεολόγημα της Ελληνικότητας στο Μεσοπόλεμο (The Metamorphoses of Nationism and the Ideology of Greekness in the Interwar Period). Athens: Odysseas.

Valtinos, Thanassis ([1963]1992). *Η Κάθοδος των Εννιά* (The Descent of the Nine). Athens: Agra.

———— ([1964]1990). *Συναξάρι Αντρέα Κορδοπάτη, Βιβλίο Πρώτο: Αμερική* (The Book of the Days of Andreas Kordopatis, Book I: America). Athens: Agra.

———— (1972). The Plaster Cast. In *Eighteen Texts*, ed. and trans. Willis Barnstone, intro. Stratis Haviaras. Cambridge: Harvard University Press.

———— ([1978]1989). *Τρία Ελληνικά Μονόπρακτα* (Three Greek One-Acts). Athens: Stigmi.

———— (1979). Εθισμός στη Νικοτίνη (Nicotine Addiction). Thessaloniki: Ausblicke.

———— (1989). *Στοιχεία για τη Δεκαετία του '60* (Data from the Decade of the Sixties). Athens: Stigmi.

———— (1991). Ιστορία Ενός Βιασμού (Story of a Rape). In *Three Portraits* (*Valtinos-Papavasileiou-Papayiorgis*), ed. Chronis Botsoglou. Athens: Kastaniotis.

———— (1994a). Ορθοκωστά (Orthokosta). Athens: Agra.

———— (1994b). Interview by Stelios Rogkakos. Η Επικίνδυνη Αναγκαιότητα της Μνήμης: Μια Συνομιλία με τον Θανάση Βαλτινό (The Dangerous Necessity of Memory: A Conversation with Thanassis Valtinos). *Anti*, August 5–September 2.

———— (1994c). Interview by Vena Georgakopoulou. Δεν Εξαγνίζω τους Ταγματασφαλίτες (I Do Not Expatiate the Security Battalionists). *Eleftherotypia*, August 24.

———— (1997). Πέρα από την Πραγματικότητα: Το Ιστορικό Γεγονός ως Στοιχείο Μύθου (Beyond Reality: The Historical Fact as an Element of Myth). In *Historical Reality and Modern Greek Prose (1945–1995)*. Etaireia Spoudon Neoellinikou Politismou kai Genikis Paideias. Athens: Moraitis School.

———— (2000a). Συναξάρι Αντρέα Κορδοπάτη, Βιβλίο Δεύτερο: Βαλκανικοί–'22 (The Book of the Days of Andreas Kordopatis, Book II: Balkan Wars–'22). Athens: Okeanida.

———— (2000b). *Data from the Decade of the Sixties: A Novel*, trans. Jane Assimakopoulos and Stavros Deligiorgis. Evanston, Ill.: Hydra Books, Northwestern University Press.

Van Boeschoten, Riki (1997). Ανάποδα Χρόνια: Συλλογική Μνήμη και Ιστορία στο Ζιάκα Γρεβενών (1900–1950) (Unruly Years: Collective Memory and History in Ziaka, Grevena [1900–1950]). Athens: Plethron.

———— (2002). Δεκαετία του 1940: Διαστάσεις της Μνήμης σε Αφηγήσεις Ζωής της Περιόδου (The Decade of the 1940s: Dimensions of Memory in Life Narratives of the Period). *The Greek Review of Social Research* (Special Issue: Perspectives on Oral History in Greece, ed. Maria Thanopoulou and Aleka Boutzouvi) 107: 135–55.

Van Den Abbeele, Georges (1992). *Travel as Metaphor from Montaigne to Rousseau*. Minneapolis: University of Minnesota Press.

Van Dyck, Karen (1998). *Kassandra and the Censors: Greek Poetry Since 1967*. Ithaca: Cornell University Press.

Varlas, Mihalis (2003). Η Διαμόρφωση της Προσφυγικής Μνήμης (The Formation of Refugee Memory). In *Beyond the Catastrophe: Asia Minor Refugees in Interwar Greece*, ed. Yiorgos Tzedopoulos. Athens: Foundation of the Hellenic World.

Varon, Odet (1994). Προφορική Ιστορία: Η Συγκρότηση και Επεξεργασία Ενός Αρχείου (Oral History: The Formation and Processing of an Archive). In *Narrativity, History and Anthropology*, ed. Rika Benveniste and Theodoros Paradellis. Mytilini: University of the Aegean, Department of Social Anthropology.

Venezis, Ilias (1931). Το Νούμερο 31328 (Number 31328). Mytilini: Maroudis.

Ventoura, Lina (1999). Έλληνες Μετανάστες στο Βέλγιο (Greek Immigrants in Belgium). Athens: Nefeli.

Verdery, Katherine (1999). *The Political Lives of Dead Bodies*. New York: Columbia University Press.

Vervenioti, Tasoula (2002). Προφορική Ιστορία και Έρευνα για τον Ελληνικό Εμφύλιο: Η Πολιτική Συγκυρία, ο Ερευνητής και ο Αφηγητής (Oral History and Research on the Greek Civil War: The Political Conjuncture, the Reseacher and the Narrator). *The Greek Review of Social Research* (Special Issue: Perspectives on Oral History in Greece, ed. Maria Thanopoulou and Aleka Boutzouvi) 107: 157–81.

Vidali, Anna (1996). Political Identity, Identification and Transmission of Trauma. *Cultural Memory* 30: 33–45.

———— (1999). Άραγε Εμείς Ήμασταν; Απαγορευμένη Ιστορία και Υποκειμενικότητα σε Τέσσερις Ιστορίες από τον Ελληνικό Εμφύλιο (Was that Really Us? Forbidden History and Subjectivity in Four Stories from the Greek Civil War). Athens: Exantas.

Vitti, Mario (1977). Η Γενιά του Τριάντα: Ιδεολογία και Μορφή (The Generation of the Thirties: Ideology and Form). Athens: Ermis.

Vlahoyiannis, Yiannis (1901). Ἀθηναϊκόν Ἀρχεῖον (Athenian Archive), vol. 1. Athens: Vlastos.

――― ([1903]1948). Καραϊσκάκης: Βιογραφία Βγαλμένη Ἀπό Ἀνέκδοτες Πηγές, Βιβλιογραφία καί Στοματικές Παραδόσεις (Karaiskakis: Biography Drawn from Unpublished Sources, Bibliography and Oral Traditions). Athens: Estia.

――― ([1907]1947). Introduction and Notes. Ἀπομνημονεύματα (Memoirs), by Yiannis Makriyiannis. Athens: Vayionakis.

――― (1907). Ἀρχεῖα τῆς Νεοτέρας Ἑλληνικῆς Ἱστορίας (Archives of Modern Greek History), 2 vols. Athens.

Vološinov, V.N. ([1929]1973). Marxism and the Philosophy of Language, trans. Ladislav Matejka and I.R. Titunik. Cambridge: Harvard University Press.

Voulgaris, Kostas (2001). Στο Ὄνειρο Πάντα ἡ Πελοπόννησο (Always in Dream the Peloponnese). Athens: Ekdoseis Gavrielidis.

――― (2004). Ἡ Παρτίδα: Ἕνα Παιχνίδι Λογοτεχνίας καί Ἱστορίας (The Deal: A Game of Literature and History). Athens: Vivliorama.

Voyiatzis, Fotis (1980). Θεσσαλική Ζωγραφική 1500–1980 (Thessalian Painting 1500–1980). Athens.

――― (1987). Θέατρο στο Βόλο (Theater in Volos). Athens: Omospondia Syllogon Apodimon Magnisioton Attikis, Mnimes.

Wallot, Jean-Pierre and Normand Fortier (1998). Archival Science and Oral Sources. In The Oral History Reader, ed. Robert Perks and Alistair Thomson. London: Routledge.

Weber, Samuel (1996). Mass Mediauras: Form, Technics, Media. Stanford: Stanford University Press.

White, Hayden (1973). Metahistory: The Historical Imagination of Nineteenth-Century Europe. Baltimore: Johns Hopkins University Press.

――― (1978). Tropics of Discourse. Baltimore: Johns Hopkins University Press.

――― (1987). The Content of the Form: Narrative Discourse and Historical Representation. Baltimore: Johns Hopkins University Press.

White, Luise (2000). Speaking with Vampires: Rumor and History in Colonial Africa. Berkeley: University of California Press.

Wieviorka, Annette (1999). From Survivor to Witness: Voices from the Shoah. In War and Remembrance in the Twentieth Century, ed. Jay Winter and Emmanuel Sivan. Cambridge: Cambridge University Press.

Williams, Raymond (1973). The Country and the City. New York: Oxford University Press.

Wolf, Eric (1982). Europe and the People Without History. Berkeley: University of California Press.

Wright, Gwendolyn (1991). The Politics of Design in French Colonial Urbanism. Chicago: University of Chicago Press.

Wright, Patrick (1985). On Living in an Old Country. London: Verso.

Xanthakis, Alkis (1985). Ἱστορία τῆς Ἑλληνικῆς Φωτογραφίας, 1839–1960 (History of Greek Photography, 1839–1960). Athens: Hellenic Literary and Historical Archive (ELIA).

Yates, Francis A. (1966). The Art of Memory. London: Routledge & Kegan Paul.

Yiannacopoulos, Yiorgos A., ed. (1992). Refugee Greece: Photographs from the Archive of the Center for Asia Minor Studies. Athens: Center for Asia Minor Studies.

――― (1993). The Reconstruction of a Destroyed Picture: The Oral History Archive of the Center for Asia Minor Studies. Mediterranean Historical Review 8(2): 201–17.

Yiasirani-Kyritsi, Vassilia (1996). Ἱστορίες Ζωῆς καί Θανάτου στο Νεκροταφείο του Βόλου (Stories of Life and Death in the Cemetery of Volos). Volos: Ekdoseis Ores.

Young, James E. (1993). The Texture of Memory: Holocaust Memorials and Meaning. New Haven, Conn.: Yale University Press.

Index